ArtScroll Tanach Series

A traditional commentary on the Books of the Bible

Rabbi Nosson Scherman / Rabbi Meir Zlotowitz
General Editors

ספר נחמיה

nechemiah

THE BOOK OF NEHEMIAH / A NEW TRANSLATION WITH A COMMENTARY ANTHOLOGIZED FROM TALMUDIC, MIDRASHIC AND RABBINIC SOURCES.

Published by

Mesorah Publications, ltd

ספר נחמיה

Translation, Commentary
and Overview by

Rabbi Yosef Rabinowitz

FIRST EDITION
First Impression . . . August, 1990

Published and Distributed by
MESORAH PUBLICATIONS, Ltd.
Brooklyn, New York 11232

Distributed in Israel by
MESORAH MAFITZIM / J. GROSSMAN
Rechov Harav Uziel 117
Jerusalem, Israel

Distributed in Europe by
J. LEHMANN HEBREW BOOKSELLERS
20 Cambridge Terrace
Gateshead, Tyne and Wear
England NE8 1RP

Distributed in Australia & New Zealand by
GOLD'S BOOK & GIFT CO.
36 William Street
Balaclava 3183, Vic., Australia

Distributed in South Africa by
KOLLEL BOOKSHOP
22 Muller Street
Yeoville 2198
Johannesburg, South Africa

THE ARTSCROLL TANACH SERIES
NECHEMIAH / THE BOOK OF NEHEMIAH

4401 Second Avenue / Brooklyn, N.Y. 11232 / (718) 921-9000

ISBN
0-89906-095-1 (hard cover)
0-89906-096-X (paperback)

Typography by CompuScribe at ArtScroll Studios, Ltd.
4401 Second Avenue / Brooklyn, N.Y. 11232 / (718) 921-9000

Printed in the United States of America by Moriah Offset
Bound by Sefercraft Quality Bookbinders, Ltd., Brooklyn, NY

Author's Preface:

The Heart of Jerusalem

נַחֲמוּ נַחֲמוּ עַמִּי . . . דַּבְּרוּ עַל לֵב יְרוּשָׁלַיִם וְקִרְאוּ אֵלֶיהָ . . .

Comfort, comfort My people ... Speak to the heart of Jerusalem, and call out to her ... (Isaiah 40:1-2).

The beauty of Jerusalem, the grace and charm of its natural setting, the elegance of form and material typical of its traditional architectural design, represent the visible outer reach of the sacred radiance which dwells within the city.

גָּדוֹל ה׳ וּמְהֻלָּל מְאֹד בְּעִיר אֱלֹהֵינוּ הַר קָדְשׁוֹ יְפֵה נוֹף מְשׂוֹשׂ כָּל הָאָרֶץ הַר צִיּוֹן.

HASHEM is great and extremely exalted in the city of our God, His sacred mount. The vision of beauty, joy of all the earth, Mount Zion ... (Psalms 48:2-3).

This theme of the sacred presence coupled with the vision of the beauty of Jerusalem molded the minds and captured the souls of the men who embodied the spirit of the city. It was to these men of Jerusalem that Jeremiah was commanded to address his prophetic call invoking the grandeur of the Exodus from Egypt into the desert, "Go forth and call out to the ears of Jerusalem saying: So says HASHEM, I remember the goodness of your youth, the ardor of your betrothal, when you followed Me into the desert, an unseeded land ..." (Jeremiah 2:2). Here, no direct appeal to the heart was required. The prophet had but to issue his call, and "... the ears of Jerusalem ..." would respond eagerly.

But the radiance dimmed, and the vision and grandeur, ground underfoot by the conquering legions, were replaced by endless humiliation and suffering, with no respite in sight. Now, it would no longer suffice to merely issue the prophetic call, for the men of Jerusalem had suffered a great, gaping inner wound, and the heart of the city had broken.

Still, the prophetic wisdom would yet convey the eternal message of comfort and solace, and the word of God through the prophet Isaiah, uttered in Jerusalem some two millennia in the past, reaches the quiet recesses of the heart in every generation. "Comfort, comfort My people ... speak to the heart of Jerusalem, and call out to her ..." Teach, in the language of the heart, that suffering cleanses and purifies. Reach out to the sacred city, and convey to her that "her sin is absolved, for she has suffered doubly, at the hand of God, for all her iniquities" (Isaiah 40:2). Make known to the men of Jerusalem that the power of the radiant presence, which heals and makes whole, will restore the beauty to their souls. "On a high mountain rise up, herald of Zion, lift your voice with power, herald of Jerusalem, lift, fear not, say to the cities of Judah, 'Behold your God!' " (ibid. v. 9).

Nechemiah's restoration of Jerusalem from the scorched rubble of the first Temple era remains as an everlasting symbol of the rejuvenation of the eternal city. At the time, the survival of Jerusalem as a Jewish enclave was in grave doubt. By the power of his personality, Nechemiah arranged for the reconstruction of the city's walls and many of its dwellings. In addition, he moved forcefully and effectively to strengthen the observance of the commandments among the people, emphasizing particularly those mitzvos related to the Temple services. Thus, through his efforts, Jerusalem regained its stature as the center of Jewish esthetic and spiritual achievement. If the book of Eichah (Lamentations), the narrative of the desolation of Jeruslaem, is the sourcebook for sorrow and lament, then the book of Nechemiah is the history of fulfillment and consolation, for it records the majestic rise of a city blessed with the beauty and grandeur of the radiant presence.

Acknowledgments

All that men accomplish, is traced to the Creator of all beings. I open my acknowledgments with an expression of gratitude to the Almighty, Master of creation, for favoring me once again with the privilege of contributing to the ArtScroll Tanach Series. As in the past my participation in this vital project is a source of deep fulfillment and satisfaction.

RABBI YAAKOV ASTOR *deserves a note of thanks for his valuable editorial work. In addition,* REB SHEAH BRANDER'S *widely acclaimed artistic talent has enhanced this book with its attractive format. Finally, a word of profound appreciation to the general editors of Mesorah Publications,* RABBI MEIR ZLOTOWITZ *and* RABBI NOSSON SCHERMAN, *for giving me the benefit of their professional excellence. I cherish their friendship and support.*

My closing remarks are dedicated to my wife, שרה שתחי׳, *in appreciation of her strength and constant encouragement. May it please Heaven that we be privileged to witness the continued growth and fulfillment of our children and grandchildren,* שיחיו.

Yosef Rabinowitz

מוצאי שבת נחמו תש״ן

An Overview /
Nehemiah — Man of Jerusalem

I. Restoration

The Architect

Nehemiah ben Hachaliah architect of the restoration of Jerusalem, exerted the immense power of his creative genius at the dawn of the Second Temple era, when the future of the entire fledgling settlement in Jerusalem hung in the balance. Nearly a century had elapsed since the Babylonian armies had razed the First Temple and destroyed Jerusalem. The Persian Empire had gained world domination, and its far-flung acquisitions included the territory of Palestine, with its capital city of Jerusalem, the focal point of Jewish longing and aspirations.

The Persian Empire had gained world domination, and its far-flung acquisitions included the territory of Palestine.

The Persian monarchy had recognized the intensity of the Jewish desire for the restoration of the Temple, and, after an abortive beginning, finally permitted its reconstruction, and the resumption of the sacrificial service (see *Ezra* 1:6). In addition, although King Cyrus had issued a call to his Jewish subjects inviting them to resettle the Holy Land (*Ezra* 1:2-4), only a fraction of the Jewish populace — 42,360 people — responded by returning to the land (*Ezra* 2:64). It was the desperate plight of these settlers that drew Nehemiah's attention.

Only a fraction of the Jewish populace — 42,360 people — responded by returning to the land.

He was particularly distressed by the grave peril facing the embattled inhabitants of Jerusalem. Ultimately, it was his deep anguish over the fate of the sacred city "... *where my forefathers are buried* ..." (*Nehemiah* 2:3) that moved him to abandon his position as attendant to the king of Persia, journey to Jerusalem, and engage, at great personal risk, in the struggle for the survival of the city.

Upon his arrival, Nehemiah discovered a vulnerable city. Jerusalem's charred walls permitted easy intrusion by the enemies of the Jews, particularly the Cuthite sect, whose members had traditionally oppressed the Jewish community and disrupted their religious observances. The area was so sparsely populated that meaningful defense was virtually impossible. Communal affairs languished in a state of near anarchy. Provisions for the Temple services were in short supply, and the tithes for the support of the Kohanim and Levites were inadequate. Intermarriage was rampant, Sabbath observance lax, and the destitute were downtrodden by wealthy moneylenders.

Intermarriage was rampant, Sabbath observance lax, and the destitute were downtrodden by wealthy moneylenders.

Nehemiah plunged directly into the welter of conflict and struggle with great courage and skill. He supervised, personally, the refurbishing of the city walls and the organization of an effective defense system. He arranged for a communal fund to provide income for the Temple needs, and encouraged the people to comply fully with their tithing obligations. He ended the practice of mixed marriage, severely punishing those who had indulged in this transgression. He also moved decisively against public desecration of the Sabbath, by closing the gates of the city to the violators. In addition, Nehemiah persuaded the affluent moneylenders to cancel the obligations of the poor, relieving them of their crushing burden of debt. And, in a ceremony symbolizing the rejuvenating effect of all of his activities, he joined with his illustrious colleague, Ezra,[1] in consecrating the revitalized city with a festive procession around its reconstructed walls. The celebration was attended by the most distinguished men of the day, as well as the general public, and was marked by the sounding of trumpets and the offering up of thanksgiving offerings amid tumultuous rejoicing.[2]

He ended the practice of mixed marriage . . . He also moved decisively against public desecration of the Sabbath.

1. For a review of his life and accomplishments, see ArtScroll *Ezra*.

2. According to one Talmudic opinion, King Solomon's original sanctification of the city had expired with the destruction of the First Temple and the nation's exile. Thus, Nehemiah's consecration ceremony actually invested the city with its special sanctity. The prevailing opinion, however, is that Solomon's sanctification is eternally effective. Accordingly, the ceremony at this time was merely symbolic, זכר בעלמא הוא. See *Shevuos* 16a, and *Rambam, Hil. Beis Habechirah* 6:14.

New Environment

The special providential protection of the Jewish people was not clearly evident when Nehemiah's activities took place.

Nehemiah's organizational talents and his gift for inspiring his countrymen created the environment that sustained Jerusalem as the nation's spiritual center throughout the period of the Second Temple. It should be noted, however, that the special providential protection of the Jewish people was not clearly evident when Nehemiah's activities took place. It was an era of Persian domination, and it was only through special royal prerogative that he was empowered to rebuild the city. Moreover, the Divine Presence did not reveal itself during the age of Nehemiah, as it had in the day of King Solomon's Second Temple tenure. As the Talmud states: Five things were in the First Temple, but not the Second; the Holy Ark with its covering and golden cherubs, the flame that descended from heaven to the Altar, the Divine Presence, prophetic inspiration, and the breastplate oracle [*Urim V'Tumim*] (*Yoma* 21b).

Thus, there emerges a fundamental divergence between the Jerusalem of King Solomon and that of Nehemiah, each of which was molded by the particular nature of the time. King Solomon's empire represents the zenith of Jewish Jerusalem; in his Temple, there dwelt revealed *Shechinah*, available for human observation. During Nehemiah's period, however, Providence concealed itself. In Nehemiah's Temple and in his Jerusalem, there resided a veiled Presence, beyond the reach of mortal perception.

In Nehemiah's Temple and in his Jerusalem, there resided a veiled Presence, beyond the reach of mortal perception.

The mystic will of Providence does not select men randomly to carry great tasks to fruition. Since Nehemiah was the master artisan of Jerusalem during the era of the Second Temple, his deepest personal level of devotion must have reflected the special sacredness of the city at that time.

How was the city's sanctity embodied in Nehemiah's worship? Indeed, what is the basis for the hallowed status of Jerusalem in every age? The answer to these fundamental questions may be found by exploring the Biblical source material regarding the status of the Holy City, beginning with the narrative of the Patriarch Jacob's dream of the ladder.

II. The Dream and the Ladder

The Center-point's Symbolism

He [Jacob] dreamt, and, behold, a ladder stood on the earth, and its head reached into heaven (*Genesis* 28:12).

As *Rashi* explains, the ladder stood in Beersheba with its centerpoint over the Temple. Beersheba is situated in southern Judah, Jerusalem is to the north bordering the territory of Benjamin, and Bethel is in northern Benjamin, bordering the territory of Joseph. Hence, a ladder based in Beersheba, with its head over Bethel, would have its midpoint over Jerusalem (*Rashi* to *Genesis* 28:17).

There must have been a reason why precisely the center of the ladder had to appear over Jerusalem.

There must have been a reason why precisely the center of the ladder had to appear over Jerusalem. As *Ramban* (ibid. v. 17) notes, the midpoint would seem to be of no greater significance than any other part of the ladder; why, then, was it chosen?

The center of the ladder is, indeed, supremely symbolic, for it represents the meeting of the heavenly and the earthly. The ladder spans the distance between heaven and earth, and serves as the passage from one to the other, signifying the union of the supernal and the worldly. Its upper half points heavenward; its lower half points earthward. It is at the ladder's centerpoint that this fusion of heaven and earth is most clearly manifested. This symbolism of heaven meeting earth corresponds perfectly with the concept of the Temple, which is shared as a Sanctuary both by the Creator and by the human beings who serve Him there. The Temple is the single location in the universe specified as a retreat where the Divine Presence visits and where mortals worship. It belongs equally to both God and man. Thus, it was the *center* of the ladder that hovered over the Temple in Jacob's dream, in accordance with the synthesis of the sublime and the mundane represented by both places (*Gur Aryeh* ibid.).

The Temple is the single location in the universe where the Divine Presence visits and where mortals worship.

This special sanctity of the Temple, radiated throughout the entire city of Jerusalem.

The Rabbinic literature suggests that this special sanctity of the Temple, based on the communion between the Divine Presence and the worshipers in the Sanctuary itself, radiated throughout the entire city of Jerusalem. This is apparent from *Rambam's* assertion that "... the Sanctuary and Jerusalem are sacred because of the Divine Presence ..." (*Hil. Beis Habechirah* 6:16). Furthermore, the city is likened to the מַחֲנֶה יִשְׂרָאֵל, the desert camp occupied by the Israelites during the forty years after the Egyptian Exodus (*Rambam, Hil. Beis Habechirah* 7:11, from *Zevachim* 116b). Clearly, the special sacred status of the Israelite camp in the desert[3] was based on its proximity to the Tabernacle. This is evident from the passage ... *let them* [the Israelites] *camp around the Tent of Meeting* (*Numbers* 2:2). Since Jerusalem's sanctity parallels that of the Israelite camp, it follows that the city's special status was founded on its proximity to the Temple. The communion between man and his Creator, which took place at the Sanctuary, enveloped the life of the city and became the focal point of its activities. It rendered all other pursuits extraneous and trivial. Jerusalem is the eternal "camp around the Tent of Meeting."

The communion between man and his Creator, which took place at the Sanctuary, enveloped the life of the city.

Malkizedek and Lot

This extended sanctity of the Temple and its environs was instituted when David and Solomon consecrated the *Beis HaMikdash* and the city of Jerusalem. Its roots, however, reach some nine centuries across the generations, to an incident that took place during the earliest epoch of Jewish history. This event was the meeting between the Patriarch Abraham and Malkizedek, king of Jerusalem. It serves as the subject of the first Biblical account concerning Jerusalem, and should be studied as an indicator of the essential character of the city.

Scripture (*Genesis* 14) relates that in the times of Abraham an alliance of four kingdoms rose to power, conquering the city of Sodom and taking its inhabitants

3. Sacrifices offered in the Wilderness were eaten only within the confines of the Tabernacle Courtyard or the Israelite camp. Similarly, the sacrifices brought in Jerusalem could be eaten only in the Temple Courtyard or within the city (see *Zevachim* 112b).

captive. Among them was Abraham's nephew Lot. Abraham led a small force against the kingdoms, and succeeded in overcoming them and rescuing Lot. When he returned from the battle, he was met by the king of Salem, who greeted him with bread and wine. וּמַלְכִּי צֶדֶק מֶלֶךְ שָׁלֵם הוֹצִיא לֶחֶם וָיָיִן, *Malkizedek, king of Salem, brought out bread and wine* (14:18). "Salem" refers to Jerusalem (*Ramban* from *Midrash*, *Ralbag* and *Radak* to *Joshua* 10:1).

The bread and wine alluded, homiletically, to the meal offerings and wine libations.

The bread and wine alluded, homiletically, to the meal offerings and wine libations that would be brought at the Temple in Jerusalem, many centuries later, by Abraham's descendants (*Rashi* from *Midrash*). Thus the Temple offerings and libations are linked with the entire city of Jerusalem. This is perfectly compatible with the thesis that the city's sacred status emanates from the Temple and the services performed there. However, the context of this link in the Biblical narrative concerning Abraham's victory over the kingdoms and his rescue of Lot deserves exploration. Midrashic interpretation is always consistent with the passage under discussion, even at its surface level. How, then, is Abraham's story relevant to the status of Jerusalem?

Throughout the book of *Genesis*, *Ramban* follows the theme of כָּל מַה שֶּׁאֵירַע לָאָבוֹת סִימָן לַבָּנִים, *the incidents in the lives of the Patriarchs portend parallel occurrences in history of their offspring* (*Ramban* to *Genesis* 12:6). Accordingly, he interprets the four kingdoms' ascension to power in Abraham's time as an allusion to the four empires — the Babylonians, Persians and Medes, Greeks, and Romans — that, respectively, would achieve world supremacy and subjugate the Jewish people. Since Lot was the ancestor of King David, the forebear of Messiah (see *Rashi* to *Numbers* 25:18), Abraham's conquest of the kingdoms and his rescue of Lot foreshadow the eventual Jewish triumph and return from exile in Messianic times.

Abraham's conquest of the kingdoms and his rescue of Lot foreshadow the eventual Jewish triumph and return from exile.

Gur Aryeh (*Genesis* 19:29) explains that, despite Lot's egregious shortcomings, as evidenced by his choice of Sodom as a dwelling place (*Rashi* 13:10,11), he harbored a hidden spark of purity and devotion. This was passed down through his progeny, reaching expression in the saintliness of King David, and will come to full fruition in the exalted character of Messiah. Thus, Lot's deliverance was supremely symbolic of the Messianic redemption, and in saving his life Abraham literally preserved the kernel of Messianic sanctity.

Messianic Goal

Rambam (*Hil. Teshuvah* 9 and *Hil. Melachim* 12) analyzes the meaning of Jewish suffering and exile, and the significance of redemption. *Eretz Yisrael* was promised as a land of plenty and luxury ... *a goodly, spacious land ... flowing with milk and honey* (*Exodus* 3:8). This abundance was offered so that the people might satisfy their physical needs and be free to occupy themselves fully with the study of Torah and the performance of the commandments.

If the people indulge themselves with temporal pleasures then the land and its blessings will have been transformed into a pitfall.

If the people indulge themselves with the temporal pleasures afforded by the land, however, thereby forsaking their devotion to the Torah, then the land and its blessings will have been transformed into a pitfall, and its benefits will be withheld. Indeed, Providence will satisfy the people's preference for abandoning Torah values. The affluence of *Eretz Yisrael*, transformed by their choice into an impediment to Torah observance, will be replaced by genuine hindrances — famine, warfare, persecution, and, finally, exile among the nations, where constant privation and suffering will effectively curtail the study of Torah and the fulfillment of *mitzvos*. The people will merit redemption only when they devote themselves intensely to the Torah, despite the obstacles presented by their suffering.

Messianic redemption is defined as freedom from the obstructions to Torah observance that are inherent in the conditions of exile.

Accordingly, Messianic redemption is defined as freedom from the obstructions to Torah observance that are inherent in the conditions of exile; and as the restoration of the blessings of the Holy Land to be utilized in accordance with their original intent, which was to provide the worldly needs needed for the people to engage fully in spiritual affairs. "Our Sages and Prophets did not long for the Messianic era in order to dominate the world, or rule over the heathens, or so that the nations might extol them, or in order to eat, drink and carouse; but so that they might avail themselves of

In that era there will be neither famine nor warfare, and all the world will engage solely in knowing God.

the Torah and its wisdom without oppression or disturbance ... In that era there will be neither famine nor warfare, envy nor contention, for worldly goods will flow affluently, with every delicacy as abundant as the dust, and all the world will engage solely in knowing God ..." (*Rambam, Hil. Melachim* 12:4,5).

The Messianic epoch, then, is a time when material satisfaction will serve as the instrument by which humanity immerses itself in the affairs of the soul. Earthly gratification will become the cornerstone upon which devotion to the spirituality of Torah is built, so that heaven and earth will interact harmoniously. This concept corresponds precisely with the theme of communion between God and man represented by the centerpoint of Jacob's ladder.[4]

The world of the Temple and Jerusalem and the kingdom of Mashiach are perfectly matched.

It is this union of the supernal and the worldly that underlies the consecration of the Temple and the city of Jerusalem. The Messianic Era, therefore, may be described as the period in human history when the sanctity of the Holy City will be realized as a universal ideal. Thus, the Torah, in describing the events following Abraham's conquest of the four kings, most appropriately cites the gift of bread and wine offered by Malkizedek, king of Jerusalem. This gift, with its intimation of the Temple sacrifices to be offered in Jerusalem, relates directly to the Messianic era foreshadowed by Abraham's victory. The world of the Temple and Jerusalem and the kingdom of Mashiach are perfectly matched.

III. Man of Jerusalem

Nehemiah's Resolve

Nehemiah's role as the dominant figure in the resurrection of Jerusalem placed him at the vortex of the city's spiritual life. Since he was chosen by Providence for this momentous task, it follows that the

4. *Ramban* (*Genesis* 28:12) cites a Midrashic interpretation identifying the angels who ascended the ladder and then descended earthward as the spirits of the four kingdoms who would subjugate the Jewish people. In the Prophetic dream, the ascent represented their rise to power, and the descent to earth their downfall, to be followed by Messianic redemption.

nature of his own devotional experience coincided with that of Jerusalem. How was the harmonious interaction between body and soul, the essence of Jerusalem's spirit, reflected in Nehemiah's worship?

Our book, narrated by Nehemiah himself, opens its account in the city of Shushan, capital of Persia, where he served as the king's personal attendant. Nehemiah learned of the suffering of the Jewish settlers in Jerusalem, and of the extent of the structural decay of the city. He was appalled, and he resolved to petition the king for permission to travel to Jerusalem and rebuild the city. Before actually making his request, he prayed.

He was appalled, and he resolved to petition the king for permission to travel to Jerusalem and rebuild the city.

The prayer itself, however, does not appear in the text. The succeeding passage describes his conversation with the king.

> "The king said to me, 'What is your request?' I then prayed to the God of heaven. And I said to the king, 'If it pleases the king, and if your servant finds favor before you, then permit me to go to Judah to the city where my ancestors are buried, so that I may build it' " (2:4,5).

The Pervasive Prayer

Why is the prayer missing from the text? *Malbim* and *Pri Tzaddik* (*Vayigash*, by *R' Menachem Azariah of Fano*) explain that the words spoken by Nehemiah to the king, as recorded in the next passage, were actually words of prayer. While beseeching the mortal king, his attention turned towards the King of the Universe:

> ". . . the God of heaven," in supplication. As he addressed the Persian ruler, Nehemiah's thoughts were directed to God: "If it pleases the King of all Creation, and if Your servant, by fulfilling Your *mitzvos*, finds favor before You, then use the king of Persia as Your instrument for sending me to Judah to the city where my ancestors are buried, so that I may build it."

What emerges here is an apparently casual prayer form, wherein the supplicant addresses God while engaged in conversation with a fellow mortal. This is seemingly inconsistent with the level of intense concentration required during prayer (see *Shulchan Aruch Orach Chaim* 98). Moreover, it seems to be at total

The supplicant addresses God while engaged in conversation with a fellow mortal.

variance with the sense of complete involvement conveyed by David in describing his own prayer — וַאֲנִי תְפִלָּה, *and I am prayer* (*Psalms* 109:4) — I am so consumed by my supplication that the prayer and I become a single entity. How, then, can Nehemiah's conversational form be reconciled with the desirable level of absorption in prayer? Particularly for men of his towering stature, it does not appear to be an acceptable form.

How, then, can Nehemiah's conversational form be reconciled with the desirable level of absorption in prayer?

The answer is that his prayer was not casual supplication during conversation, but quite the reverse. While engrossed in supplication, Nehemiah engaged in casual conversation. His statements to the Persian king involved mere lip service, while the full force of his attention was directed heavenward. But the question persists, why did he choose this particular prayer form, rather than the conventional one in which the supplicant withdraws from all mundane activity and addresses God alone?

Because the conversational prayer form was the expression of Nehemiah's surpassing love of God, as described by *Rambam:*

> "... one should love Hashem with an immense, surpassing, exceedingly powerful passion, so that the soul is entwined with the love of Hashem, and is always preoccupied with it, like a lovesick person who is unable to turn his mind from the object of his ardor ..." (*Hil. Teshuvah* 10:3).

A *tzaddik* is so captivated by the love of God that he attends to mundane matters almost casually, preoccupied, as he is, with far more exalted interests. During ordinary discussion his mind relates the subject at hand to God by natural transfer, like a lover whose every experience reminds him of his beloved. Conversational prayer is characteristic of those who love God in this way, so Nehemiah's interview with the king is transformed instantaneously into communion with the Creator, and entreaty before the emperor becomes prayer before God. Nehemiah's concurrent prayer and conversation shows that he was infatuated with God. By the force of this passion, his meeting with the king

During ordinary discussion his mind relates the subject at hand to God by natural transfer.

of Persia became communion with the Master of the universe.

This clarifies the dynamic of Nehemiah's position at the fulcrum of power during the rebirth of Jerusalem. At that time earthly and heavenly activities, in accordance with the sanctity emanating from the Temple, were joined harmoniously. However, because the *Shechinah's* visitation remained imperceptible throughout the period of the second Temple, the Divine Presence was not discernible.

His commonplace activity was transformed into spiritual experience; for him, therefore, nothing was secular.

Nehemiah's personality, revealed by his preoccupation with prayer while he conversed with the king, was similarly patterned. His commonplace activity was transformed into spiritual experience; for him, therefore, nothing was secular. In his character, the mundane and the sacred converged as a single whole. His life, representing the confluence of heaven and earth, mirrored the special sanctity typical of Jerusalem. His sanctification of the commonplace, however, was conducted neither in the Sanctuary nor in the halls of learning. It took place, rather, during ordinary activities generally unworthy of attention, in the seclusion of Nehemiah's mind. The process, therefore, was imperceptible to the observer, and, in this way, resembled the particular sanctity indigenous to Jerusalem during the era of the Second Temple, when the Sacred Presence was concealed.

Thus was Nehemiah chosen, by Providential design, as the instrument for the rejuvenation of Jerusalem.

Thus was Nehemiah chosen, by Providential design, as the instrument for the rejuvenation of Jerusalem. By the energy of his surpassing love of God, he embodied the union of the worldly and the supernal which belongs to the spirit of the Holy City. He was the man of Jerusalem.

IV. The Sabbath

A Major Impetus

In his struggle to create a viable communal structure in Jerusalem, Nehemiah, naturally, turned his attention to matters most critical for the survival of the commonwealth. Hence, Scripture (ch. 10) records that he led the people in signing a declaration guaranteeing their intent to refrain from intermarriage, and to faithfully keep the Temple-related *mitzvos*. In addition, it is related, he placed great stress on Sabbath observance. In the declaration of intent, he included a clause mandating strict adherence to the Sabbath restrictions (10:32), and, later, he admonished the people for their laxity in observing the Sabbath, and threatened the transgressors with severe punishment (13:15-22).

The preservation of the Sabbath commandment served as a major impetus to the rejuvenation of Jerusalem.

Evidently, the preservation of the Sabbath commandment served as a major impetus to the rejuvenation of the community in Jerusalem. Why this particular commandment?

Obviously, Sabbath desecration constitutes a grave breach of Torah law. Beyond this, however, Nehemiah's emphasis of the matter in the context of the restoration of Jerusalem indicates that this transgression is particularly antithetic to the status of the city. This may be explained by examining the dual nature of the Sabbath day. On the Sabbath, the Rabbis assert, an "extra" soul descends, surpassing the ordinary weekday soul in its scope (*Beitzah* 16a).

Rabbeinu Chananel there remarks that the pleasures of the soul were created on the Sabbath day, representing the pleasure of the World to Come, where *tzaddikim* delight in the radiance of the *Shechinah*. Presumably, activity involving the gratification of the soul during the Sabbath would be in order. Yet, the *oneg Shabbos*, or enjoyment of the Sabbath precept, requires indulging in material pleasure on the Sabbath, such as eating and drinking, rather than exclusively in the affairs of the soul. Evidently, the Torah prefers actual physical experience as the Sabbath observer's means of creating a worldly example of the delights of the soul in *Olam Haba*, the World to Come.

Yet, the oneg Shabbos, or enjoyment of the Sabbath precept, requires indulging in material pleasure on the Sabbath.

Moreover, material gratification is, in itself, directly related to the joys of the World to Come. *Ramban* teaches that the eternal bliss of the afterworld, referred to by the Rabbis as "the day of everlasting Shabbos," is to be shared by both body and soul, reunited after death, through the process of resurrection. Delight in the radiance of the *Shechinah*, rather than food and drink, will then serve as the source of nourishment. Having attained a state of soul-like purification, the body itself will derive its sustenance from this spiritual ecstasy. Accordingly, the material pleasures of *Oneg Shabbos* represent the corporal delights of "the day of everlasting Shabbos," when the body is enraptured by Divine radiance (*Toras HaAdam, Chavel,* p. 303). [*Rashi* (*Beitzah*) states that the additional Sabbath soul actually causes greater eating enjoyment.]

The Sabbath ideal, then, represents the perfect fusion of body and soul.

The Sabbath ideal, then, represents the perfect fusion of body and soul, when corporal, earthly experience reaches the level of the spiritual and the heavenly. It is this interaction of heaven and earth that places Sabbath observance first among the precepts necessary for the proper development of the sanctity of the Holy City. The sacred status of Jerusalem, as indicated by the centerpoint of the ladder in Jacob's dream, is the application of the identical concept in the personal observance of the Sabbath.

Nehemiah understood that the community is, after all, the sum of its constituents. He took pains, therefore, to enforce Sabbath observance to the fullest extent of his powers, so that the sanctification of the city would follow.

Nehemiah's legacy of sanctity through the Sabbath and Jerusalem remains a source of inspiration for all Jews in every generation.

Nehemiah's legacy of sanctity through the Sabbath and Jerusalem remains a source of inspiration for all Jews in every generation. In actual practice, Sabbath observance has served as the mainstay for the preservation of the Jewish concept of sacredness throughout the centuries of wandering and persecution that followed the destruction of the Temple. In longing and faith, the image of a radiant Jerusalem, vibrant in its dual role as Sanctuary of God and man, is the centerpiece of the Jewish vision of redemption and triumphant return.

ספר נחמיה

א א דִּבְרֵי נְחֶמְיָה בֶּן־חֲכַלְיָה וַיְהִי בְחֹדֶשׁ־כִּסְלֵו
א שְׁנַת עֶשְׂרִים וַאֲנִי הָיִיתִי בְּשׁוּשַׁן הַבִּירָה׃

I

The events described in *Nehemiah*[1] took place fourteen years after the completion of the construction of the Second Temple in the sixth year of the Persian king Darius, son of Ahasuerus and Queen Esther (*Ezra*, 6:15).[2]

A year after the Temple was erected, Ezra had ascended from Babylon to the Holy Land bearing Darius' directive ordering support for the Temple and empowering him to implement Torah law (*Ezra* 7). Ezra did so, successfully ridding the Jewish people of their non-Jewish wives and children.

The Book of *Nehemiah* opens with the information that, although the Temple stood, the Jewish enclave in Jerusalem suffered great privation, humiliation, and lived under the threat of enemy attack (ch. 4). Nehemiah left his position in the service of the king (1:11) and journeyed to Jerusalem to reconstruct the city's walls and rejuvenate its community.

1. דִּבְרֵי נְחֶמְיָה — *The words of Nehemiah.* The following book was written by Nehemiah ben Hachaliah (*Rashi*; *Sanhedrin* 93b).

Rashi's statement must be understood against the backdrop of the Talmud. The Book of *Nehemiah*, as defined in the order of Scriptures and in Talmudic literature, is not a separate book. Rather, it is considered part of the Book of *Ezra* [see *Gilyon HaShas, Succah* 12a]. Indeed, it was Ezra, the Rabbis assert, who authored the volume bearing his name: 'Ezra composed his book' (*Bava Basra* 15a). However, an apparently conflicting Rabbinical statement indicates that Nehemiah, not Ezra, composed the Book of *Ezra*. *Sanhedrin* 93b states: 'All of *Ezra* was composed by Nehemiah.'

This discrepancy is resolved by *Rashi* (*Sanhedrin* 93b). To the Talmud's statement that all of *Ezra* was composed by Nehemiah, *Rashi* interjects: 'The major portion of *Ezra* and *Nehemiah*.' Evidently troubled by the conflict with *Bava Basra's* statement that Ezra composed his book, *Rashi* determined that the statement: 'All of Ezra was composed by Nehemiah,' is not intended literally, but as a reference to that section of the work now known as the Book of *Nehemiah*. In the order of Scripture, however, both *Ezra* and *Nehemiah* are regarded as *one* book, which is called *Ezra*. [See prologue to ArtScroll *Ezra*.] The *Nehemiah* portion of the book is nearly double the *Ezra* portion. Because it comprises the bulk of the combined book of *Ezra/Nehemiah*, the Talmud refers to it by the term 'all of *Ezra*,' although the reference is only to *Nehemiah* [see *Chochmas Shlomo, Bava Basra*, 15a].

נְחֶמְיָה — *Nehemiah*. The Talmud (*Sanhedrin* 38a) identifies Nehemiah as Zerubabel, the scion of the royal house of David (*I Chronicles* 3:19) mentioned in the Books of *Haggai* (1:1, 2:2), *Zechariah* (ch. 4), and *Ezra* (2:2). He was among the leaders who ascended to Jerusalem in the days of King Cyrus.[3] *Malbim* (*Haggai*

1. Since *Ezra* and *Nehemiah* are essentially one book (see comm. below), many pertinent issues of *Nehemiah* have already been discussed in our commentary to *Ezra*. To avoid needless repetition, the commentary here where appropriate refers the reader to where these same issues have been elaborated upon in *Ezra*.

2. This follows *Rashi* (1:1) and one opinion in *Tosafos* (*Rosh Hashanah* 3b). According to another opinion in *Tosafos*, however, the story of Nehemiah took place in the third year of Darius, before the completion of the Temple (see comm. 1:1).

3. Cyrus, king of Persia, granted permission for the Jews to return from Babylon to *Eretz Yisrael* and begin rebuilding the Temple (*Ezra* 1:1-4). He later revoked the grant (*Ezra* 4:21-24), and the Temple construction was not resumed until the Persian king Darius renewed

I
1-2
The words of Nehemiah ben Hachaliah: it came
to pass in the month of Kislev of the twentieth
year, that I was in the capital city of Shushan. 2 Hanani,

1:1) goes so far as to say that, had all Israel merited it, Zerubabel would have been the Messiah.[1] The name Zerubabel is composed of the words נְזְרַע בְּבָבֶל, *implanted in Babylon*, referring to the fact that Nehemiah was conceived and born in Babylon (see Overview and ArtScroll *Ezra* 2:2, 3:2).

However, *Rambam* (intro. to *Commentary on Mishnah* and *intro. to Mishneh Torah*), *Meiri* (intro. to *Avos*), *Abarbanel*, and *R' Ovadiah Bertinoro* (*Avos* 1:1) assume that Nehemiah and Zerubabel were not the same person. [Presumably, this is based on the straight-forward reading of *Ezra* 2:2 which lists the names of Nehemiah and Zerubabel as if they were two separate individuals.][2] [See *B'Shaar HaMelech* by *R' Chaim Kanievsky* who cites *Targum* to *Shir HaShirim* in support of *Rambam's* view.]

Nehemiah was also known by the title Hatirshatha (see comm. 7:65; ArtScroll *Ezra* 2:63).

בְחֹדֶשׁ־כִּסְלֵו — *In the month of Kislev. Ramban* (*Exodus* 12:2, *Drashas Rosh Hashanah*) observes that the months of the year are referred to by number (e.g., *the first month*) in all the books of Scripture [see *Exodus* 40:17; *Numbers* 10:11, 29:1] except those which discuss the period after the return from Babylon. In those books they are referred to by their Persian names — *Adar* (*Ezra* 6:15); *Kislev* (*Nehemiah* 1:1); *Shevat* (*Zechariah* 1:7), *Nissan* (*Esther* 3:7).

Prior to this change, the Torah referred to the months exclusively by number, starting with *Nissan* in keeping with the command, *This month [Nissan] shall be for you, the first of the months* (*Exodus* 12:2). This established *Nissan* as the first month, in commemoration of the Exodus from Egypt, which took place on the fifteenth of *Nissan*. The Persian names of the months were brought to the Holy Land as a memento of the captivity, and incorporated into Scripture to commemorate the redemption from the Babylonian-Persian exile.

Ramban explains that this follows *Jeremiah's* prophecy giving preference to the commemoration of redemption from the Babylonian exile over the remembrance of the deliverance from Egypt: ... *Days shall come ... when it shall no longer be said: 'Hashem ... Who brought the Children of Israel up from the land of Egypt, but, Hashem ... Who brought the Children of Israel up from the land to the North'* [Babylon] (*Jeremiah* 16:14,15).

שְׁנַת עֶשְׂרִים — *Of the twentieth year. Rashi* (*Rosh Hashanah* 3b) notes that Scripture does not specify the event which serves as the reference point from which the twentieth year was reckoned. According to *Rashi*, therefore, this verse refers to the twentieth year of the Persian king Darius, son of Ahasuerus and Queen Esther, who had renewed the construction of the Temple edifice in the the permit (*Ezra* 6:14). Eighteen years passed from Cyrus' grant until Darius' (see pref. ArtScroll *Ezra*).

1. *Malbim* (ibid.) writes: "Despite the prophecies of Daniel and others who envisioned the redemption as an event of the far distant future, the potential for the ultimate redemption existed at the time of Zerubabel — had the people returned (in *teshuvah*) with full hearts to *Hashem* ... In any event, the Messiah in the end of days will be a descendant of Zerubabel."

2. This argument is not conclusive. It can be countered that the Nehemiah mentioned with Zerubabel is not the Nehemiah of the Book of *Nehemiah*, but a different person of the same name. See further ArtScroll *Ezra* 2:2.

א ב וַיָּבֹא חֲנָנִי אֶחָד מֵאַחַי הוּא וַאֲנָשִׁים מִיהוּדָה
ב וָאֶשְׁאָלֵם עַל־הַיְּהוּדִים הַפְּלֵיטָה אֲשֶׁר־

second year of his reign (*Ezra* 4:24), and completed it in his sixth year (ibid. 6:15).

This is derived through the hermeneutic device known as the גְּזֵירָה שָׁוָה, *comparison analysis*, which reveals the meaning of a Biblical phrase by comparing it with an identical phrase appearing in a different passage. The phrase שְׁנַת עֶשְׂרִים, *the twentieth year*, appears in the next chapter (2:1) with the clarification לְאַרְתַּחְשַׁסְתְּא הַמֶּלֶךְ, *of King Artahshast*, a reference to the Persian king Darius who is called Artahshast in *Ezra* 8:1. Similarly, *the twentieth year* in our verse also refers to that year in the reign of Darius-Artahshast.[1]

Malbim explains why our verse fails to specify whose reign is the starting point of *the twentieth year.* Scripture assumes that the reader will identify the monarch of Nehemiah's opening verse as Darius-Artahshast, mentioned in the latter portion of *Ezra* (chs. 6-8). This is in keeping with the Talmudic statement (*Bava Basra* 14b) that *Nehemiah* is an extension of the Book of *Ezra* (see comm. v. 1).

Tosafos (*Rosh Hashanah* 3b, first opinion), however, contends that by the twentieth year of Darius' reign, when the Temple had been standing for twelve years [and Ezra had arrived in Jerusalem with the royal edict supporting the Temple and the Torah], the Jewish community was securely established and peaceful. Therefore, *Tosafos* argues, *the twentieth year of King Artahshast* (2:1), when the Jews in Jerusalem suffered at the hands of their enemies, refers to an earlier date. It was the twentieth year *since* King Cyrus, who is called Artahshast, a general name for all Persian kings in *Ezra* 4:7. That year was Darius' third and the events described in *Ne-*

The Four Events

According to Rashi		According to Tosafos	
Event	**Year of Darius' Reign**	**Event**	**Year of Darius' Reign**
1. Resumption of Second Temple construction	2 (3408)	1. Resumption of Second Temple construction	2 (3408)
		2. Nehemiah's twentieth year of Artahshast/Cyrus	3 (3409)
2. Completion of Second Temple construction	6 (3412)	3. Completion of Second Temple construction	6 (3412)
3. Ezra's arrival in Jerusalem	7 (3413)	4. Ezra's arrival in Jerusalem	7 (3413)
4. Nehemiah's twentieth year of Artahshast/Darius	20 (3426)		

1. [Ezra had arrived in Jerusalem during the seventh year of Darius' reign (*Ezra* 7:8) bearing the king's command for support of the Temple and for the establishment of the Torah laws as the law of the land (*Ezra* 7). However, Nehemiah was informed in Darius' twentieth year that the walls of the city lay in ruins and the Jews suffered greatly at the hands of their gentile neighbors. Apparently, the king's decree was ineffective in quelling the animosity towards the Jews.]

one of my brethren, came with men from Judah; I inquired of them concerning the survivors of the Jews

hemiah preceded the occurrences of the latter portion of *Ezra* [chs. 6-10], which took place in the sixth and seventh years of Darius.

בְּשׁוּשַׁן הַבִּירָה — *In the capital city of Shushan.* This refers to the city where the king's palace was situated (*Metzudos*). [The literal meaning of בִּירָה is *palace city*, i.e., the seat of the monarchy.]

Nehemiah was in Shushan as a servant of the king (*Ri Mitrani* see v. 11). [Although Nehemiah had ascended to the Holy Land in response to Cyrus' proclamation (*Ezra* 1:1-4), he now appears in the Persian capital of Shushan. Evidently, he departed from *Eretz Yisrael* when Cyrus rescinded his grant for the Temple construction (*Ezra* 4:21-24), and traveled to the seat of the Persian monarchy in Shushan to attempt to regain the king's permission to build the Sanctuary. *Ralbag* (*Ezra* 2:2) similarly explains Mordechai's appearance in Shushan, as described in *Esther* 2:5, after he had emigrated to Jerusalem when Cyrus issued his invitation to the Jews. *Ran* (*Megillah* 2a) suggests that many Jews returned to the Diaspora when Cyrus' decree was withdrawn.]

☙ News of Jerusalem

2. Verse 2 details the arrival of a message informing Nehemiah (who was in Shushan, Persia at the time) that the protective wall around Jerusalem was in ruins. As a result, the Jewish community there was 'suffering great evil and humiliation.' The chapter describes (and the next three chapters detail) how Nehemiah took up the mission to rebuild the wall, and successfully resisted enemy plots and threats. A question arises, however, as the events of this chapter unfold. Why did not Ezra take charge and rebuild the wall?

Ezra was the leading Torah sage of his generation and would have been worthy of bringing the Torah to Israel had Moses not preceded him (*Sanhedrin* 21b; see further ArtScroll *Ezra* 7:6,10). Furthermore, Ezra, apparently, was already in the Holy Land (*Ezra* chapter 7, but see further comm. to 7:73). Why, then, did the Jewish community wait for Nehemiah to begin rebuilding the wall of Jerusalem?

Ri Mitrani (see *comm.* to 7:73) addresses this problem. He observes that King Artahshast merely sanctioned Ezra to return to *Eretz Yisrael* as a religious leader, instructing him to organize religious observance in the Holy Land (*Ezra* 7:12-16). Thus, Ezra performed a religious mission sanctioned by the king, nothing more. Nehemiah, on the other hand, was the royal representative. He had been the king's "cup-bearer", a trusted advisor. He came to *Eretz Yisrael* as the governor (5:15) with Persian soldiers at his disposal (unlike *Ezra*; see footnote to 2:8). Thus, Nehemiah came with the support of Persian military power. Ezra, however, did not have political carte blanche. *Ri Mitrani* concludes that Ezra feared that should he overstep his bounds, the enemies of the Jews would accuse him before the Persian monarch. This, in turn, would jeopardize his own mission. He, therefore, refrained from any involvement in the construction.

[An additional factor may have prevented Ezra from resuming the construction. *Rashi* to *Berachos* 4a points out that by Divine decree, the Jewish return to Zion was destined to come about only under Persian dominion (see ArtScroll *Ezra* 1:2 and Overview there). Since Ezra lacked the full authority of the Persian government, he was not Divinely sanctioned to restore the protective walls of Jerusalem. It remained for Nehemiah, who could conscript Persian might for the Jewish cause, to take charge of the

א
ג־ה

ג נִשְׁאֲרוּ מִן־הַשְּׁבִי וְעַל־יְרוּשָׁלִָם׃ וַיֹּאמְרוּ לִי
הַנִּשְׁאָרִים אֲשֶׁר־נִשְׁאֲרוּ מִן־הַשְּׁבִי שָׁם
בַּמְּדִינָה בְּרָעָה גְדֹלָה וּבְחֶרְפָּה וְחוֹמַת
ד יְרוּשָׁלִַם מְפֹרָצֶת וּשְׁעָרֶיהָ נִצְּתוּ בָאֵשׁ׃ וַיְהִי
כְּשָׁמְעִי | אֶת־הַדְּבָרִים הָאֵלֶּה יָשַׁבְתִּי וָאֶבְכֶּה
וָאֶתְאַבְּלָה יָמִים וָאֱהִי צָם וּמִתְפַּלֵּל לִפְנֵי
ה אֱלֹהֵי הַשָּׁמָיִם׃ וָאֹמַר אָנָּא יהוה אֱלֹהֵי הַשָּׁמַיִם
הָאֵל הַגָּדוֹל וְהַנּוֹרָא שֹׁמֵר הַבְּרִית וָחֶסֶד

military-political needs of the people (see further, preface to chapter 5).]

הַיְּהוּדִים הַפְּלֵיטָה אֲשֶׁר־נִשְׁאֲרוּ מִן־הַשֶּׁבִי — *The survivors of the Jews who remained of the captivity.* The survivors who remained in Jerusalem, who were spared exile in Babylon (*Rashi*). Nehemiah was not concerned for the Jews who had ascended from Babylon after Cyrus' proclamation — they had been provided with their own Jewish governor (*Ezra* 5:14) who held them under his protective custody. Nehemiah's inquiries were directed, rather, towards those who had dwelt in the Land of Israel *before* Cyrus' reign — those *who remained of the captivity,* i.e., who had remained in the Holy Land and had never been part of the Diaspora in Babylon. They were ruled by a gentile satrap (3:7) and suffered humiliation and persecution (*Malbim*).

According to *Metzudos*, however, the reference is to those who returned from Babylon to *Eretz Yisrael*. They are referred to as merely the remnant of the captivity, because they constituted only a fraction of the Jewish population, most of whom remained in the Diaspora.

This opinion concurs with *Ran* (*Megillah* 2a), who states that the majority of the Jews remained in the Diaspora, including many who left the Holy Land when Cyrus' permit for the construction of the Temple was withdrawn. *Ramban* (Megillah 2a), however, states that most of the Jewish people returned to the Land of Israel following Cyrus' proclamation, and remained there even after its revocation. [See ArtScroll *Ezra* 2:64.]

וְעַל יְרוּשָׁלָם — *And concerning Jerusalem.* Nehemiah inquired about the city itself (*Rashi*), specifically whether the city's walls were built (*Metzudos*).

3. הַנִּשְׁאָרִים — *The remaining ones.* Nehemiah's first question, concerning the remaining Jews, was answered first. His second question, about the city of Jerusalem, was answered next (*Rashi*).

בְּרָעָה גְדֹלָה וּבְחֶרְפָּה — *Suffer great evil and humiliation.* They are despoiled by the gentiles (*Rashi*), who humiliate them (*Metzudos*).

As noted above, *Malbim* explains this as a reference to the Jews who had remained in the land of Israel at the time of the Babylonian exile (comm. v. 2). Although the returning Jews had their own Jewish governor, the original inhabitants remained subject to Persian satraps who persecuted their subjects.

וּשְׁעָרֶיהָ נִצְּתוּ בָאֵשׁ — *And its gates were set afire.* The gates remained as they were after Nebuchadnezzar set them afire at the time of the destruction of the

who remained of the captivity, and concerning
Jerusalem. [3] *They said to me, 'The remaining ones*
who remained of the captivity there in the territory,
suffer great evil and humiliation; the wall of
Jerusalem is breached, and its gates were set
afire.' [4] *When I heard these words I sat and wept*
and grieved [for some] days, and I fasted and prayed
before the God of heaven. [5] *I said, 'I beseech You,*
HASHEM, God of heaven, the great, awe-inspiring God,
Keeper of the covenant and of kindness for those who

First Temple [*II Kings* 25:10] (*Ri Mitrani*). *Ralbag* agrees, noting that those who had returned from the Babylonian exile had been permitted to rebuild the Temple (*Ezra* 6) but not the gates and walls of Jerusalem.

◆§ Nehemiah's Distress

4-11. Like all great leaders of the Jewish people, Nehemiah was primarily spiritually orientated (see Overview). Even though he was an unequaled political and military leader, his first reaction to the threat toward his people was to turn in prayer to God. His communion with God was the source of his political and military success.

4. יָשַׁבְתִּי — *I sat.* I sat on the ground [as is customary during mourning; see *Yoreh Deah* 387:1] (*Ibn Ezra*); I sat, stunned (*Ibn Ezra; Metzudos;* see *Ezra* 9:3).

וָאֱהִי צָם וּמִתְפַּלֵּל — *And I fasted and prayed.* In the face of danger, one should weep, mourn, fast, and pray (*Ralbag*; see *Orach Chaim* 566; ArtScroll *Ezra* 9:3-5).

5. הָאֵל הַגָּדוֹל וְהַנּוֹרָא — *The great, awe-inspiring God.* This introduction to Nehemiah's prayer is identical with the introduction to Daniel's prayer [*Daniel* 9:4] (*Malbim*).

Yoma [69b] notes that Moses praised God with the words *great, powerful*, and *awe-inspiring* [*Deut.* 10:17], while Daniel (*Daniel* 9:4) praised God as *great* and *awe-inspiring*, but deleted *powerful* because God withheld His power in permitting the gentile nations to subjugate the Jewish people [this, presumably, is why our verse also omits *powerful*]. Later, however, *Anshei Knesses HaGedolah [the Men of the Great Assembly*, the supreme Rabbinical court of which Ezra and Nehemiah were leading members] praised God with the words *great, powerful* and *awe-inspiring*. [See further comm. to 9:32.]

שֹׁמֵר הַבְּרִית — *Keeper of the covenant.* This refers to the reward which God promised in the covenant (*Metzudos*). [Evidently, *Metzudos* alludes to the covenant with Abraham (בְּרִית בֵּין הַבְּתָרִים) wherein God promised that Abraham's descendants would inherit the Holy Land as a reward for Abraham's righteousness (*Genesis* 15). Nehemiah now asked God to allow the children of Abraham to inhabit the land in peace. In addition, God promised, at Sinai, to reward the descendants of those who love Him (*Exodus* 20:6). Since the Torah was referred to, at Sinai, as *The Book of the Covenant* (*Exodus* 24:7), this constitutes a covenant to reward the descendants of those who accepted the Torah at Sinai.]

א
ו־ז

ו לְאֹהֲבָיו וּלְשֹׁמְרֵי מִצְוֺתָיו: תְּהִי נָא אָזְנְךָ־
קַשֶּׁבֶת וְעֵינֶיךָ פְתוּחוֹת לִשְׁמֹעַ אֶל־תְּפִלַּת
עַבְדְּךָ אֲשֶׁר אָנֹכִי מִתְפַּלֵּל לְפָנֶיךָ הַיּוֹם יוֹמָם
וָלָיְלָה עַל־בְּנֵי יִשְׂרָאֵל עֲבָדֶיךָ וּמִתְוַדֶּה
עַל־חַטֹּאות בְּנֵי־יִשְׂרָאֵל אֲשֶׁר חָטָאנוּ לָךְ
ז וַאֲנִי וּבֵית־אָבִי חָטָאנוּ: חֲבֹל חָבַלְנוּ לָךְ

וָחֶסֶד לְאֹהֲבָיו וּלְשֹׁמְרֵי מִצְוֺתָיו — *And of kindness for those who love Him and observe His commandments.* [This passage is nearly identical with *Exodus* 20:6: *And [I] perform kindness ... for those who love Me and those who observe My commandments. Ramban* there explains that the phrase *those who love Me* refers to those whose love of God leads them to risk their lives for the sake of His *mitzvos*, in keeping with the commandment *Love Hashem your God with all your soul* (*Deut*. 6:5). Loving God with all the soul alludes to the willingness to give up one's soul — i.e. one's life, rather than commit idol worship or for any transgression — when the entire Torah is threatened (*Sanhedrin* 74a). The phrase *those who observe My commandments, Ramban* concludes, refers to all the other righteous ones who observe the Torah.

Our verse is also identical with *Deuteronomy* 7:9: *[God] keeps the covenant and kindness for those who love Him and observe His commandments.*

Both Biblical passages refer to God's rewarding the descendants of those who love Him and observe His commandments. Accordingly, Nehemiah's prayer may be understood: 'I beseech You, HASHEM — Keeper of the covenant and of kindness for those who love Him and observe His commandments — help their descendants.']

6. תְּהִי נָא אָזְנְךָ־קַשֶּׁבֶת — *Please, may Your ear listen.* The translation follows *Rashi* who understands the word קַשֶּׁבֶת as a variant form of the verb קוֹשֶׁבֶת, *she hears.*

Ibn Ezra and *Malbim*, however, understand קַשֶּׁבֶת as an adjective modifying the noun *ear*. Their translation is *May Your ear be a listening one.*

וְעֵינֶיךָ פְתוּחוֹת — *And Your eyes remain open.* May Your eyes observe my tears (*Metzudos*) and see our needs so that You may give us Your immediate providential assistance (*Malbim*) [see *Daniel* 9:18]. This interpretation corresponds with *Ramban's* statement (*Genesis* 18:19) that the passage *the eye of* HASHEM *is on those who fear Him* (*Psalms* 33:18) refers to the special providential protection which God gives to *tzaddikim*. [See *Ezra* 5:5.]

הַיּוֹם יוֹמָם וָלָיְלָה — *Today, day and night.* Listen to the prayer which I say today, i.e., at this time [*Metzudos*], and which I repeat constantly, day and night [*Ibn Ezra; Malbim*].

וּמִתְוַדֶּה — *And I confess.* [The sense of this verse is: *Listen to the prayer which I pray before You today, and* (to the confession) *which I confess* ...] *Shaarei Teshuvah* (1:40) lists confession as one of the major components of repentance, from the passage ... *Let him confess to that which he transgressed* (*Leviticus* 5:5). *Rambam* (*Hilchos Teshuvah* 1:1) states that the confession is a commandment in the Torah: *They shall confess to the sins which they committed* (*Numbers* 5:7). [See further ArtScroll *Ezra* 10:11.]

I
6-7

love Him and observe His commandments: [6] *Please, may Your ear listen and Your eyes remain open to hear Your servant's prayer which I pray before You today, day and night for Your servants, the Children of Israel; and I confess to the transgressions of the Children of Israel that we have committed against You: I and my father's house have sinned.* [7] *We have been destructive towards You;*

וַאֲנִי וּבֵית־אָבִי חָטָאנוּ — *I and my father's house have sinned.* I confess that I and my father's house have sinned (*Metzudos; Malbim*). [Nehemiah's mention of his father's sins together with his own follows *Leviticus* 26:40, *They shall confess to their sins and the sins of their father;* and *Psalms* 106:6, *We have sinned with our fathers.* The confession recorded by *Rambam* (*Seder Tefillos Kol Hashanah*) and the confession we recite on Yom Kippur also mentions the father's sins.]

Shaarei Teshuvah (1:40) explains: [The penitent] should mention [in his confession] his own sins and the sins of his fathers, since the children who commit the same sins as their fathers are punished for the father's transgressions as well as for their own (*Berachos* 7a).

Maharsha (*Yoma* 36b) qualifies this: The father's sins are mentioned only when the son confesses to misdeeds committed through ignorance of the law. The father is then held culpable for his son's transgression, since it was his own failure to educate his son properly which brought about the misdeed. [See further ArtScroll *Ezekiel* 18:2.]

7. חֲבֹל חָבַלְנוּ לָךְ — *We have been destructive towards You.* The translation follows *Rashi, Ralbag, Ibn Ezra* and *Metzudos*.

Ralbag stresses that the evildoers do not affect God who is perfect, but destroy only themselves. [This is stated in *Deuteronomy* 32:5, *He destroyed — not Him. Rashi* comments: They [the wicked] destroy themselves, but not God.] The expression, *we have been destructive towards You,* means that we have been destructive of ourselves by transgressing commandments which relate to *God* (בֵּין אָדָם לַמָּקוֹם), such as idol worship and lack of faith, rather than those which relate to man (בֵּין אָדָם לַחֲבֵרוֹ), such as robbery and assault.

Midrash Rabbah (*Exodus* 51:3) translates חֲבֹל חָבַלְנוּ לָךְ as *we have given You a security* (see *Deut*. 24:6). The reference is to a security deposited with the lender as collateral until the loan is repaid. At that time, the security is returned. The security in our verse refers to the Temple which is also called מִשְׁכָּן, *Sanctuary,* from מַשְׁכּוֹן, *security*. It was taken from the Jewish nation and deposited with God — i.e., destroyed — until the people honor their obligation to observe the Torah; then the Temple will be returned. [See *Rashi* to *Exodus* 38:21.]

The double verb חֲבֹל חָבַלְנוּ alludes to the First and Second Temples, both of which were destroyed by God until the Jews would repent. (*Razav* explains that, although our verse was spoken by Nehemiah when the Second Temple was newly established, the words were prophetically inspired to intimate its eventual destruction.)

Malbim, following *Midrash Rabbah,* explains our verse as follows: *We have given You a security* — the Temple — which was taken from us when we failed in our obligation to fulfill the Torah, for

וְלֹא־שָׁמַרְנוּ אֶת־הַמִּצְוֹת וְאֶת־הַחֻקִּים וְאֶת־
הַמִּשְׁפָּטִים אֲשֶׁר צִוִּיתָ אֶת־מֹשֶׁה עַבְדֶּךָ׃
ח זְכׇר־נָא אֶת־הַדָּבָר אֲשֶׁר צִוִּיתָ אֶת־מֹשֶׁה
עַבְדְּךָ לֵאמֹר אַתֶּם תִּמְעָלוּ אֲנִי אָפִיץ אֶתְכֶם
ט בָּעַמִּים׃ וְשַׁבְתֶּם אֵלַי וּשְׁמַרְתֶּם מִצְוֹתַי
וַעֲשִׂיתֶם אֹתָם אִם־יִהְיֶה נִדַּחֲכֶם בִּקְצֵה
הַשָּׁמַיִם מִשָּׁם אֲקַבְּצֵם °והבואתים אֶל־ °וַהֲבִיאֹתִים ק׳
הַמָּקוֹם אֲשֶׁר בָּחַרְתִּי לְשַׁכֵּן אֶת־שְׁמִי שָׁם׃
י וְהֵם עֲבָדֶיךָ וְעַמֶּךָ אֲשֶׁר פָּדִיתָ בְּכֹחֲךָ הַגָּדוֹל
יא וּבְיָדְךָ הַחֲזָקָה׃ אָנָּא אֲדֹנָי תְּהִי נָא אׇזְנְךָ־

we have not kept the commandments . . . [Although the Temple was already rebuilt, Nehemiah spoke of the transgressions which brought about its destruction because the people continued to commit them. *Malbim* (see ArtScroll *Ezra* 9:7-9) asserts that Ezra, in his prayers, pointed out that the people persisted in the very sins which had caused the destruction of the First Temple, and were given the Second Temple as an undeserved gift. Similarly, Nehemiah now mentioned the sins which had caused the destruction of the Sanctuary because the people still committed them.]

וְאֶת־הַחֻקִּים וְאֶת־הַמִּשְׁפָּטִים — *The precepts, and the laws. Yoma* (67b) defines חֻקִּים as the precepts given by God without explanation, such as the restriction against eating pork or wearing *shatnez* (a garment of wool and linen); and מִשְׁפָּטִים as the laws which the human mind understands, such as the prohibition against murder or robbery. [See further ArtScroll *Ezra* 7:10.]

8. אֲשֶׁר צִוִּיתָ — *Which You commanded.* This refers to the Biblical obligation for the sinner to repent (*Malbim*). [See above comm. to v. 6.]

אַתֶּם תִּמְעָלוּ — *If you should sin. Malbim* explains that מַעַל in the Torah refers to one of two transgressions: 1) The sin of one who is entrusted with an object but denies that he is safeguarding it for its owner and keeps the article for himself (וּמָעֲלָה מַעַל בַּה׳ וְכִחֵשׁ בַּעֲמִיתוֹ) [*Leviticus* 5:21]; and 2) the profanation of a sacred object (הֶקְדֵּשׁ) through its use for secular purposes (נֶפֶשׁ כִּי תִמְעֹל מַעַל וְחָטְאָה בִּשְׁגָגָה מִקׇּדְשֵׁי ה׳) [*Leviticus* 5:15]. In our verse, both meanings are intended: 'If the people should sin by denying the obligation which they have assumed, and by desecrating the *mitzvos* . . .'

אֲנִי אָפִיץ אֶתְכֶם בָּעַמִּים — *And I disperse you among the nations.* Moses warned the people a number of times that their sins would cause them to be dispersed among the nations, as in the verse, *And Hashem shall disperse you among all the nations* (*Deut*. 28:64) [see also *Lev.* 26:33 and *Deuteronomy* 11:17].

9. וּשְׁמַרְתֶּם מִצְוֹתַי וַעֲשִׂיתֶם אֹתָם — *And observe My commandments and perform them.* [*Ramban* (*Exodus* 20:8), citing the Talmud (*Eruvin* 96a), asserts that שָׁמוֹר, *observe*, refers to the observance of the negative commandments (לֹא תַעֲשֶׂה).

we have not kept the commandments, the precepts, and the laws which You commanded to Your servant Moses.
8 *Remember, please, the word which You commanded Your servant Moses, saying, 'If you should sin and I disperse you among the nations,*
9 *And then you return to Me and observe My commandments and perform them; [then] even if the banished among you reach the ends of heaven, I shall gather them from there and bring them to the place which I have chosen as the resting place for My Name.'*
10 *For they are Your servants and Your people whom You redeemed with Your great strength and Your powerful hand.*
11 I *beseech You, my God, may Your ear please*

Accordingly, we may interpret וּשְׁמַרְתֶּם מִצְוֹתַי, *And observe My commandments,* in our passage as a reference to the observance of the negative commandments and וַעֲשִׂיתֶם אֹתָם, *And perform them,* as a reference to the positive commandments (עֲשֵׂה).]

אִם־יִהְיֶה נִדַּחֲכֶם בִּקְצֵה הַשָּׁמַיִם — *[Then] even if the banished among you reach the ends of heaven.* This follows *Deuteronomy* 30:4: *Even if the banished among you reach the ends of heaven,* HASHEM, *Your God, shall gather you from there* (*Rashi*).

שְׁמִי — *My Name.* This refers to the *Shechinah,* Divine Presence (*Metzudos*).

10. אֲשֶׁר פָּדִיתָ — *Whom You redeemed.* This refers to the redemption from Egypt. Nehemiah invoked the memory of the *great strength* and *powerful hand* God exhibited in taking His people out of Egypt in the hope that He would do the same for His people now. True, they had returned to the Holy Land, but only as subjects of the Persian kings. Perhaps God would free them from this subjugation and lead them Himself as He had when they left Egypt (*Malbim*).

וּבְיָדְךָ הַחֲזָקָה — *And Your powerful hand.* [This follows *Deuteronomy* 26:8: HASHEM *took us out of Egypt with a powerful hand* ... and *Deuteronomy* 34:12: *And for all of the powerful hand ... which Moses did ... Ramban* there interprets it as a reference to the splitting of the Red Sea, where Scripture states, *And Israel saw the great hand ...* (*Exodus* 14:30). Or [quoting *Sifre, Berachah*], as a reference to God's smiting of the firstborn Egyptians, when the Torah says ... *For he* [Pharaoh] *shall send them away with a powerful hand ...* [when the firstborn are smitten] (*Exodus* 6:1). In our passage, both interpretations may be used. Nehemiah spoke of *God's powerful hand* in splitting the sea or in smiting the firstborn. [See also *Rashi* to *Deut.* 7:19.]

11. אָנָּא אֲדֹנָי — *I beseech You, my God.* Nehemiah opened (v. 5) and closed his prayer with the words *I beseech You* (*Rashi*). [*Rashi* alludes to *Berachos* 29b, which states that a person should use beseeching terms in his prayers. Based on this, *Shulchan Aruch Orach Chaim* 98:3 instructs that a person should pray in a beseeching way, like a poor man begging at the door.]

קַשֶּׁבֶת אֶל־תְּפִלַּת עַבְדְּךָ וְאֶל־תְּפִלַּת עֲבָדֶיךָ
הַחֲפֵצִים לְיִרְאָה אֶת־שְׁמֶךָ וְהַצְלִיחָה־נָּא
לְעַבְדְּךָ הַיּוֹם וּתְנֵהוּ לְרַחֲמִים לִפְנֵי הָאִישׁ הַזֶּה
וַאֲנִי הָיִיתִי מַשְׁקֶה לַמֶּלֶךְ: א וַיְהִי ׀
בְּחֹדֶשׁ נִיסָן שְׁנַת עֶשְׂרִים לְאַרְתַּחְשַׁסְתְּא
הַמֶּלֶךְ יַיִן לְפָנָיו וָאֶשָּׂא אֶת־הַיַּיִן וָאֶתְּנָה
ב לַמֶּלֶךְ וְלֹא־הָיִיתִי רַע לְפָנָיו: וַיֹּאמֶר לִי הַמֶּלֶךְ

אֶל־תְּפִלַּת עַבְדְּךָ — *To the prayer of Your servant.* This refers to Nehemiah himself (*Metzudos*).

וְאֶל־תְּפִלַּת עֲבָדֶיךָ הַחֲפֵצִים לְיִרְאָה אֶת־שְׁמֶךָ — *And to the prayer of Your servants, who wish to fear Your Name.* Accept, also, the prayers of the people who wish to fear Your Name. Help them for two reasons: 1) Because of their prayers, and 2) because of their desire to fear You.

This is related to v. 10, where Nehemiah requested that God redeem the nation miraculously as He had in Egypt. Nehemiah added that on the strength of their prayers and desire to fear God, the people were as deserving of miracles now as they were in Egypt (*Malbim*).

וְהַצְלִיחָה־נָּא לְעַבְדְּךָ הַיּוֹם — *Please grant Your servant success this day.* Nehemiah now prayed for his own success [in persuading the king to allow him to aid the Jews] (*Rashi*).

וּתְנֵהוּ לְרַחֲמִים — *Make him [i.e., Nehemiah] the object of compassion.* Nehemiah now explained what *success* he requested — that the king might be compassionate towards him and grant his wish (*Metzudos*).

לִפְנֵי הָאִישׁ הַזֶּה — *Before this man.* I.e., before the king (*Rashi*).

וַאֲנִי הָיִיתִי מַשְׁקֶה לַמֶּלֶךְ — *I was the king's wine-servant* [lit. *I gave drink to the king*]. The commentaries disagree as to whether this statement is related to Nehemiah's prayer. *Ri Mitrani* interprets: 'With this prayer, I acted as the king's wine-servant.' [With my thoughts on this prayer, I served the king.]

According to *Metzudos*, however, the statement, *I was the king's wine-servant* is not related to the prayer, but is intended as a preface to the next chapter, where Nehemiah describes his experiences when placing the wine before the king.

Malbim understands the mention of Nehemiah's service to the king as an explanation of the previous phrase, *before this man.* Nehemiah now explains that *the man* referred to was the king whom he served.

Rashi, citing the Talmud [*Yerushalmi, Kiddushin* 4:1], notes that Nehemiah was called Hatirshatha, meaning *permitted to drink* [*hatir shathah*]. Because of his position as wine-servant to the king, the Rabbis *permitted him to drink* wine touched by a non-Jew, which is otherwise prohibited.[1] See comm. 2:1, 7:65.

1. *Ri Mitrani* states that permission was granted because of the danger to Nehemiah's life should he have refused the king's order to drink. [Although even Biblical prohibitions may be transgressed to save a life, a special dispensation was needed to allow Nehemiah to take the office and place himself in a position where he would be forced to drink the wine. This permission was granted so that he could work for the welfare of his people.]

listen to the prayer of Your servant and to the prayer of Your servants, who wish to fear Your Name; please grant Your servant success this day, and make him the object of compassion before this man.' I was the king's wine-servant.

It came to pass in the month of Nissan of the twentieth year of King Artahshast; [they brought] wine before him. I carried the wine and gave it to the king; I had never appeared downcast before him. 2 *The king said to*

II

⥈ Nehemiah's Plea to the King

1. שְׁנַת עֶשְׂרִים — *The twentieth year.* This was the same as the *twentieth year* mentioned in 1:1 (*Rosh Hashanah* 3b; see *comm.* 1:1).

לְאַרְתַּחְשַׁסְתְּא — *Of King Artahshast.* This was King Darius. *Artahshast* was the name given to all of the Persian kings, like Pharaoh to the Egyptians (*Rashi, Metzudos*). [Darius was the son of Ahasuerus and Queen Esther, and he completed the construction of the Temple in the sixth year of his reign (*Ezra* 6:15).] According to *Tosafos* (*Rosh Hashanah* 3b), however, the name *Artahshast* here refers to King Cyrus, who ruled a number of years earlier. This was the twentieth year *since* King Cyrus, actually the *third* year of King Darius. [See comm. and table, 1:1.]

יַיִן לְפָנָיו — *[They brought] wine before him.* I.e. to the courtyard where he sat (*Rashi*).

Malbim connects our verse with the final verse of ch. 1, וַאֲנִי הָיִיתִי מַשְׁקֶה לַמֶּלֶךְ, *I gave drink to the king*. These words are to be combined with those in our verse, producing the phrase וַאֲנִי הָיִיתִי מַשְׁקֶה לַמֶּלֶךְ, יַיִן לְפָנָיו — *I gave wine to drink to the king, wine before him.*

וָאֶשָּׂא אֶת־הַיַּיִן וָאֶתְּנָה לַמֶּלֶךְ — *I carried the wine and gave it to the king*. The custom was for one person to deliver the wine to the king's courtyard and for the wine servant then to give it to the king (*Rashi*; see preceding comm.).

וְלֹא־הָיִיתִי רַע לְפָנָיו — *I had never appeared downcast* [lit. *bad*] *before him.* The translation follows *Rashi: I had previously always been cheerful before him,* but now I looked angry and dejected.

Malbim, however, translates, *I was not downcast before him* at this time. I was careful, when I brought the wine, not to appear downcast. I knew that the king required that his servants appear before him in good humor, and that the appearance of dejection would cause him to suspect that I had evil intentions.

Ri Mitrani's rendition is *I was never bad to him* — I did not refuse to obey the Persian law requiring that I drink some of the wine before giving it to him, since my refusal would have aroused the king's suspicion. The law required that the wine-servant taste the wine intended for the king as a precaution against poisoning. The Sages, however, prohibited the drinking of wine touched by a gentile (סתם יינם, see *Shulchan Aruch Yoreh De'ah*, 123:1). Nehemiah ruled[1] that the prohibition may be waived in the case of

1. [The Jerusalem Talmud (*Kiddushin* 4:1) states that the Rabbis, and not Nehemiah, permitted him to drink the wine. However, *Ri Mitrani* here and in his notes to *Ezra* 2:63 quotes Rabbinical sources as stating that Nehemiah himself issued the ruling.]

מַדּוּעַ ׀ פָּנֶיךָ רָעִים וְאַתָּה אֵינְךָ חוֹלֶה אֵין זֶה
ג כִּי־אִם רֹעַ לֵב וָאִירָא הַרְבֵּה מְאֹד׃ וָאֹמַר
לַמֶּלֶךְ הַמֶּלֶךְ לְעוֹלָם יִחְיֶה מַדּוּעַ לֹא־יֵרְעוּ
פָנַי אֲשֶׁר הָעִיר בֵּית־קִבְרוֹת אֲבֹתַי חֲרֵבָה
ד וּשְׁעָרֶיהָ אֻכְּלוּ בָאֵשׁ׃ וַיֹּאמֶר
לִי הַמֶּלֶךְ עַל־מַה־זֶּה אַתָּה מְבַקֵּשׁ וָאֶתְפַּלֵּל
ה אֶל־אֱלֹהֵי הַשָּׁמָיִם׃ וָאֹמַר לַמֶּלֶךְ אִם־עַל־
הַמֶּלֶךְ טוֹב וְאִם־יִיטַב עַבְדְּךָ לְפָנֶיךָ אֲשֶׁר
תִּשְׁלָחֵנִי אֶל־יְהוּדָה אֶל־עִיר קִבְרוֹת אֲבֹתַי

the king's wine-servant, since refusal could antagonize the king, and place the servant (and perhaps the entire Jewish people) in mortal danger. [See footnote above to 1:11; ArtScroll *Ezra* 2:63.]

Ibn Ezra's interpretation is *I was not unacceptable to him* as a servant. He desired my service.

2. מַדּוּעַ פָּנֶיךָ רָעִים — *Why is your face downcast* [lit. *bad*]? Nehemiah appeared downcast and angry as a result of his fasting and weeping [1:4] (*Ri Mitrani*). *Metzudos* explains that dejection causes the face to lose its brightness, making it look bad.

Ibn Ezra translates רָעִים as *broken* [see *Isaiah* 24:19], or *weakened* like someone ill.

Although Nehemiah attempted to appear before the king in good spirits [see comm. v. 1], the effects of his fasting and weeping could be discerned in his face. Alternatively, Divine Providence caused his face to appear downcast, so that the king would initiate the discussion which eventually resulted in the rejuvenation of the community in Jerusalem (*Malbim*).

וְאַתָּה אֵינְךָ חוֹלֶה — *You are not ill.* [Apparently the king recognized that, although Nehemiah's expression was one of haggardness and dejection, he was not physically ill.]

רֹעַ לֵב — *Evil intention* [lit. *heart*]. Your dark look indicates that you have poisoned the wine and intend to murder me (*Rashi; Metzudos*). *Ri Mitrani* translates רֹעַ לֵב as *hatred*; you look as if you hate me.

According to *Ralbag*, the king did not suspect Nehemiah of evil intent, but was merely inquiring solicitously after his well-being. רֹעַ לֵב means *heartache*. The king thought that some great worry had caused Nehemiah's downcast look. Nehemiah, however, misunderstood, and thought that the king suspected him of evil intentions.

וָאִירָא הַרְבֵּה מְאֹד — *I became extremely frightened.* I was afraid of the king's false accusation (*Rashi*).

According to *Malbim* [see comm. to v. 1 and 2], Nehemiah was frightened because he had violated the requirement that the king's servants appear in good humor, and the king, who was offended and angry, had absolute power over his life.

3. הַמֶּלֶךְ לְעוֹלָם יִחְיֶה — *May the king live forever!* Protocol required that the

me, 'You are not ill. Why is your face downcast? This could only be your evil intention.' I became extremely frightened.
3 *So I said to the king, 'May the king live forever! Why should my face not be downcast when the city where my ancestors are buried is desolate, and its gates are consumed by fire?'*
4 *The king said to me, 'What is your request?' I then prayed to the God of heaven.*
5 *And I said to the king, 'If it please the king, and if your servant finds favor before you, then permit me to go to Judah to the city where my*

king be blessed at the outset of one's remarks (*Metzudos*).

הָעִיר בֵּית־קִבְרוֹת אֲבֹתַי — *The city where my ancestors are buried*. This refers to Jerusalem (*Rashi*). Nehemiah expressed his concern for Jerusalem in this manner because the Persians revered ancestral burial grounds (*Malbim*).

חֲרֵבָה — *Desolate*. I am downcast because the city and its gates are desolate [but not because of any evil intentions towards you] (*Metzudos*).

☙ The King's Reply

4. עַל־מַה־זֶּה אַתָּה מְבַקֵּשׁ — *What is your request?* Tell me your request, so that I may fulfill it (*Rashi*).

וָאֶתְפַּלֵּל — *I then* [lit. *and I*] *prayed*. Nehemiah's prayer does not appear in the text. *Rashi* and *Metzudos* explain that, before opening his request to the king (v. 5), Nehemiah uttered a short prayer for Divine aid in achieving his purpose.

Ibn Ezra, however, renders *I had prayed* [referring to the prayer recorded in 1:5-11].

Malbim and *Pri Tzaddik* (*Vayigash*, quoting *R' Menachem Azariah of Panu*) present a novel interpretation: While uttering the words in the next verse (v. 5), Nehemiah turned his heart toward "the God of heaven". [This is indicated by the insertion of the clause וָאֶתְפַּלֵּל אֶל־אֱלֹהֵי הַשָּׁמָיִם, *I then prayed to the God of heaven*, between the king's question (v. 4) and Nehemiah's reply (v. 5).] The king heard the words of v. 5, but Nehemiah's thoughts addressed the supreme King, HASHEM, in prayer.

☙ Nehemiah's Request

5. אִם־עַל־הַמֶּלֶךְ טוֹב — *If it please the king*. The translation follows *Metzudos*. According to *Malbim* and *Pri Tzaddik*, although Nehemiah uttered the words before King Darius, his thoughts were directed towards God. 'If it please the King of the universe ...'

In a similar view, *Pri Tzaddik* interprets Judah's statement to Joseph "... *I beseech you, my master*..." (*Genesis* 44:18) as a prayer. In Judah's thoughts, *my master* referred to *God*, the Master of the universe.

וְאִם־יִיטַב עַבְדְּךָ לְפָנֶיךָ — *And if your servant finds favor before you*. According to *Malbim*, this was not merely a polite redundancy, but a double request: (1) *If it please the king*, i.e., that the king acquiesce to let the city be rebuilt, even if he does not approve of my participation; and (2) *If your servant finds favor before you*, i.e., that you choose me to carry out this rebuilding.

ו וְאֶבְנֶנָּה: וַיֹּאמֶר לִי הַמֶּלֶךְ וְהַשֵּׁגַל ׀ יוֹשֶׁבֶת
אֶצְלוֹ עַד־מָתַי יִהְיֶה מַהֲלָכְךָ וּמָתַי תָּשׁוּב
וַיִּיטַב לִפְנֵי־הַמֶּלֶךְ וַיִּשְׁלָחֵנִי וָאֶתְּנָה לוֹ זְמָן:
ז וָאוֹמַר לַמֶּלֶךְ אִם־עַל־הַמֶּלֶךְ טוֹב אִגְּרוֹת
יִתְּנוּ־לִי עַל־פַּחֲווֹת עֵבֶר הַנָּהָר אֲשֶׁר יַעֲבִירוּנִי
ח עַד אֲשֶׁר־אָבוֹא אֶל־יְהוּדָה: וְאִגֶּרֶת אֶל־אָסָף
שֹׁמֵר הַפַּרְדֵּס אֲשֶׁר לַמֶּלֶךְ אֲשֶׁר יִתֶּן־לִי

◆§ The King's Reply

6. וְהַשֵּׁגַל — *With the queen. Rashi* here and in *Daniel* 5:2 translates שֵׁגַל as the *king's wife*, or *queen*. *Rashi* to *Deuteronomy* 28:30 translates שֵׁגַל as *concubine*.

Malbim suggests that the queen mentioned here was the king's mother, Queen Esther (see comm. below).

According to one opinion in *Rosh Hashanah* 4a, שֵׁגַל refers to a female dog with whom the king had unnatural relations. The practice of this abomination indicates that King Darius, who was previously righteous, had now "soured". [See ArtScroll *Ezra*, footnotes to 6:4 and 7:8.] None of the commentators to our verse, however, cite this opinion, evidently preferring the prevailing interpretation in the Talmud of שֵׁגַל as *queen*.

וְהַשֵּׁגַל יוֹשֶׁבֶת אֶצְלוֹ — *With the queen sitting beside him.* Our translation follows *Rashi*, who comments that the queen sat beside the king while he spoke.

Malbim, however, renders *the king, and the queen sitting beside him, said to me*, noting that the singular וַיֹּאמֶר, *he said*, is sometimes used in describing a statement made by two people (see *Genesis* 21:22). Perhaps, *Malbim* adds, *the queen* refers to Esther, whom the Rabbis identify as Darius' mother. Out of her great love for her people, she immediately granted Nehemiah's request, merely asking him for the time of his departure.

עַד־מָתַי יִהְיֶה מַהֲלָכְךָ — *When* [lit. *until when*] *will you depart?* The translation follows *Rashi*. *Metzudos*, however, translates, *until when*, i.e., how long will your trip last? The next question — *when will you return?* — is merely a clarification of the first inquiry.

וַיִּיטַב לִפְנֵי־הַמֶּלֶךְ וַיִּשְׁלָחֵנִי — *The king was favorable and permitted me to go.* Nehemiah had not yet replied to the inquiry concerning the times of his intended departure and return, when the king interjected his permission. Nehemiah then replied, informing the king when his departure and return would take place (*Malbim*).

7. אִגְּרוֹת יִתְּנוּ־לִי — *Let them give me letters.* Let the king's scribes give me letters sealed with the royal signet (*Rashi*).

עֵבֶר הַנָּהָר — *Trans-River.* This refers to the Land of Israel, which lay across the river [Euphrates] from Persia (see ArtScroll *Ezra* 4:10).

אֲשֶׁר יַעֲבִירוּנִי — *So that they will bring me across.* They will accompany me and protect me (*Rashi*). The letter requested by Nehemiah directed the satraps to provide guards to accompany him (*Metzudos*).

Malbim observes that the king provided a military escort for Nehemiah until the borders of the Holy Land (v. 9). He now requested an armed escort

ancestors are buried, so that I may build it.'
6 *The king said to me with the queen sitting beside him, 'When will you depart and when will you return?' The king was favorable and permitted me to go, and I gave him a time.*
7 *Then I said to the king, 'If it please the king, let them give me letters to the Trans-River satraps, so that they will bring me across until I arrive in Judah;*
8 *And a letter to Asaph, the king's forester, so that he will give me*

for the remainder of the journey.[1]

Ralbag explains that Nehemiah was concerned that the *enemies of Judah and Benjamin*, who had halted the Temple construction [*Ezra* ch. 4] and traditionally oppressed the Jews, would now attack him.

8. וְאִגֶּרֶת אֶל־אָסָף — *And a letter to Asaph*. Let the king himself dispatch a letter to Asaph (*Rashi*), or give it to Nehemiah, who would give it to Asaph (*Metzudos*).

שֹׁמֵר הַפַּרְדֵּס — *The king's forester*. Our translation follows *Rashi*. Asaph was the keeper of the forests of Lebanon, which belonged to the king (*Malbim*). [See ArtScroll *Ezra* 3:7.]

אֲשֶׁר יִתֶּן־לִי עֵצִים — *So that he will give me timbers*. The Talmud (*Arachin* 6a) asserts that donations from non-Jews are not acceptable for the construction of the Temple, either because their offer may mask a hidden intent to disrupt the Temple construction (as in the case of *The enemies of Judah and Benjamin — Ezra* ch. 4, *Rashi; Arachin*), or because their participation in the construction could lead them to later claim ownership of the Temple (*Tosafos*). [See also ArtScroll *Ezra* 4:3.] Why, then, asks the Talmud, was it permitted to accept timbers from Asaph?[2] The Talmud answers that donations may be accepted from a king since it is unlikely that imperial policy, once instituted, would be reversed. 'Shemuel said: *If the imperial power undertakes to uproot a mountain, then it will uproot it, and never reverse itself!*' Thus, it could be assumed that, once the king used the power of his throne to promote the rebuilding of the Temple, he would not later reverse himself and hinder its construction [see *Esther* 8:8]. Nor was it likely that the king would later claim sovereignty over the Temple, once he had publicly proclaimed that its con-

1. *Ezra* 8:22 records that Ezra ascended to *Eretz Yisrael* without the king's military support. *Malbim* (ibid.) explains that Ezra did not request military aid because the king had been told that the returning exiles enjoyed special Divine protection. Otherwise, Ezra would not have relied solely on God's protection, and would have asked for troops (as Nehemiah did twelve years later in our verse). [Even though Ezra and his entourage were engaged in fulfilling a major *mitzvah* — that of going up to the Holy Land — nevertheless, אֵין סוֹמְכִים עַל הַנֵּס, *we do not rely on miracles*. As the Talmud (*Pesachim* 8a) states, even while engaged in performing a *mitzvah* (when the merit of the *mitzvah* provides a protective shield), it is improper to expose oneself to *likely* danger.]

2. [Asaph acted under the instructions of Darius, who was the son of Ahasuerus and Queen Esther (*Midrash Rabbah* 13:5), hence, a bona fide Jew. Why, then, does *Arachin* treat Darius' donation as that of a non-Jew? Evidently, the reason is that he acted in his capacity as king of Persia. A gift bestowed by the monarch of a gentile nation is, in effect, a gift given by gentiles.]

ב
ט־י

עֵצִים לְקָרוֹת אֶת־שַׁעֲרֵי הַבִּירָה אֲשֶׁר־
לַבַּיִת וּלְחוֹמַת הָעִיר וְלַבַּיִת אֲשֶׁר־אָבוֹא
אֵלָיו וַיִּתֶּן־לִי הַמֶּלֶךְ כְּיַד־אֱלֹהַי הַטּוֹבָה עָלָי׃
ט וָאָבוֹא אֶל־פַּחֲווֹת עֵבֶר הַנָּהָר וָאֶתְּנָה לָהֶם
אֵת אִגְּרוֹת הַמֶּלֶךְ וַיִּשְׁלַח עִמִּי הַמֶּלֶךְ שָׂרֵי
י חַיִל וּפָרָשִׁים׃ וַיִּשְׁמַע
סַנְבַלַּט הַחֹרֹנִי וְטוֹבִיָּה הָעֶבֶד הָעַמֹּנִי וַיֵּרַע

struction was for the Jewish people.

This comment is apparently contradicted by the events in *Ezra* (ch. 4), when the enemies of Judah and Benjamin persuaded the king to withdraw his sanction for the Temple's reconstruction. *Malbim*, however, to *Ezra* 4:21, explains that the enemies convinced the king, through a slanderous misrepresentation of the activities in Jerusalem, that the Jews had grossly overstepped the terms of the edict. The decree had specified that they were granted permission only to rebuild the Temple. Instead, the enemies alleged, they were actually rebuilding and fortifying the entire city with its surrounding walls, indicating that they planned a rebellion. The king accepted the slander and halted the work in Jerusalem because he assumed that the construction taking place was unauthorized by his edict. Thus, the enemies were successful in circumventing the objective of the proclamation without actually repealing it (see further ArtScroll *Ezra* 4:21).

שַׁעֲרֵי הַבִּירָה אֲשֶׁר־לַבַּיִת — *The palace gates of the Temple*. The *palace* (בִּירָה) refers to the Temple [see *I Chronicles* 29:1] (*Metzudos*). The Talmudic Sage, Resh Lakish, holds that the term בִּירָה connotes the entire Temple complex. By contrast, R' Yochanan thinks that it refers only to a citadel which stood on the Temple Mount. [See *Yerushalmi, Pesachim* 7:8 and *Zevachim* 104b. See also *Aruch HaShalem* under בִּירָה.]

The palace gates were the gates of the wall which surrounded the Temple Mount (הַר הַבַּיִת) and the gates of the wall which surrounded the Temple Courtyard (עֲזָרָה). The Temple itself had been built but not the gates of these walls (*Rashi*; see *Middos* 1:3, 4).

Ralbag explains that שַׁעֲרֵי הַבִּירָה, *palace gates*, refers not to the gates themselves, but to the vestibules [of wood] which were built before the gates and led to them.

וּלְחוֹמַת הָעִיר — *And for the walls of the city*. The beams were to be used in constructing the walls of the city (*Rashi*). *Ibn Ezra* and *Metzudos* (to *Ezra* 6:4) explain, in regard to the Temple complex (of Solomon), that wooden tiers used in unison with marble tiers actually fortify the structure. [This is apparently *Rashi's* intention — that the wood was to be used along with stone for the city's walls.] According to *Ralbag*, the wood was to be used in constructing the roofs over the gates of the city walls.

וְלַבַּיִת אֲשֶׁר־אָבוֹא אֵלָיו — *And for the home into which I will enter*. Nehemiah also requested beams to build a house for his personal use (*Rashi*). The royal representative in a foreign country lived in a house which belonged to the king. Nehemiah requested such a house, referring to it as *the* home, but not *my* home, since it would belong to the king (*Malbim*).

וַיִּתֶּן־לִי הַמֶּלֶךְ כְּיַד־אֱלֹהַי הַטּוֹבָה עָלָי — *The king gave me [this] by my God's beneficence* [lit. *good hand*] *to me*. God's beneficence gave me success and enabled

timbers to roof the palace gates of the Temple, and for the
walls of the city, and for the home into which I will enter.'
The king gave me [this] by my God's beneficence to me.
9 *So I came to the Trans-River satraps, and gave them*
the king's letters. The king had sent army officers and
cavalrymen with me.
10 *Now, when Sanballat the Horonite and Tobiah the*

me to find favor before the king (*Rashi*, *Metzudos*).

☙ Nehemiah's Journey

9. אִגְּרוֹת הַמֶּלֶךְ — *The king's letters*. I gave the satraps the king's letters instructing them to accompany me (*Rashi*).

וַיִּשְׁלַח עִמִּי הַמֶּלֶךְ שָׂרֵי חַיִל וּפָרָשִׁים — *The king had sent army officers and cavalrymen with me*. The officers and cavalrymen were sent for my honor and protection (*Rashi*).

Malbim explains that they accompanied Nehemiah until his meeting with the satraps. Although the text mentions only Nehemiah's request for protection *after* his arrival in the Trans-River territory (v. 7), it is obvious that he must have also asked for the soldiers who accompanied him to the satraps.

Metzudos offers an alternative interpretation: Our verse refers to the party now sent by the satraps to protect Nehemiah in *Eretz Yisrael*. The army officers and cavaliers are described as those whom *the king had sent* because the satraps sent them under instructions from the king.

☙ The Enemies

10. סַנְבַלַּט הַחֹרֹנִי — *Sanballat the Horonite*. *Ri Mitrani* identifies him as a Jewish apostate from the city of Beth Horon (בֵּית חוֹרוֹן).

Wertheimer (notes on *Ri Mitrani*), however, cites *Josephus* (ch. 5), who asserts that Sanballat was a gentile whose daughter had married a Jewish *Kohen*. When the *Kohanim* who had intermarried expelled their gentile wives in the times of Ezra (*Ezra* 10:18), Sanballat's Jewish son-in-law refused, and was disqualified from the priesthood.

According to *Josephus*, Sanballat lived to witness the fall of the Persian empire to the Greeks, and enlisted the aid of Alexander the Great in setting up a rival temple for his son-in-law on Mount Gerizim.

וְטוֹבִיָּה הָעֶבֶד הָעַמֹּנִי — *And Tobiah the Ammonite slave*. The Talmud (*Kiddushin* 70a) identifies Tobiah the Ammonite slave as the Tobiah [mentioned later 6:18] whose father-in-law was Shechaniah ben Aruch, and whose son had married the daughter of Meshullam ben Berachiah. Tobiah's marriage (as well as his son's) was not recognized by Torah law because a slave is disqualified from marrying into the Jewish community. [The Talmud does not clarify whether Tobiah was the slave of gentile or Jewish masters. In either case he would have been forbidden to marry a Jewish woman, since gentiles or even gentile slaves owned by a Jew may not marry into the Jewish people (see *Rambam*, *Isurei Biah* 12:1, 11-13).]

Rashi (6:17) remarks that Tobiah was a Jew, albeit wicked. This statement apparently conflicts with the Talmud's contention that he was disqualified from marrying a Jewish woman. The conflict may be resolved by interpreting *Rashi's* statement to mean that Tobiah was a gentile slave owned by a Jew, and had undergone immersion in the *mikveh*. Such a slave achieves a degree of

ב
יא־יג

לָהֶם רָעָה גְדֹלָה אֲשֶׁר־בָּא אָדָם לְבַקֵּשׁ טוֹבָה
יא לִבְנֵי יִשְׂרָאֵל: וָאָבוֹא אֶל־יְרוּשָׁלָ͏ִם וָאֱהִי־שָׁם
יב יָמִים שְׁלֹשָׁה: וָאָקוּם ׀ לַיְלָה אֲנִי וַאֲנָשִׁים ׀
מְעַט עִמִּי וְלֹא־הִגַּדְתִּי לְאָדָם מָה אֱלֹהַי נֹתֵן
אֶל־לִבִּי לַעֲשׂוֹת לִירוּשָׁלָ͏ִם וּבְהֵמָה אֵין עִמִּי
יג כִּי אִם־הַבְּהֵמָה אֲשֶׁר אֲנִי רֹכֵב בָּהּ: וָאֵצְאָה
בְשַׁעַר־הַגַּיְא לַיְלָה וְאֶל־פְּנֵי עֵין הַתַּנִּין וְאֶל־
שַׁעַר הָאַשְׁפֹּת וָאֱהִי שֹׂבֵר בְּחוֹמֹת יְרוּשָׁלַ͏ִם

Jewish sanctity. He must observe most of the *mitzvos* which apply to Jewish people, and not just the seven precepts incumbent upon all non-Jews. See *Rambam, Isurei Biah*, 12:11.

In addition to being a slave, Tobiah is identified as an Ammonite. Male Ammonites, even after converting to Judaism, are forbidden to marry into the Jewish community. [See comm. to v. 13:1,3.]

Rashi and *Metzudos* identify Sanballat and Tobiah as *the enemies of Judah and Benjamin* who had previously succeeded in disrupting the reconstruction of the Temple (*Ezra* ch. 4). [The *enemies of Judah and Benjamin* were idolatrous gentiles who had been transplanted by the Assyrian king, Sennacherib, from their homelands to Samaria in the Land of Israel (*II Kings* 17:24). Thus, they became known as Samaritans. In Talmudic terminology they are referred to as Cuthites (כּוּתִים). They were a constant source of attacks upon the Jews. See comm. to 3:34; ArtScroll *Ezra* 4:1 and footnote to 4:3.]

אֲשֶׁר־בָּא אָדָם — *That a person had come.* Our translation follows *Rashi*, who sees the syntax of the verse as unusual and to be understood as if its order were rearranged to read: *When Sanballat...and Tobiah...heard that a person had come...they were extremely chagrined.*

The translation of *Metzudos*, however, assumes the verse's syntax to be in sequence: *When Sanballat...and Tobiah...heard* [about my request to rebuild the city], *they were extremely chagrined that a person had come to seek the benefit of the Children of Israel.*

◄§ Nehemiah Arrives

11. יָמִים שְׁלֹשָׁה — *For three days.* After three days in Jerusalem, I began the activities described in the following verses (*Rashi*).

[Similarly, Ezra waited three days to prepare for the intense concentration necessary in examining his followers' genealogical records (see ArtScroll *Ezra* 8:15). Nehemiah, too, waited for three days before beginning the arduous task of examining and rebuilding the city walls.]

Ralbag explains that Nehemiah waited three days to avoid attention, so that he could conduct his activities without arousing the enemies' suspicion.

12. וָאָקוּם לַיְלָה... — *I then arose at night* ... Nehemiah conducted his activities under cover of darkness and in the company of just a few men held to secrecy to avoid detection. The enemies of the Jews, indeed, later attempted to halt the reconstruction [ch. 4] (*Malbim*). To further minimize the chance of discovery, he took no animals with his party

II
11-13

Ammonite slave heard that a person had come to seek the benefit of the Children of Israel, they were extremely chagrined. 11 *I arrived in Jerusalem, and was there for three days.* 12 *I then arose at night, accompanied by a few men, without telling anyone what my God had inspired me to do for Jerusalem. There were no beasts with me, save for the beast upon which I rode.* 13 *I went out in the night through the Gate of the Valley to Ein HaTanin and to the Refuse Gate; I broke the walls of Jerusalem*

for fear that their noise would alert his enemies (*Rashi*).

13. וָאֵצְאָה — *I went out*. I went out, accompanied by my companions (*Rashi*).

בְשַׁעַר־הַגַּיְא — *Through the Gate of the Valley*. The translation follows *Ralbag*, who explains that this gate led to an area known as גֵּיא בֶן־הִנֹּם, *the valley of Ben Hinom*. [The valley of *Ben Hinom* is mentioned by *Jeremiah* (19:2). *Rashi*, there, states that this valley stood next to the Refuse Gate.]

Malbim asserts that Nehemiah's home was adjacent to the Gate of the Valley, at the western side of the wall. He moved southward to *Ein HaTanin*, and from there to the Refuse Gate.

As proof that Nehemiah's home was adjacent to the Gate of the Valley, *Malbim* cites 3:11,13, where it is recorded that the Gate of the Valley was situated between the Tower of Ovens and the Refuse Gate. Ch. 12 describes how Nehemiah arranged for two groups to march around the city walls, one group to the right side towards the Refuse Gate (v. 31), and a second group to the left, to the Tower of Ovens (v. 38). Although the text does not identify the starting point from which the two groups marched, logic dictates that it was Nehemiah's home, at the Gate of the Valley, which stood between the Tower of Ovens and the Refuse Gate.

וְאֶל־שַׁעַר הָאַשְׁפֹּת — *And to the Refuse Gate*. I passed the place known as *Ein HaTanin*, and proceeded from there to the Refuse Gate, one of the gates of the Jerusalem wall, situated 1000 cubits away from the Gate of the Valley [3:13] (*Malbim*).

The city's garbage was carried out through the Refuse Gate, which led to the area used as the refuse heap (*Ralbag*). [Although identical in name (שַׁעַר הָאַשְׁפּוֹת), this gate, apparently, is not identical with the gate today commonly called the "Dung Gate." That gate faces the south. The Refuse Gate mentioned here evidently faced west. See *Malbim* to 3:12,13.]

וָאֱהִי שֹׁבֵר בְּחוֹמֹת יְרוּשָׁלַם — *I broke the walls of Jerusalem*. *Rashi*, *Metzudos* and *Ri Mitrani* read שֹׁבֵר, with the letter *shin* (שׁ), meaning *broke*.

Rashi and *Ri Mitrani* explain that Nehemiah and his group increased the damage to the walls so that the people could be easily aroused to action in repairing them. *Metzudos* thinks that the purpose of the breakage was to give the impression that the enemies of the Jews had inflicted more damage, thus arousing the Jewish community to quickly rebuild them.

However, *Ibn Ezra* and *Ralbag* read שֹׂבֵר, with the letter *sin* (שׂ), meaning *contemplated* or *studied*. Their interpretation is that Nehemiah studied the city's walls in order to determine the extent of the repairs needed.

According to *Malbim*, Nehemiah first attempted breaking the walls merely to

°הֵם | פְּרוּצִים ק׳

אֲשֶׁר־°הֵמפרוּצִים וּשְׁעָרֶיהָ אֻכְּלוּ בָאֵשׁ׃
יד וָאֶעֱבֹר אֶל־שַׁעַר הָעַיִן וְאֶל־בְּרֵכַת הַמֶּלֶךְ
טו וְאֵין־מָקוֹם לַבְּהֵמָה לַעֲבֹר תַּחְתָּי׃ וָאֱהִי
עֹלֶה בַנַּחַל לַיְלָה וָאֱהִי שֹׂבֵר בַּחוֹמָה
טז וָאָשׁוּב וָאָבוֹא בְּשַׁעַר הַגַּיְא וָאָשׁוּב׃ וְהַסְּגָנִים
לֹא יָדְעוּ אָנָה הָלַכְתִּי וּמָה אֲנִי עֹשֶׂה
וְלַיְּהוּדִים וְלַכֹּהֲנִים וְלַחֹרִים וְלַסְּגָנִים
וּלְיֶתֶר עֹשֵׂה הַמְּלָאכָה עַד־כֵּן לֹא הִגַּדְתִּי׃

test their strength. That portion of the walls which crumbled easily needed to be replaced. Where they held fast, they would be left intact and merely strengthened. Indeed, 4:1 indicates that only the breached portions were replaced. The walls' solid portions were left in place and strengthened. *Malbim's* interpretation, therefore, fits both readings of שבר: *he broke* the walls in order *to study* them.

אֲשֶׁר־הֵמפְּרוּצִים וּשְׁעָרֶיהָ אֻכְּלוּ בָאֵשׁ — *Which were breached, and the gates consumed by fire.* I caused additional breakage to those areas which were breached and consumed by fire, and were therefore more susceptible to further damage (*Rashi*).

Ralbag interprets, I studied those areas which were breached and consumed by fire, to determine the extent of the repairs needed [see comm. above].

Minchas Shai notes that הֵם פְּרוּצִים (*they were breached*) is written (כְּתִיב) as one word — הֵמפְּרוּצִים, without a space between the הֵמ and פְּרוּצִים, and with the letter *mem* (מ) open as normally used in the middle of the word; but it is read (קְרִי) separately — הֵם פְּרוּצִים, with a space between הֵם and פְּרוּצִים, and with the closed *mem* (ם), as used at the end of a word. *Ibn Ezra* suggests that the purpose of the open *mem* in our verse is to indicate homiletically the open or breached state of the walls.

Ibn Ezra cites a similar case of combined words in *Exodus* 4:2. [See *Rashi* there.]

14. וָאֶעֱבֹר אֶל — *I then desired to cross* [lit. *I crossed*] *to*. This is *Rashi's* translation. *Ralbag* renders *I crossed to* those places, but could not pass through them.

שַׁעַר הָעַיִן — *The Gate of the Spring*. This gate led to a spring which served as a water supply (*Ralbag*).

Malbim places the Gate of the Spring to the south of the Refuse Gate, based on 3:15. [See comm. there.]

וְאֶל־בְּרֵכַת הַמֶּלֶךְ — *And the King's Pool*. This was a gate which led to a pool used either for watering the king's horses and as a general water supply for the king or as the water supply for the king's gardens (*Ralbag*).

[The text describes Nehemiah's movements along the wall. Thus, *the King's Pool* cannot mean the pool itself, but a gate in the wall leading to the pool.]

וְאֵין־מָקוֹם — *But there was no place*. I could not pass through the breaches there, as they were too narrow for a person riding a beast (*Rashi*), and the place was strewn with stones which had fallen from the wall (*Metzudos*).

Ralbag explains that the ground was broken up, making it impassible for an animal. [*No place for the beast* means no place *suitable* for the beast.]

In any case, Nehemiah did not pass through the difficult breaches, but went on to the valley mentioned in the follow-

II
14-16

which were breached, and the gates consumed by fire.
14 *I then desired to cross to the Gate of the Spring and the King's Pool, but there was no place for the beast under me to pass.*
15 *I went up the valley in the night, and broke the wall. Then I turned back, came to the Gate of the Valley and returned.*
16 *Now the nobles did not know where I had gone and what I was doing, for I had not, until now, informed the Jews, Kohanim, aristocrats, nobles, and the remainder who did the work.*

ing verse. *Malbim*, however, states that Nehemiah dismounted and visited the narrow breaches on foot.

לַבְּהֵמָה לַעֲבֹר תַּחְתָּי — *For the beast under me to pass* [lit. *to pass under me*]. The translation follows *Metzudos*.

15. וָאֱהִי עֹלֶה בַנַּחַל — *I went up the valley*. This refers to the area described later as *the hills descending from the city of David* [3:15] (*Malbim*).

וָאֱהִי שֹׂבֵר בַּחוֹמָה — *And broke the wall*. I broke the wall, together with those who accompanied me (*Rashi*). As above, *Ralbag* translates, *studied the wall* [see comm., v. 13].

וָאָשׁוּב...וָאָשׁוּב — *Then I turned back...and returned*. Now Nehemiah *turned* back and headed northward along the same route he had come. Then he *returned* to his home (*Malbim*).

16. וְהַסְּגָנִים — *Now the nobles*. The nobles were aware that Nehemiah had left his home, but did not know where he had gone (*Malbim*).

[The nobles in this first part of the verse are different nobles from those mentioned in the latter part. The second part of the verse lists those dignitaries (among them, a group identified as *nobles*) whom Nehemiah had not informed. The first part, which states separately that *the nobles did not know*, indicates that these nobles' lack of knowledge was different from the others' — they *did not know* where Nehemiah had gone, but they knew Nehemiah had left his home. Thus, there were two sets of nobles.]

וּמָה אֲנִי עֹשֶׂה — *And what I was doing* [lit. *am doing*]. The nobles did not know where Nehemiah had gone during the night, or even what he was doing in Jerusalem. They were unaware of his mission to rebuild the walls (*Malbim*).

וְלַחֹרִים — *Aristocrats*. This refers to the lords (*Ri Mitrani*). *Metzudos* explains that the word is derived from חוּר, *white* or *bright*, and refers to great leaders.

וְלַסְּגָנִים — *Nobles*. This refers to the noblemen of the cities of Judah (*Metzudos*). [But not of Jerusalem, already mentioned in the first phrase of the verse.]

עַד־כֵּן — *Until now* [lit. *until thus*]. The translation follows *Rashi*, who understands כֵּן as כָּאן, *now*. [*Until now*, Nehemiah did not inform them of his plans to request that the walls be rebuilt. Now he did, as explained in the next verse.]

Ibn Ezra and *Metzudos*, however, translate כֵּן as *thus*, referring to Nehemiah's plan of rebuilding the walls. *Until* my intentions were actually carried out *thus*, i.e., according to plan, I did not inform them that I had broken the walls. Later, when the plan was carried out and the walls were built (ch. 7), I informed

ב
יז־כ

יז וָאוֹמַר אֲלֵהֶם אַתֶּם רֹאִים הָרָעָה אֲשֶׁר
אֲנַחְנוּ בָהּ אֲשֶׁר יְרוּשָׁלַם חֲרֵבָה וּשְׁעָרֶיהָ
נִצְּתוּ בָאֵשׁ לְכוּ וְנִבְנֶה אֶת־חוֹמַת יְרוּשָׁלַם
יח וְלֹא־נִהְיֶה עוֹד חֶרְפָּה׃ וָאַגִּיד לָהֶם אֶת־יַד
אֱלֹהַי אֲשֶׁר־הִיא טוֹבָה עָלַי וְאַף־דִּבְרֵי
הַמֶּלֶךְ אֲשֶׁר אָמַר־לִי וַיֹּאמְרוּ נָקוּם וּבָנִינוּ
יט וַיְחַזְּקוּ יְדֵיהֶם לַטּוֹבָה׃ וַיִּשְׁמַע
סַנְבַלַּט הַחֹרֹנִי וְטֹבִיָּה ׀ הָעֶבֶד הָעַמּוֹנִי וְגֶשֶׁם
הָעַרְבִי וַיַּלְעִגוּ לָנוּ וַיִּבְזוּ עָלֵינוּ וַיֹּאמְרוּ
מָה־הַדָּבָר הַזֶּה אֲשֶׁר אַתֶּם עֹשִׂים הַעַל
כ הַמֶּלֶךְ אַתֶּם מֹרְדִים׃ וָאָשִׁיב אוֹתָם דָּבָר
וָאוֹמַר לָהֶם אֱלֹהֵי הַשָּׁמַיִם הוּא יַצְלִיחַ לָנוּ

them that I had previously broken the walls.

17. וָאוֹמַר אֲלֵהֶם — *So I said to them.* The following day I said to them (*Rashi*).

הָרָעָה אֲשֶׁר אֲנַחְנוּ בָהּ — *How badly off we are* [lit. *the badness in which we are*]. We are so badly off because of the oppression of the enemies of Judah (*Malbim*).

אֲשֶׁר יְרוּשָׁלַם חֲרֵבָה — *That Jerusalem is desolate.* Because Jerusalem is desolate we are not fortified against our enemies (*Malbim*). And because its gates have been ruined by fire, anyone may easily add to the breakage [as someone did last night] (*Metzudos*).

לְכוּ וְנִבְנֶה אֶת־חוֹמַת יְרוּשָׁלַם וְלֹא־נִהְיֶה עוֹד חֶרְפָּה — *Come, let us build the wall of Jerusalem so that we shall no longer be humiliated.* Let us strengthen the walls so that 1) we will be protected (*Malbim*) and 2) passers-by will no longer humiliate us by breaking them (*Metzudos*).

◆§ The People Accept

18. אֱלֹהַי אֲשֶׁר־הִיא טוֹבָה עָלַי — *Of my God's beneficent hand towards me.* I told them how God had granted me favor and success before the king [who granted my requests for permission to rebuild the wall and for aid in doing so (vs. 6-8)] (*Rashi*).

וְאַף־דִּבְרֵי הַמֶּלֶךְ אֲשֶׁר אָמַר־לִי — *And also of the king's words which he had spoken to me.* This refers to words of comfort not recorded in the text (*Metzudos*). [The king's permission for Nehemiah to visit Jerusalem and his letters aiding Nehemiah (vs. 6-8) are already referred to in the opening phrase of our verse *I told them of my God's beneficent hand towards me. The king's words ... to me*, therefore, refers to words of comfort, not alluded to in the statement about God's beneficence.]

וַיְחַזְּקוּ יְדֵיהֶם לַטּוֹבָה — *And they strengthened their hands for the good.* Their intentions were for the good; they strengthened themselves to accomplish a good thing — the construction of the city wall (*Rashi; Metzudos*).

Ibn Ezra disagrees, translating, *They*

II 17-20

[17] *So I said to them, 'You see how badly off we are; that Jerusalem is desolate and its gates were set afire. Come, let us build the wall of Jerusalem so that we shall no longer be humiliated.'* [18] *I told them of my God's beneficent hand towards me, and also of the king's words which he had spoken to me. They said, 'Let us arise and build,' and they strengthened their hands for the good.*

[19] *When Sanballat the Horonite, Tobiah the Ammonite slave, and Geshem the Arab heard, they ridiculed and disparaged us, and said, 'What is this thing you are doing? Are you rebelling against the king?'* [20] I *answered them, and said to them, 'The God of heaven shall grant us success; and we, His servants,*

gathered strength from the goodness — from the king's goodness to me.

◆§ The Enemies' Reaction

19. וַיִּשְׁמַע — *Heard. Rashi* comments: When they heard that we planned to reconstruct the city walls...

וְגֶשֶׁם הָעַרְבִי — *And Geshem the Arab.* Geshem was an Arabian enemy of the Jews (*Ri Mitrani*).

הַעַל הַמֶּלֶךְ אַתֶּם מֹרְדִים — *Are you rebelling against the king?* Are you building the walls of the city as a fortress so that you can rebel against the king? (*Rashi; Ralbag; Metzudos*).

Malbim's interpretation of the alleged rebellion differs slightly. King Cyrus had issued a decree halting the reconstruction of the city (*Ezra* 4:21), and the decree of a Persian king could not be repealed (see *Esther* 8:8). Thus the enemies alleged that the reconstruction of the walls constituted rebellion against Cyrus' decree.

◆§ Nehemiah's Reply

20. וָאָשִׁיב אוֹתָם דָּבָר — *I answered them [a word].*

Malbim explains that this phrase alludes to Nehemiah's unrecorded answer to the accusation that the Jews were rebelling against the king (v. 19). The Jews were accused of disregarding Cyrus' instructions (*Ezra* 4:21) not to rebuild the city of Jerusalem (see comm. v. 19). Nehemiah replied that Cyrus had merely ordered that the city not be rebuilt *until a decree is issued by me* [the king] (*Ezra* 4:21). Since the Jews now had King Darius' permission to reconstruct the city walls (2:6), Cyrus' prohibition no longer applied.

According to *Malbim*, this argument is alluded to by the phrase *I answered them*. The remainder of the verse — *And said to them ...* — is not an explanation of the opening phrase, but an independent statement made by Nehemiah.

אֱלֹהֵי הַשָּׁמַיִם הוּא יַצְלִיחַ לָנוּ — *The God of heaven shall grant us success.* Even if you should slander us before the king by falsely accusing us of rebellion (v. 19), your efforts will fail, since God is with us (*Metzudos*).

The God of heaven shall cause our activities of rebuilding to succeed and stand as our memorial (*Malbim*).

ג וַאֲנַחְנוּ עֲבָדָיו נָקוּם וּבָנִינוּ וְלָכֶם אֵין־חֵלֶק
א וּצְדָקָה וְזִכָּרוֹן בִּירוּשָׁלָםִ׃
א וַיָּקָם אֶלְיָשִׁיב הַכֹּהֵן הַגָּדוֹל וְאֶחָיו הַכֹּהֲנִים
וַיִּבְנוּ אֶת־שַׁעַר הַצֹּאן הֵמָּה קִדְּשׁוּהוּ וַיַּעֲמִידוּ

וַאֲנַחְנוּ עֲבָדָיו — *And we, His servants.* Because we are His servants, God will cause the king to reject your slander (*Metzudos*). We are His servants exclusively — but you worship idols in addition to Him [see *II Kings* 17:33], and are therefore not considered His servants (*Ralbag*). [See ArtScroll *Ezra* 4:2.]

Because we shall build as His servants — for the sake of His glory, not for personal gain — we shall be granted success (*Malbim*).

וְלָכֶם אֵין־חֵלֶק — *But you have no portion.* Why do you involve yourselves in our construction of the city's wall, when you have no portion in Jerusalem? (*Rashi*). *Malbim* explains that Sanballat and the others had no portion in the city because they were gentiles. The city of Jerusalem is the inheritance of Abraham, Isaac and Jacob, forefathers of the Jewish people (see *Exodus* 32:13).

Ralbag translates: *You have no part in building Jerusalem*. With these words, Nehemiah pronounced Sanballat and the other enemies of the Jews unfit for taking part in the construction of the city's walls, just as the elders of Israel had disqualified *the enemies of Judah and Benjamin* from aiding in the rebuilding of the Temple construction in the time of King Cyrus (*Ezra* 4:3). Nehemiah's statement indicates that Sanballat and his companions had offered to aid in constructing the city walls, as the *enemies of Judah and Benjamin* had offered to aid in constructing the Temple (*Ezra* 4:2). Although the offer is not recorded in the text, it is evident from Nehemiah's assertion that Sanballat, Tobiah, and Geshem *have no part* in the city of Jerusalem. The Talmud (*Shekalim* 1:4) derives from this verse that contributions offered by any gentiles for the construction of the city of Jerusalem are not to be accepted, just as their contributions for the Temple construction are unacceptable [see comm. 2:8; ArtScroll *Ezra* 4:3].

Ralbag presents an alternate interpretation: Your interference with the construction of Jerusalem indicates that you have no portion in Jerusalem.

וּצְדָקָה — *Or merit. Ibn Ezra* defines *tzedakah* here as a righteous act: You may not take part in the righteous act of constructing Jerusalem.

Ralbag refers to his interpretation that the preceding phrase *you have no part* excluded them from taking part in the construction. He explains that the phrase *or merit* [lit. *charity*] was intended to disqualify them from contributing funds, i.e. *charity*, for the reconstruction of the walls (*Ralbag*).

Metzudos understands the mention of merit as an oblique reference to the king's generosity in permitting the Jews to return to Jerusalem. It was the king's grant which allowed the Jews to return to Jerusalem. *He* was charitable to Jerusalem, but you were not. You cannot claim credit for any meritorious act towards Jerusalem.

וְזִכָּרוֹן — *Or memorial*. The *memorial* refers to the sacred objects used [at the Temple] in Jerusalem, which stand as a memorial to those who donated them. The enemies could not make such a donation (*Ralbag*).

Ibn Ezra comments that the righteous act of building Jerusalem causes its par-

III *shall arise and build — but you have no portion or merit*
1 *or memorial in Jerusalem.'*

Then Eliashib the Kohen Gadol and his brothers, the Kohanim, arose and built the Sheep Gate — they sanctified it and erected its doors — until the Tower of

ticipants to be remembered before God.[1] The enemies of the Jewish people, who were disqualified from performing the *mitzvah* of rebuilding Jerusalem, would not be remembered before God. They had no memorial in Jerusalem.

According to *Malbim*, the walls themselves would serve as a *memorial* to their builders. Only the Jews would be granted the Divine aid in completing the act of construction. Therefore, only they could have this memorial.

III

Verse 18, near the end of chapter 2, recorded the Jewish leaders' positive response to Nehemiah's call to begin rebuilding the protective wall around Jerusalem. After a brief exchange of words between Nehemiah and the enemies of the Jewish settlers (vs. 19,20), chapter 3 begins where verse 18 left off. It details the names of those who lead the rebuilding of the wall, and describes how the work was organized.

See Appendix: *Map of Jerusalem.*

1. אֶלְיָשִׁיב הַכֹּהֵן הַגָּדוֹל — *Eliashib the Kohen Gadol.* Eliashib is listed later in *Nehemiah* (12:10) among the descendants of Jeshua, the first *Kohen Gadol* of the Second Temple (*Ezra* 3:2, 8).

אֶת־שַׁעַר הַצֹּאן — *The Sheep Gate. Ralbag* suggests that the sheep used as Temple sacrifices were brought in through this gate. The Sheep Gate was situated at the center of the eastern wall (see map), facing the Temple (12:39,40), and was therefore chosen as the starting point for reconstruction and resanctification (*Malbim*).

הֵמָּה קִדְּשׁוּהוּ — *They sanctified it.* They invested the gate with the special sanctity of the city of Jerusalem (*Rashi*). [The special sanctity pertaining to Jerusalem qualified it as the place where the fruits of *maaser sheini*,[2] the second tithe, and the meat of the *kodashim kalim*,[3] offerings of lesser holiness, could be eaten.]

This is not to be confused with the sanctification required for use of the altar in the Temple. A number of years earlier, in the days of Cyrus, the original settlers had brought sacrifices on the altar. [See ArtScroll *Ezra* 3:6.]

1. God's 'remembering' refers to His recognition of the good deeds of righteous people, which results in His kindness towards them (see *Rosh Hashanah* 16a — *God says, "... say 'rememberings'* (זִכְרוֹנוֹת) *before Me* [on Rosh Hashanah] *so that your memory may appear before Me for the good").*

2. Fruits and vegetables grown in the Holy Land are subject to several tithes known as מַעַשְׂרוֹת, *maasros*. After the first of these, *maaser rishon*, is removed for the Levite (*Terumos* 3:7; *Rambam, Hilchos Maaser* 1:1), a tenth of the remaining produce is taken. This tithe, known as *maaser sheini* [second tithe], must be brought by its owner to Jerusalem and eaten there (*Rambam, Deut.* 14:22-27; *Maaser Sheini* 2:1).

3. *Kodashim kalim* were sacrifices such as the *todah*, thanksgiving, and *shelamim*, peace offerings, whose meat could be eaten anywhere within the confines of the city of Jerusalem (*Zevachim* 55a).

ג
ב־ה

דַּלְתֹתָיו וְעַד־מִגְדַּל הַמֵּאָה קִדְּשׁוּהוּ עַד
ב מִגְדַּל חֲנַנְאֵל׃ וְעַל־יָדוֹ בָנוּ אַנְשֵׁי יְרֵחוֹ
ג וְעַל־יָדוֹ בָּנָה זַכּוּר בֶּן־אִמְרִי׃ וְאֵת שַׁעַר
הַדָּגִים בָּנוּ בְּנֵי הַסְּנָאָה הֵמָּה קֵרוּהוּ וַיַּעֲמִידוּ
ד דַּלְתֹתָיו מַנְעוּלָיו וּבְרִיחָיו׃ וְעַל־יָדָם הֶחֱזִיק
מְרֵמוֹת בֶּן־אוּרִיָּה בֶּן־הַקּוֹץ וְעַל־יָדָם הֶחֱזִיק
מְשֻׁלָּם בֶּן־בֶּרֶכְיָה בֶּן־מְשֵׁיזַבְאֵל וְעַל־יָדָם
ה הֶחֱזִיק צָדוֹק בֶּן־בַּעֲנָא׃ וְעַל־יָדָם הֶחֱזִיקוּ
הַתְּקוֹעִים וְאַדִּירֵיהֶם לֹא־הֵבִיאוּ צַוָּרָם

The Talmud (*Shevuos* 16a) presents two opinions concerning the sanctification of Jerusalem. One opinion is that its sanctification was created by King Solomon and is everlastingly effective, despite the destruction of the Sanctuary and the city and the exile of the people, קְדֻשָּׁה רִאשׁוֹנָה קִדְּשָׁה לְשַׁעְתָּהּ וְקִדְּשָׁה לֶעָתִיד לָבֹא (see *Rambam, Beis HaBechirah* 6:15; see also intro. to ArtScroll *Ezra* part VI). Accordingly, it was unnecessary, in the times of Nehemiah, to resanctify Jerusalem. A second opinion is that King Solomon's original sanctification expired when Nebuchadnezzar destroyed the Temple and the city and exiled the nation, קְדֻשָּׁה רִאשׁוֹנָה קִדְּשָׁה לְשַׁעְתָּהּ וְלֹא קִדְּשָׁה לֶעָתִיד לָבֹא. According to this view, Nehemiah resanctified the city by marching around its walls and offering the two תּוֹדוֹת, *thanksgiving offerings*, described later (ch. 12). According to both opinions, there was no apparent point in sanctifying the gate and the walls at the time of their construction. How is this reconciled with *Rashi's* statement that the builders sanctified the Sheep Gate now?

Ri Mitrani, however, explains that the sanctification of the gate and the walls invested them with a sanctity particular to the Temple. The gate was designated as Temple property; henceforth it was sinful for anyone to derive personal benefit from it, as it is a transgression to desecrate any Temple property by turning it to secular use (מְעִילָה). [*Ri Mitrani* evidently follows the opinion recorded in the Talmud (*Kiddushin* 54a) that the walls were Temple property. According to another opinion in the Talmud, they were not. See *Wertheimer*, notes to *Ri Mitrani*.]

Ralbag renders קִדְּשׁוּהוּ, *they prepared it* [see *Exodus* 19:10 — וְקִדַּשְׁתָּם, *prepare them (Rashi)*]. They prepared both sides of the gate for the extension of the city wall. At one side, they extended it until the Tower of Hameiah; at the other, they extended it in the opposite direction until the Tower of Hananel.

מִגְדַּל הַמֵּאָה — *The Tower of Hameiah.* All of the towers mentioned in this chapter (v. 11, 25) were built into the city walls (*Rashi*). *Ralbag* suggests that the Tower of Hameiah, literally *one hundred*, derived its name from the fact it was built and occupied by a hundred well-known people during the period of the First Temple.

וְעַד־מִגְדַּל הַמֵּאָה קִדְּשׁוּהוּ עַד מִגְדַּל חֲנַנְאֵל — *They sanctified it . . . until the Tower of Hameiah [and] until the Tower of Hananel*. The translation follows *Metzudos*. After erecting the doors of the Sheep Gate, they built the wall until the Tower of Hameiah, and then sanctified the wall as they had sanctified the gate. Then they extended the wall further, past the Tower of Hameiah, until

III
2-5

Hameiah [and] until the Tower of Hananel. [2] *The men of*
Jericho built adjacent to him, and Zaccur the son of Imri
adjacent to him. [3] *The sons of Hasenaah built the Fish*
Gate — they roofed it and erected its doors, its locks and
bars. [4] *Meremoth the son of Uriah the son of Hakoz*
strengthened [the area] adjacent to them, and Meshul-
lam the son of Berachiah the son of Meshezabel
strengthened [the area] adjacent to them, and Zadok
the son of Baanah strengthened [the area] adjacent to
them. [5] *The Tekoans strengthened adjacent to them but*
their powerful [ones] did not accept the yoke of their

it reached the Tower of Hananel (*Metzudos*).

Malbim (v. 6) states that the Tower of Hameiah and the Tower of Hananel stood north of the Sheep Gate, along the eastern wall. However, *Ralbag* places the Sheep Gate between the Tower of Hameiah and the Tower of Hananel.

2. וְעַל־יָדוֹ — *Adjacent to him* [lit. *upon his hand*]. This translation follows *Rashi* who cites וְעָלָיו מַטֵּה מְנַשֶּׁה, *adjacent to him, the tribe of Menasseh* (*Numbers* 2:20), as an indication that וְעַל may be translated *adjacent*. Next to every one of the *Kohanim* building the Sheep Gate, stood the men of Jericho, building their portion. [The singular — *adjacent to him* — refers to *every one* of the *Kohanim*.]

Rashi explains that the entire wall was built this way. Each group worked independently at the construction of its own section. In this manner, the wall around the entire city was completed.

Metzudos translates *adjacent to his* — Eliashib's — *place*, i.e., next to the Sheep Gate, the men of Jericho built their section of the wall. According to *Malbim*, the men of Jericho built the section of the wall between the Tower of Hananel (v. 1) and the Fish Gate (v. 3).

בָּנוּ — *Built*. *Malbim* asserts that the word בָּנוּ, built, refers to the complete reconstruction of a section of wall which had collapsed, whereas the term הֶחֱזִיק, *strengthened* (see vs. 4-6), refers to the strengthening of a portion of the wall by closing its breaches.

3. הֵמָּה קֵרוּהוּ — *They roofed it*. They constructed a shelter before the gate to protect those who sat there from the elements (*Ralbag*).

וּבְרִיחָיו — *And bars*. The bars were placed behind the doors, stretching across their entire width to prevent their opening (*Ralbag; Metzudos*).

4. וְעַל־יָדָם — *Adjacent to them*. Adjacent to the spot where the sons of Hasenaah (in v. 3) built (*Metzudos*). [See comm. to v. 3.]

5. הַתְּקוֹעִים — *The Tekoans*. Those who came from the city of *Tekoah* [a city in Judah mentioned several times in Scripture; see *II Samuel* 14:2] (*Rashi*).

וְאַדִּירֵיהֶם לֹא־הֵבִיאוּ צַוָּרָם בַּעֲבֹדַת אֲדֹנֵיהֶם — *But their powerful [ones] did not accept the yoke of [*lit. *bring their necks into] their Master's labor*. The rich among them did not aid in the construction of the wall, *their Master's* [i.e., God's] labor, a labor for the sake of God (*Rashi; Metzudos*).

Ibn Ezra and *Ralbag*, however, under-

ג
ו־ח

ו בַּעֲבֹדַת אֲדֹנֵיהֶם: וְאֵת שַׁעַר הַיְשָׁנָה הֶחֱזִיקוּ
יוֹיָדָע בֶּן־פָּסֵחַ וּמְשֻׁלָּם בֶּן־בְּסוֹדְיָה הֵמָּה
קֵרוּהוּ וַיַּעֲמִידוּ דַּלְתֹתָיו וּמַנְעֻלָיו וּבְרִיחָיו:
ז וְעַל־יָדָם הֶחֱזִיק מְלַטְיָה הַגִּבְעֹנִי וְיָדוֹן
הַמֵּרֹנֹתִי אַנְשֵׁי גִבְעוֹן וְהַמִּצְפָּה לְכִסֵּא פַּחַת
ח עֵבֶר הַנָּהָר: עַל־יָדוֹ הֶחֱזִיק עֻזִּיאֵל בֶּן־חַרְהֲיָה
צוֹרְפִים וְעַל־יָדוֹ הֶחֱזִיק חֲנַנְיָה בֶּן־הָרַקָּחִים
וַיַּעַזְבוּ יְרוּשָׁלִַם עַד הַחוֹמָה הָרְחָבָה:

stand *their master* as a reference to a mortal — a family member (*Ibn Ezra*); a taskmaster (*Ralbag*) who was appointed to supervise their construction work. The rich Tekoans did not aid the overseer in building the wall.

According to *Malbim*, this verse states quite the reverse. The powerful Tekoans did engage in the construction work. Those Jews who lived in *Eretz Yisrael* before King Cyrus permitted the Jews to return to their homeland (*Ezra* ch. 1) were under the jurisdiction of gentile satraps [see comm., v. 7, 1:3]. The Tekoans were among them and were therefore obligated to follow the instructions of *their master*, the satrap. But the rich, powerful Tekoans freed themselves from this satrap and were able to join in the construction. Alternatively, the Tekoans followed the instruction of the Jewish taskmaster appointed over them. The rich ones, however, refused to accept him, and chose, instead, to construct a different section of the wall. The work of this second, rich group of Tekoans is described later (v. 27; see comm. there).

6. שַׁעַר הַיְשָׁנָה — *The Old Gate*. The Old Gate was so called because it had been standing in Jerusalem since antiquity (*Ralbag*). According to *Ibn Ezra*, the adjective *old* modified a noun which was part of the name of the gate. The object described as old, however, is deleted in the text.

Malbim places the Old Gate at the northeastern corner of the city wall, and identifies it as the *Corner Gate* (שַׁעַר הַפִּנָּה) mentioned in *II Chronicles* 26:9 (see comm., v. 8). Accordingly, the Scriptural description of the work of construction begins with the Sheep Gate, which stood at the center of the Eastern wall (comm., v. 1), moves northward through the Towers of Hameiah and Hananel (v. 1) and the Fish Gate (v. 3), and now reaches the northeastern corner at the Old Gate.

7. אַנְשֵׁי גִבְעוֹן וְהַמִּצְפָּה — *[And] men of Gibeon and Mizpah*. The translation follows *Ibn Ezra* and *Metzudos*. In addition to Melatiah and Jadon, men of Gibeon and Mizpah also strengthened the wall.

In a second interpretation, *Ibn Ezra* does not add the word *and*. In this rendition, Melatiah and Jadon are identified as men of Gibeon and Mizpah.

וְעַל־יָדָם הֶחֱזִיק — *Strengthened [the area] adjacent to them*. The text now describes the construction work which took place along the city's northern border, moving from east to west (*Malbim*).

לְכִסֵּא פַּחַת עֵבֶר הַנָּהָר — *Until* [the site of] *the chair of the governor of Trans-River*. The translation follows *Rashi*, *Ralbag*, and *Metzudos*, who explain that a chair

Master's labor. 6 *Joiada the son of Paseah and Meshullam*
the son of Besodiah strengthened the Old Gate — they
roofed it and set in its doors, locks, and bars; 7 *Melatiah*
the Gibeonite and Jadon the Meronothite strengthened
[the area] adjacent to them, [and] men of Gibeon and
Mizpah until [the site of] the chair of the governor of
Trans-River. 8 *Uzziel the son of Harhaiah Zorphim*
strengthened [the area] adjacent to him and Hananiah,
one of the perfumers, strengthened [the area] adjacent to
him — they fortified Jerusalem until the Broad Wall;

stood in Jerusalem for the use of the governor of Trans-River when he visited the city. [פֶּחָה (Pahah) refers, generally, to a gentile governor, i.e., satrap (*Radak* to *Haggai* 1:1).] The builders strengthened the wall until the spot facing the area or building in which the chair stood.

In an alternate interpretation, *Ralbag* reads: *Gibeon and Mizpah, the seat of the governor of Trans-River,* i.e., the cities of Gibeon and Mizpah were under the jurisdiction of the governor of Trans-River. Scripture praises the merit of the men of Gibeon and Mizpah. Although they were subjects of the gentile governor of Trans-River, they aided in the construction of the city wall.

Malbim explains why only the members of Gibeon and Mizpah were subjects of the governor of Trans-River. As noted above, only those who returned from Babylon after Cyrus' proclamation were placed under the jurisdiction of Jewish governors (*Ezra* 5:14). Those who dwelt in *Eretz Yisrael* before Cyrus' time, however, remained under the rule of gentile governors appointed by the king (see comm. 1:3). Thus, the men of Jericho (v. 2) and the children of Hasenaah (v. 3), whose names are mentioned among those who ascended in the days of Cyrus (*Ezra* 2:34,35), were ruled by the Jewish governor. But the men of Gibeon and Mizpah are not mentioned among the immigrants who responded to Cyrus' proclamation. Evidently, they had lived in the Holy Land prior to Cyrus' reign. Hence, they were governed by the satrap of Trans-River. Similarly, the Tekoans mentioned above (v. 5), who are not listed among Cyrus' returnees, were also under the rule of the Trans-River satrap (see comm., v. 5).

8. צוֹרְפִים — *Zorphim.* The family was called by the name *Zorphim* because this was their occupation (*Rashi*), literally they purified gold and silver (*Metzudos*).

וַיַּעַזְבוּ יְרוּשָׁלִַם — *They fortified Jerusalem.* They filled the spaces between the beams with earth in order to strengthen the wall (*Rashi; Ibn Ezra; Metzudos*). *Metzudos* explains that this interpretation is based on the term מַעֲזִיבָה used in the Mishnah (*Bava Metzia* 116b) in reference to the cement used to cover the beams of a ceiling (see *Tosefos Yom Tov, Succah* 1:7).

עַד הַחוֹמָה הָרְחָבָה — *Until the Broad Wall. Malbim* notes that the Gate of Ephraim stood between the area of the wall known as the Broad Wall, and the Old Gate (12:38,39). However, Scripture here mentions the Old Gate (v. 6) and then the Broad Wall, with no reference to the intervening Gate of Ephraim. Evidently, *Malbim* reasons, the Gate of Ephraim was not in need of major repair, and is, therefore, not mentioned specifically in our chapter's record of the

ט וְעַל־יָדָם הֶחֱזִיק רְפָיָה בֶן־חוּר שַׂר חֲצִי פֶּלֶךְ
י יְרוּשָׁלָ͏ִם׃ וְעַל־יָדָם הֶחֱזִיק יְדָיָה בֶן־חֲרוּמַף
וְנֶגֶד בֵּיתוֹ וְעַל־יָדוֹ הֶחֱזִיק חַטּוּשׁ בֶּן־
יא חֲשַׁבְנְיָה׃ מִדָּה שֵׁנִית הֶחֱזִיק מַלְכִּיָּה בֶן־חָרִם
וְחַשּׁוּב בֶּן־פַּחַת מוֹאָב וְאֵת מִגְדַּל הַתַּנּוּרִים׃
יב וְעַל־יָדוֹ הֶחֱזִיק שַׁלּוּם בֶּן־הַלּוֹחֵשׁ שַׂר חֲצִי
יג פֶּלֶךְ יְרוּשָׁלָ͏ִם הוּא וּבְנוֹתָיו׃ אֵת שַׁעַר הַגַּיְא
הֶחֱזִיק חָנוּן וְיֹשְׁבֵי זָנוֹחַ הֵמָּה בָנוּהוּ וַיַּעֲמִידוּ
דַּלְתֹתָיו מַנְעֻלָיו וּבְרִיחָיו וְאֶלֶף אַמָּה בַּחוֹמָה

reconstruction of the wall.

In addition, *Malbim* notes that the Gate of Ephraim was followed by the Corner Gate, as recorded in *Chronicles* (*II* 25:23) . . . *And he* [Joash, king of Israel] *broke through the wall of Jerusalem from the Gate of Ephraim until the Corner Gate, four hundred cubits.* Yet Nehemiah (12:39) records that the Gate of Ephraim was followed by the Old Gate, and does not mention the Corner Gate at all. This indicates, *Malbim* continues, that the Old Gate mentioned in Nehemiah was actually the Corner Gate of *Chronicles*, so called because it stood at the northeastern corner of the Jerusalem Wall (see comm. v. 6).

Finally, *Malbim* explains why it was necessary at this point to strengthen the wall with earth. After recording the repair of the Old Gate at the northeastern corner, the text describes the construction along the northern border of the city, traveling from east to west. Unlike the other sides of Jerusalem, which were surrounded by mountains, the northern area faced a level plain. Hence, it was necessary to strengthen the wall with earth to provide additional protection until the Broad Wall, where the breadth of the wall itself was sufficient.

9. שַׂר חֲצִי פֶּלֶךְ יְרוּשָׁלַם — *The governor of half the district of Jerusalem.* פֶּלֶךְ refers to a district apportioned to a ruler. Rephaiah governed half the people in Jerusalem (*Rashi*).

10. וְנֶגֶד בֵּיתוֹ — *[And] opposite his home.* The translation follows *Rashi*, who explains that the portion of the wall which Jedaiah built, described in the verse as being adjacent to Rephaiah's, was opposite Jedaiah's home.

Metzudos and *Malbim*, however, translate *and opposite his home.* In addition to the section adjacent to Rephaiah, Jedaiah also built that part of the wall which was opposite his home.

11. מִדָּה שֵׁנִית — *A similar* [lit. *a second*] *measure*. The translation follows *Rashi*. The section of wall built by Malchijah and Hashub was the same length as that of Hattush [v. 10] (*Rashi; Metzudos*). *Rashi* adds that *a similar measure* applies only to the section of the wall built by Malchijah and Hashub, but not to the Tower of Ovens, which they also constructed.

Malbim explains that there were no gates or towers along this stretch of wall (the northern wall west of the area known as the Broad Wall). Hence the length of wall was divided into two equal sections, and each group undertook to construct one section.

III
9-13

[9] *Rephaiah the son of Hur, the governor of half the district of Jerusalem, strengthened [the area] adjacent to them.*
[10] *Jedaiah the son of Harumaph strengthened [the area] adjacent to them [and] opposite his home; Hattush the son of Hashabneiah strengthened [the area] adjacent to him.*
[11] *Malchijah the son of Harim and Hashub the son of the governor of Moab strengthened a similar measure and the Tower of the Ovens.* [12] *Shallum the son of Hallohesh, the governor of half the district of Jerusalem, strengthened [the area] adjacent to him — he and his daughters.*
[13] *Hanun and the inhabitants of Zanoah strengthened the Gate of the Valley — they built it and erected its doors, its locks and bars — and one thousand cubits of the wall*

בֶּן־פַּחַת מוֹאָב — *The son of the governor of Moab* [lit. *the son of the ruler of Moab*]. The Talmud (*Taanis* 28a) identifies the *Pahath Moab,* literally *the governor of Moab,* as King David, or his nephew Joab, both of whom were descended from the Moabite princess Ruth [see *Ruth* 14:22; ArtScroll *Ezra* 2:6].

מִגְדַּל הַתַּנּוּרִים — *The Tower of the Ovens.* [Hashub] also built the Tower of the Ovens (*Rashi*). This tower stood at the northwestern corner of the wall (*Malbim*).

12. וְעַל־יָדוֹ הֶחֱזִיק — *Strengthened [the area] adjacent to him.* The text now describes the construction of the western wall of Jerusalem, running from north to south (*Malbim*).

הַלּוֹחֵשׁ — *Hallohesh. Ibn Ezra* suggests that the opening letter ה is not part of the name, but is the prefix הַ meaning *the,* i.e., *the Lohesh.* [הַלּוֹחֵשׁ, *halohesh,* translated literally, is *the whisperer.* The word לַחַשׁ, *whispering,* sometimes refers to *the whispered prayer* (*Isaiah* 26:16). It may also refer to the kabbalistic secrets of the Torah, which may only be whispered (*Isaiah* 3:3). Sometimes, it is associated with the snake charmer, who whispers incantations which prevent the snake from striking (*Rashi, Psalms* 58:6; *Jeremiah* 8:17).]

According to *Malbim,* however, the letter ה is not a prefix, but is part of the name *Hallohesh.*

הוּא וּבְנוֹתָיו — *He and his daughters.* The translation follows *Ralbag* and *Malbim,* who comment that Shallum's daughters aided him in the work of construction.

Ralbag presents an alternate translation, rendering הוּא וּבְנוֹתָיו as, *with its nearby towns.* The reference is to the district of Jerusalem and the surrounding smaller towns, of which Shallum was the governor. [See *Numbers* 21:25 for a similar usage: וּבְכָל־בְּנֹתֶיהָ, *all of its surrounding towns* (*Rashi*).]

13. שַׁעַר הַגַּיְא — *The Gate of the Valley.* The gate leading to the valley of *Ben Hinom* (*Ralbag*; see comm. 2:13).

הֵמָּה בָנוּהוּ — *They built it.* Strengthening the gate was not sufficient, so they rebuilt it completely (*Malbim;* see comm. v. 2).

וְאֶלֶף אַמָּה בַּחוֹמָה — *And one thousand cubits of the wall.* In addition to the Gate of the Valley, they built 1000 cubits of the wall (*Metzudos*) heading south *until the Refuse Gate.*

יד עַד שַׁעַר הָשְׁפוֹת: וְאֵת | שַׁעַר הָאַשְׁפּוֹת
הֶחֱזִיק מַלְכִּיָּה בֶן־רֵכָב שַׂר פֶּלֶךְ בֵּית־הַכָּרֶם
הוּא יִבְנֶנּוּ וְיַעֲמִיד דַּלְתֹתָיו מַנְעֻלָיו וּבְרִיחָיו:
טו וְאֵת שַׁעַר הָעַיִן הֶחֱזִיק שַׁלּוּן בֶּן־כָּל־חֹזֶה
שַׂר פֶּלֶךְ הַמִּצְפָּה הוּא יִבְנֶנּוּ וִיטַלְלֶנּוּ
°ויעמידו דַּלְתֹתָיו מַנְעֻלָיו וּבְרִיחָיו וְאֵת °וְיַעֲמִיד ק׳
חוֹמַת בְּרֵכַת הַשֶּׁלַח לְגַן־הַמֶּלֶךְ וְעַד־
טז הַמַּעֲלוֹת הַיּוֹרְדוֹת מֵעִיר דָּוִיד: אַחֲרָיו הֶחֱזִיק
נְחֶמְיָה בֶן־עַזְבּוּק שַׂר חֲצִי פֶּלֶךְ בֵּית־צוּר
עַד־נֶגֶד קִבְרֵי דָוִיד וְעַד הַבְּרֵכָה הָעֲשׂוּיָה
יז וְעַד בֵּית הַגִּבֹּרִים: אַחֲרָיו הֶחֱזִיקוּ הַלְוִיִּם
רְחוּם בֶּן־בָּנִי עַל־יָדוֹ הֶחֱזִיק חֲשַׁבְיָה שַׂר־

עַד שַׁעַר הָשְׁפוֹת — *Until the Refuse Gate.* They built up to, but not including, the Refuse Gate [which was built by Malchijah (v. 14)] (*Rashi*).

Ibn Ezra, followed by *Minchas Shai*, notes that the text reads הָשְׁפוֹת, rather than הָאַשְׁפּוֹת, as in the following verse. The deleted א (*aleph*) is still heard because it is an extension of the pronunciation of the prefix הָ.

14. הוּא יִבְנֶנּוּ — *He built it* [lit. *shall build it*]. The translation follows *Metzudos.*

15. שַׁעַר הָעַיִן — *The Gate of the Spring.* This gate led to the spring which provided water for the king (*Ralbag* 2:14).

יִבְנֶנּוּ — *He built it* [lit. *shall build it*]. The translation follows *Ibn Ezra*, who also offers an alternative interpretation: The future tense is used to indicate that Shallum caused others to build the wall. *He,* i.e., someone else, *shall build* as a result of Shallum's efforts.

וִיטַלְלֶנּוּ — *Covered it.* He placed a roof on it (*Ralbag*).

וְאֵת חוֹמַת בְּרֵכַת הַשֶּׁלַח — *And the wall of the Pool of Shelah.* The waters of this pool were used to irrigate the king's gardens. *Shelah,* literally, *which sends forth* or *spreads,* alludes to the trees of the garden which grew from the waters of the pool and sent forth their branches (*Metzudos*; see *Song of Songs* 4:13).

Malbim identifies the Pool of Shelah as the pool of the king mentioned in 2:14, and the stream of *Shiloah* in *Isaiah* 8:6. The Mishnah (*Succah* 48a) relates that the water for the Temple celebration of the drawing of water (שִׂמְחַת בֵּית הַשּׁוֹאֵבָה) was taken from the *Shiloah*.

The pool was situated in the inner or eastern side of the wall (*Malbim*).

לְגַן־הַמֶּלֶךְ — *Towards the royal garden.* The pool faced the king's garden (*Rashi*). It watered the royal orchard and garden in the days of the kings of Judah [i.e., of the First Temple] (*Ralbag*).

וְעַד־הַמַּעֲלוֹת הַיּוֹרְדוֹת מֵעִיר דָּוִיד — *Until the steps descending from the City of David. Malbim* explains that the City of David lay on the eastern flank of Mount Zion, situated between the walls of the

until the Refuse Gate. [14] *Malchijah the son of Rechab, the*
governor of the district of Beth Cherem, strengthened
the Refuse Gate — he built it and erected its doors from
its locks and bars. [15] *Shallun the son of Kal Hozeh, the*
governor of the district of Mizpah, strengthened the Gate
of the Spring — he built it, covered it, and erected its
doors, its locks and bars — and the wall of the Pool of
Shelah towards the royal garden until the steps
descending from the City of David. [16] *After him,*
Nehemiah the son of Azbuk, the governor of half the
district of Beth Zur, strengthened [the area] until
opposite the graves of David [and] until the man-made
pool [and] until the House of the Mighty. [17] *After him, the*
Levites strengthened: Rehum the son of Bani; [the area]
adjacent to him strengthened Hashabiah, the governor of

mountain. Steps sloping downward from the city led directly to the Pool of Shelah and the royal gardens. Shallun built the wall of Jerusalem until the point reached by those steps (*Ralbag*).

16. עַד־נֶגֶד קִבְרֵי דָוִיד — *Until opposite the graves of David.* The western wall of the city was extended further southward beyond the wall of the Pool of Shelah until the area opposite the graves of David. This lay across the Valley of Ben Hinom on the slopes of Mount Zion (*Malbim*).

וְעַד הַבְּרֵכָה הָעֲשׂוּיָה — *[And] until the man-made* [lit. *made*] *pool*. The translation follows *Metzudos*.

Malbim translates, *the pool made afterward*, explaining that the reference is to a pool in the Valley of Ben Hinom which was constructed as an extension of an old canal, i.e., it was *made after* the old canal. This is alluded to in *Isaiah* 22:11 — *You have made a pool between the double wall and the waters of the old canal.* The western wall of the city was now extended even further southward until the area adjacent to the *pool made afterward* in the Valley of Ben Hinom.

Malbim notes that *Isaiah* 22:11 refers to the *double wall* near the pool that was made. Thus, it may be concluded that the section of wall described in our verse was doubled [either of double thickness, or two parallel walls].

According to *Ralbag's* interpretation, the wall was extended from steps descending from the City of David (v. 15) until the area opposite the graves of David which was *also* adjacent to the man-made pool. *Malbim*, however, holds that two extensions were made — the first, from the steps until the graves; the second, from the area of the graves until the man-made pool.

וְעַד בֵּית הַגִּבֹּרִים — *[And] until the House of the Mighty.* The wall was extended further from the man-made pool until the House of the Mighty (*Ralbag; Metzudos*).

The House of the Mighty was a building where King David's גִבּוֹרִים,

יח חֲצִי־פֶּלֶךְ קְעִילָה לְפִלְכּוֹ: אַחֲרָיו הֶחֱזִיקוּ
אֲחֵיהֶם בַּוַּי בֶּן־חֵנָדָד שַׂר חֲצִי פֶּלֶךְ קְעִילָה:
יט וַיְחַזֵּק עַל־יָדוֹ עֵזֶר בֶּן־יֵשׁוּעַ שַׂר הַמִּצְפָּה
מִדָּה שֵׁנִית מִנֶּגֶד עֲלֹת הַנֶּשֶׁק הַמִּקְצֹעַ:
כ אַחֲרָיו הֶחֱרָה הֶחֱזִיק בָּרוּךְ בֶּן־°זבי מִדָּה — זַכַּי ק׳
שֵׁנִית מִן־הַמִּקְצוֹעַ עַד־פֶּתַח בֵּית אֶלְיָשִׁיב
כא הַכֹּהֵן הַגָּדוֹל: אַחֲרָיו הֶחֱזִיק מְרֵמוֹת בֶּן־
אוּרִיָּה בֶּן־הַקּוֹץ מִדָּה שֵׁנִית מִפֶּתַח בֵּית
כב אֶלְיָשִׁיב וְעַד־תַּכְלִית בֵּית אֶלְיָשִׁיב: וְאַחֲרָיו
כג הֶחֱזִיקוּ הַכֹּהֲנִים אַנְשֵׁי הַכִּכָּר: אַחֲרָיו הֶחֱזִיק
בִּנְיָמִן וְחַשּׁוּב נֶגֶד בֵּיתָם אַחֲרָיו הֶחֱזִיק
עֲזַרְיָה בֶּן־מַעֲשֵׂיָה בֶּן־עֲנָנְיָה אֵצֶל בֵּיתוֹ:
כד אַחֲרָיו הֶחֱזִיק בִּנּוּי בֶּן־חֵנָדָד מִדָּה שֵׁנִית
מִבֵּית עֲזַרְיָה עַד־הַמִּקְצוֹעַ וְעַד־הַפִּנָּה:

mighty warriors (see *II Samuel* 23:8-39), used to gather (*Ralbag*). It was, therefore, near the armory, due south of it [see v. 19] (*Malbim*).

17. לְפִלְכּוֹ — *With* [lit. *to*] *his district.* Hashabiah, together with the constituents of his district, strengthened the walls (*Metzudos*).

18. אֲחֵיהֶם — *Their brothers.* This refers to their fellow Levites (*Rashi; Metzudos*).

19. מִדָּה שֵׁנִית — *A similar* [lit. *second*] *measure*. Ezer built a section of the wall similar in size to that of Bavvai [v. 18] (*Metzudos*; *Malbim*; see comm. v. 11).

Malbim translates *a twofold measure.* Ezer, Malchijah (v. 11), Baruch (v. 20), Meremoth (v. 21), Binnui (v. 24), the Tekoans (v. 27), and Hanun (v. 30) each undertook to construct double the amount of the work done by the other groups.

מִנֶּגֶד עֲלֹת הַנֶּשֶׁק — *Opposite the ascent to the armory.* The wall was now built adjacent to the entrance to the armory of the mighty warriors (v. 16) (*Rashi*). *Ralbag* asserts that the arms were manufactured in this building.

According to *Ibn Ezra*, however, עֲלֹת הַנֶּשֶׁק, *Aloth HaNeshek*, was simply the name of a place.

הַמִּקְצֹעַ — *[In the] corner.* The armory stood at the corner of the wall (*Rashi*), specifically, the southwest corner of the city wall (*Malbim*).

20. הֶחֱרָה — *Buttressed.* The translation follows *Rashi*. *Ri Mitrani* and *Ralbag* translate *heatedly* or *ardently* — i.e., Baruch worked to strengthen the wall with great fervor.

Ibn Ezra interprets הֶחֱרָה as *angrily*, as in חֲרוֹן אַף, *anger*. Baruch was angry at himself at the delay in the construction.

According to *Malbim*, הֶחֱרָה, *Heherah*, is the name of a person. The passage

half the district of Keilah — with his district. 18 *After*
him, their brothers, Bavvai the son of Henadad, the
governor of half the district of Keilah, strengthened.
19 *And [the area] adjacent to him, Ezer the son of Jeshua,*
the governor of Mizpah, strengthened a similar measure,
opposite the ascent to the armory [in the] corner. 20 *After*
him, Baruch the son of Zakkai buttressed [and]
strengthened a similar measure from the corner until the
entrance of the house of Eliashib the Kohen Gadol.
21 *After him, Meremoth the son of Uriah the son of Hakoz*
strengthened a similar measure from the entrance of the
house of Eliashib until the end of the house of Eliashib.
22 *And after him, the Kohanim, men of the Plain,*
strengthened [the area]. 23 *After it, Benjamin and Hashub*
strengthened [the area] opposite their houses [and] after
it, Azariah the son of Maaseaiah the son of Ananiah
strengthened [the area] by his house. 24 *After him, Binnui*
the son of Henadad strengthened a similar measure from
the house of Azariah until the corner, and until the tower.

After him, Heherah Baruch ben Zakkai strengthened (אַחֲרָיו הֶחֱרָה הֶחֱזִיק בָּרוּךְ בֶּן זַכָּי) is read, *After him, Heherah* [strengthened]; *Baruch ben Zakkai strengthened [after him]* (אַחֲרָיו [הֶחֱזִיק] הֶחֱרָה [אַחֲרָיו] הֶחֱזִיק בָּרוּךְ).

מִן הַמִּקְצוֹעַ עַד־פֶּתַח בֵּית אֶלְיָשִׁיב — *From the corner until the entrance of the house of Eliashib.* The text now describes the construction of the southern wall, beginning from the southwest corner and moving eastward (*Malbim*).

21. מְרֵמוֹת . . . מִדָּה שֵׁנִית — *Meremoth . . . a similar measure.* Meremoth is mentioned previously (v. 4) as one of the builders. He now built an additional section of the wall, in the same measure as Baruch of v. 20 (*Metzudos*).

מִפֶּתַח בֵּית אֶלְיָשִׁיב וְעַד־תַּכְלִית בֵּית אֶלְיָשִׁיב — *From the entrance of the house of Eliashib until the end of the house of Eliashib.* Meremoth repaired the entire area of the wall opposite the home of the *Kohen Gadol* Eliashib (*Rashi*).

23. אַחֲרָיו — *After it.* The translation follows *Metzudos*, who explains: after the section of the wall already built [by the *Kohanim*, men of the Plain]. [Although אַחֲרָיו is generally translated *after him*, the translation here is *after it* because there is no mention of an individual in v. 22, the preceding verse.]

24. עַד־הַמִּקְצוֹעַ — *Until the corner.* I.e., the southeastern corner, which was now reached (*Malbim*). According to *Malbim*, the corner referred to in v. 19 — the armory — was in the southwest (see there).

וְעַד־הַפִּנָּה — *and until the tower* [lit. *corner*]

כה פָּלָל בֶּן־אוּזַי מִנֶּגֶד הַמִּקְצוֹעַ וְהַמִּגְדָּל
הַיּוֹצֵא מִבֵּית הַמֶּלֶךְ הָעֶלְיוֹן אֲשֶׁר לַחֲצַר
כו הַמַּטָּרָה אַחֲרָיו פְּדָיָה בֶן־פַּרְעֹשׁ׃ וְהַנְּתִינִים
הָיוּ יֹשְׁבִים בָּעֹפֶל עַד נֶגֶד שַׁעַר הַמַּיִם
כז לַמִּזְרָח וְהַמִּגְדָּל הַיּוֹצֵא׃ אַחֲרָיו הֶחֱזִיקוּ
הַתְּקֹעִים מִדָּה שֵׁנִית מִנֶּגֶד הַמִּגְדָּל הַגָּדוֹל
כח הַיּוֹצֵא וְעַד חוֹמַת הָעֹפֶל׃ מֵעַל ׀ שַׁעַר
הַסּוּסִים הֶחֱזִיקוּ הַכֹּהֲנִים אִישׁ לְנֶגֶד בֵּיתוֹ׃

Metzudos explains that פִּנָּה, literally *corner*, sometimes means *tower* (as in *Zephaniah* 1:16), because the towers are generally located at the corners of the wall.

25. פָּלָל בֶּן־אוּזַי מִנֶּגֶד הַמִּקְצוֹעַ וְהַמִּגְדָּל — *Palal the son of Uzai, opposite the corner and the tower.* Palal began constructing the wall opposite the corner, as well as the tower which extended from the royal palace (*Metzudos*).

According to *Malbim*, however, it means that Palal built the wall near the tower. The Nethinites built the tower itself (see comm. v. 26).

הַיּוֹצֵא — *Which extended.* This tower, which was built into the wall, jutted out from the inside face of the wall [towards the city] (*Rashi*).

מִבֵּית הַמֶּלֶךְ — *From the royal palace* [lit. *from the king's house*]. The text now describes the construction of the eastern wall of the city, beginning with the southeastern corner (v. 24), and moving northward. The tower extended from the royal palace, which stood near the eastern wall (*Malbim*).

הָעֶלְיוֹן — *On the heights.* The palace stood on a high hill (*Metzudos*).

אֲשֶׁר לַחֲצַר הַמַּטָּרָה — *Which is [adjacent] to the prison courtyard.* The place was adjacent to the prison courtyard (*Metzudos*).

According to *Malbim*, however, the rendition is *belonging to the prison courtyard*, i.e., the tower was part of the courtyard. *Malbim* notes that the prison courtyard near the palace in our verse is unrelated to the *Prison Gate* (12:39) which stood near the Temple.

26. וְהַנְּתִינִים — *And the Nethinites.* The Nethinites were descendants of the Canaanite inhabitants of the city of Gibeon, who deceived Joshua into allowing them to convert to Judaism. In consequence, they were designated by Joshua to serve as water carriers and woodcutters (*Joshua* ch. 9). They were exiled and many returned to the Holy Land with the entire nation when Cyrus permitted the Jews to return to Jerusalem. [See further ArtScroll *Ezra* 2:43.]

בָּעֹפֶל — *In Ophel.* The Nethinites were in the place called Ophel (*Rashi*). *Ophel* literally means *the heights* (*Ralbag*) or, *the high stronghold* [as in *Numbers* 14:44, וַיַּעְפִּלוּ לַעֲלוֹת — *They ascended with strength;* see also *Micah*, 4:8] (*Ibn Ezra*).

עַד נֶגֶד שַׁעַר הַמַּיִם לַמִּזְרָח — *Until opposite the Water Gate to the east.* The Water Gate located on the eastern side of the city. This gate adjoined the Temple (*Yoma* 69b; *Malbim*).

The Nethinites dwelt in the heights adjoining the wall. They therefore constructed the wall from the area adjoining

III
25-28

[25] *Palal the son of Uzai, opposite the corner and the tower which extended from the royal palace on the heights, which is [adjacent] to the prison courtyard; after him, Pedaiah the son of Parosh.* [26] *And the Nethinites dwelt in Ophel until opposite the Water Gate to the east and the extending tower.* [27] *After it, the Tekoans strengthened [the area] a similar measure from opposite the large, extending tower until the wall of Ophel.* [28] *Above the Horses' Gate, the Kohanim strengthened [the area] each opposite his home.*

their homes in Ophel until the Water Gate (*Rashi*).

Malbim reads the word *strengthened* (הֶחֱזִיק) from v. 24 into this passage, and combines our verse with the preceding one (v. 25): Pedaiah and the Nethinites strengthened from the area adjacent to the royal palace until the Water Gate to the east.

וְהַמִּגְדָּל הַיּוֹצֵא — *And the extending tower.* In addition, they built the tower which extended, i.e., jutted out from the inside of the wall [towards the city] (*Rashi*), or from the outside of the wall [away from the city] (*Metzudos*).

Malbim identifies the *extending tower* as the *tower which extended from the royal palace* (v. 25). Palal built the wall from the corner until the area of the tower which extended from the royal palace. The Nethinites built the tower itself.

27. מִדָּה שֵׁנִית — *A similar measure.* In addition to the Tekoans' construction mentioned above (v. 5), they now strengthened a section of wall *the same length* as that repaired by the Nethinites (*Metzudos*).

According to *Malbim*, one group of Tekoans built the section of wall described in v. 5 while a richer, more powerful group constructed the section described here, v. 27. [See comm. v. 5.]

וְעַד חוֹמַת הָעֹפֶל — *Until the wall of Ophel.* According to *Rashi* (v. 26), *Ophel* was the name of the section in which the Nethinites lived. They therefore built that section of the wall. Our verse [27] states that the Tekoans built another section of the wall which was linked with the wall at *Ophel*. According to *Ralbag*, עֹפֶל means the highest point of the city. The Tekoite effort was to complete the wall up to that plateau.

Malbim translates חוֹמַת הָעֹפֶל as the *wall of the fortress*, explaining that a fortress was attached to the *tower which extended from the royal palace* (v. 25), also referred to as the *extending tower* (v. 26). The Nethinites constructed the wall until the Water Gate and rebuilt the extending tower (v. 26). Then the Tekoites built the city wall from opposite the extending tower [at the Water Gate] until they reached the wall of the fortress.

28. מֵעַל שַׁעַר הַסּוּסִים — *Above the Horses' Gate.* This gate was used as an entrance for the horses (*Ralbag*). *Malbim* notes that *II Kings* 11:16 describes a Horses' Gate which led into the king's palace. This corresponds with our verse, which mentions the Horses' Gate in the area of the tower extending from the palace (vs. 25-27).

אִישׁ לְנֶגֶד בֵּיתוֹ — *Each opposite his home.* The homes of the *Kohanim* were in this area (*Metzudos*).

ג
כט־לד

כט אַחֲרָיו הֶחֱזִיק צָדוֹק בֶּן־אִמֵּר נֶגֶד בֵּיתוֹ
וְאַחֲרָיו הֶחֱזִיק שְׁמַעְיָה בֶן־שְׁכַנְיָה שֹׁמֵר
ל שַׁעַר הַמִּזְרָח: °אחרי הֶחֱזִיק חֲנַנְיָה בֶן־ °אַחֲרָיו ק׳
שֶׁלֶמְיָה וְחָנוּן בֶּן־צָלָף הַשִּׁשִּׁי מִדָּה שֵׁנִי
אַחֲרָיו הֶחֱזִיק מְשֻׁלָּם בֶּן־בֶּרֶכְיָה נֶגֶד נִשְׁכָּתוֹ:
לא °אחרי הֶחֱזִיק מַלְכִּיָּה בֶּן־הַצֹּרְפִי עַד־בֵּית °אַחֲרָיו ק׳
הַנְּתִינִים וְהָרֹכְלִים נֶגֶד שַׁעַר הַמִּפְקָד וְעַד
לב עֲלִיַּת הַפִּנָּה: וּבֵין עֲלִיַּת הַפִּנָּה לְשַׁעַר הַצֹּאן
לג הֶחֱזִיקוּ הַצֹּרְפִים וְהָרֹכְלִים: וַיְהִי
כַּאֲשֶׁר שָׁמַע סַנְבַלַּט כִּי־אֲנַחְנוּ בוֹנִים אֶת־
הַחוֹמָה וַיִּחַר לוֹ וַיִּכְעַס הַרְבֵּה וַיַּלְעֵג עַל־
לד הַיְּהוּדִים: וַיֹּאמֶר ׀ לִפְנֵי אֶחָיו וְחֵיל שֹׁמְרוֹן

29. צָדוֹק בֶּן־אִמֵּר — *Zadok the son of Immer.* Since Zadok was not a *Kohen*, he is mentioned separately (*Metzudos*). Like the *Kohanim*, he built the section of the wall opposite his home.

שַׁעַר הַמִּזְרָח — *The Eastern Gate.* This refers to the Eastern Gate of the Temple, known as the Gate of HaMiphkad (v. 31) (*Malbim*).

30. בֶּן־צָלָף הַשִּׁשִּׁי — *The sixth son of Zalaph.* The translation follows *Rashi*.

מִדָּה שֵׁנִי — *A similar* [lit. *second*] *measure*. The grammar here is unusual, since the masculine form — שֵׁנִי — is used for a feminine noun [מִדָּה], rather than the grammatically correct שֵׁנִית (feminine) used in the remainder of the chapter (e.g., vs. 11, 19-21). A similar usage is found in *Esther* 2:14 (*Ibn Ezra*).

נִשְׁכָּתוֹ — *His chamber.* This word has the same meaning as לִשְׁכָּתוֹ (*Rashi; Ralbag, Metzudos; Malbim; Ri Mitrani*). *Metzudos* notes that Scripture sometimes substitutes the letter *nun* (נ) for *lamed* (ל). [See 13:7.] (See *Rashi* to *Leviticus* 19:16.)

Malbim observes that Meshullam's chamber stood at the city's eastern wall now being described [see comm., v. 25], near the Temple Courtyard (עֲזָרָה).

31. בֶּן־הַצֹּרְפִי — *Son of the metalsmith.* His father was a metalsmith, known by the name of his trade (*Rashi*). Alternatively, the word should be understood as if the letter *mem* (ם) were added, to form the plural הַצֹּרְפִים, *the metalsmiths* (*Ralbag*). [See comm. v. 8.]

עַד־בֵּית הַנְּתִינִים — *Until the home of the Nethinites.* [Besides the Nethinites who lived in Ophel, other Nethinites lived here.]

נֶגֶד שַׁעַר הַמִּפְקָד — *Opposite the Gate of HaMiphkad.* The strengthening of the wall continued past the home of the Nethinites and the peddlers (v. 31), until the area opposite the Gate of HaMiphkad (*Metzudos*).

וְעַד עֲלִיַּת הַפִּנָּה — *And until the tower ascent.*

This was a fortification which stood on a high spot (*Malbim*).

32. לְשַׁעַר הַצֹּאן — *The Sheep Gate.* The

III
29-34

[29] *After him, Zadok the son of Immer strengthened [the area] opposite his house and, after him, Shemaiah the son of Shechaniah, guard of the Eastern Gate, strengthened.* [30] *After him, Hananiah the son of Shelemiah and Hanun the sixth son of Zalaph strengthened [the area] a similar measure; after him Meshullam the son of Berachiah opposite his chamber.* [31] *After him, Malchijah the son of the metalsmith strengthened [the area] until the home of the Nethinites and peddlers [until] opposite the Gate of HaMiphkad and until the tower ascent.* [32] *The metalsmiths and peddlers strengthened [the area] between the tower ascent and the Sheep Gate.*

[33] *When Sanballat heard that we were building the wall he became enraged, extremely angry, and he ridiculed the Jews.* [34] *Then he spoke before his brothers and the populace of Samaria and said, 'Why are the*

Sheep Gate had been the starting point for the construction of the wall (v. 1). Thus, the builders ringed the entire city with a completely connected wall (*Rashi; Metzudos*).

☙ The Enemies' Reaction

33. וַיִּחַר לוֹ וַיִּכְעַס הַרְבֵּה — *He became enraged, extremely angry.* The translation follows *Metzudos*, who explains וַיִּחַר, *he became enraged*, as a reference to his inner feelings, and וַיִּכְעַס, *he became angry*, as a reference to the open expression of that anger (*Metzudos*). *Malbim* translates the first clause *He was displeased* (as in *Genesis* 4:5).

34. אֶחָיו — *His brothers.* I.e., his companions (*Rashi*).

וְחֵיל שֹׁמְרוֹן — *And the populace of Samaria.* The Samaritans were the enemies of Judah (*Rashi*). [See also comm. to 2:10 and ArtScroll *Ezra* 4:1.]

The Samaritans were a large populace of pagans transplanted to *Eretz Yisrael* who converted to Judaism but continued to worship idols (*II Kings* 17:24-41). For centuries, the authenticity of their conversion was questioned and, thus, their status as Jews was often tenuous. Not surprisingly, incidents of conflict between the Samaritans and the Jews in the Holy Land often erupted. At times, the tension threatened to break into outright war. *Pirkei d'R' Eliezer* (ch. 38) and *Yalkut Shimoni* (to *II Kings* 17) report that in the days of Darius' decree allowing the Jews to rebuild the Temple, the Samaritans mounted an army of 180,000 men and threatened to attack the builders. As a result of this, and because of their role in the original disruption of the Temple construction (*Ezra* ch. 4), the Jewish leaders excommunicated them (see ArtScroll *Ezra* footnote to 4:3). In the days of Rabbi Meir (c. 160 C.E., over 500 years after the events in *Nehemiah*), a bird-like idol was discovered in their midst. Finally, in the days of R' Ami and R' Assi (c. 300 C.E.), the Samaritans were decreed non-Jews in all aspects of Torah law (*Chullin* 6a).

וַיֹּ֣אמֶר מָ֗ה הַיְּהוּדִ֣ים הָאֲמֵלָלִ֔ים עֹשִׂ֑ים
הֲיַעַזְב֨וּ לָהֶ֜ם הֲיִזְבָּ֗חוּ הַיְכַלּ֣וּ בַיּ֔וֹם הַיְחַיּ֧וּ
אֶת־הָאֲבָנִ֛ים מֵעֲרֵמ֥וֹת הֶעָפָ֖ר וְהֵ֥מָּה שְׂרוּפֽוֹת׃
לה וְטוֹבִיָּ֥ה הָעַמֹּנִ֖י אֶצְל֑וֹ וַיֹּ֗אמֶר גַּ֚ם אֲשֶׁר־הֵ֣ם
בּוֹנִ֔ים אִם־יַעֲלֶ֣ה שׁוּעָ֔ל וּפָרַ֖ץ חוֹמַ֥ת אַבְנֵיהֶֽם׃
לו שְׁמַ֤ע אֱלֹהֵ֙ינוּ֙ כִּֽי־הָיִ֣ינוּ בוּזָ֔ה וְהָשֵׁ֥ב חֶרְפָּתָ֖ם
אֶל־רֹאשָׁ֑ם וּתְנֵ֥ם לְבִזָּ֖ה בְּאֶ֥רֶץ שִׁבְיָֽה׃
לז וְאַל־תְּכַס֙ עַל־עֲוֺנָ֔ם וְחַטָּאתָ֖ם מִלְּפָנֶ֣יךָ
אַל־תִּמָּחֶ֑ה כִּ֥י הִכְעִ֖יסוּ לְנֶ֥גֶד הַבּוֹנִֽים׃

מָה — *Why* [lit. *what*]? The translation follows *Rashi*; others translate as *what* (*Ralbag*).

Metzudos explains the intent of this phrase: What can the Jewish weaklings accomplish?

הֲיַעַזְבוּ לָהֶם — *Will they let them?* This interpretation is *Rashi's*: Do they think that the gentiles will leave them alone, and allow them to build?

However, *Ralbag, Ibn Ezra, Ri Mitrani, Metzudos,* and *Malbim* translate the root עזב as *strengthen,* as in v. 8, where it meant that the wall was strengthened by filling in its openings with dirt (see comm., v. 8). The translation here is *will they strengthen the wall for themselves?*

הֲיִזְבָּחוּ — *Will they bring sacrifices?* Will they be permitted to constantly bring their sacrifices, as they think? (*Rashi*).

Ralbag's interpretation is: 'Will they bring sacrifices to celebrate the completion of the construction of the wall?' The inference was that the wall was so puny and insignificant that its completion would not warrant rejoicing (*Metzudos*).

הַיְכַלּוּ בַיּוֹם — *Can they finish in a* [lit. *the*] *day*? Can they finish their work in a day, and thus avoid interruption by their enemies? Surely they cannot, and they will be interrupted (*Rashi*; *Ralbag*). *Ibn Ezra* and *Metzudos* render, *Can they finish on the day?* Can they successfully complete their project on the intended day according to plan? They cannot; they are too weak.

Malbim reads הֲיִזְבָּחוּ הַיְכַלּוּ together, rendering, *Will they bring sacrifices in order to finish in a day?* Will their sacrifices make them worthy of a miracle, allowing them to finish in a day? Surely not.

Ri Mitrani translates these words as a statement rather than a question: *Even if they finish in a day, they will not bring sacrifices,* for the king will banish them the same day. [Sanballat and his cohorts accused the Jews of reconstructing the city's walls in order to rebel against the king, 2:19.]

הַיְחַיּוּ אֶת־הָאֲבָנִים — *Can they restore the stones?* The word יְחַיּוּ literally means to *bring to life.* It is used in the sense of *to restore* (*Rashi*; see *Exodus* 22:3; *Bava Kamma* 65a). *Ri Mitrani* comments that bringing the stones to life is a figure of speech for building successfully with those stones. He cites a similar expression in 4:1, *The wall of Jerusalem was healed.*

מֵעֲרֵמוֹת הֶעָפָר וְהֵמָּה שְׂרוּפוֹת — *Out of the mounds of charred dust* [lit. *mound of*

Jewish weaklings doing this? Will they let them? Will they bring sacrifices? Can they finish in a day? Can they restore the stones out of the mounds of charred dust?'
35 *Tobiah the Ammonite was near him and he said, 'Even that which they build, if [even] a fox were to go up, he would break their stone wall.'* 36 *'Hear, our God, for we are ridiculed. Return their anger to their heads. May they be despoiled in a land of captivity.* 37 *Do not cover up their sins, nor may their transgressions be eradicated from before You, for they have reviled the builders;*

dust, and they are burnt]. The stones of Jerusalem's walls were burnt during the destruction of the city and collapsed in heaps of charred ruins. Sanballat now ridiculed the Jews' effort to reconstruct the wall as an attempt to bring the stones back out of the dust of their ruins (*Rashi; Ri Mitrani*).

35. אֶצְלוֹ — *Was near him.* Tobiah was near Sanballat (*Rashi*).

וַיֹּאמֶר גַּם אֲשֶׁר־הֵם בּוֹנִים — *And he said, 'Even that which they build.'* The translation follows *Rashi* and *Malbim*, who translate גַּם as *even*. Tobiah added that even if they were to succeed in building, the wall would be easily crushed (*Malbim*).

Metzudos, however, reads וַיֹּאמֶר גַּם, *And he also said*, i.e., in addition to Sanballat, Tobiah also added the following remarks.

אִם־יַעֲלֶה שׁוּעָל — *If [even] a fox were to go up.* The wall is so weak that anyone can destroy it (*Rashi*); even the fox, a weak lazy animal (*Ralbag*). It is not uncommon for foxes to cause breaks in ruined structures, as stated in *Ezekiel* (13:14), *like foxes in the ruins* ... (*Malbim*).

◆§ Nehemiah's Prayer

36. שְׁמַע — *Hear.* When I (Nehemiah) heard their ridicule, I uttered the following prayer, *'Hear, our God ...'* (*Rashi*).

וּתְנֵם לְבִזָּה — *May they be despoiled.* This is *Ralbag*'s translation. *Metzudos*, however, translates, *May they be humiliated.*

בְּאֶרֶץ שִׁבְיָה — *In a land of captivity.* May they be exiled, as we have been (*Rashi*). [They are hindering the reconstruction of our homeland after our return from exile — let them be exiled themselves.]

37. וְאַל־תְּכַס עַל־עֲוֹנָם — *Do not cover up their sins.* In the preceding verse, Nehemiah requested that God punish the enemies for their verbal abuse, *For we have been humiliated.* In our verse, Nehemiah prayed that God punish them for the sin of attempting to interrupt the construction — *For they have incensed the builders,* in an effort to make them cease their work.

וְחַטָּאתָם מִלְּפָנֶיךָ אַל־תִּמָּחֶה — *Nor may their transgressions be eradicated from before You.* Nehemiah's request is twofold: (1) Do not cover up their sins, i.e., do not fail to punish them for their sins; (2) and may their transgressions not be eradicated before you — even after the punishment is meted out, remember their transgressions eternally (*Malbim*). Although the punishment has already occurred, the memory of the transgression before God is significant. Because of it, God will not favor the sinners with His good will and benevolence (see *Shaarei Teshuvah* 1:42).

כִּי הִכְעִיסוּ לְנֶגֶד הַבּוֹנִים — *For they have reviled* [lit. *against*] *the builders.* Our

ג
לח

לח וַנִּבְנֶה֙ אֶת־הַ֣חוֹמָ֔ה וַתִּקָּשֵׁ֥ר כָּל־הַחוֹמָ֖ה עַד־
חֶצְיָ֑הּ וַיְהִ֥י לֵ֛ב לָעָ֖ם לַעֲשֽׂוֹת׃

ד
א־ב

א וַיְהִ֡י כַּאֲשֶׁ֣ר שָׁמַ֣ע סַנְבַלַּ֣ט וְ֠טוֹבִיָּה וְהָֽעַרְבִ֞ים
וְהָעַמֹּנִ֣ים וְהָֽאַשְׁדּוֹדִ֗ים כִּֽי־עָלְתָ֨ה אֲרוּכָ֜ה
לְחֹמ֤וֹת יְרוּשָׁלִַ֙ם֙ כִּי־הֵחֵ֥לּוּ הַפְּרֻצִ֖ים לְהִסָּתֵ֑ם
ב וַיִּ֥חַר לָהֶ֖ם מְאֹֽד׃ וַיִּקְשְׁר֤וּ כֻלָּם֙ יַחְדָּ֔ו לָב֖וֹא
לְהִלָּחֵ֣ם בִּירוּשָׁלִָ֑ם וְלַעֲשׂ֥וֹת ל֖וֹ תּוֹעָֽה׃

translation follows *Rashi*, who takes הִכְעִיסוּ לְנֶגֶד as an idiom for *showing contempt* or *ridiculing.*

Metzudos translates, *For they raged against the builders.* While ridiculing the builders (vs. 34,35), Tobiah and Sanballat also expressed their rage, thereby hoping to intimidate the Jews and cause them to abandon the construction. [This concludes Nehemiah's prayer.]

38. וַנִּבְנֶה אֶת־הַחוֹמָה — *Yet we built the wall.* Despite the abuse and the rage against us, we persisted in building (*Metzudos*).

וַתִּקָּשֵׁר כָּל־הַחוֹמָה — *When the entire wall was joined.* The breaches resulted in gaps in the wall. When they were filled, the wall was joined (*Ibn Ezra; Metzudos*).

עַד־חֶצְיָהּ — *Halfway.* The breaches were completely filled in for half the perimeter of the city.

Verse 32 records the completion of the wall at the Sheep Gate, yet the text now states that the wall was only half complete. *Metzudos* reconciles the discrepancy. After making the general statement that the wall was completed [v. 32], the narrative now returns to the time when it was only half finished, and describes in detail [ch. 4] how the enemies then threatened to attack, and how the Jews defended themselves and continued to build.

וַיְהִי לֵב לָעָם לַעֲשׂוֹת — *The people were eager to proceed* [lit. *act*]. The joining of half the wall made the people enthusiastic about continuing the construction (*Rashi; Metzudos*). Not only were the people undeterred by their enemies, but they were enthusiastic about proceeding — there was no fear or lethargy on their part (*Malbim*).

IV

The events recorded in this chapter occurred some time after the beginning of the construction effort described in chapter 3 (*Ibn Ezra*) but before the actual completion of the wall as recorded in 3:32 (*Metzudos*). [See comm. to 3:38.]

1. The Enemies

עָלְתָה אֲרוּכָה לְחֹמוֹת יְרוּשָׁלַםִ — *The walls of Jerusalem were healing.* The walls were being rebuilt (*Rashi*).

Malbim observes that אֲרוּכָה, *healing*, refers in particular to the healing of fractured bones (see *Jeremiah* 30:15). Hence, it is used here to describe the repair of the broken walls (see comm. to 3:34; *I Kings* 18:30).

כִּי־הֵחֵלּוּ הַפְּרֻצִים לְהִסָּתֵם — *That those who had been exposed had begun to be*

III 38 [38] *yet we built the wall.' When the entire wall was joined halfway, the people were eager to proceed.*

IV 1-2 *Now when Sanballat, Tobiah, the Arabs, the Ammonites, and the Ashdodites heard that the walls of Jerusalem were healing, [and] that those who had been exposed had begun to be sheltered, they grew extremely angry.* [2] *So they all banded together to come and do battle in Jerusalem, and cause its destruction.*

sheltered. The translation follows *Rashi*, who explains that the people themselves were now finally getting protection. *Ralbag*, however, translates *the breaches had begun to be closed*, referring to the wall, which had been breached and was now repaired.

וַיִּחַר לָהֶם מְאֹד — *They grew extremely angry.*

This follows *Metzudos'* translation of וַיִּחַר; see comm. to 3:33.

[Note the gradual progression of hostility on the part of Sanballat and his accomplices. In 2:10, when Nehemiah first arrived, *they were extremely chagrined.* Next, in 2:19, when Nehemiah declared his purpose in coming, they *ridiculed and disparaged.* Finally, here (and in 3:33), with the wall better than halfway complete, *they grew extremely angry.* Not even the enemies of the settlers believed at first that this one man, Nehemiah, could make a difference. As they watched the efforts of his labor bear fruit, their concern turned to mockery and, finally, extreme anger. The realization that the Jews were actually completing the wall enraged them.]

Ramban (*Megillah* 2a) comments that the decree issued by Ahasuerus and Haman ordering the massacre of all the Jews in the kingdom (*Esther* 3:13) was far more threatening to the Jews living in open cities than to those protected by walls. In support of this, *Ramban* cites our passage describing the deep chagrin of Sanballat and his companions over the reconstruction of the wall, thereby restoring Jerusalem to the status of a fortified city. Consequently, *Ramban* contends, the Purim celebration was at first accepted spontaneously only by the inhabitants of the open cities, who had been delivered from greater danger. The walled cities were not included until later, when Purim was declared a national holiday.

2. וְלַעֲשׂוֹת לוֹ תּוֹעָה — *And cause its destruction* [lit. *do destruction to it*]. The translation follows *Rashi*. This makes it clear that the primary objective of the enemies was to destroy the wall (*Rashi*).

Ralbag and *Malbim*, however, translate *and cause* [the Jewish nation] *to be misled.* The word תּוֹעָה is related to טָעוּת, *error.* The enemies of the Jews did not wish to attack openly, inasmuch as the sizable Jewish population, with the support of the king, would have resisted successfully. Instead, the plan was to lull the Jews into a false sense of security and destroy them with a sudden attack (see v. 5).

Other ways of understanding תּוֹעָה in the verse are *cause* [Nehemiah or the Jewish nation] *confusion* (*Ibn Ezra, Metzudos*) or *and cause* [the Jewish nation] *provocation*, תּוֹעָה being a variation of תְּעְתּוּעַ, *ridicule*, or *provocation* (*Ri Mitrani*). [All of the interpretations are related to the definition of תּוֹעָה as טָעוּת,

ג וַנִּתְפַּלֵּל אֶל־אֱלֹהֵינוּ וַנַּעֲמִיד מִשְׁמָר עֲלֵיהֶם
ד יוֹמָם וָלַיְלָה מִפְּנֵיהֶם׃ וַיֹּאמֶר יְהוּדָה כָּשַׁל כֹּחַ
הַסַּבָּל וְהֶעָפָר הַרְבֵּה וַאֲנַחְנוּ לֹא נוּכַל לִבְנוֹת
ה בַּחוֹמָה׃ וַיֹּאמְרוּ צָרֵינוּ לֹא יֵדְעוּ וְלֹא יִרְאוּ
עַד אֲשֶׁר־נָבוֹא אֶל־תּוֹכָם וַהֲרַגְנוּם וְהִשְׁבַּתְנוּ
ו אֶת־הַמְּלָאכָה׃ וַיְהִי כַּאֲשֶׁר־בָּאוּ הַיְּהוּדִים
הַיֹּשְׁבִים אֶצְלָם וַיֹּאמְרוּ לָנוּ עֶשֶׂר פְּעָמִים

error or *mistake*. Destruction (*Rashi*) turns an object into a shambles of itself — i.e., a mistaken version. Confusion (*Ibn Ezra*) is based on error. Ridicule (*Ri Mitrani*) creates an erroneous caricature of the person or object being maligned.]

3. Prayer and Guards

וַנַּעֲמִיד מִשְׁמָר עֲלֵיהֶם — And *established a guard over them.* Soldiers were assigned to watch the builders (*Rashi, Ri Mitrani; Metzudos; Ralbag*). Alternatively, *them* refers to the enemies. *We established sentries over the enemies*, to watch for signs of attack and warn the builders (*Ralbag; Malbim*).

מִפְּנֵיהֶם — *Because of them.* Because of Sanballat and his companions (*Rashi; Metzudos*).

4. וַיֹּאמֶר יְהוּדָה כָּשַׁל כֹּחַ הַסַּבָּל — *Then Judah said, 'The strength of the bearer is spent.'* סַבָּל is a bearer of heavy weights as in *II Chronicles* 2:1, *I Kings* 5:29 (*Malbim; Metzudos*). The men of Judah complained that one particular group of workers, the bearers of heavy weights, were weakened, from their fear of the enemy (*Rashi*), and from their strenuous physical exertion (*Metzudos*). Their energy was now spent.

Midrash Rabbah (*Eichah* 1:43) interprets this verse as an indication that the Babylonian monarchy sapped the strength of the Jews. 'Four things,' the Midrash remarks, 'sap a man's strength: (1) fasting, (2) travel, (3) sin, (4) and the Babylonian monarchy ... as it is written: כָּשַׁל כֹּחַ הַסַּבָּל, *the strength of the bearer is spent.*' [*Razav* explains that they were exhausted from the pressures of the exorbitant taxes levied upon them by the Persian conquerors who now presided over the Babylonian empire (*Daniel* 5:29, 6:1.]

וְהֶעָפָר הַרְבֵּה וַאֲנַחְנוּ לֹא נוּכַל לִבְנוֹת בַּחוֹמָה — *But there is much earth; we are unable to construct the wall.* Much earth has already been assembled to fill in the wall (*Ri Mitrani*), but this arduous task remains to be done. Yet the workers are too weakened from fear (*Rashi*) and exhaustion (*Ri Mitrani; Metzudos*) to complete the task of constructing the wall.

5. וַיֹּאמְרוּ צָרֵינוּ — *And our enemies*[1] *said.*

According to *Rashi* and *Ri Mitrani*,

1. *Ramban* (*Leviticus* 26:41) questions the apparently incongruous sequence of events in Scripture's prophetic description of the exile. First, the Torah portrays the punishment and exile to be visited upon the Jewish people (vs. 14-39), followed by their repentance (v. 40). But this is followed, once again, by the visitation of God's punishment: *I shall bring them to the land of their enemies* (v. 41). Why, after repentance, should they be brought to enemy land?

*3 We prayed to our God, and established a guard over
them day and night because of them. 4 Then Judah
said, 'The strength of the bearer is spent, but there
is much earth; we are unable to construct the wall.'
5 And our enemies said, 'They shall neither know nor
see before we come among them and kill them,
thus halting the work.' 6 Then, when the Jews who
lived among them came and warned us ten times,*

Nehemiah's portrayal of the complaints of the men of Judah is limited to v. 4 while v. 5 now narrates the enemies' plan.

Ralbag and *Malbim*, however, interpret our verse as part of the complaint of the men of Judah. First, the men of Judah asserted that they were unable to construct the wall (v. 4). Then, in our verse, they attempt to further substantiate their complaint by pointing out that the enemies planned to attack them. [Of course, from the moment the reconstruction effort began, attack was a possibility. Nevertheless, the men of Judah related that now it was imminent in light of the fact that plans for a surprise enemy attack had been uncovered. See v. 6 and v. 9.]

לֹא יֵדְעוּ וְלֹא יִרְאוּ — *They shall neither know nor see.* The enemies planned a surprise attack. They (the Jews) shall not see our forces approaching, for we will fall upon them from a hidden place (*Malbim*).

☙ The Jews Give Warning

6. כַּאֲשֶׁר־בָּאוּ הַיְּהוּדִים הַיֹּשְׁבִים אֶצְלָם — *When the Jews who lived among them came.* Nehemiah now relates that the enemies who gathered to attack included, in their forces, Jews who lived among them. These Jews arrived prior to the army to speak to us. By this subterfuge they were able to outwit our enemies and warn us (*Rashi*).

[These Jews were apparently part of the enemy army, yet they risked their lives to warn their brethren. Perhaps, since Jerusalem was a city in ruins, desolate and unprotected, many Jews lived in the surrounding towns and villages among the enemies. Fearing for their own lives and the lives of their families, they joined the army of the gentiles. When, at the critical moment, they realized that their brethren were in imminent danger, they summoned the courage to warn them.

Alternatively, even if these Jews were traitors, nevertheless, their sympathies for their brothers lay dormant. Faced with the prospect of participating in the destruction of their own people, they broke down and relayed the information of a surprise attack.]

וַיֹּאמְרוּ לָנוּ עֶשֶׂר פְּעָמִים — *And warned us ten times.* Ten times is a figure of speech meaning many times a day (*Ralbag; Ri Mitrani*). The repetition of the warning many times indicated that the threat of attack was very real (*Malbim*).

Ramban answers that *the land of their enemies* is not a reference to the exile, but to the Holy Land itself, which is to be occupied by the enemies of the Jews even after the redemption. The repentance mentioned in v. 40 is not complete, and is thus followed by only a partial redemption. This alludes to the resettlement of the Land of Israel in the days of Nehemiah, when the enemies lived in the land, and attempted to attack the Jews, as described here by Nehemiah.

ד ז־ח

ז מִכָּל־הַמְּקֹמוֹת אֲשֶׁר־תָּשׁוּבוּ עָלֵינוּ: וָאַעֲמִיד
מִתַּחְתִּיּוֹת לַמָּקוֹם מֵאַחֲרֵי לַחוֹמָה
°בצחחיים וָאַעֲמִיד אֶת־הָעָם לְמִשְׁפָּחוֹת
ח עִם־חַרְבֹתֵיהֶם רָמְחֵיהֶם וְקַשְּׁתֹתֵיהֶם: וָאֵרֶא
וָאָקוּם וָאֹמַר אֶל־הַחֹרִים וְאֶל־הַסְּגָנִים וְאֶל־
יֶתֶר הָעָם אַל־תִּירְאוּ מִפְּנֵיהֶם אֶת־אֲדֹנָי
הַגָּדוֹל וְהַנּוֹרָא זְכֹרוּ וְהִלָּחֲמוּ עַל־אֲחֵיכֶם
ט בְּנֵיכֶם וּבְנֹתֵיכֶם נְשֵׁיכֶם וּבָתֵּיכֶם: וַיְהִי
כַּאֲשֶׁר־שָׁמְעוּ אוֹיְבֵינוּ כִּי־נוֹדַע לָנוּ וַיָּפֶר

°בְּצִחִיחִים ק׳

מִכָּל־הַמְּקֹמוֹת אֲשֶׁר־תָּשׁוּבוּ עָלֵינוּ — *Gather together from all the places against us* [lit. *from all the places which you turn upon us*]. The Jews who dwelt among the enemies warned of the impending attack: 'Take care to gather together from all the scattered sites along the construction area to do battle against our forces' (*Rashi*).

Ibn Ezra translates the warning: *From all the places to which you return* [they will fall] *upon us*. They informed the workers that the enemies planned a surprise attack in which they would ambush them at the places to which the workers *returned* at night.

Ralbag offers yet another interpretation, translating, *they warned us ten times of all the places from which they would turn upon us*. The Jewish members of the gentile forces revealed the enemy hiding places from which they intended to launch their attacks. The verb תָּשׁוּבוּ, in the future (feminine) tense, is translated, *they would turn*, denoting the enemies' constant shifting from one hiding place to another, in order to find the most suitable spot from which to launch their ambush. [The future tense may sometimes be used to denote repeated action; see *Rashi, Job* 1:5; *Ezekiel* 37:7.]

◆§ The Defense

7. וָאַעֲמִיד — *I set up*. When I heard of the plan to attack us, I set up the people (*Rashi*).

מִתַּחְתִּיּוֹת לַמָּקוֹם — *Underneath the place*. לַמָּקוֹם, *the place*, can refer either to the wall or the area where the enemies lay in ambush. Accordingly, Nehemiah posted the warriors *underneath the place* of the construction of the wall (*Metzudos*). [Evidently, the wall was built on a hill, and the warriors stood on the hill below the construction site.] Or Nehemiah *removed* his men *from underneath the* (hiding) *place* to a more advantageous position (*Ralbag*); or *placed* his warriors *underneath the* (hiding) *place*, i.e., *among the rocks*, בְּצְחִיחִים, to do battle from there (*Malbim*).

בְּצְחִיחִים — *On the cliffs*. The translation follows *Rashi*. *Malbim* translates *among the rocks* and understands it as a reference to the place where Nehemiah set up his own men to ambush the enemy forces (see above).

Ralbag interprets בְּצְחִיחִים as a reference to sentinels who were placed on high spots to observe the activities of the enemies in their hidden places, and to signal if they began their attack.

'Gather together from all the places against us,' 7 *I set*
up underneath the place behind the wall on the cliffs —
I set up the people by families with their swords,
spears, and bows. 8 *When I saw, I arose and said to the*
aristocrats, the nobles, and the rest of the people, 'Do not
fear them. Remember the great, awesome God, and
battle for your brothers, sons, daughters, wives, and
homes.'
9 *But then, when our enemies heard that we knew,*

וָאַעֲמִיד אֶת־הָעָם לְמִשְׁפָּחוֹת — *I set up the people by families.* The verse now elaborates upon its opening phrase, *I set up underneath the place.* The repetition of a clause in such a manner is not unusual; see *Exodus* 4:9; *Psalms* 92:10, 115:1; *Judges* 5:12 (*Rashi*).

Ralbag, however, interprets the opening phrase to describe the stationing of sentinels. The families of the second part of the verse were set up as warriors. These were better suited as warriors because they naturally formed a tighter fighting group. Nehemiah understood that members of the same family would offer one another maximum aid.

Malbim, too, interprets the two portions of the verse as referring to two different groups. One group *set up underneath the spot behind the wall and among the rocks,* hidden in ambush. The other group, *set up . . . by families,* stood ready for open warfare.

עִם־חַרְבֹתֵיהֶם רָמְחֵיהֶם וְקַשְּׁתֹתֵיהֶם — *With their swords, spears, and bows.* All of the people stood armed to protect the city (*Ri Mitrani*). [This indicates that the construction had stopped.] *Metzudos* and *Malbim*, however, comment that all the warriors stood armed to protect the workers [indicating that the construction continued].

8. וָאֵרֶא — *When I saw.* When I saw the enemy approaching (*Rashi*), implying that Nehemiah himself was one of those who watched the enemy's activities (*Malbim*). Alternatively, Nehemiah *saw* or *understood* that this was the proper time to encourage the people (*Metzudos*).

הַחֹרִים — *The aristocrats.* This is *Ralbag's* translation. See comm. to 2:16.

The aristocrats and the nobles were among those armed (*Ri Mitrani*). [Note that the verse continues וְאֶל־יֶתֶר הָעָם, *and the rest of the people,* whereas in 2:16 they are called יֶתֶר עֹשֵׂה הַמְּלָאכָה, *the remainder who did the work.* Now that their lives were seriously threatened they are called הָעָם, a people, having banded together more than before. They are also no longer the עֹשֵׂה הַמְּלָאכָה, *those who did the work,* because they were now too busy protecting themselves to do more work. See comm. v. 7.]

אַל־תִּירְאוּ מִפְּנֵיהֶם — *Do not fear them.* [This parallels the Biblically commanded speech recited by the *Kohen* anointed for war (מְשׁוּחַ מִלְחָמָה) before the Jewish warriors entered into battle: *'Let your hearts not soften, do not be afraid'* (*Deut.* 20:3). See *Rambam, Melachim* 7.]

עַל־אֲחֵיכֶם — *For* [lit. *over*] *your brothers.* For the sake of your brothers (*Rashi*).

The Return to Work

9. כִּי־נוֹדַע לָנוּ — *That we knew.* The enemies heard that we knew of their plans to attack us (*Rashi*), and that we were armed and prepared (*Metzudos; Malbim*).

ד
י־יב

°וַנָּשָׁב ק׳ הָאֱלֹהִים אֶת־עֲצָתָם °ונשוב כֻּלָּנוּ אֶל־
י הַחוֹמָה אִישׁ אֶל־מְלַאכְתּוֹ: וַיְהִי | מִן־
הַיּוֹם הַהוּא חֲצִי נְעָרַי עֹשִׂים בַּמְּלָאכָה
וְחֶצְיָם מַחֲזִיקִים וְהָרְמָחִים הַמָּגִנִּים
וְהַקְּשָׁתוֹת וְהַשִּׁרְיֹנִים וְהַשָּׂרִים אַחֲרֵי כָּל־
יא בֵּית יְהוּדָה: הַבּוֹנִים בַּחוֹמָה וְהַנֹּשְׂאִים
בַּסֶּבֶל עֹמְשִׂים בְּאַחַת יָדוֹ עֹשֶׂה בַמְּלָאכָה
יב וְאַחַת מַחֲזֶקֶת הַשָּׁלַח: וְהַבּוֹנִים אִישׁ חַרְבּוֹ

וַיָּפֶר הָאֱלֹהִים אֶת־עֲצָתָם — *God upset their plans.* They retreated, no longer determined to attack and halt the construction (*Metzudos; Malbim*).

This demonstrates one of the ways God bestows kindness on the Jewish people. Although the enemies planned to ambush the Jews, God caused the secret plan to be revealed. Then, the enemies, realizing that God was with the Jews, abandoned their plan (*Ralbag*). This is consistent with the change in the nature of Divine Providence, symbolized by the story of Purim (which occurred a short time earlier). 'In the days of Esther there was a concealment of the Divine countenance' (*Rashi* to *Chullin* 139b). God's control of the affairs of man, from the time of Esther onward, took place on a hidden level, in the form of apparent coincidence and 'natural' happenstance. See further, Overview to ArtScroll *Esther*, and author's preface to *Ezra*.

וַנָּשָׁב כֻּלָּנוּ . . . אִישׁ אֶל־מְלַאכְתּוֹ — *Then we all returned ... each to his work.* Although we returned, we still prepared for a possible attack [see vs. 10-12] (*Ralbag*).

◆§ Workers and Warriors

Malbim understands vs. 10-15 as follows: Immediately following the abortive enemy attack (vs. 8,9), the Jews feared renewed onslaughts. Therefore, the majority of the builders did not disperse to their accustomed building places along the length of the wall. They remained together near the place where they had prepared to engage the enemy and worked there, laboring with one hand and holding weapons with the other (vs. 11,12). Only Nehemiah's personal servants, who were skilled warriors, dispersed, half of them doing the work and half standing guard with weapons (v. 10). Later, when it became evident that a renewed enemy attack was not imminent, all of the builders dispersed and returned to their separate construction sites along the wall. Then (v. 15), half of the entire work force worked and half patrolled the city armed with spears.

10. וַיְהִי מִן־הַיּוֹם הַהוּא — [Lit. *it came to pass*] *from that day onward.* From the day it was discovered that the enemies planned to attack (*Metzudos*).

נְעָרַי — *My servants* [lit. *youths*]. This is *Ri Mitrani's* translation. [*Ramban* (*Exodus* 33:11) cites a number of verses where נַעַר is translated *servant*.] *Rashi* identifies them as warriors.

חֲצִי ... עֹשִׂים בַּמְּלָאכָה וְחֶצְיָם מַחֲזִיקִים וְהָרְמָחִים הַמָּגִנִּים — *Half . . . did the work, and half held* [lit. *and*] *spears, shields.* Half the warriors worked, and half the warriors stood armed to protect the builders (*Rashi*). The phrase מַחֲזִיקִים וְהָרְמָחִים, *held and the spears,* is to be understood as if it read מַחֲזִיקִים הָרְמָחִים, *held the spears*. The prefix וְ, *and*, is

IV 10-12

God upset their plans; then, we all returned to the wall, each to his work. [10] *From that day onward, half of my servants did the work, and half held spears, shields, bows, and armor, with the lords joining the entire house of Judah.* [11] *Those who built the wall and those who carried and bore the weights worked with one hand and held the sword with the other.* [12] *The builders built with*

ignored (*Rashi, Ibn Ezra, Ralbag*). [*Rashi* cites a precedent for this in *Genesis* 36:24.]

וְהַקְּשָׁתוֹת וְהַשִּׁרְיֹנִים — *Bows, and armor.* The list of arms reveals why the youths carrying the weapons could not work. Those armed with *spears* also had *shields*, so that both hands were occupied, and those who carried *bows* wore suits of *armor*, which made it impossible for them to work (*Malbim*).

וְהַשָּׂרִים אַחֲרֵי כָּל־בֵּית יְהוּדָה — *With the lords joining* [lit. *to the rear of*] *the entire house of Judah.* The lords joined behind the tribe of Judah to do battle (*Rashi; Metzudos*); or, the lords stood behind the tribe of Judah, i.e., they encouraged them and urged them to work quickly (*Ri Mitrani*).

Ralbag reads the entire latter portion of the passage together: *the shields, the bows, the armor and the lords* [stood] *to the rear of the entire house of Judah.* The weapons and the lords stood in the rear, ready for battle if necessary.

Malbim, however, reads the verse: *and the lords and the entire house of Judah remained behind*, explaining that they were the builders mentioned in the next verse (v. 11). Except for Nehemiah's warriors, the people were not trained in archery, and did not disperse into small groups to work at the various construction sites. They remained behind with Nehemiah at the site of the anticipated attack. This needed special protection because of its particular vulnerability. There, holding tools in one hand and a sword in the other (v. 11), they built the wall. [See prefatory remarks to 10-15.]

11. הַבּוֹנִים בַּחוֹמָה — *Those who built the wall.* According to *Malbim* [v. 10], these builders included the lords. However, according to the commentators above who explained that the lords stood in the rear, they were not included among the builders.

וְהַנֹּשְׂאִים בַּסֶּבֶל עֹמְשִׂים — *Those who carried and bore the weights.* The translation follows *Rashi* and *Metzudos*, who translate סֶבֶל, *the weight. Ralbag*, however, explains that סֶבֶל is rendered *cushion*, referring to a small cushion placed on the shoulders of the weight bearer underneath the load. His translation is *those who carried* [the weights] *which are loaded onto the cushion.*

Malbim interprets עֹמְשִׂים as *loading: Those who carried the weights which were loaded* by others. The need for loading by others is explained by the next phrase of the verse: [they] *worked with one hand and held the sword with the other.* Since only one hand was free for working, the weight bearers could not load themselves, but were forced to load one another.

הַשָּׁלַח — *The sword.* שֶׁלַח, an unusual synonym of חֶרֶב, *sword*, is found in *Job* 33:18 and in *II Chronicles* 32:5 (*Rashi; Metzudos*).

Malbim explains that שֶׁלַח refers to *a double-edged sword* which is not placed in a scabbard, but held in the hand for use against the enemy. חֶרֶב refers to the single-edged sword carried in a scabbard.

אֲסוּרִים עַל־מָתְנָיו וּבוֹנִים וְהַתּוֹקֵעַ בַּשּׁוֹפָר
יג אֶצְלִי: וָאֹמַר אֶל־הַחֹרִים וְאֶל־הַסְּגָנִים
וְאֶל־יֶתֶר הָעָם הַמְּלָאכָה הַרְבֵּה וּרְחָבָה
וַאֲנַחְנוּ נִפְרָדִים עַל־הַחוֹמָה רְחוֹקִים אִישׁ
יד מֵאָחִיו: בִּמְקוֹם אֲשֶׁר תִּשְׁמְעוּ אֶת־
קוֹל הַשּׁוֹפָר שָׁמָּה תִּקָּבְצוּ אֵלֵינוּ אֱלֹהֵינוּ
טו יִלָּחֶם לָנוּ: וַאֲנַחְנוּ עֹשִׂים בַּמְּלָאכָה וְחֶצְיָם
מַחֲזִיקִים בָּרְמָחִים מֵעֲלוֹת הַשַּׁחַר עַד צֵאת
טז הַכּוֹכָבִים: גַּם בָּעֵת הַהִיא אָמַרְתִּי לָעָם אִישׁ
וְנַעֲרוֹ יָלִינוּ בְּתוֹךְ יְרוּשָׁלָםִ וְהָיוּ־לָנוּ הַלַּיְלָה

The bearers of weights could not carry single-edged swords as did the builders (v. 12), since it would have been difficult for them to draw the swords from the scabbard quickly. Instead, they grasped the double-edged שֶׁלַח in one hand as they carried the load on their backs.

12. וְהַבּוֹנִים אִישׁ חַרְבּוֹ אֲסוּרִים עַל־מָתְנָיו וּבוֹנִים — *The builders built with each man's sword secured at his hips.* The builders, unlike the weight bearers, could easily draw the single-edged sword, חֶרֶב, from the scabbard to do battle. Therefore, the builders carried the חֶרֶב strapped at the hips. The load carriers, however, held the שֶׁלַח in one hand (*Malbim*).

וְהַתּוֹקֵעַ בַּשּׁוֹפָר אֶצְלִי — *And the one who sounded the shofar was next to me.* The *shofar* blast would alert the people to gather together (*Ralbag*), and signal the fighters' moves during battle (*Malbim*).

☙ The Workers Dispersed

13. הַרְבֵּה וּרְחָבָה — *Large and extensive* [lit. broad]. This is *Rashi's* interpretation. *Ri Mitrani*, however, renders this as *extremely extensive.* Since the work involves an extensive area, we must disperse to cover all of it (*Malbim*).

וַאֲנַחְנוּ נִפְרָדִים עַל־הַחוֹמָה — *And we are dispersed along* [lit. *upon*] *the wall.* Immediately following the enemies' intended attack, the majority of the builders had gathered to build together at one site [see pref. remarks 10-15]. Now that some time had passed, and it became evident that the threat of imminent attack was over, the laborers dispersed, each to his particular construction site. Nehemiah then issued the instructions described in our verse (*Malbim*).

רְחוֹקִים אִישׁ מֵאָחִיו — *Distant from one another.* We are too distant to see or hear one another (*Metzudos*).

14. תִּקָּבְצוּ אֵלֵינוּ — *Gather to us.* Rally to us so that we may battle the enemy as a unified group (*Metzudos*).

15. וַאֲנַחְנוּ עֹשִׂים בַּמְּלָאכָה — *Then we did the work.* According to *Malbim*, these are more of Nehemiah's actual words instructing the people. *Metzudos*, however, understands these words as the narrative voice of Nehemiah, describing the work done after he organized everyone and gave instructions to assemble at the sound of the *shofar* (v. 14).

וְחֶצְיָם מַחֲזִיקִים בָּרְמָחִים — *With half of them holding spears.* Half of the people, or, perhaps, half of Nehemiah's personal

IV 13-16

each man's sword secured at his hips, and the one who
sounded the shofar was next to me. 13 *Then I said to the*
aristocrats, the nobles, and the rest of the people, 'The work is large and extensive, and we are dispersed along the wall, distant from one another.
14 *At the place where you hear the sound of the shofar, gather to us there. Our God will do battle for*
us.' 15 *Then we did the work, with half of them holding*
spears, from dawn until nightfall. 16 *At that time I also*
said to the people: 'Let each man with his servants pass the nights in Jerusalem.' We spent the nights

servants, (v. 10) held spears (*Metzudos*).

The spear holders were to patrol the city, on the alert against enemy attack. Previously, when all the workers had gathered at the same spot to build (v. 11), they had worked with one hand and carried swords with the other. However, now that the builders dispersed to various points along the wall (v. 13), they could not possibly defend themselves. Instead, a large group of armed men patrolled the city, on the alert against the enemy (*Malbim*).

Ralbag observes that Nehemiah knew that the enemies were trying to delay the construction, and then persuade the king to halt it completely. The Jewish leader therefore hastened the building process in every way possible. Thus, he stationed guards for protection so that the work could continue despite the threat of enemy attack.

מֵעֲלוֹת הַשַּׁחַר עַד צֵאת הַכּוֹכָבִים — *From dawn until nightfall.* In their hurry to complete the construction, they worked with all possible diligence, beginning at dawn and ending at nightfall (*Ralbag*).

עֲלוֹת הַשַּׁחַר, *dawn,* refers to the first ray of morning light, even before the appearance of the sun (*Metzudos*).

Rambam (Commentary to *Berachos* 1:1) explains that עֲלוֹת הַשַּׁחַר takes place an hour and a fifth before sunrise. The length of one 'hour' (שָׁעָה זְמַנִּית), defined as one-twelfth of the length of that particular day, varies from day to day. (See *Tosefos Yom Tov, Berachos* 1:1.)

צֵאת הַכּוֹכָבִים refers to the appearance of three medium-sized stars. This constitutes nightfall (*Tosafos, Pesachim* 2a).[1]

16. בָּעֵת הַהִיא — *At that time. Metzudos* explains: during the construction, when the wall was still incomplete. According to *Ri Mitrani*, however, *at that time* refers to a later time, after the wall had been completed.

יָלִינוּ בְּתוֹךְ יְרוּשָׁלָם — *Pass the nights in Jerusalem.* During the construction, they stayed in Jerusalem at night to guard against the enemy (*Metzudos*).

1. The Talmud (*Berachos* 2b) derives from this verse that a halachic 'day' (יוֹם) is not defined as the period from sunrise (נֵץ הַחַמָּה) until sunset (שְׁקִיעָה). It is defined, rather, as a much longer period, beginning from the first ray of light, before the sun appears over the horizon, and lasting until the fall of darkness, long after the sun has set. Accordingly, the *mitzvos* which must be performed during the day (e.g., circumcision, reading of the *Megillah*) are valid (בְּדִיעֲבַד, *after the fact*) if carried out before sunrise, so long as the first ray of light has already appeared (*Megillah* 20a; *Ralbag*).

ד יז מִשְׁמָר וְהַיּוֹם מְלָאכָה: וְאֵין אֲנִי וְאַחַי וּנְעָרַי
יז וְאַנְשֵׁי הַמִּשְׁמָר אֲשֶׁר אַחֲרַי אֵין־אֲנַחְנוּ
פֹּשְׁטִים בְּגָדֵינוּ אִישׁ שִׁלְחוֹ הַמָּיִם:
ה א וַתְּהִי צַעֲקַת הָעָם וּנְשֵׁיהֶם גְּדוֹלָה אֶל־אֲחֵיהֶם
א־ג ב הַיְּהוּדִים: וְיֵשׁ אֲשֶׁר אֹמְרִים בָּנֵינוּ וּבְנֹתֵינוּ
ג אֲנַחְנוּ רַבִּים וְנִקְחָה דָגָן וְנֹאכְלָה וְנִחְיֶה: וְיֵשׁ

Ri Mitrani, however, interprets our verse as a reference to the time when the wall had already been completed and the threat of attack had disappeared. The verse means that Nehemiah now permitted the people to spend their nights freely in Jerusalem. [*Ri Mitrani* agrees, however, that the next phrase *we spent the nights on watch, and the days at work* and the following verse (17) revert to the time of danger while the wall was under construction.]

וְהָיוּ־לָנוּ הַלַּיְלָה מִשְׁמָר — *We spent the nights on watch* [lit. *the night was watch to us*]. *Rashi* and *Ibn Ezra* explain the words מִשְׁמָר and מְלָאכָה as if they had included the prefix לְ — *for. The nights were* לְמִשְׁמָר, *for watching, while the days were* לִמְלָאכָה, *for working. Malbim* explains the verse as if it were rearranged to read בַּלַּיְלָה [הָיָה לָנוּ] מִשְׁמָר — *at night* [we had] *the watch*, וּבַיּוֹם [הָיָה לָנוּ] מְלָאכָה, *and by day* [we had] *work*.

At night they guarded against enemy attack, and by day they built the walls (*Ralbag*). *Rashi* notes that since the nights were spent watching and the days working, virtually no time was left for sleep.

17. אֵין־אֲנַחְנוּ פֹּשְׁטִים בְּגָדֵינוּ — *[We] did not disrobe.* My companions and I laid down to rest fully clothed, in case of enemy attack (*Metzudos*).

אִישׁ שִׁלְחוֹ הַמָּיִם — *[Not even] to disrobe for water.* The translation follows *Rashi*, who applies the negative אֵין, *did not*, from the beginning of the verse to our phrase. *None of us disrobed*[1] *[even to launder our garments] in water*, since we were constantly on the alert for enemy attacks.

An alternative rendition is [*we*] *did not disrobe except each man for water* — when crossing a body of water, laundering the garments (*Ralbag, Ri Mitrani*), washing oneself, or immersing in the *mikveh* (*Ibn Ezra*; see *Metzudos*).

Another translation is שִׁלְחוֹ, *his sword* [see v. 11]. אִישׁ שִׁלְחוֹ הַמָּיִם is rendered *each [held] his sword, even with the water*. Even when they finished their duties and went to eat and drink in the evening, they held their swords, for fear of the enemy (*Ibn Ezra*). [מָיִם here is not just *water*, but any liquid used for drinking.] Alternatively, *each* [held] *his sword in the water*. Even when crossing a body of water, each held his sword, in case of attack.

The story of the enemy threats to Jerusalem's Jews and Nehemiah's resistance ends here. Although chapter 6 tells of the enemies' attempt to discredit Nehemiah through feigned friendship, and chapter 7 (vs. 3-5) describes precautions taken against possible enemy incursions, the text no longer talks of arming the Jews and organizing them into battle positions. Apparently, once the protective wall was completed, large-scale en-

1. See *Targum* to *Leviticus* 6:4, where שלח is used in this sense. *Malbim* understands the verse in much the same manner. However, he translates שִׁלְחוֹ in its more usual sense — *send it: nor did any man send his garment [to be laundered] in water.*

on watch, and the days at work. 17 *I, my brothers, my*
servants, and the watchmen who followed me did not
disrobe, [not even] to disrobe for water.

Now, the outcry of the people and their wives con-
cerning their Jewish brothers was great. 2 *Some said,*
'We [and] our sons and daughters are numerous, and we
must buy grain to eat and remain alive.' 3 *Others said,*

emy attacks were no longer to be feared. The Book of *Nehemiah* goes on to record other important improvements made by Nehemiah.

V

Chapter five begins by depicting the desperate plight of the poverty-stricken among the Jews, and their resulting outcry. The narrative then informs us of Nehemiah's reaction and his immediate implementation of measures to correct the situation. The question, however, arises: Why could not Ezra deal with these problems?

Earlier (comm. to 1:2), a similar question was raised regarding Ezra's failure to organize the reconstruction of the wall of Jerusalem. Citing *Ri Mitrani*, it was noted that Ezra was sanctioned by the king only as a religious leader. The events of chapter five, however, detail internal difficulties — Jews who did not fully support their more destitute brethren. For internal problems such as these, why did the people not come to Ezra, as they did in *Ezra*, chapter nine?

According to *Malbim* (*Ezra* 7:6), there was a natural distribution of leadership functions. Jeshua, the *Kohen Gadol*, oversaw the needs of the Temple; Ezra organized the spread of Torah scholarship and strict adherence to its principles; and Nehemiah was engaged in social reforms and in meeting the immediate needs of the people. These responsibilities fell upon Nehemiah because he was the representative of Persian royalty. Moreover, he was a descendant of the royal line of David, and, thus, naturally looked upon as the leader who would rectify the injustices among the people.

1. וַתְּהִי צַעֲקַת הָעָם — *Now, the outcry of the people.* צְעָקָה refers to a loud outcry of complaint (*Ramban*, *Exodus* 14:10).

The poor people cried out about their impoverished state (*Rashi*). The difficult conditions that prevailed had so reduced them that many were forced to sell their lands — and some even their sons and daughters — to pay for food (vs. 2-5).

Not all the people were impoverished; some still prospered. In their desperation the poor now cried out to their more fortunate brethren to come to their aid (*Ri Mitrani*).

Other commentators explain that the outcry described in the next few verses was directed to Nehemiah himself, to complain about the failure of the rich to save them from ruin (*Rashi*). The translation, *concerning their Jewish brothers*, follows this latter view.

2. בָּנֵינוּ וּבְנֹתֵינוּ אֲנַחְנוּ רַבִּים וְנִקְחָה דָגָן וְנֹאכְלָה וְנִחְיֶה — *We [and] our sons and daughters are numerous, and we must buy grain to eat and remain alive.* This verse represents the first of three groups of poor to voice their anguish (*Malbim*). The first complaint was made by those who had no fields to yield grain. They needed money to buy grain in the market. 'We have many children,' they said, 'therefore the expense of supporting our families is high' (*Metzudos*). *Ralbag* understands the intent of the verse in a similar fashion

אֲשֶׁר אֹמְרִים שְׂדֹתֵינוּ וּכְרָמֵינוּ וּבָתֵּינוּ
ד אֲנַחְנוּ עֹרְבִים וְנִקְחָה דָגָן בָּרָעָב: וְיֵשׁ אֲשֶׁר
אֹמְרִים לָוִינוּ כֶסֶף לְמִדַּת הַמֶּלֶךְ שְׂדֹתֵינוּ
ה וּכְרָמֵינוּ: וְעַתָּה כִּבְשַׂר אַחֵינוּ בְּשָׂרֵנוּ כִּבְנֵיהֶם
בָּנֵינוּ וְהִנֵּה אֲנַחְנוּ כֹבְשִׁים אֶת־בָּנֵינוּ וְאֶת־
בְּנֹתֵינוּ לַעֲבָדִים וְיֵשׁ מִבְּנֹתֵינוּ נִכְבָּשׁוֹת
וְאֵין לְאֵל יָדֵנוּ וּשְׂדֹתֵינוּ וּכְרָמֵינוּ לַאֲחֵרִים:

but translates רַבִּים as *raising* (not *numerous*). *We are raising our sons and daughters,* and therefore need food for their support.

Malbim renders רַבִּים, *borrow usuriously* (see *Habakuk* 2:6): We must offer our sons and daughters as security in obtaining usurious loans to buy food (see v. 5). [*Malbim* does not specify whether the usurious loans were from Jews or non-Jews. Jewish law, naturally, forbids usurious loans among Jews (*Ex.* 22:24; *Lev.* 25:37).]

3. וְיֵשׁ אֲשֶׁר אֹמְרִים שְׂדֹתֵינוּ . . . אֲנַחְנוּ עֹרְבִים — *Others said, We must offer our fields . . . as security.* Now a second group of poor complained — those who owned fields and homes, but who would soon have to mortgage them to pay for their basic sustenance (*Rashi*; *Malbim*). The lender could then confiscate the property as security, and collect their yearly produce or rent (*Malbim*). The result would be that these poor owners would remain without means of support.

Metzudos, however, translates *we have already* [past tense] *given our fields, vineyards, and homes as security.* Like the first group (v. 2), these poor lacked property. However, they (v. 3) had once owned fields, vineyards, and homes.

וְנִקְחָה דָגָן בָּרָעָב — *To buy grain in the famine.* Although we own fields, the yield is insufficient in this year of famine (*Metzudos*; *Malbim*). Though there is food to be had, we shall be forced to give up our fields to buy grain from our rich Jewish brothers (*Ibn Ezra*).

4. לָוִינוּ כֶסֶף . . . שְׂדֹתֵינוּ וּכְרָמֵינוּ — *We borrowed money* [*against*] *our fields and vineyards.* The groups voicing the previous complaints (vs. 2,3) were expressing their concern over the immediate future. A third group was already destitute, having previously mortgaged their fields to pay their taxes (*Malbim*).

The term עֹרְבִים, *offer as security*, used in verse 3, is applied to this verse as well: [וְעָרַבְנוּ] שְׂדֹתֵינוּ וּכְרָמֵינוּ, [*we offered as security*] *our fields and vineyards* (*Malbim*).

לְמִדַּת הַמֶּלֶךְ — *For the king's taxes.* מִדַּת is understood as מִנְדָּה, *taxes*, used in *Ezra* 4:13 (*Rashi; Ri Mitrani; Metzudos*). *R' Asher* (*Nedarim* 62b) specifies that מִנְדָּה refers to property tax levied upon estates.

Although there had been no famine the previous year, these people had given their fields as security to borrow money for the king's taxes (*Malbim*). Now that they no longer had fields, they expressed their fear of lacking means to obtain food (*Metzudos*).

5. כִּבְשַׂר אַחֵינוּ בְּשָׂרֵנוּ — *Our flesh is like the flesh of our brothers.* We are as worthy as they, and of equally distinguished lineage (*Rashi*), so why should we be their servants? Let them rather be charitable towards us, and support us through this difficult time (*Metzudos*). Alternatively, *Our flesh is like theirs.* We,

*'We must offer our fields, vineyards, and homes as secu-
rity to buy grain in the famine.'*
4 *Still others said, 'We
borrowed money [against] our fields and vineyards for the
king's taxes.*
5 *Now, our flesh is like the flesh of our
brothers and our sons like theirs; yet we must press our
sons and daughters into servitude with some of our daugh-
ters already pressed [into servitude], and we are power-
less; and our fields and vineyards are given to others.'*

too, deserve to be able to eat (*Malbim*).

Although we have borrowed from them, they have overstepped their rights. The Torah prohibits the lender from unduly pressuring the borrower for repayment [*Exodus* 22:24; *Choshen Mishpat* 97:1], yet they hold our daughters as slaves (*Ibn Ezra*).

וְהִנֵּה אֲנַחְנוּ כֹבְשִׁים אֶת־בָּנֵינוּ וְאֶת־בְּנֹתֵינוּ לַעֲבָדִים — *Yet we must press our sons and daughters into servitude.*

The Torah provides for a Jew in desperate circumstances to sell himself or his daughters to a fellow Jew as servants[1] (*Exodus* ch. 21, *Lev.* 25:39ff). However, *Malbim* to *Leviticus* 25:39 (based on *Kiddushin* 20a) enumerates the various steps a man must undertake before resorting to this drastic alternative. First, he must sell all his movable property; if that does not suffice, his fields; after that, his house; then he must borrow [even] with interest [from a non-Jew]. Only if he is destitute does the Torah permit him to sell his young daughter. *R' Hirsch* comments on the verse (*Exodus* 21:7): . . . *if a Jewish man sells his young daughter to become a maidservant* . . . 'only the most bitter, compelling necessity could have driven him to do so. He must have sold his house, home, and all his land, even his last shirt, before he is permitted to take such a step' (*Kiddushin* 20a; *Rambam, Hilchos Avadim* 4:2). If even that does not help, he sells himself into servitude.

[The verse is nevertheless puzzling. Jewish law does not empower a man to sell his sons and mature daughters, yet the verse implies that they, too, would be sold. Apparently, the situation had become so dire that the people countenanced offending Torah law in order to save their own and their children's lives.]

וְיֵשׁ מִבְּנֹתֵינוּ נִכְבָּשׁוֹת — *With some of our daughters already pressed [into servitude].* This is *Rashi's* explanation. *Malbim* suggests another interpretation. נִכְבָּשׁוֹת is translated *ravished* (as in *Esther* 7:8 — לִכְבּוֹשׁ אֶת הַמַּלְכָּה). Some of our enslaved daughters have been subjected to immoral treatment.

וְאֵין לְאֵל יָדֵנוּ — *And we are powerless* [lit. *there is no power in our hand*]. We are powerless to redeem them (*Rashi; Ri Mitrani*). [The word אֵל used in this idiom means *strength* or *power*; see *Genesis* 31:29.]

וּשְׂדֹתֵנוּ וּכְרָמֵינוּ לַאֲחֵרִים — *And our fields and vineyards are given to others.* Our

1. This is the institution of עֶבֶד עִבְרִי, literally, a *Hebrew slave* or bondservant. Although an עֶבֶד, *slave*, he is still an עִבְרִי, *Hebrew*, i.e., a fellow citizen (*Hirsch*). The master must treat his Hebrew servant as an equal with regard to food, clothes, and living conditions (even so far as to let the Hebrew servant sleep on his master's bed, if only one bed is available). He may not make him perform demeaning work, such as washing the master's feet, taking off his shoes, etc. Nor is he permitted to assign him to a task the servant is not qualified to perform, i.e., he can not ask a gardener to lay bricks (*Leviticus* 25:39, *Toras Kohanim* and *Mechilta; Hirsch*). Indeed, the Talmud remarks that one who buys an עֶבֶד עִבְרִי, *Hebrew servant*, has bought himself a master (*Kiddushin* 20a).

ה ו וַיִּחַר לִי מְאֹד כַּאֲשֶׁר שָׁמַעְתִּי אֶת־זַעֲקָתָם
ו־ט ז וְאֵת הַדְּבָרִים הָאֵלֶּה׃ וַיִּמָּלֵךְ לִבִּי עָלַי וָאָרִיבָה
אֶת־הַחֹרִים וְאֶת־הַסְּגָנִים וָאֹמְרָה לָהֶם מַשָּׁא
°נֹשִׁים ק׳ אִישׁ־בְּאָחִיו אַתֶּם °נשְׁאים וָאֶתֵּן עֲלֵיהֶם
ח קְהִלָּה גְדוֹלָה׃ וָאֹמְרָה לָהֶם אֲנַחְנוּ קָנִינוּ
אֶת־אַחֵינוּ הַיְּהוּדִים הַנִּמְכָּרִים לַגּוֹיִם כְּדֵי בָנוּ
וְגַם־אַתֶּם תִּמְכְּרוּ אֶת־אֲחֵיכֶם וְנִמְכְּרוּ־לָנוּ
°וָאֹמַר ק׳ ט וַיַּחֲרִישׁוּ וְלֹא מָצְאוּ דָּבָר׃ °ויאמר לֹא־טוֹב
הַדָּבָר אֲשֶׁר־אַתֶּם עֹשִׂים הֲלוֹא בְּיִרְאַת
אֱלֹהֵינוּ תֵּלֵכוּ מֵחֶרְפַּת הַגּוֹיִם אוֹיְבֵינוּ׃

fields and vineyards have been given over to others, leaving us with no source of sustenance (*Rashi*), and no means to redeem our enslaved children (*Malbim*).

⸎ Nehemiah Confronts the Lords

6. אֶת־זַעֲקָתָם — *Their outcry.* The outcry of the destitute who would be forced to sell their children and property (*Malbim*).

וְאֵת הַדְּבָרִים הָאֵלֶּה — *And these matters.* This second clause refers to those who had already given their fields and children as security and now complained of their mistreatment (*Malbim*).

7. וַיִּמָּלֵךְ לִבִּי עָלַי — *I followed my heart's advice* [lit. *my heart advised me*]. My heart told me to be strong in opposing the lords (*Metzudos, Malbim*).

Malbim proposes another interpretation: The heart is viewed as the seat of the passions. Although Nehemiah was angered, he did not permit his anger to motivate the dispute with the lords. His heart controlled the anger, and advised him, on the basis of rationality, to follow the path of justice in disputing the lords.[1]

מַשָּׁא אִישׁ־בְּאָחִיו אַתֶּם נֹשִׁים — *You are moneylenders to your brothers?* Why are you moneylenders? You should support your brothers with charity rather than lend them money and then confiscate their children and their property (*Rashi; Metzudos*).

Ri Mitrani and *Malbim* translate, *Are you coercive in regard to your brothers' loans?* The word נֹשִׁים, *coercive*, alludes to the Biblical injunction לֹא־תִהְיֶה לוֹ כְּנֹשֶׁה, *Do not coerce him* (*Exodus* 22:24). This prohibits the moneylender from exerting undo pressure on the borrower to force repayment. [See comm. to v. 5.] Nehemiah also used the word נֹשִׁים to remind the lords of two other *mitzvos* mentioned in the Torah together with the prohibition against coercion: the prohibition against usury (נֶשֶׁךְ, *Exodus* 22:24) and the requirement for the mon-

1. *Rambam* (*Dayos* 2:3) discusses the control of anger. 'One should learn never to become angered even when a worthy matter is involved. If a parent wishes to admonish his child ... or a leader his congregation, let him give the impression of anger, but maintain his inner calm, like a person feigning anger, but not truly angry.'

[6] I was angered when I heard their outcry and these matters. [7] I followed my heart's advice and confronted the aristocrats and the nobles, saying to them, 'You are moneylenders to your brothers?' I also gathered a large crowd around them. [8] And I said to them, 'We ransomed, according to our means, our brothers, the Jews, who were sold to gentiles; now you too will sell your brothers, to be sold to us!' They were silent, unable to find an answer. [9] I also said to them, 'The thing you are doing is not good; better that you walk with the fear of our God, because of the insult of the nations who are our enemies.

eylender to permit the borrower to reclaim and use his possessions taken as security, תְּשִׁיבֶנּוּ לוֹ (*Exodus* 22:25).

וָאֶתֵּן עֲלֵיהֶם קְהִלָּה גְדוֹלָה — *I also gathered a large crowd around them.* This follows *Rashi*, who comments that Nehemiah gathered a large crowd to join him in crying out against the lords, so that they would be more deeply embarrassed.

Alternatively, the people gathered together on the spot because they heard Nehemiah publicly admonishing the lords (*Malbim*).

8. אֲנַחְנוּ קָנִינוּ — *We ransomed.* We previously ransomed our brothers (*Rashi*) who had been sold to gentiles.

כְּדֵי בָנוּ — *According to our means* [lit. *as sufficient in us*]. I.e., each gave the amount he deemed sufficient according to his means (*Rashi; Metzudos*). *Ralbag* translates *with all that was in us* — with our fullest efforts.

Malbim's translation is *as are sufficient among us*. Aren't there already enough people among us who were redeemed from captivity of the gentiles?

וְגַם־אַתֶּם תִּמְכְּרוּ אֶת־אֲחֵיכֶם וְנִמְכְּרוּ־לָנוּ — *Now you too will sell your brothers, to be sold to us!* Nehemiah showed the rich Jews the absurdity of the situation: You, who now own Jewish slaves [whom you have taken from your fellow Jews], will sell them to the gentiles [when your own wealth begins to wane]. Then, as in the past, the Jewish community to which you belong will redeem them. Thus, you, yourselves, will eventually pay the gentiles for the very slaves you sold to them (*Rashi*)!

Ri Mitrani translates: *Now you too, will sell your brothers; they will be sold to us!* We are forced to redeem the slaves from your hands, just as we were forced to redeem them from the gentiles.

According to *Metzudos*, Nehemiah spoke sarcastically, saying: *Sell your brothers to be sold to us.* It is not befitting to redeem a slave from the hands of your own brother. Better sell your slaves to the gentiles, so that we may redeem them from your hands.

וַיַּחֲרִישׁוּ — *They were silent* from embarrassment (*Rashi*).

9. הֲלוֹא בְּיִרְאַת אֱלֹהֵינוּ תֵּלֵכוּ מֵחֶרְפַּת הַגּוֹיִם אוֹיְבֵינוּ — *Better that you walk with the fear of our God, because of the insult of the nations who are our enemies.* The translation follows *Rashi*, *Ri Mitrani* and *Malbim*, who render מֵחֶרְפַּת, *be-*

י וְגַם־אֲנִי אַחַי וּנְעָרַי נֹשִׁים בָּהֶם כֶּסֶף וְדָגָן
יא נַעַזְבָה־נָּא אֶת־הַמַּשָּׁא הַזֶּה: הָשִׁיבוּ נָא לָהֶם
כְּהַיּוֹם שְׂדֹתֵיהֶם כַּרְמֵיהֶם זֵיתֵיהֶם וּבָתֵּיהֶם
וּמְאַת הַכֶּסֶף וְהַדָּגָן הַתִּירוֹשׁ וְהַיִּצְהָר אֲשֶׁר
יב אַתֶּם נֹשִׁים בָּהֶם: וַיֹּאמְרוּ נָשִׁיב וּמֵהֶם לֹא
נְבַקֵּשׁ כֵּן נַעֲשֶׂה כַּאֲשֶׁר אַתָּה אוֹמֵר וָאֶקְרָא
אֶת־הַכֹּהֲנִים וָאַשְׁבִּיעֵם לַעֲשׂוֹת כַּדָּבָר הַזֶּה:
יג גַּם־חָצְנִי נָעַרְתִּי וָאֹמְרָה כָּכָה יְנַעֵר הָאֱלֹהִים

cause of the insult. Behave in a God-fearing manner in order to avoid the insults of the nations. Follow God's commands, Nehemiah told the lords, even if you are not inwardly truly fearful of Heaven. Otherwise, the enemy nations will ridicule you for being irreligious[1] (*Malbim*).

However, *Ralbag, Ibn Ezra*, and *Metzudos* translate מֵחֶרְפַּת, *from the insult.* With the fear of God, *you shall walk [away] from the insult of the nations.* Nehemiah instructed the lords to fear God, and, despite their rights as debtors, free the children of their fellow Jews from bondage. God would then respond by forgoing the 'debts' incurred by the Jewish people through their transgressions, and free them from their humiliating enslavement to the enemy nations. This is in accordance with the precept of *measure for measure* [מִדָּה כְּנֶגֶד מִדָּה], wherein God treats his creatures as they treat each other.

Ibn Ezra adds that the outcry of the poor Jewish debtors took place during the *Shemittah* [Sabbatical] year, when the Torah prohibits collecting one's debts [see *Deut*. 15: 1-6; *Choshen Mishpat* 67].

10. וְגַם־אֲנִי אַחַי וּנְעָרַי — *I, my brothers, and my servants also.* וּנְעָרַי is translated *servants* as in 4:10.

Do not think that I criticize you so freely because I have nothing to lose personally — I and my companions will join you in suffering a loss (*Malbim*).

נַעַזְבָה־נָּא אֶת־הַמַּשָּׁא הַזֶּה — *We will now relinquish this debt. Rashi* and *Malbim* explain that this refers to Nehemiah and his companions. *Metzudos*, however, translates *let us now relinquish this debt.* Nehemiah referred to the lords as well as himself and his companions. Let us, together, relinquish the debt.

11. הָשִׁיבוּ נָא לָהֶם — *Restore to them now.* Having announced his own intention to relinquish the debts owed to him (v. 10), Nehemiah now urged the others to join him and do the same.

כְּהַיּוֹם — *This very day* [lit. *as this day*]. Now is a time of great need. Since there is a famine (v. 3) and the people are involved in constructing the wall, they have become impoverished and in need of food (*Malbim*).

וּמְאַת הַכֶּסֶף — *And the hundreds in silver.* Large sums of money (*Rashi;*

1. Rav Yehudah said in the name of Rav: One should always engage in Torah and *mitzvos*, even without the purest intentions [שֶׁלֹּא לִשְׁמָהּ, not solely for the sake of carrying out the will of God], for this leads, ultimately, to pure intention [לִשְׁמָהּ] (*Pesachim* 50b).

[10] I, my brothers, and my servants also lent them money and grain; we will now relinquish this debt. [11] Restore to them now, this very day, their fields, vineyards, olive orchards, and homes; and the hundreds in silver, grain, wine, and oil which you hold against them.' [12] They said, 'We shall restore and make no demands of them — we shall do as you say.' Then I called the Kohanim and adjured them to do the same. [13] I also shook the corner of my garment and said, 'So may God shake

Ralbag, see *Ramban, Genesis* 20:16); מְאַת, lit. *the hundred*, is understood as מֵאוֹת, *the hundreds* (*Ri Mitrani*).

Metzudos and *Malbim* translate *the hundred [shekalim] of silver.* The inordinately large sum of one hundred was chosen to stress that the loans must be relinquished no matter how large, even up to the sum of one hundred silver pieces.

אֲשֶׁר אַתֶּם נֹשִׁים בָּהֶם — *Which you hold against them.* The loans of silver, grain, wine, and oil must be relinquished. Although the relinquishing of these loans is not spelled out in the text [only the restoration of the fields, vineyards, and olive orchards is mentioned specifically], it is evident that this was Nehemiah's request, since the lords replied in the next verse (v. 12), *We shall restore [the fields] and make no demands of them* [for repayment of the loans] (*Ibn Ezra*).

12. נָשִׁיב וּמֵהֶם לֹא נְבַקֵּשׁ — *We shall restore and make no demands of them.* We shall restore the fields, and make no demands for repayment of the loans (*Ibn Ezra, Metzudos*).

כֵּן נַעֲשֶׂה כַּאֲשֶׁר אַתָּה אוֹמֵר — *We shall do as you say.* This is a repetition of the preceding statement, uttered by the lords to stress their intent to comply (*Metzudos*).

וָאֶקְרָא אֶת־הַכֹּהֲנִים וָאַשְׁבִּיעֵם — *Then I called the Kohanim and adjured them.* Nehemiah bade the *Kohanim* swear that they, too, would relinquish the debts owed to them (*Rashi*).

According to *Ibn Ezra, Metzudos,* and *Malbim,* however, the *Kohanim* were called to administer the oath to the lords who had agreed to relinquish the debts. The presence of the *Kohanim* added to the solemnity, and hence the binding commitment of the oath. Administering oaths was on certain occasions a function of the *Kohen,* as in the case of the suspected adulteress [סוֹטָה] (see *Numbers* 5:19-22).

13. נָעַרְתִּי — *I shook* the dust off my garment (*Ralbag; Metzudos*).

חָצְנִי — *The corner of my garment*. Our translation follows *Rashi*, who translates this word as in *Isaiah* 49:22. *Ralbag* identifies חָצְנִי as the garment covering the arms. To *Malbim*, the reference is to the pocket of the garment, which Nehemiah shook and emptied. *Ibn Ezra*, however, suggests *I shook my arms.*

כָּכָה יְנַעֵר הָאֱלֹהִים — *So may God shake.* Just as I shook the dust from my garment, so may God shake loose anyone [who will not comply with this oath] from his home, i.e., may He destroy his home and everything else he has toiled for (*Malbim*).

[*Ramban* to *Genesis* 12:6 observes that the prophets sometimes enacted symbolic

ה
יד־טו

אֶת־כָּל־הָאִישׁ אֲשֶׁר לֹא־יָקִים אֶת־הַדָּבָר
הַזֶּה מִבֵּיתוֹ וּמִיגִיעוֹ וְכָכָה יִהְיֶה נָעוּר וָרֵק
וַיֹּאמְרוּ כָל־הַקָּהָל אָמֵן וַיְהַלְלוּ אֶת־יהוה
יד וַיַּעַשׂ הָעָם כַּדָּבָר הַזֶּה: גַּם מִיּוֹם | אֲשֶׁר־צִוָּה
אוֹתִי לִהְיוֹת פֶּחָם בְּאֶרֶץ יְהוּדָה מִשְּׁנַת
עֶשְׂרִים וְעַד שְׁנַת שְׁלֹשִׁים וּשְׁתַּיִם
לְאַרְתַּחְשַׁסְתְּא הַמֶּלֶךְ שָׁנִים שְׁתֵּים עֶשְׂרֵה
טו אֲנִי וְאַחַי לֶחֶם הַפֶּחָה לֹא אָכַלְתִּי: וְהַפַּחוֹת
הָרִאשֹׁנִים אֲשֶׁר־לְפָנַי הִכְבִּידוּ עַל־הָעָם

portrayals of the events which they foretold (see *Jeremiah* 51:63,64; *II Kings* 13:17). This insured the eventual fulfillment of the prophecy which otherwise might not have been fulfilled. (For example, concerning punishment for the wicked, God's mercy might have intervened; in the case of reward for the righteous, a future misdeed might have stood in the way. See further ArtScroll *Genesis* 32:8 and *Rashi* 32:11.) However, a heavenly decree, once enacted on earth, albeit symbolically, is never rescinded.]

אֶת־הַדָּבָר הַזֶּה — *This matter.* The relinquishing of the debts (*Rashi*).

מִבֵּיתוֹ — *Away from his home.* He shall be removed from this world (*Rashi*) or *from the members of his household* — from his family (*Ralbag; Metzudos*).

וּמִיגִיעוֹ — *And his toil.* He shall lose his possessions (*Rashi; Ralbag*).

וְכָכָה יִהְיֶה נָעוּר וָרֵק — *And so may he remain, shaken and empty.* So may he remain forever, bereft of all possessions (*Metzudos*). May he always remain empty, even when the natural course of events would lead him to success (*Malbim*).

וַיְהַלְלוּ אֶת־ה׳ — *And* [lit. *they*] *praised HASHEM.* They praised God in their hearts for inspiring them to carry out this matter (*Ibn Ezra; Metzudos*).

According to *Malbim*, *[they] praised Hashem and ... carried out the matter.* The praise was uttered as a blessing pronounced before 'the matter,' i.e., before performing the *mitzvos* of charity and returning the security to the borrower.[1]

וַיַּעַשׂ הָעָם כַּדָּבָר הַזֶּה — *And the people carried out the matter.* They returned the fields and relinquished the debts (*Metzudos*). Two *mitzvos* were now performed: (1) charity, and (2) the return of the security to the borrower.

14. גַּם — *Moreover.* This verse begins a new subject, depicting Nehemiah's refusal to derive any personal benefit from his position as royal governor (*Ri Mitrani*). This follows thematically from

1. *Malbim* notes that the Rabbis devote much discussion to the question of pronouncing a blessing before fulfilling the commandments of charity and returning the security (see *Teshuvos HaRashba* 18; *Abudraham* pp. 17-21). [The prevailing opinion is that the blessings are not required. Although it is forbidden to pronounce any blessing when it is not required (בְּרָכָה לְבַטָּלָה), this applies only when the words ה׳ אֱלֹהֵינוּ, *Hashem our God*, are used. Evidently, the people here praised God without uttering these words.]

any man failing to fulfill this matter away from his home and his toil; and so may he remain, shaken and empty.' The entire congregation answered, 'Amen,' and praised HASHEM; *and the people carried out the matter.* [14] *Moreover, from the day he appointed me governor of the land of Judah, from the twentieth until the thirty-second year of King Artahshast, twelve years, my brothers and I did not eat of the governor's stipend.* [15] *But the earlier governors who preceded me burdened the people*

the previous section, since both recount Nehemiah's efforts to ease the burden of the Jews in Jerusalem. The previous narrative described his aid to the indigent; our verse portrays his easing of the burden of taxes for all the people (*Metzudos*). Because of Nehemiah's benevolence in refusing the governor's stipend despite his great expenditure in feeding his household (vs. 17,18), God aided him and crowned his activities with success (*Ralbag*).

According to *Malbim*, our verse provides the explanation for Nehemiah's success in convincing the wealthy Jews to relinquish their claims against their brothers (v. 12). Because Nehemiah had eased the burden of taxes from the wealthy, they were favorably disposed towards him, and heeded his advice to relinquish their debts.

צִוָּה אוֹתִי — *He appointed me.* From the day the king appointed me (*Ri Mitrani*). Although צִוָּה is generally translated *he commanded*, here the meaning is *he appointed*, as in *I Samuel* 13:14 (*Ramban, Numbers* 27:19).

לִהְיוֹת פֶּחָם — *Governor* [lit. *to be governor*]. The root is פֶּחָה, *governor* (see *Ezra* 5:14); the letter *'mem'* (מ) is added (*Rashi; Ri Mitrani; Ralbag*). However, *Ibn Ezra, Metzudos*, and *Malbim* render *their governor* (פֶּחָה שֶׁלָּהֶם), although the more proper usage in this sense would be פֶּחָתָם.

מִשְּׁנַת עֶשְׂרִים ... לְאַרְתַּחְשַׁסְתְּא הַמֶּלֶךְ — *From the twentieth ... year of King Artahshast.* This refers to the twentieth year of King Darius, when Nehemiah ascended to the Holy Land [see comm. to 2:1] (*Rashi*).

אֲנִי וְאַחַי — *My brothers and I.* Nehemiah and his brothers, the *Kohanim* (*Ibn Ezra*, v. 16).

לֶחֶם הַפֶּחָה — *The governor's stipend* [lit. *bread*]. This refers to food which the governor was empowered to collect by taxing the people (*Rashi; Ibn Ezra; Metzudos*). I refrained from collecting this stipend in order the lighten the people's burden (*Ri Mitrani*).

15. וְהַפַּחוֹת הָרִאשֹׁנִים — *But* [lit. *and*] *the earlier governors.* This includes Daniel, who was governor over the Jews before Nehemiah (*Sanhedrin* 93b; see ArtScroll *Ezra* 5:14).

הִכְבִּידוּ עַל־הָעָם — *Burdened* [lit. *placed weight upon*] *the people.* They placed the *weight of taxes* upon the people (*Rashi*).

The Talmud (*Sanhedrin* 93b) asserts that although Nehemiah was the author of the book describing his activities, it is nevertheless entitled the Book of *Ezra* (see comm. to 1:1). Nehemiah's name was deleted from the title of his book as a punishment for his criticism of the earlier governors, particularly Daniel, who was greater than he. Another opinion at-

וַיִּקְחוּ מֵהֶם בְּלֶחֶם וָיַיִן אַחַר כֶּסֶף־שְׁקָלִים
אַרְבָּעִים גַּם נַעֲרֵיהֶם שָׁלְטוּ עַל־הָעָם וַאֲנִי
טז לֹא־עָשִׂיתִי כֵן מִפְּנֵי יִרְאַת אֱלֹהִים: וְגַם
בִּמְלֶאכֶת הַחוֹמָה הַזֹּאת הֶחֱזַקְתִּי וְשָׂדֶה לֹא
קָנִינוּ וְכָל־נְעָרַי קְבוּצִים שָׁם עַל־הַמְּלָאכָה:
יז וְהַיְּהוּדִים וְהַסְּגָנִים מֵאָה וַחֲמִשִּׁים אִישׁ
וְהַבָּאִים אֵלֵינוּ מִן־הַגּוֹיִם אֲשֶׁר־סְבִיבֹתֵינוּ
יח עַל־שֻׁלְחָנִי: וַאֲשֶׁר הָיָה נַעֲשֶׂה לְיוֹם אֶחָד
שׁוֹר אֶחָד צֹאן שֵׁשׁ־בְּרֻרוֹת וְצִפֳּרִים נַעֲשׂוּ־לִי
וּבֵין עֲשֶׂרֶת יָמִים בְּכָל־יַיִן לְהַרְבֵּה וְעִם־זֶה

tributes the deletion of Nehemiah's name to his request for God's recognition of his good deeds (v. 19).

בְּלֶחֶם וָיַיִן אַחַר כֶּסֶף־שְׁקָלִים אַרְבָּעִים — *Bread and wine, in addition to* [lit. *after*] *forty silver shekels.* The yearly tax was forty silver shekels. In addition, the governors collected bread and wine from the people (*Rashi; Metzudos*). *Ralbag's* opinion is that the sum of forty silver shekels was a weekly, rather than yearly, tax. [This was presumably a communal rather than personal tax.]

Malbim's interpretation is that the text refers to different governors. His reading is as follows: *The earlier governors who preceded me burdened the people and took from them bread and wine* — This refers to the early governors, who took only food. אַחַר, *another governor*, i.e., the one immediately preceding me, took no food, but collected *forty silver shekels.*

16. וְגַם בִּמְלֶאכֶת הַחוֹמָה הַזֹּאת הֶחֱזַקְתִּי — *I also sustained* [lit. *upheld*] *the work of this wall.* I constantly urged the workers to apply themselves to the work of building the wall (*Rashi; Metzudos*). [The term הֶחֱזַקְתִּי, *sustained*, indicates a sustained program to maintain an effort.]

Ri Mitrani translates *I also held [my money] for the construction of the wall.* I made no other expenditure, but spent all of my money for the construction of the wall.

לֹא קָנִינוּ — *We did not buy.* 'We' refers to Nehemiah and his companions (*Rashi*), the *Kohanim*, according to *Ibn Ezra*.

וְשָׂדֶה — *Fields.* My companions and I did not buy the fields of those who were involved in the construction of the wall, although they were in need of funds. Instead, we donated money to them so that they might keep their fields and continue building the wall (*Rashi; Metzudos*).

According to *Ralbag*, the explanation is *we did not buy fields*, for this would have required that the fields be cultivated, and we were completely involved in the work of the wall. Nehemiah stressed his inability to buy fields in order to indicate that he was, at that time, without an income — yet he refused to accept the governor's stipend (vs. 14,18).

עַל־הַמְּלָאכָה — *At work.*

and took from them bread and wine, in addition to
forty silver shekels, and their servants ruled over the
people; I, however, did not do so for fear of God. 16 *I*
also sustained the work of this wall and we did
not buy fields; all of my servants were gathered there
at work. 17 *Jews and nobles — one hundred and fifty*
men, in addition to those who came to us from the
surrounding nations, were at my table. 18 *One day's*
fare was an ox, six selected sheep, and fowl, prepared
for me, plus wine enough for ten days; despite this

They were building constantly (*Rashi*).

☙ Nehemiah's Expenditure

17. וְהַבָּאִים אֵלֵינוּ מִן־הַגּוֹיִם אֲשֶׁר־סְבִיבֹתֵינוּ — *In addition to those who came to us from the surrounding nations.* This refers to proselytes who came to the Jews (*Rashi; Metzudos*).

עַל־שֻׁלְחָנִי — *Were at my table*. The one hundred and fifty men and those who came from the nations ate at my table (*Rashi*). I supported them, since they were engaged in the construction of the wall (*Ri Mitrani*). As a result of my support of these people, my expenses were enormous [v. 18] (*Ralbag; Malbim*).

18. וַאֲשֶׁר הָיָה נַעֲשֶׂה לְיוֹם אֶחָד — *One day's fare* [lit. *that which was done for one day*]. *Rashi* explains: the amount of food for those who ate at my table for one day.

וְצִפֳּרִים — *And fowl.* A large number of fowl (*Rashi*).

נַעֲשׂוּ־לִי — *Prepared* [lit. *made*] *for me.* Although נַעֲשׂוּ is generally translated *made*, here the rendition is *prepared*, as in *Genesis* 18:8 (*Rashi; Ralbag*).

וּבֵין עֲשֶׂרֶת יָמִים בְּכָל־יַיִן לְהַרְבֵּה — *Plus wine enough for ten days* [lit. *among ten days, with all wine to a great amount*]. Each day my guests drank a ten days' supply of wine (*Rashi*). Alternatively, so much wine was drunk that the wine cellars had to be refilled every ten days (*Ralbag*).

Ibn Ezra translates *one day's fare was an ox ... prepared for me, every ten days, with all wine abundant.* The meal described in this verse, together with abundant wine, was given every ten days. The wine was generally limited, since too much drinking would have caused interruption of the work. It was only once every ten days that the wine was provided in abundance, to be drunk freely.

Malbim presents an original interpretation. *Between the tenth days, all wine was abundant.* Nehemiah's custom was to 'tithe' his days. He spent every tenth day in devotion and fasting, just as one tenth of the produce of the land is tithed and given to the Levite. On this day wine was not provided. *Between the tenth days* of fasting, however, the wine was abundant.

וְעִם־זֶה — *Despite this.* Despite the great expenditure (and my lack of income), I did not request the governor's stipend (*Ralbag; Ri Mitrani; Metzudos; Malbim*).

ה לֶחֶם הַפֶּחָה לֹא בִקַּשְׁתִּי כִּי־כָבְדָה הָעֲבֹדָה
יט יט עַל־הָעָם הַזֶּה: זָכְרָה־לִּי אֱלֹהַי לְטוֹבָה כֹּל
ו א אֲשֶׁר־עָשִׂיתִי עַל־הָעָם הַזֶּה: וַיְהִי
א־ב כַאֲשֶׁר נִשְׁמַע לְסַנְבַלַּט וְטוֹבִיָּה וּלְגֶשֶׁם
הָעַרְבִי וּלְיֶתֶר אֹיְבֵינוּ כִּי בָנִיתִי אֶת־
הַחוֹמָה וְלֹא־נוֹתַר בָּהּ פָּרֶץ גַּם עַד־הָעֵת
הַהִיא דְּלָתוֹת לֹא־הֶעֱמַדְתִּי בַשְּׁעָרִים:
ב וַיִּשְׁלַח סַנְבַלַּט וְגֶשֶׁם אֵלַי לֵאמֹר לְכָה
וְנִוָּעֲדָה יַחְדָּו בַּכְּפִירִים בְּבִקְעַת אוֹנוֹ וְהֵמָּה

לֶחֶם הַפֶּחָה לֹא בִקַּשְׁתִּי — *I did not request the governor's stipend* [lit. *bread*]. I did not request the stipend which the governor was entitled to collect as a tax from the people (*Rashi; Ri Mitrani; Ralbag*). *Ibn Ezra's* interpretation, however, is *I did not request the governor's bread.* The governor's meat and wine was collected from the people since they had sufficient supplies of these. It was the *bread*, which was in short supply because of the famine (v. 2), which Nehemiah did not collect from the people. In contrast to this, the earlier governors also taxed the people for bread (v. 15).

כִּי־כָבְדָה הָעֲבוֹדָה עַל־הָעָם הַזֶּה — *For the labor weighed heavily on this people.* This refers to their labor in constructing the wall (*Rashi*), and for the king's taxes (*Metzudos*).

19. זָכְרָה־לִּי אֱלֹהַי לְטוֹבָה — *Remember in my favor, my God.* Consider my actions as a source of merit for me (*Metzudos*).

One opinion in *Sanhedrin* (93b) asserts that Nehemiah was punished for this request by the deletion of his name as the author of his book (see comm. to v. 15). Although King David made a similar request in *Psalms* (106:4) — *Remember me,* HASHEM, *when You favor Your people* — David's request was acceptable, since he called on God to exercise mercy in remembering his good deeds.

Nehemiah, however, erred in thinking that his good deeds *in themselves* made him deserving of merit, even without God's compassion. No man may justifiably make this assumption, and for this Nehemiah was punished (see *Maharsha, Sanhedrin* 93b).[1] *Anaf Yosef* in *Ein Yaakov* explains that David addressed God using the four-letter name, HASHEM, which denotes mercy. Nehemiah, however, invoked the name אֱלֹהַי, a reference to God as the dispenser of justice.

עַל־הָעָם הַזֶּה — *For* [lit. *upon*] *this people.* Remember all that I did for the good of this people (*Metzudos*).

Malbim presents an alternative explanation: *Remember, in my favor, all that I did upon this people* — let my good

1. *Anaf Yosef* explains that David was deserving of merit even by the exacting standards of Divine justice. Nevertheless, he based his entreaty on the mercy of God, as if he himself had not earned merit, recognizing that no man becomes righteous without God's help. Nehemiah, too, earned his exalted station according to the righteousness inherent in his life. His entreaty, in which he neglected to call upon God's mercy, reflected this and was found wanting. For this shortcoming, he was punished.

V
19
I did not request the governor's stipend, for the labor
weighed heavily on this people. [19] *Remember in my*
favor, my God, all that I did for this people.

VI
1-2
Now, when Sanballat, Tobiah, Geshem the Arab, and
our remaining enemies heard that I had built the
wall, and no breaches remained, and also that up until
that time, I had not erected doors in the gateways;
[2] *Sanballat and Geshem sent [word] to me, saying, 'Go,*
and let us meet at Kefirim in the plain of Ono.' But they

deeds be accredited, not to me, but to the entire people. Let the favor I enjoy because of my good deeds be visited *upon this people*. Nehemiah's request is based on the principle that the merits of the saintly protect the entire Jewish people (זְכוּת הַצַּדִּיקִים מְגִינָּה). [This is still consistent with the Talmud's statement that Nehemiah was punished for asking God to credit him (see preceding comm.). Nehemiah thought he was *deserving* of credit, and asked that his credit be transferred to the people. This was an improper assumption, since no man is *deserving* of credit, but may gain favor only through God's mercy.]

VI

Chapter six returns to the subject of the narrative in chapter four — the enemies' resistance to the establishment of a viable Jewish community centered in Jerusalem. However, while chapter four deals with the enemies' threat to the reconstruction effort, our chapter depicts their endeavors against Nehemiah. Realizing that he was the driving force behind the dramatic rise in the fortunes of the Jewish community, they determined to destroy him.

☙ Sanballat's Invitation

1. גַּם עַד־הָעֵת הַהִיא דְּלָתוֹת לֹא־הֶעֱמַדְתִּי בַשְּׁעָרִים — *And also that up until that time I had not erected doors in the gateways. Metzudos* explains why the information that the doors were not erected is now relevant. Shemaiah, in collusion with the enemies, attempted to draw Nehemiah into the Sanctuary, arguing that he needed the protection of the Sanctuary's locked doors against those who wished to murder him (v.10). This argument was valid only because the city walls did not offer protection, since the doors had not been erected.

Malbim explains the mention of the missing doors differently. So long as the doors were not in place, the construction was not fully completed, and the enemies still had hopes of stopping it. Later, however, when it was completed, they became despondent (v.16) and abandoned this hope. Thus, we are informed of their final effort to halt the construction before the doors were erected and the city's wall was fully in place.

2. בַּכְּפִירִים — *At Kefirim. Kefirim* was the name of a place (*Rashi; Metzudos*), a city in the territory of the tribe of Benjamin as mentioned in *Joshua* 18:26 (*Malbim*). *Ibn Ezra* and *Ralbag*, however, translate כְּפִירִים as *one of the towns*, from the word כְּפַר, *town* (see *I Chronicles* 27:25).

ו
ג־ז

ג חֹשְׁבִים לַעֲשׂוֹת לִי רָעָה: וָאֶשְׁלְחָה עֲלֵיהֶם
מַלְאָכִים לֵאמֹר מְלָאכָה גְדוֹלָה אֲנִי עֹשֶׂה
וְלֹא אוּכַל לָרֶדֶת לָמָּה תִשְׁבַּת הַמְּלָאכָה
ד כַּאֲשֶׁר אַרְפֶּהָ וְיָרַדְתִּי אֲלֵיכֶם: וַיִּשְׁלְחוּ
אֵלַי כַּדָּבָר הַזֶּה אַרְבַּע פְּעָמִים וָאָשִׁיב
ה אוֹתָם כַּדָּבָר הַזֶּה: וַיִּשְׁלַח אֵלַי סַנְבַלַּט
כַּדָּבָר הַזֶּה פַּעַם חֲמִישִׁית אֶת־נַעֲרוֹ וְאִגֶּרֶת
ו פְּתוּחָה בְּיָדוֹ: כָּתוּב בָּהּ בַּגּוֹיִם נִשְׁמָע
וְגַשְׁמוּ אֹמֵר אַתָּה וְהַיְּהוּדִים חֹשְׁבִים לִמְרוֹד
עַל־כֵּן אַתָּה בוֹנֶה הַחוֹמָה וְאַתָּה הֹוֶה
ז לָהֶם לְמֶלֶךְ כַּדְּבָרִים הָאֵלֶּה: וְגַם־נְבִיאִים
הֶעֱמַדְתָּ לִקְרֹא עָלֶיךָ בִירוּשָׁלִַם לֵאמֹר מֶלֶךְ
בִּיהוּדָה וְעַתָּה יִשָּׁמַע לַמֶּלֶךְ כַּדְּבָרִים הָאֵלֶּה

וְהֵמָּה חֹשְׁבִים לַעֲשׂוֹת לִי רָעָה — *But they planned* [lit. *thought to do*] *evil towards me.* I understood that they were plotting to murder me in Kefirim (*Rashi*).

3. מְלָאכָה גְדוֹלָה — *A great work.* The construction of the city (*Rashi*) is vital and there is much to do (*Metzudos*).

לָמָּה תִשְׁבַּת הַמְּלָאכָה כַּאֲשֶׁר אַרְפֶּהָ — *Why should the work cease while I leave it* [lit. *become weak in it*]? If I were to leave the work, it would come to a halt (*Metzudos*). [As noted above, only Nehemiah's ceaseless efforts and dynamic leadership kept the project moving forward when others would have despaired.]

◆§ The Enemies Persist

5. כַּדָּבָר הַזֶּה . . . אֶת־נַעֲרוֹ — *This* [lit. *like this word*] . . . *with his servant*. Sanballat sent a fifth invitation, conveyed orally by his servant, to meet at Kefirim (*Malbim*).

וְאִגֶּרֶת פְּתוּחָה — *And an open letter.* In addition to the invitation, the servant carried an *open letter*, i.e., unsealed (*Metzudos*), and unrolled (*Ibn Ezra*). Sanballat wished to show that he was not being secretive, but had sent the letter openly, so that anyone might read it.

◆§ Contents of the Letter

6. כָּתוּב בָּהּ . . . כַּדְּבָרִים הָאֵלֶּה — *In it was written . . . the following* [lit. *like these words*]. The phrase כַּדְּבָרִים הָאֵלֶּה appears at the end of this verse, but in the translation, which follows *Rashi*, it appears in the beginning of the passage. *Rashi* explains the verse as if the word order were rearranged, and this phrase attached to the beginning of the verse: כָּתוּב בָּהּ כַּדְּבָרִים הָאֵלֶּה, *in it was written the following*. Other commentators interpret the phrase in the context of the end of the passage (see below there).

בַּגּוֹיִם נִשְׁמָע וְגַשְׁמוּ אֹמֵר — *It has become known among the nations, and Gashmu says [this].* Gashmu is *Geshem* the Arab [v. 1] (*Rashi; Ralbag; Malbim*).

The letter ו is added to the end of גֶּשֶׁם as it is in the Biblical name יֶתֶר which is changed to יִתְרוֹ with the additional ו (*Ibn Ezra*).

planned evil towards me. [3] So I sent envoys to them,
saying, 'I am involved in a great work and will be unable
to come down. Why should the work cease while I leave
it and come down to you?' [4] They sent this correspon-
dence to me four times and I made this reply. [5] Then San-
balat sent this to me a fifth time with his servant and an
open letter in his hand. [6] In it was written the following:
It has become known among the nations, and Gashmu
says [this], that you and the Jews plan to rebel, and [you]
are, therefore, building the wall; and that you are becom-
ing their king. [7] You have also set up speakers to proc-
laim concerning you in Jerusalem, announcing, 'A king is
in Judah.' Now such things will be heard by the king.

The phrase about Gashmu is parenthetical. The story circulating among the nations that you wish to rebel is confirmed by Gashmu (*Rashi, Metzudos*).

עַל־כֵּן אַתָּה בוֹנֶה הַחוֹמָה — *And [you] are, therefore, building the wall.* You intend to use the city as a fortress for your rebellion (*Metzudos*).

וְאַתָּה הֹוֶה לָהֶם לְמֶלֶךְ — *And that you are becoming their king.* This follows the translation of *Metzudos. Ibn Ezra*, however, translates *you desire to be their king.*

The verse ends with the words כַּדְּבָרִים הָאֵלֶּה, lit. *like these words. Rashi* interprets this phrase as if it were written at the beginning of the passage (see above). Other commentators, however, interpret the phrase in its context at the close of the verse. Accordingly, 'Your intention to rebel, your becoming king' — *words like these* have been heard among the nations (*Metzudos*).

Malbim renders, *your becoming king says words like these,* i.e., your becoming king proves that the nations' talk of a Jewish rebellion is based on fact and not on unfounded suspicion. Sanballat supported this accusation by pointing to the false prophets (v. 7) allegedly hired by Nehemiah to proclaim him king.

7. וְגַם — *You have also.* This entire verse is part of the letter (*Rashi*).

נְבִיאִים — *Speakers.* Although נְבִיאִים is generally rendered *prophets*, here *Rashi* and *Metzudos* translate *speakers* (cf. נִיב שְׂפָתָיִם, *the lips' speech*, in *Isaiah* 57:19). The word נְבָא, literally *prophecy*, need not refer to predicting the future. It may also be translated as speech (see further, intro. to ArtScroll *Joshua*; ArtScroll *I Chronicles* 25:1,2).

Sanballat claimed that Nehemiah had set up public speakers to address the people and proclaim him king.

Malbim, however, renders נְבִיאִים, *prophets*, referring to the false prophet Shemaiah (vs.10,12), who actually had been hired by Sanballat and Tobiah to proclaim Nehemiah king. Sanballat now alleged that Nehemiah himself had paid the false prophet to make the announcement, indicating that Nehemiah planned a rebellion against the Persian throne.

וְעַתָּה יִשָּׁמַע לַמֶּלֶךְ כַּדְּבָרִים הָאֵלֶּה — *Now such things will be heard by the king.* The Persian monarch will hear that you have been proclaimed king (*Rashi*), and you will be accused of building the wall for the sake of your rebellion (*Malbim*). You will then be severely punished by the king (*Metzudos*).

ח וְעַתָּה לְכָה וְנִוָּעֲצָה יַחְדָּו: וָאֶשְׁלְחָה אֵלָיו
לֵאמֹר לֹא נִהְיָה כַּדְּבָרִים הָאֵלֶּה אֲשֶׁר אַתָּה
ט אוֹמֵר כִּי מִלִּבְּךָ אַתָּה בוֹדָאם: כִּי כֻלָּם
מְיָרְאִים אוֹתָנוּ לֵאמֹר יִרְפּוּ יְדֵיהֶם מִן־
הַמְּלָאכָה וְלֹא תֵעָשֶׂה וְעַתָּה חַזֵּק אֶת־
י יָדָי: וַאֲנִי בָאתִי בֵּית שְׁמַעְיָה בֶן־דְּלָיָה
בֶן־מְהֵיטַבְאֵל וְהוּא עָצוּר וַיֹּאמֶר נִוָּעֵד אֶל־
בֵּית הָאֱלֹהִים אֶל־תּוֹךְ הַהֵיכָל וְנִסְגְּרָה
דַּלְתוֹת הַהֵיכָל כִּי בָּאִים לְהָרְגֶךָ וְלַיְלָה
יא בָּאִים לְהָרְגֶךָ: וָאֹמְרָה הַאִישׁ כָּמוֹנִי

לְכָה וְנִוָּעֲצָה יַחְדָּו — *Let us . . . go and take counsel together.*

Sanballat feigned friendship for Nehemiah, and offered to aid him in covering up the announcement that he would be king, so that he would not be executed for planning a rebellion (*Ri Mitrani; Ralbag; Metzudos*).

◆§ Nehemiah's Reply

8. לֹא נִהְיָה כַּדְּבָרִים הָאֵלֶּה — *These things . . . have never happened.* Your claim that the nations have heard that I plan to rebel is false (*Metzudos*), as is your allegation that I set up false prophets who would proclaim me king (*Malbim*).

9. כִּי כֻלָּם — *For they all.* All of the gentiles (*Rashi*), including you (*Malbim*), fear us.

מְיָרְאִים אוֹתָנוּ — *Are afraid of us.* The translation follows *Rashi*, who renders מְיָרְאִים אוֹתָנוּ as מִתְיָרְאִים מִמֶּנּוּ, *frightened of us. Ibn Ezra*, however, translates: *You are only trying to intimidate us* into halting the work. In the past you have tried to frighten us into stopping the work. Do you expect us to trust your claim of friendship? (*Metzudos*).

וְעַתָּה חַזֵּק אֶת־יָדָי — *And now you strengthen my hand!* Nehemiah is incredulous at Sanballat's offer of friendly advice (v.7). 'Your desire has always been to halt the work — now you suddenly encourage me!?' (*Metzudos; Malbim*).

Others, however, understand this verse as a conciliatory remark. *Now strengthen my hand* — forget the past, halt your opposition, strengthen my hand! (*Ibn Ezra; Metzudos*).

Alternatively, this phrase is a description of Nehemiah's own feelings. *Now strengthen my hand:* Their intentions are to weaken our work, but the effect is the opposite — the letter only strengthens my resolve (*Ri Mitrani; Ralbag*).

◆§ Shemaiah

10. וַאֲנִי בָאתִי בֵּית שְׁמַעְיָה — *I then came to the home of Shemaiah.* Nehemiah then began an investigation of Shemaiah, the supposed 'prophet' who had proclaimed him king [v. 7] (*Malbim*).

Rashi states that he was a false prophet [claiming to speak in the name of *Hashem*] who had been hired by Sanballat and his cohorts as part of their plot to destroy Nehemiah. According to *Malbim*, it was not yet public knowledge that Shemaiah was a false prophet. Thus, Nehemiah entertained the possibility

Let us, at this time, go and take counsel together. [8] *I sent to him, saying: These things which you claim have never happened but you have fabricated them in your heart.* [9] *For they all are afraid of us, saying, 'Let them leave off the work, let it not be done' — and now you strengthen my hand!* [10] *I then came to the home of Shemaiah the son of Deliah the son of Mehetabel who was within. He said, 'Let us meet at God's Temple, inside the Sanctuary, and close the Sanctuary doors, for they are coming to kill you. During the night they are coming to kill you.'* [11] *But I said,*

that Shemaiah's prophecy (that Nehemiah would become king) was true (*Malbim* to v. 12).

וְהוּא עָצוּר — *Who was within* [lit. *and he was shut in*]. The translation follows *Rashi*, who explains that Nehemiah found Shemaiah at home.

Ibn Ezra, following the more literal translation of *shut in*, explains that Shemaiah seemed to have given up worldly interests and had shut himself in his house to devote himself to spiritual pursuits, as was the custom of those aspiring to prophecy [*Ralbag; see Rambam*, *Yesodei HaTorah* 7:1].

According to *Malbim*, Shemaiah was ill, and confined to his home. Therefore, Nehemiah could not summon Shemaiah to appear before him, and was forced to conduct his investigation at Shemaiah's home.

נִוָּעֵד אֶל־בֵּית הָאֱלֹהִים — *Let us meet at God's Temple.* Shemaiah claimed that he had been told, in a prophetic vision, to instruct Nehemiah to meet him at the Temple. The plotters expected Nehemiah to heed the prophet's word and enter the Temple, where they would kill him (*Ralbag*).

Malbim maintains that Shemaiah did not now claim prophetic knowledge. He asserted that informers had told him of the plan to murder Nehemiah, and offered his personal advice to Nehemiah to meet in the Temple behind the doors of the Sanctuary [see comm. v. 12].

אֶל־תּוֹךְ הַהֵיכָל — *Inside the Sanctuary.* [The *Heichal*, Sanctuary, was the Temple building, consisting of the אוּלָם, *Antechamber*, קֹדֶשׁ, *Holy*, and the קֹדֶשׁ קָדָשִׁים, *Holy of Holies*. This building — together with the עֲזָרָה, *Courtyard*, around it — constituted the Temple (*Rambam, Beis HaBechirah*, 1:5). Non-*Kohanim* were forbidden to enter the *Heichal* (*Mishnah Keilim* 1:8,9; *Rambam, Beis HaBechirah* 7:19,20).]

וְנִסְגְּרָה דַּלְתוֹת הַהֵיכָל — *And close the Sanctuary doors.* Since the doors of the city had not yet been completed [v. 1 see comm.], the only protection would be behind the doors of the *Heichal*, i.e., the Temple building (*Rashi; Metzudos; Malbim*). [Shemaiah argued that the only safe place was in the *Heichal* itself. Apparently, the gates of the wall surrounding the Temple Mount and the Temple Courtyard had not yet been built (see comm. to 2:8).]

כִּי בָאִים — *For they are coming.* Sanballat and his accomplices are coming (*Rashi; Metzudos*).

וְלַיְלָה בָּאִים לְהָרְגֶךָ — *During the night they are coming to kill you.* In the dark of night you will be defenseless against

ו יִבְרָ֑ח וּמִ֥י כָמ֛וֹנִי אֲשֶׁר־יָב֥וֹא אֶל־הַהֵיכָ֖ל וָחָ֑י
יב לֹ֥א אָבֽוֹא׃ יב וָֽאַכִּ֕ירָה וְהִנֵּ֥ה לֹא־אֱלֹהִ֖ים שְׁלָח֑וֹ
כִּ֤י הַנְּבוּאָה֙ דִּבֶּ֣ר עָלַ֔י וְטוֹבִיָּ֥ה וְסַנְבַלַּ֖ט שְׂכָרֽוֹ׃

them (*Metzudos*); tonight they are coming to kill you (*Ri Mitrani*).

☙ Nehemiah Refuses

11. הַאִישׁ כָּמוֹנִי יִבְרָח — *Does a man like me run away?* I am the governor (*Ri Mitrani*). Does a man like me show cowardice and flee (*Malbim; Metzudos*)?

וּמִי כָמוֹנִי אֲשֶׁר־יָבוֹא אֶל־הַהֵיכָל וָחָי — *And who, being like me, may enter the Sanctuary and live?* 'How can a non-*Kohen* like myself enter the *Heichal* and remain alive?' Nehemiah was not a *Kohen* [the Talmud (*Sanhedrin* 38a) identifies him as a scion of the House of David, who was descended from Judah. Priests are descended from Aaron, himself a descendant of Levi]. Therefore, by entering the Sanctuary, he would incur the penalty of 'death at the hands of Heaven'[1] as *Numbers* 3:10 states: וְהַזָּר הַקָּרֵב יוּמָת, *The stranger who approaches shall die*. This verse prohibits non-*Kohanim* from entering the *Heichal* on pain of death (*Rashi*).

Meshech Chochmah (*Numbers* 3:10) disputes this interpretation, noting that the Rabbis apply that warning only to the non-*Kohen* who 'approaches' by performing the Temple rituals reserved for the *Kohanim* [*Sanhedrin* 81b, 83b; *Rambam, Bias HaMikdash* 9:1; *Mishneh LaMelech* 9:15]. A non-*Kohen* who merely enters the Sanctuary without performing the Temple services is not punished with death, although he is guilty of a transgression.

Meshech Chochmah, therefore, offers a different translation of our verse by rendering וָחָי, *in order to live*, not simply *and live*. Nehemiah stated that it was unbecoming for someone such as himself to enter the Temple building *for the purpose of living*, i.e., to escape the assault of Sanballat and his accomplices.

According to *Ri Mitrani*, however, Nehemiah was a *Kohen* and was thus permitted to enter the *Heichal*. [*Ri Mitrani's* source is v. 10:2, where Nehemiah is listed as the first of a group signing a statement of allegiance to God (see comm. 10:1). The chapter continues (10:9), *These are the Kohanim*, referring to all those listed previously, including Nehemiah (*Wertheimer*). According to this view, although he was a *Kohen*, Nehemiah asserted that he could not enter the *Heichal* because he had become *tamei* (ritually contaminated) through contact with a dead body (טְמֵא מֵת).]

Ralbag, too, assumes that Nehemiah was a *Kohen*, and interprets his statement that he could not enter the *Heichal* and live as a reference to the verse (*Leviticus* 16:2): וְאַל יָבֹא בְכָל־עֵת אֶל־הַקֹּדֶשׁ, *Let him not enter the Holy place at all times*. This prohibition enjoins the *Kohanim*, on pain of death, from entering the *Heichal* at any time except for the purpose of performing the Temple services. [The Talmud (*Menachos* 27b), however, states that a *Kohen* entering the *Heichal* for purposes other than performing the Temple services was not punished by death, but with lashes (מלקות). The death punishment applied only to entering the Holy of Holies (קֹדֶשׁ קָדָשִׁים), the innermost chamber of the *Heichal*. See *Rambam, Beis HaMikdash* 2:2-4.]

12. וָאַכִּירָה וְהִנֵּה לֹא־אֱלֹהִים שְׁלָחוֹ — *I recognized that God had not sent him.* I recognized at that time that he was a false prophet. His advice to save my life by

1. The punishment of death mentioned in connection with our verse is not the capital punishment meted out by the courts [מִיתַת בֵּית דִּין], but death by Divine affliction [כָּרֵת, מִיתָה בִּידֵי שָׁמַיִם] (see *Sanhedrin* 81b; *Rambam, Bias HaMikdash* 3:12-14; 9:1). This refers to the premature death of the transgressor or his children, or the destruction of the soul after death.

'Does a man like me run away? And who, being like me,
may enter the Sanctuary and live? I shall not come.' 12 *I*
recognized that God had not sent him, for he spoke
prophetically to me; Tobiah and Sanballat had hired him.

committing a sin was not the word of God (*Rashi*; *Ralbag*), because it contradicted the Torah's commandments (*Metzudos*).

כִּי הַנְּבוּאָה דִּבֶּר עָלַי — *For he spoke prophetically to me.* He claimed that the advice to hide in the Sanctuary was prophecy (*Rashi*). This claim proved that Shemaiah was a false prophet. Had Shemaiah suggested the flight to the Sanctuary as personal advice, it would have been acceptable. Although entering the Sanctuary is forbidden to non-*Kohanim*, all Torah prohibitions are waived in cases of mortal danger [except for the cardinal sins of adultery and incest, murder, and idolatry] (*Sanhedrin* 74a; *Rambam, Yesodei HaTorah* 5:1,2). However, Shemaiah's claim that God had *commanded* Nehemiah to flee inside the Sanctuary was unacceptable. God, Who in His Omnipotence could have rescued Nehemiah in an infinite number of ways, would not have chosen the one method which required the violation of a prohibition (*Metzudos*). Furthermore, while Nehemiah might have entered the Sanctuary for self-preservation, why would Shemaiah, whose life was not endangered, have been permitted to meet with him in the Sanctuary (v. 10)? It was obvious to Nehemiah, then, that Shemaiah had lied. His advice was not prophetic, but was part of a plan to trap Nehemiah (*Ralbag*).

[A prophet who commands, in the name of God, that the people temporarily violate any of the Torah's commandments (except for idol worship) must be obeyed, provided that he has already been proven to be a true messenger of God (through the fulfillment of his prophecies) (see *Yevamos* 90b; *Sanhedrin* 89b; *Rambam, Yesodei HaTorah* 9:3). Shemaiah was unproven as a prophet — indeed, Nehemiah was suspicious of him from the first — and his present unacceptable 'prophecy' confirmed the suspicions. Nehemiah, therefore, ignored his alleged command in the name of God.]

According to *Ibn Ezra* and *Ri Mitrani*, Scripture presupposes the falsity of Shemaiah's prophecy. Thus, it is self-understood that the word *false* is inserted in the verse: *for he spoke the* [*false*] *prophecy to me*, i.e., for it was his own fabrication.

As noted in the commentary to v. 10, *Malbim's* understanding is that Shemaiah's advice for Nehemiah to escape to the Sanctuary was personal rather than prophetic. According to *Malbim*, the verse now refers to two distinct matters: 1) Shemaiah's advice, and 2) the statement that Nehemiah would be king. Although Shemaiah's suggestion to hide in the Sanctuary was not offered as prophecy, his pronouncement that Nehemiah would be king of the Jews (v. 7) was presented as a prophetic revelation. Until now, Nehemiah had not known whether to accept it as the word of God, or reject it as false prophecy. The question was now clarified. Nehemiah recognized that Shemaiah was a false prophet because his advice contradicted his own prophecy. If God truly intended to make Nehemiah king, then Providence would protect him. It would then be unnecessary for Nehemiah to violate the sanctity of the Temple in order to escape harm at the hands of Sanballat.

Nehemiah's refusal to accept Shemaiah's warning teaches careful consideration before accepting advice. By refusing to follow Shemaiah's proposal, Nehemiah thwarted his enemies' plan to murder him and malign him for violating the ban against entering the Sanctuary (*Ralbag*).

וְטוֹבִיָּה וְסַנְבַלַּט שְׂכָרוֹ — *Tobiah and Sanballat had hired him.* Now that Nehemiah realized that God had not sent

יג לְמַ֫עַן שָׂכ֥וּר ה֛וּא לְמַֽעַן־אִירָ֥א וְאֶֽעֱשֶׂה־כֵּ֖ן
וְחָטָ֑אתִי וְהָיָ֤ה לָהֶם֙ לְשֵׁ֣ם רָ֔ע לְמַ֖עַן
יד יְחָרְפֽוּנִי׃ זָכְרָ֧ה אֱלֹהַ֛י לְטוֹבִיָּ֥ה
וּלְסַנְבַלַּ֖ט כְּמַעֲשָׂ֣יו אֵ֑לֶּה וְגַ֨ם לְנֽוֹעַדְיָ֤ה
הַנְּבִיאָה֙ וּלְיֶ֣תֶר הַנְּבִיאִ֔ים אֲשֶׁ֥ר הָי֖וּ מְיָֽרְאִ֥ים
טו אוֹתִֽי׃ וַתִּשְׁלַם֙ הַחוֹמָ֔ה בְּעֶשְׂרִ֥ים וַחֲמִשָּׁ֖ה
טז לֶאֱל֑וּל לַחֲמִשִּׁ֥ים וּשְׁנַ֖יִם יֽוֹם׃ וַיְהִ֗י
כַּאֲשֶׁ֤ר שָֽׁמְעוּ֙ כָּל־א֣וֹיְבֵ֔ינוּ וַיִּֽרְא֖וּ כָּל־

Shemaiah, the logical conclusion was that Tobiah and Sanballat had hired him.

The verb שְׂכָרוֹ, *[he] hired him,* seems incompatible with the plural subject, Tobiah and Sanballat. *Rashi* explains that each of the aforementioned — Tobiah and Sanballat — had hired Shemaiah separately. *Ibn Ezra* and *Metzudos* translate *Tobiah 'or' Sanballat had hired him.*

13. לְמַעַן שָׂכוּר הוּא — *Because he was a hireling.* Because he was their hireling, Shemaiah had told me that I was to be murdered, and should seek refuge in the Sanctuary (*Rashi; Ri Mitrani; Ibn Ezra; Metzudos*).

לְמַעַן־אִירָא וְאֶעֱשֶׂה־כֵּן וְחָטָאתִי — *So that I would be frightened, do so, and sin.* There was no truth at all to Shemaiah's message; its purpose was simply to frighten me into sinning by entering the Sanctuary (*Rashi; Ralbag; Metzudos*). This would have brought Divine punishment upon me (*Malbim*).

וְהָיָה לָהֶם לְשֵׁם רָע לְמַעַן יְחָרְפוּנִי — *And then they would have a calumny with which to humiliate me.* Their plot was to humiliate me by advertising my sin (*Rashi; Metzudos; Ri Mitrani*); or by advertising my cowardly behavior in taking flight behind the locked doors of the Sanctuary (*Ibn Ezra*).

Malbim's approach to this verse varies slightly from the others. According to *Malbim*, the last phrase of the previous verse, וְטוֹבִיָּה וְסַנְבַלַּט שְׂכָרוֹ, *Tobiah and Sanballat had hired him*, explains only the motivation behind Shemaiah's actions — he was bribed. This verse goes one step further, and explains the plan to entrap Nehemiah. This plan had a twofold purpose: 1) to accuse Nehemiah of hiring a false prophet for his own personal gain; 2) to frighten him into sin and ultimate humiliation.

Malbim's reasoning is based on the following: The phrase לְמַעַן שָׂכוּר הוּא is understood *so that [it might be claimed that] he was a hireling,* i.e., so that it could be claimed that Nehemiah had hired Shemaiah to proclaim him as king (v. 7). The phrase beginning לְמַעַן־אִירָא, *so that I would be frightened,* expresses the second purpose — to frighten Nehemiah into entering the Sanctuary. This would cause Nehemiah to sin and suffer Divine punishment (thus, the words *and sin)*, and it would create a *calumny* against him. His enemies would advertise that he had desecrated the sanctity of the Temple building by entering it illegally.

14. זָכְרָה אֱלֹהַי לְטוֹבִיָּה וּלְסַנְבַלַּט כְּמַעֲשָׂיו אֵלֶּה — *Remember, my God, Tobiah and Sanballat, according to these deeds by each.* Remember them by punishing each of them according to his deeds (*Metzudos*), bribing the false prophets (*Malbim*).

נוֹעַדְיָה הַנְּבִיאָה וּלְיֶתֶר הַנְּבִיאִים — *Noadiah the prophetess and the other prophets.* Tobiah and Sanballat bribed them all to frighten Nehemiah with false prophecies (*Rashi; Metzudos*).

Ibn Ezra wonders why Shemaiah is not

13 *Because he was a hireling — so that I would be frightened, do so, and sin, and then they would have a calumny with which to humiliate me.*
14 *Remember, my God, Tobiah and Sanballat, according to these deeds by each; also Noadiah the prophetess and the other prophets who [tried to] frighten me.*
15 *The wall was completed on the twenty-fifth of Elul, after fifty-two days.*
16 *Now, when all our enemies heard, and all of the*

included in Nehemiah's request that God remember these people for punishment. To reconcile this, *Ibn Ezra* identifies Noadiah as Shemaiah (v.10). He is called Noadiah from נעד, *to meet*, because he said נִוָּעֵד אֶל־בֵּית אֱלֹהִים, *Let us meet at God's Temple* (v.10). The feminine נְבִיאָה, *prophetess*, appears in conjunction with the feminine *Noadiah*, but actually refers to *Shemaiah* the prophet.

In another interpretation, *Ibn Ezra* acknowledges that Noadiah was not Shemaiah, but simply *a prophetess*. However, the inclusion of Shemaiah in this statement is implicit and self-explanatory, as indicated by the word וְגַם, *also*. Noadiah and the other false prophets should *also* be held accountable for their false prophecies — certainly Shemaiah, the primary false prophet, should be *remembered* for punishment.

Malbim adds that Noadiah is singled out because she joined Shemaiah in prophesying falsely that Nehemiah would be the king of the Jews (v.7), while the others merely uttered prophecies intended to intimidate him.

⤙§ The Wall Completed

15. וַתִּשְׁלַם הַחוֹמָה — *The wall was completed.* Although the wall was now completed, its doors were not fixed until the seventh of Iyar. That date was celebrated afterward as a minor holiday, on which eulogies were forbidden (*Wertheimer* to *Ri Mitrani* citing *Megillas Taanis*,[1] ch. 2).

בְּעֶשְׂרִים וַחֲמִשָּׁה לֶאֱלוּל — *On the twenty-fifth of Elul.* This occurred in the twentieth year of King Darius, the year that Nehemiah had arrived in Jerusalem (2:1,11). He completed the wall within that year (*Rashi*).

לַחֲמִשִּׁים וּשְׁנַיִם יוֹם — *After fifty-two days.* The wall was completed fifty-two days after it was begun (*Rashi; Ri Mitrani*). According to *Ibn Ezra*, however, the fifty-two days are reckoned from the sending of Sanballat's letter (vs. 5,6). In any case, the threats made by Sanballat and the enemies caused Nehemiah to strengthen his resolve, and complete the wall in only fifty-two days (*Ralbag*).

16. וַיְהִי כַּאֲשֶׁר שָׁמְעוּ כָּל־אוֹיְבֵינוּ — *Now, when all our enemies heard.* They heard that the wall was finished (*Rashi*) in such a short time (*Metzudos*).

1. מְגִלַּת תַּעֲנִית [*Megillas Taanis*], *Scroll of Fasts*, is an ancient document written by Chananiah ben Chizkiah and his colleagues (*Shabbos* 13b) during the period of the Second Temple. It records all the days when miracles occurred for the Jewish people during the Second Commonwealth. These days were celebrated as minor festivals. [See Mishnah, *Taanis*, 2:8.]

ו הַגּוֹיִם אֲשֶׁר סְבִיבֹתֵינוּ וַיִּפְּלוּ מְאֹד בְּעֵינֵיהֶם
יז־יט וַיֵּדְעוּ כִּי מֵאֵת אֱלֹהֵינוּ נֶעֶשְׂתָה הַמְּלָאכָה
יז הַזֹּאת: גַּם ׀ בַּיָּמִים הָהֵם מַרְבִּים חֹרֵי יְהוּדָה
אִגְּרֹתֵיהֶם הוֹלְכוֹת עַל־טוֹבִיָּה וַאֲשֶׁר
יח לְטוֹבִיָּה בָּאוֹת אֲלֵיהֶם: כִּי־רַבִּים בִּיהוּדָה
בַּעֲלֵי שְׁבוּעָה לוֹ כִּי־חָתָן הוּא לִשְׁכַנְיָה
בֶן־אָרַח וִיהוֹחָנָן בְּנוֹ לָקַח אֶת־בַּת־מְשֻׁלָּם
יט בֶּן בֶּרֶכְיָה: גַּם טוֹבֹתָיו הָיוּ אֹמְרִים לְפָנַי
וּדְבָרַי הָיוּ מוֹצִיאִים לוֹ אִגְּרוֹת שָׁלַח טוֹבִיָּה
לְיָרְאֵנִי:

ז א וַיְהִי כַּאֲשֶׁר נִבְנְתָה הַחוֹמָה וָאַעֲמִיד
א הַדְּלָתוֹת וַיִּפָּקְדוּ הַשּׁוֹעֲרִים וְהַמְשֹׁרְרִים

וַיִּרְאוּ כָּל־הַגּוֹיִם אֲשֶׁר סְבִיבֹתֵינוּ וַיִּפְּלוּ מְאֹד בְּעֵינֵיהֶם — *And all of the nations surrounding us saw, they fell greatly in their own eyes.* When they witnessed the speed of the construction (*Metzudos*), their sense of superiority collapsed. They now feared the Jews (*Rashi*).

Ralbag and *Ri Mitrani*, however, translate, *they marveled greatly* (from the root פֶּלֶא). They marveled at the miraculous speed of the construction.

וַיֵּדְעוּ כִּי מֵאֵת אֱלֹהֵינוּ נֶעֶשְׂתָה הַמְּלָאכָה הַזֹּאת — *For they knew that this work was done by our God.* They understood that Divine Providence [see comm. to 4:9] had enabled the Jews to complete the construction so quickly (*Metzudos*), and prevent the enemies from halting the work (*Malbim*).

◆§ Tobiah's Friends

17. גַּם בַּיָּמִים הָהֵם — *But even* [lit. *also*] *in those days.* Even in those days, when it was evident that the hand of God had caused the wall of the city to be completed rapidly (v.16), some Jews sided with Tobiah and communicated with him (*Metzudos*). For this reason, Nehemiah found it necessary to post a guard (7:2,3) around the city (*Malbim*).

וַאֲשֶׁר לְטוֹבִיָּה בָּאוֹת אֲלֵיהֶם — *And Tobiah's came to them.* The exchange of letters indicated the warm relationship between Tobiah and the luminaries of Judah (*Metzudos*).

18. כִּי־רַבִּים בִּיהוּדָה בַּעֲלֵי שְׁבוּעָה לוֹ — *For many in Judah had sworn allegiance to him* [lit. *were principals in an oath to him*]. Many lords in Judah had sworn allegiance to him, having joined him in a covenant sealed by a solemn oath (*Rashi*).

כִּי־חָתָן הוּא לִשְׁכַנְיָה בֶן־אָרַח וִיהוֹחָנָן בְּנוֹ לָקַח אֶת־בַּת־מְשֻׁלָּם בֶּן בֶּרֶכְיָה — *Since he was the son-in-law of Shechaniah the son of Arach, and his son Jehohanan had married* [lit. *taken*] *the daughter of Meshullam the son of Berechiah.* They joined in a covenant with him because he was closely related to two respected lords: his own father-in-law Shechaniah (*Metzudos*), and his son's father-in-law Meshullam (*Rashi*). Tobiah himself was

nations surrounding us saw, they fell greatly in their
own eyes, for they knew that this work was done by our
God. 17 *But even in those days the aristocrats of Judah*
sent many letters to Tobiah, and Tobiah's came to them.
18 *For many in Judah had sworn allegiance to him, since*
he was the son-in-law of Shechaniah the son of Arah,
and his son Jehohanan had married the daughter of
Meshullam the son of Berechiah. 19 *They also recited his*
merits before me and passed along my remarks to him;
Tobiah sent letters to intimidate me.

Now it came to pass that when the wall was built and
I set up its doors, the gatekeepers and singers —

a Jew, albeit a wicked one (*Rashi*). [See comm. to 2:10.]

19. גַּם טוֹבֹתָיו הָיוּ אֹמְרִים לְפָנַי — *They also recited his merits before me.* Tobiah's friends recited his merits before me in order to cause me vexation (*Metzudos*). According to *Malbim*, however, the lords had joined in a covenant with Tobiah (v.18), because they considered him a good person. For the same reason, they recited his merits before Nehemiah.

וּדְבָרַי הָיוּ מוֹצִיאִים לוֹ — *And passed along my remarks to him.* They related my disparaging remarks concerning Tobiah to him (*Metzudos*). Or, Tobiah's friends served as his spies, releasing Nehemiah's private statements to him (*Malbim*).

אִגְּרוֹת שָׁלַח טוֹבִיָּה לְיָרְאֵנִי — *Tobiah sent letters to intimidate me.* Tobiah made it a practice to send me intimidating letters in an effort to halt the construction of the wall (*Rashi*). Because his friends related my disparaging remarks to him, Tobiah constantly sent letters to frighten me (*Metzudos*).

Ibn Ezra translates, [they] *passed along my remarks to him [that] Tobiah had sent letters to frighten me.* The remarks released to Tobiah consisted of Nehemiah's statement that Tobiah had sent letters to frighten him.

VII

◆§ The Appointments

1. כַּאֲשֶׁר נִבְנְתָה הַחוֹמָה וָאַעֲמִיד הַדְּלָתוֹת — *When the wall was built and I set up its doors.* When the wall and the doors were completed [the doors were completed several months after the completion of the wall (see comm. 6:15)], I appointed the Levites to their positions at the Temple (*Rashi*). Until this time, they had been occupied with constructing the wall and could not assume their duties at the Temple (*Malbim*). [The Temple was completed fourteen years before the wall. See comm. 1:1.]

הַשּׁוֹעֲרִים וְהַמְשֹׁרְרִים — *The gatekeepers and singers.* The gatekeepers and the singers were Levites (*Rashi*). [The Mishnah, *Middos* 1:1, delineates the locations in the Temple where the Levites stood guard.]

ז
ב־ה

ב וְהַלְוִיִּם: וָאֲצַוֶּה אֶת־חֲנָנִי אָחִי וְאֶת־חֲנַנְיָה
שַׂר הַבִּירָה עַל־יְרוּשָׁלִָם כִּי־הוּא כְּאִישׁ אֱמֶת
ג וְיָרֵא אֶת־הָאֱלֹהִים מֵרַבִּים: °ויאמר לָהֶם לֹא   °וָאֹמַר ק׳
יִפָּתְחוּ שַׁעֲרֵי יְרוּשָׁלִַם עַד־חֹם הַשֶּׁמֶשׁ וְעַד
הֵם עֹמְדִים יָגִיפוּ הַדְּלָתוֹת וֶאֱחֹזוּ וְהַעֲמֵיד
מִשְׁמְרוֹת יֹשְׁבֵי יְרוּשָׁלִַם אִישׁ בְּמִשְׁמָרוֹ
ד וְאִישׁ נֶגֶד בֵּיתוֹ: וְהָעִיר רַחֲבַת יָדַיִם וּגְדֹלָה
ה וְהָעָם מְעַט בְּתוֹכָהּ וְאֵין בָּתִּים בְּנוּיִם: וַיִּתֵּן
אֱלֹהַי אֶל־לִבִּי וָאֶקְבְּצָה אֶת־הַחֹרִים

וְהַלְוִיִּם — *Levites*. The translation follows *Ralbag* who understands our phrase as a parenthetic insert explaining that the aforementioned gatekeepers and singers were Levites. *Ri Mitrani* and *Metzudos*, however, interpret וְהַלְוִיִּם as *and the Levites.* Gatekeepers, singers, and other Levites were appointed to various communal tasks throughout the city. *Metzudos* states that they were charged with overseeing the Temple treasury and similar Temple offices.

2. וָאֲצַוֶּה — *I then appointed.* צוה, literally, commanded, can be understood as appointed. I appointed Hanani and Hananiah (*Metzudos*). [Similarly, the root צוה is translated *appoint* by *Sforno* to *Exodus* 6:13 (וַיְצַוֵּם אֶל־בְּנֵי יִשְׂרָאֵל). See *Chiddushei Maran R' Yitzchak Zev HaLevi* there.]

הַבִּירָה — *The palace.* [See comm. to 2:8.]

הוּא כְּאִישׁ אֱמֶת — *For he was a man of truth. Ibn Ezra* and *Ralbag* do not translate the prefix כְּ. *Metzudos*, however, interprets, *for he was* [seen] *as a man of truth.* He was obviously a man of truth who feared God.

וְיָרֵא אֶת־הָאֱלֹהִים מֵרַבִּים — *And long* [lit. *from many*] *God fearing.* He had been God fearing for a long time (*Rashi*). *Ralbag* translates *and God fearing more than many*, i.e., more God fearing than most people. *Malbim's* interpretation is *he feared God* more than [he feared] *many*. Hananiah was chosen for this critical position because his fear of God outweighed his fear of the many lords who supported Tobiah (6:7-19).

3. וָאֹמַר לָהֶם — *And I said to them.* To the gatekeepers (*Ri Mitrani*).

עַד־חֹם הַשֶּׁמֶשׁ — *Until the heat of the day* [lit. *of the sun*]. I.e., midday, when the sun is hottest (*Rashi; Metzudos*). The gates were to be kept closed until midday to avoid enemy infiltration (*Ralbag; Malbim*).

יָגִיפוּ הַדְּלָתוֹת וֶאֱחֹזוּ — *Let them hold the doors and lock them* [lit. *lock the doors and hold them*]. Let the watchmen stand at the doors throughout the time they are opened, not leaving for the night until the doors are locked and secured with crossbars (*Ralbag*).

Malbim suggests that the gates to the city had two sets of doors — larger outside doors, and smaller inner portals large enough for only one person at a time. The instructions to the watchmen were as follows: *While* the outer doors are open, and the people entering *are standing* in the gateway, let the watchmen hold the inner, smaller *doors*,

Levites — were designated. [2] *I then appointed my*
brother Hanani and Hananiah, lord of the palace over
Jerusalem, for he was a man of truth, and long God
fearing. [3] *And I said to them, 'Let the gates of Jerusalem*
not be opened until the heat of the day, and while they
are standing let them hold the doors and lock them;
and establish watches by the inhabitants of Jerusalem,
each at his watch, and each opposite his home.'
[4] *Now the city was spacious, large, the people in it*
were few, and no houses were built. [5] *Then my God*
gave me inspiration, and I assembled the aristocrats

which should be locked, and examine each individual before allowing him to enter.

וְהַעֲמִיד מִשְׁמְרוֹת — *And establish watches.* Let Hanani and Hananiah establish watches (*Ralbag*).

אִישׁ בְּמִשְׁמָרוֹ — *Each at his watch.* Let each man keep his particular watch at the city gates at the specified time (*Metzudos*). No one may appear at a different watch than the one assigned to him, since such changes would result in inadequate protection (*Malbim*).

וְאִישׁ נֶגֶד בֵּיתוֹ — *And each opposite his home.* In addition to the specified watch at the city gates, let each man keep watch near his own home (*Metzudos*).

Ralbag, however, combines the two phrases: *each at his watch, each opposite his home.* People were to keep watch opposite their own homes. Thus, at the very least, each homeowner was responsible to keep watch over the darkened streets and alleyways near his home.

◆§ Insufficient Inhabitants

4. רַחֲבַת יָדַיִם — *Spacious* [lit. *broad of hands*]. The word יָדַיִם, ordinarily translated *hands*, is used idiomatically here to mean *place* (*Rashi, Ri MiTrani*; see *Numbers* 2:17).

וְהָעָם מְעַט בְּתוֹכָהּ וְאֵין בָּתִּים בְּנוּיִם — *The people in it were few, and no houses were built.* According to *Metzudos*, this verse provides the reason for the special precautions taken in guarding the city (vs. 2,3). The city was difficult to defend because it was spacious, its inhabitants were few, and the houses were not built strongly to provide protection against the enemies. Careful guarding was therefore necessary.

Ralbag and *Malbim*, however, refer the mention of the lack of inhabitants and housing to Nehemiah's examination of the people's family histories, as recorded in the remainder of our chapter (vs. 5-73). Nehemiah realized that the city needed more inhabitants who would build more houses. He wished to ask each family group to send some of its members to settle in Jerusalem. For this purpose it was necessary for him to examine the family records and approach the families. Hence, the lack of people and houses is recorded in the text as a preface to the examination of the genealogical records.

◆§ Tracing the Lineage

5. וַיִּתֵּן אֱלֹהַי אֶל־לִבִּי — *Then my God gave me inspiration* [lit. *gave to my heart*]. God placed the idea in my heart (*Malbim*).

וְאֶת־הַסְּגָנִים וְאֶת־הָעָם לְהִתְיַחֵשׂ וָאֶמְצָא
סֵפֶר הַיַּחַשׂ הָעוֹלִים בָּרִאשׁוֹנָה וָאֶמְצָא כָּתוּב
ו בּוֹ: אֵלֶּה ׀ בְּנֵי הַמְּדִינָה הָעֹלִים
מִשְּׁבִי הַגּוֹלָה אֲשֶׁר הֶגְלָה נְבוּכַדְנֶצַּר מֶלֶךְ
בָּבֶל וַיָּשׁוּבוּ לִירוּשָׁלַםִ וְלִיהוּדָה אִישׁ לְעִירוֹ:
ז הַבָּאִים עִם־זְרֻבָּבֶל יֵשׁוּעַ נְחֶמְיָה עֲזַרְיָה

לְהִתְיַחֵשׂ — *To trace their lineage.* After the wall was completed, Nehemiah showed the people the records of their lineage. He did this in order to prevent gentiles from becoming intermingled with the Jews (*Ibn Ezra*); or so that he could ask each family to settle some of its members in Jerusalem (*Ralbag; Malbim;* see comm. v. 4).

הָעוֹלִים בָּרִאשׁוֹנָה — *Those who had ascended first.* [More than one wave of immigration had ascended from the Babylonian exile to the Holy Land. Eighteen years after Zerubabel led the first group of immigrants (*Ezra* chs. 1,2), another group went up to the Land, headed by Ezra (*Ezra* chs. 5,8).] Now, fourteen years after the dedication of the Sanctuary, Nehemiah found the genealogical records of those who had ascended first with Zerubabel [*Ezra* 2:3] (*Metzudos*).

Rashi comments that our verse refers to those who had *ascended first* with Ezra. [The explanation in *Rashi* is difficult because Ezra's name is not included in the list of the first returnees (*Ezra* ch. 2). Evidently, according to *Rashi*, Ezra did, indeed, ascend with the first group, although his name is not mentioned (see further comm. 7:73).]

וָאֶמְצָא כָּתוּב בּוֹ — *And found written in it.* The following passages were written in the document found by Nehemiah (*Rashi; Metzudos*).

Rashi's opinion is that the text of the document continues through 10:35. *Ralbag* and *Ri Mitrani*, however, hold that the document ends with the close of our chapter. (See comm. 7:73.)

☙ The Book of Lineage

6. The Book of Lineage recorded here is virtually identical with the list of returnees which appears in *Ezra* ch. 2. The reader is referred to ArtScroll *Ezra* for a comprehensive treatment of the subject. Our commentary here deals mainly with the differences between the two lists.

Rashi notes that although the total of 42,360 immigrants recorded in *Nehemiah* (v. 66) coincides with the total recorded in *Ezra* (2:64), the numbers listed for some individual families conflict [as in the case of the children of Arah, who number 652 here and 775 in *Ezra* (2:5).] A table listing the differences between *Ezra* and *Nehemiah* can be found in an appendix at the end of this volume.

Ralbag explains the discrepancies in the numbers of family members. *Ezra's* list was compiled during the reign of King Cyrus. Nehemiah discovered the list a number of years later, in the twentieth year of King Darius. By this time, some of the original immigrants had returned to the Diaspora, while new immigrants had arrived in the Holy Land. Nehemiah adjusted the numbers in his list accordingly, adding to the enlarged families, and subtracting from those whose numbers had diminished through emigration. *Ibn Ezra* explains the changes in the family totals as reflective of births and deaths (rather than immigration and emigration). *Metzudos* adds that families too small to be considered separately had been counted by Ezra as part of other, related families.

*and lords and the people to trace their lineage; I found
the Book of Lineage of those who had ascended first,
and found written in it:*
6 *These are the children of the province ascending
from the captivity of the exile which Nebuchadnezzar,
king of Babylon, had exiled; they now returned to
Jerusalem and to Judah, each to his city.* 7 *[Those] who
came with Zerubabel: Jeshua, Nehemiah, Azariah,*

By the time Nehemiah discovered the list, some of these had grown large enough to be counted as separate families. Conversely, some of those who had been counted separately by Ezra had now diminished, and Nehemiah did not mention them individually, but included them in other families.

Metzudos notes also that the names listed in *Nehemiah* sometimes differ slightly from those in *Ezra*, because both names were in use. [See appendix for table at the end of this volume.]

אֵלֶּה בְּנֵי הַמְּדִינָה הָעֹלִים מִשְּׁבִי הַגּוֹלָה — *These are the children of the province ascending from the captivity of the exile. Metzudos* (here and *Rashi* to *Ezra* 2:1) identifies *the children of the province* as the Jews in the Land of Israel. The list records the names of the Jews who had been exiled from the Holy Land to Babylon, and later returned from the exile.

Ibn Ezra (to *Ezra* 2:1) identifies *the children of the province* as the Jews who were in exile in Babylon. Why, then, did Nehemiah also list those who were born afterward, in the land of Israel? The phrase *children of the province, Ibn Ezra* answers, refers to the great majority of those listed, but not to the few who were born later. Nehemiah included this phrase in his rendition of the document in order to invite comparison with the list in *Ezra* (ch. 2), so that the reader might observe which families had grown in number and which had declined.

וַיָּשׁוּבוּ לִירוּשָׁלַם וְלִיהוּדָה — *They now returned to Jerusalem and to Judah.* They now returned to Jerusalem and to the territory of Judah (*Rashi*). [The territory of Judah refers to the part of the Land of Israel that was ruled by Judean kings in the time of the First Temple. For another interpretation see ArtScroll *Ezra* 2:1.]

אִישׁ לְעִירוֹ — *Each to his city.* Each man returned to the city from which he [or his family] had been exiled (*Metzudos*).

☙§ The List

7. הַבָּאִים — *[Those] who came.* The list of people who came from the captivity of the Diaspora with Zerubabel (*Rashi; Metzudos*).

In the parallel verse in *Ezra* (2:2) the phrase is in the past tense, אֲשֶׁר־בָּאוּ, *those who had come. Maharsha* (to *Megillah* 16b) explains the difference as an allusion to the fact that some of the people mentioned here came twice: once during the initial emigration, after which they returned to Babylon; and again with Nehemiah.

זְרֻבָּבֶל — *Zerubabel.* He was the Jewish community leader mentioned prominently in *Ezra* (2:2, 3:2, 5:2). One opinion in *Sanhedrin* 38a identifies him as Nehemiah. [See comm. 1:1.]

יֵשׁוּעַ — *Jeshua. Rashi* and *Metzudos* identify Jeshua as the *Kohen Gadol* Jehoshua Ben Jehozadak (*Ezra* 3:2,8; 10:18; see ArtScroll *Ezra*).

ז רַעַמְיָה נַחֲמָנִי מָרְדֳּכַי בִּלְשָׁן מִסְפֶּרֶת בִּגְוַי

ח־כ נְחוּם בַּעֲנָה מִסְפַּר אַנְשֵׁי עַם יִשְׂרָאֵל: בְּנֵי ח

פַרְעֹשׁ אַלְפַּיִם מֵאָה וְשִׁבְעִים וּשְׁנָיִם: בְּנֵי ט

שְׁפַטְיָה שְׁלֹשׁ מֵאוֹת שִׁבְעִים וּשְׁנָיִם: בְּנֵי י

אָרַח שֵׁשׁ מֵאוֹת חֲמִשִּׁים וּשְׁנָיִם: בְּנֵי־פַחַת יא

מוֹאָב לִבְנֵי יֵשׁוּעַ וְיוֹאָב אַלְפַּיִם וּשְׁמֹנֶה

מֵאוֹת שְׁמֹנָה עָשָׂר: בְּנֵי עֵילָם אֶלֶף מָאתַיִם יב

חֲמִשִּׁים וְאַרְבָּעָה: בְּנֵי זַתּוּא שְׁמֹנֶה מֵאוֹת יג

אַרְבָּעִים וַחֲמִשָּׁה: בְּנֵי זַכָּי שְׁבַע מֵאוֹת יד

וְשִׁשִּׁים: בְּנֵי בִנּוּי שֵׁשׁ מֵאוֹת אַרְבָּעִים טו

וּשְׁמֹנָה: בְּנֵי בֵבָי שֵׁשׁ מֵאוֹת עֶשְׂרִים וּשְׁמֹנָה: טז

בְּנֵי עַזְגָּד אַלְפַּיִם שְׁלֹשׁ מֵאוֹת עֶשְׂרִים יז

וּשְׁנָיִם: בְּנֵי אֲדֹנִיקָם שֵׁשׁ מֵאוֹת שִׁשִּׁים יח

וְשִׁבְעָה: בְּנֵי בִגְוָי אַלְפַּיִם שִׁשִּׁים וְשִׁבְעָה: יט

בְּנֵי עָדִין שֵׁשׁ מֵאוֹת חֲמִשִּׁים וַחֲמִשָּׁה: כ

נַחֲמָנִי — *Nahamani*. Nahamani was not included among the dignitaries listed in *Ezra* 2:2. *Metzudos* (to 7:66) explains. When the first Jewish immigrants arrived in the Holy Land during the days of King Cyrus, Nahamani was a young man, not yet worthy of being counted among the leaders of his people. Now, thirty-six years later, when Nehemiah listed those who had emigrated, Nahamani had developed into one of the great men of the times. Therefore, Nehemiah added his name to the list of distinguished men.

מָרְדֳּכַי בִּלְשָׁן — *Mordechai Bilshan*. The Talmud (*Megillah* 16b) identifies him as the Mordechai who was the leader of the Jews during the Purim episode. The Talmud (*Menachos* 65a) states that בִּלְשָׁן, *Bilshan*, was an additional name for Mordechai. The name is derived from two Aramaic words בַּיִל לִשְׁנֵי, meaning *he mixed languages*. Mordechai was a master of language. He alone could decipher the jargon spoken by some of the witnesses who came before the Rabbis, and even the sign language of mutes (see *Shekalim* 5:1).

In the list recorded in *Ezra* (2:2), Mordechai is mentioned fifth whereas in our list his name appears sixth (*Megillah* 16b).[1] The Talmud explains that Mordechai's standing among the great men of the generation was reduced from fifth to sixth because his diligence in studying Torah was reduced as a result

1. This can only be understood if we do not count Zerubabel. Thus, according to the Talmudic rendition, the verse is read, *those who came with Zerubabel: Jeshua* . . ..

Raamiah, Nahamani, Mordechai Bilshan, Mispereth
Bigvai, Nehum, Baanah; the number of the distinguished
men of the people of Israel. 8 *The children of Parosh, two*
thousand one hundred and seventy-two. 9 *The children*
of Shephatiah, three hundred and seventy-two: 10 *The*
children of Arah, six hundred and fifty-two. 11 *The*
children of the governor of Moab — of the children of
Jeshua and Joab — two thousand eight hundred and
eighteen. 12 *The children of Elam, one thousand two*
hundred and fifty-four. 13 *The children of Zattu, eight*
hundred and forty-five. 14 *The children of Zaccai, seven*
hundred and sixty. 15 *The children of Binui, six hundred*
and forty-eight. 16 *The children of Bebai, six hundred and twenty-eight.* 17 *The children of Azgad, two*
thousand three hundred and twenty-two. 18 *The*
children of Adonikam, six hundred and sixty-seven.
19 *The children of Bigvai, two thousand and sixty-seven.*
20 *The children of Adin, six hundred and fifty-five.*

of his exalted position in the Persian court. R' Yosef said, 'The study of Torah surpasses even the saving of lives.' Although Mordechai used his influence at court to preserve Jewish lives, his standing fell because his devotion to Torah study was diminished.[1]

אַנְשֵׁי — *The distinguished men.* The word אֲנָשִׁים, literally *men*, is used in Scripture to denote distinguished men (*Metzudos*; see *Rashi*, *Numbers* 13:3).

8. בְּנֵי פַרְעֹשׁ — *The children of Parosh.* Some of the immigrants [such as the children of Parosh] are listed according to the name of the head of their family. Others [such as the men of Bethlehem (v. 26) or Anathoth (v. 27)] are listed by the city of their origin (*Metzudos*; see ArtScroll *Ezra* 2:3).

11. פַּחַת מוֹאָב — *The governor of Moab.* This is the *Metzudos'* translation (to *Ezra* 2:6; see ArtScroll *Ezra* 2:6).

לִבְנֵי יֵשׁוּעַ וְיוֹאָב — *Of the children of Jeshua and Joab.* The children of Jeshua and Joab were, themselves, children of the governor of Moab (*Metzudos*).

1. The general rule that saving a life takes precedence over all the Torah's precepts [except for the three cardinal sins] applies only where there is an imminent threat to life. In Mordechai's case, that threat had already been averted with the death of Haman and the destruction of his followers. Mordechai, however, continued to occupy the post of chief minister in order to guard against any *potential* future threats. Although this, too, was a great *mitzvah*, it did not take precedence over the study and teaching of Torah, since no clear threat actually existed at that time (*R' Yosef Chaim* in his comm. *Ben Yehoyada* to *Megillah*).

כא־כב בְּנֵי־אָטֵר לְחִזְקִיָּה תִּשְׁעִים וּשְׁמֹנָה׃ בְּנֵי
כג חָשֻׁם שְׁלֹשׁ מֵאוֹת עֶשְׂרִים וּשְׁמֹנָה׃ בְּנֵי בֵצָי
כד שְׁלֹשׁ מֵאוֹת עֶשְׂרִים וְאַרְבָּעָה׃ בְּנֵי חָרִיף
כה מֵאָה שְׁנֵים עָשָׂר׃ בְּנֵי גִבְעוֹן תִּשְׁעִים
כו וַחֲמִשָּׁה׃ אַנְשֵׁי בֵית־לֶחֶם וּנְטֹפָה מֵאָה
כז שְׁמֹנִים וּשְׁמֹנָה׃ אַנְשֵׁי עֲנָתוֹת מֵאָה עֶשְׂרִים
כח וּשְׁמוֹנָה׃ אַנְשֵׁי בֵית־עַזְמָוֶת אַרְבָּעִים וּשְׁנָיִם׃
כט אַנְשֵׁי קִרְיַת יְעָרִים כְּפִירָה וּבְאֵרוֹת שְׁבַע
ל מֵאוֹת אַרְבָּעִים וּשְׁלֹשָׁה׃ אַנְשֵׁי הָרָמָה וָגָבַע
לא שֵׁשׁ מֵאוֹת עֶשְׂרִים וְאֶחָד׃ אַנְשֵׁי מִכְמָס
לב מֵאָה וְעֶשְׂרִים וּשְׁנָיִם׃ אַנְשֵׁי בֵית־אֵל וְהָעָי
לג מֵאָה עֶשְׂרִים וּשְׁלֹשָׁה׃ אַנְשֵׁי נְבוֹ אַחֵר
לד חֲמִשִּׁים וּשְׁנָיִם׃ בְּנֵי עֵילָם אַחֵר אֶלֶף
לה מָאתַיִם חֲמִשִּׁים וְאַרְבָּעָה׃ בְּנֵי חָרִם שְׁלֹשׁ
לו מֵאוֹת וְעֶשְׂרִים׃ בְּנֵי יְרֵחוֹ שְׁלֹשׁ מֵאוֹת
לז אַרְבָּעִים וַחֲמִשָּׁה׃ בְּנֵי־לֹד חָדִיד וְאֹנוֹ שְׁבַע
לח מֵאוֹת וְעֶשְׂרִים וְאֶחָד׃ בְּנֵי סְנָאָה שְׁלֹשֶׁת
לט אֲלָפִים תְּשַׁע מֵאוֹת וּשְׁלֹשִׁים׃ הַכֹּהֲנִים בְּנֵי
יְדַעְיָה לְבֵית יֵשׁוּעַ תְּשַׁע מֵאוֹת שִׁבְעִים
מ־מא וּשְׁלֹשָׁה׃ בְּנֵי אִמֵּר אֶלֶף חֲמִשִּׁים וּשְׁנָיִם׃ בְּנֵי

21. בְּנֵי־אָטֵר לְחִזְקִיָּה — *The children of Ater of Hezekiah.* Ater was a descendant of Hezekiah [and this verse describes his branch of the family]. Alternatively, the phrase should be understood: the children of Ater and the children of Hezekiah (*Metzudos*).

22. בְּנֵי חָשֻׁם — *The children of Hashum.* In our text, the children of Hashum are listed before the children of Bezai (v. 23). In *Ezra* (2:17, 19) the order is reversed.

24. בְּנֵי חָרִיף — *The children of Hariph.* This family is not mentioned at all in *Ezra*; and the children of Jorah, counted in *Ezra's* list (v. 18), do not appear in *Nehemiah* (*Ralbag; Ibn Ezra; Metzudos*). *Ibn Ezra* suggests that Harif and Jorah may have been different names for the same person.

27. אַנְשֵׁי עֲנָתוֹת — *The people of Anathoth.* These were the descendants of the men of Anathoth who were cursed by Jeremiah (11:21-23) and later repented (*Yalkut* to *Ezra* 2:27; see ArtScroll *Ezra* 2:23).

21 *The children of Ater of Hezekiah, ninety-eight.* 22 *The*
children of Hashum, three hundred and twenty-eight.
23 *The children of Bezai, three hundred and twenty-*
four. 24 *The children of Hariph, one hundred and*
twelve. 25 *The children of Gibeon, ninety-five.* 26 *The*
people of Bethlehem and Netophah, one hundred and
eighty-eight. 27 *The people of Anathoth, one hundred*
and twenty-eight. 28 *The people of the house of Az-*
maveth, forty-two. 29 *The people of Kiriath Je'arim,*
Chephirah, and Beeroth, seven hundred and forty-
three. 30 *The people of Haramah and Gaba, six hun-*
dred and twenty-one. 31 *The people of Michmas, one*
hundred and twenty-two. 32 *The people of Beth El and*
Ai, one hundred and twenty-three. 33 *The people of*
Nebo Aher, fifty-two. 34 *The children of a different*
Elam, one thousand two hundred and fifty-four. 35 *The*
children of Harim, three hundred and twenty. 36 *The*
children of Jericho, three hundred and forty-five.
37 *The children of Lod, Hadid, and Ono, seven hundred*
and twenty-one. 38 *The children of Senaah, three*
thousand nine hundred and thirty. 39 *The Kohanim:*
The children of Jedaiah — of the house of Jeshua —
nine hundred and seventy-three. 40 *The children of*
Immer, one thousand and fifty-two. 41 *The children of*

28. אַנְשֵׁי בֵית־עַזְמָוֶת — *The people of the house of Azmaveth.* [*Ezra* 2:24 refers to them as the children of Azmaveth.]

29. אַנְשֵׁי קִרְיַת יְעָרִים כְּפִירָה וּבְאֵרוֹת — *The people of Kiriath Je'arim, Chephirah, and Beeroth.* [*Ezra* (2:25) identifies these people as the children of Kiriath Arim, Kefirah and Beeroth.]

30. אַנְשֵׁי הָרָמָה וָגָבַע — *The people of Haramah and Gaba.*

[*Ezra* 2:26 refers to them as the children of Haramah and Geba.]

34. עֵילָם אַחֵר — *A different Elam.* The children of Elam, numbering 2,254, were already counted [v. 12]. This is not a repetition, but the listing of a different Elam (*Metzudos*).

36. בְּנֵי יְרֵחוֹ — *The children of Jericho.* [In our chapter, the children of Jericho precede the children of Lod, Chadid, and Ono (v. 37). *Ezra* (2:33,34) reverses this order.]

◆§ The Kohanim

39. הַכֹּהֲנִים — *The Kohanim.* The following is the list of the *Kohanim* (*Metzudos*).

ז
מב־נט

מב פַשְׁחוּר אֶלֶף מָאתַיִם אַרְבָּעִים וְשִׁבְעָה׃ בְּנֵי
מג חָרִם אֶלֶף שִׁבְעָה עָשָׂר׃ הַלְוִיִּם בְּנֵי־יֵשׁוּעַ
לְקַדְמִיאֵל לִבְנֵי לְהוֹדְוָה שִׁבְעִים וְאַרְבָּעָה׃
מד הַמְשֹׁרְרִים בְּנֵי אָסָף מֵאָה אַרְבָּעִים וּשְׁמֹנָה׃
מה הַשֹּׁעֲרִים בְּנֵי־שַׁלֻּם בְּנֵי־אָטֵר בְּנֵי־טַלְמֹן בְּנֵי־
עַקּוּב בְּנֵי חֲטִיטָא בְּנֵי שֹׁבָי מֵאָה שְׁלֹשִׁים
מו וּשְׁמֹנָה׃ הַנְּתִינִים בְּנֵי־צִחָא בְנֵי־חֲשֻׂפָא בְּנֵי
מז טַבָּעוֹת׃ בְּנֵי־קֵירֹס בְּנֵי־סִיעָא בְּנֵי פָדוֹן׃
מח־מט בְּנֵי־לְבָנָה בְנֵי־חֲגָבָה בְּנֵי שַׁלְמָי׃ בְּנֵי־חָנָן
נ בְּנֵי־גִדֵּל בְּנֵי־גָחַר׃ בְּנֵי־רְאָיָה בְנֵי־רְצִין בְּנֵי
נא־נב נְקוֹדָא׃ בְּנֵי־גַזָּם בְּנֵי־עֻזָּא בְּנֵי פָסֵחַ׃ בְּנֵי־בֵסַי
נג בְּנֵי־מְעוּנִים בְּנֵי °נפושסים׃ בְּנֵי־בַקְבּוּק בְּנֵי־ °נְפִישְׁסִים ק׳
נד חֲקוּפָא בְּנֵי חַרְחוּר׃ בְּנֵי־בַצְלִית בְּנֵי־מְחִידָא
נה בְּנֵי חַרְשָׁא׃ בְּנֵי־בַרְקוֹס בְּנֵי־סִיסְרָא בְּנֵי־
נו־נז תָמַח׃ בְּנֵי נְצִיחַ בְּנֵי חֲטִיפָא׃ בְּנֵי עַבְדֵי
שְׁלֹמֹה בְּנֵי־סוֹטַי בְּנֵי־סֹפֶרֶת בְּנֵי פְרִידָא׃
נח־נט בְּנֵי־יַעְלָא בְנֵי־דַרְקוֹן בְּנֵי גִדֵּל׃ בְּנֵי שְׁפַטְיָה
בְנֵי־חַטִּיל בְּנֵי פֹּכֶרֶת הַצְּבָיִים בְּנֵי אָמוֹן׃

42. בְּנֵי חָרִם — *The children of Harim.* Verse 35 has already listed a Harim. *Metzudos* explains that this is a different Harim. Alternatively, the first listing (v. 35) enumerates Harim's non-*Kohen* descendants. Our verse lists Harim's descendants who married *Kohanim* and were counted among his family members.

◆§ The Levites

43. לְקַדְמִיאֵל — *And* [lit. *to*] *Kadmiel.* The translation follows *Metzudos*.

לִבְנֵי לְהוֹדְוָה — *Of the children of Lehodiah.* Jeshua and Kadmiel are identified as the children of Lehodiah (*Metzudos*).

45. הַשֹּׁעֲרִים — *The gatekeepers. Metzudos* identifies the gatekeepers as the families of those that had been gatekeepers in the First Temple before the exile. [They could not have been gatekeepers when they returned to Jerusalem to build the Second Temple, since at that time the gates were in ruins.]

[*Ezra* 2:42 lists them as the children of the gatekeepers.]

◆§ The Nethinites

46. הַנְּתִינִים — *The Nethinites.* The Nethinites were originally Gibeonites who were appointed by Joshua to serve

Pashhur, one thousand two hundred and forty-seven.
42 *The children of Harim, one thousand and seventeen.*
43 *The Levites: The children of Jeshua and Kadmiel — of*
the children of Lehodiah — seventy-four. 44 *The singers:*
the children of Asaph, one hundred and forty-eight.
45 *The gatekeepers: The children of Shallum, the chil-*
dren of Ater, the children of Talmon, the children of
Akkub, the children of Hatita, the children of Shobai,
one hundred and thirty-eight. 46 *The Nethinites: The*
children of Ziha, the children of Hasupha, the children
of Tabbaoth. 47 *The children of Keros, the children of Sia,*
the children of Padon. 48 *The children of Lebanah, the*
children of Hagabah, the children of Slamai. 49 *The*
children of Hanan, the children of Giddel, the children
of Gahar. 50 *The children of Reaiah, the children of*
Rezin, the children of Nekoda. 51 *The children of*
Gazzam, the children of Uzza, the children of Paseah:
52 *The children of Besai, the children of Meunim, the*
children of Nephishsim. 53 *The children of Bakbuk, the*
children of Hakupha, the children of Harhur. 54 *The*
children of Batzlith, the children of Mehida, the children
of Harsha. 55 *The children of Barkos, the children of*
Sisera, the children of Tamah. 56 *The children of Neziah,*
the children of Hatipha. 57 *The children of Solomon's*
slaves: The children of Sotai, the children of Sofereth,
the children of Ferida. 58 *The children of Jaala, the*
children of Darkon, the children of Giddel: 59 *The*
children of Shephatiah, the children of Hattil, the
children of Pochereth Hazzebaim, the children of Amon.

as woodcutters and water carriers. The name Nethinites (נְתִינִים) is taken from the passage (*Joshua* 9:27): וַיִּתְּנֵם יְהוֹשֻׁעַ, *and Joshua appointed them* (*Metzudos*; see comm. 3:26; ArtScroll *Ezra* 2:43).

53. בַּקְבּוּק ... חֲקוּפָא ... חַרְחוּר — *Bakbuk ... Hakupha ... Harhur ...* These names represent negative qualities (cynicism, bullying, combativeness) which the settlers overcame in ascending to the Holy Land and constructing the Temple. See ArtScroll *Ezra* 2:51.

ז
ס-סה

ס כָּל־הַנְּתִינִים וּבְנֵי עַבְדֵי שְׁלֹמֹה שְׁלֹשׁ מֵאוֹת
סא תִּשְׁעִים וּשְׁנָיִם׃ וְאֵלֶּה הָעוֹלִים
מִתֵּל מֶלַח תֵּל חַרְשָׁא כְּרוּב אַדּוֹן וְאִמֵּר וְלֹא
יָכְלוּ לְהַגִּיד בֵּית־אֲבוֹתָם וְזַרְעָם אִם מִיִּשְׂרָאֵל
סב הֵם׃ בְּנֵי־דְלָיָה בְנֵי־טוֹבִיָּה בְּנֵי נְקוֹדָא שֵׁשׁ
סג מֵאוֹת וְאַרְבָּעִים וּשְׁנָיִם׃ וּמִן־
הַכֹּהֲנִים בְּנֵי חֳבַיָּה בְּנֵי הַקּוֹץ בְּנֵי בַרְזִלַּי אֲשֶׁר
לָקַח מִבְּנוֹת בַּרְזִלַּי הַגִּלְעָדִי אִשָּׁה וַיִּקָּרֵא
סד עַל־שְׁמָם׃ אֵלֶּה בִּקְשׁוּ כְתָבָם הַמִּתְיַחְשִׂים
סה וְלֹא נִמְצָא וַיְגֹאֲלוּ מִן־הַכְּהֻנָּה׃ וַיֹּאמֶר
הַתִּרְשָׁתָא לָהֶם אֲשֶׁר לֹא־יֹאכְלוּ מִקֹּדֶשׁ
הַקֳּדָשִׁים עַד עֲמֹד הַכֹּהֵן לְאֻרִים וְתֻמִּים׃

❧ The Base-born

61. וְאֵלֶּה — *The following.* This refers to those listed in the next verse: *the children of Delaiah, the children of Tobiah* (*Metzudos*).

תֵּל מֶלַח תֵּל חַרְשָׁא כְּרוּב אַדּוֹן וְאִמֵּר — *Tel Melah, Tel Harsha, Cherub, Addon, and Immer.* These are the names of places in Babylon. Those listed here were base-born, and, according to Jewish law, were not permitted to marry into the Jewish community (*Kiddushin* 70a). For the symbolic meaning of these names, see ArtScroll *Ezra* 2:59.

וְלֹא יָכְלוּ לְהַגִּיד — *But they could not state.* They did not know from whom they were descended (*Metzudos*; see ArtScroll *Ezra* 2:59).

בֵּית־אֲבֹתָם וְזַרְעָם — *Ancestry* [lit. *the house of their father and their seed*]. The translation follows *Metzudos.*

63. אֲשֶׁר לָקַח מִבְּנוֹת בַּרְזִלַּי הַגִּלְעָדִי אִשָּׁה — *Who married one of the daughters of Barzillai the Gileadite.* This family of *Kohanim* were known as the children of Barzillai the Gileadite because their ancestor had married a daughter of Barzillai and then assumed his family name (*Metzudos*). [See ArtScroll *Ezra* 2:61-62.]

4. אֵלֶּה בִּקְשׁוּ כְתָבָם הַמִּתְיַחְשִׂים וְלֹא נִמְצָא — *These searched for their genealogical record, but it was not found.* These *Kohanim* searched for some record of their names in the genealogical tables but none was found (*Metzudos*).

וַיְגֹאֲלוּ מִן הַכְּהֻנָּה — *So* [lit. *and*] *they were banned from the priesthood.* This translation follows *Rashi* on *Ezra* 2:62.

Metzudos translates *they were found repugnant for the priesthood*, substituting the root געל, *repugnant*, for גאל, *to ban*. [See ArtScroll *Ezra*.]

65. הַתִּרְשָׁתָא — *Hatirshatha. Metzudos* identifies him as Nehemiah, citing the passage [8:9] *Nehemiah — he was Hatirshatha.* The name *Hatirshatha* is derived from the words הַתִּיר שְׁתֹא, *permission to drink.* As the king's chamberlain (2:1), Nehemiah was required to taste the wine, to insure that

[60] *All of the Nethinites and the children of Solomon's slaves, three hundred and ninety-two.*

[61] *The following went up from Tel Melah, Tel Harsha: Cherub Addon, and Immer, but they could not state whether they were of Israelite ancestry.* [62] *The children of Delaiah, the children of Tobiah, the children of Nekoda, six hundred and forty-two.*

[63] *Of the Kohanim: The children of Habaiah, the children of Hakkoz, the children of Barzillai, who married one of the daughters of Barzillai the Gileadite and assumed their name.* [64] *These searched for their genealogical record, but it was not found, so they were banned from the priesthood.* [65] *And Hatirshatha instructed them to refrain from eating of sacrificial food until the Kohen of the Urim and Tumim arises.*

the king would not be poisoned. Although the Rabbis decreed that wine touched by a gentile (סְתָם יֵינָם) may not be drunk[1] (*Yoreh Deah* 123), they granted special permission to Nehemiah to drink the king's wine, since his refusal to do so would have aroused the king's suspicion and thereby endangered his life (*Metzudos* from *Yerushalmi Kiddushin* 4:1; see comm. 2:1, ArtScroll *Ezra* 2:63).

מִקֹּדֶשׁ הַקֳּדָשִׁים — *From ... sacrificial food. Metzudos*, citing *Kiddushin* 69b, interprets this as a reference to *terumah*, the portion taken from the produce of the Holy Land to be given to a *Kohen*, and קָדְשֵׁי מִזְבֵּחַ, *sacrifices brought to the Temple.* Legitimate *Kohanim* are commanded to eat certain portions of the sacrifices (see *Lev.* 2:3, 6:22, 7:6,31-34), but those who were now disqualified from the priesthood were not permitted to partake of them. [*Kiddushin* 69b quotes an additional opinion; see ArtScroll *Ezra* 2:63.]

עַד עֲמֹד הַכֹּהֵן לְאוּרִים וְתֻמִּים — *Until the Kohen of the Urim and Tumim arises.* The *Urim and Tumim* is the Biblical name for the parchment bearing the Ineffable Name of God which was inserted into the breastplate (חֹשֶׁן) worn by the *Kohen Gadol* (*Exodus* 28:30). When Divine revelation was requested, the *Urim and Tumim* would cause certain letters on the breastplate to illuminate, spelling out the prophetic message (*Rashi*, *Exodus* 28:30; *Yoma* 73b).

[The *Kohanim* were told not to eat of the sacrificial food until the *Kohen Gadol* of the *Urim and Tumim* would arise to clarify their status. He would request Divine revelation as to the nature of their ancestry, and would be answered by the *Urim and Tumim*.]

The *Urim and Tumim* was lost to the Jewish people when the first Temple was

1. *Pnei Moshe* (*Yerushalmi Kiddushin* 4:1) observes that this Rabbinical decree was legislated by Daniel, a senior contemporary of Nehemiah (see Daniel 1:8, *Avodah Zarah* 36a; *Beis Yosef; Tur Yoreh Deah* 123).

סו כָּל־הַקָּהָל כְּאֶחָד אַרְבַּע רִבּוֹא אַלְפַּיִם שְׁלֹשׁ־
סז מֵאוֹת וְשִׁשִּׁים׃ מִלְּבַד עַבְדֵיהֶם וְאַמְהֹתֵיהֶם
אֵלֶּה שִׁבְעַת אֲלָפִים שְׁלֹשׁ מֵאוֹת שְׁלֹשִׁים
וְשִׁבְעָה וְלָהֶם מְשֹׁרְרִים וּמְשֹׁרְרוֹת מָאתַיִם
סח וְאַרְבָּעִים וַחֲמִשָּׁה׃ גְּמַלִּים אַרְבַּע מֵאוֹת
שְׁלֹשִׁים וַחֲמִשָּׁה חֲמֹרִים שֵׁשֶׁת אֲלָפִים שְׁבַע
סט מֵאוֹת וְעֶשְׂרִים׃ וּמִקְצָת
רָאשֵׁי הָאָבוֹת נָתְנוּ לַמְּלָאכָה הַתִּרְשָׁתָא
נָתַן לָאוֹצָר זָהָב דַּרְכְּמֹנִים אֶלֶף מִזְרָקוֹת
חֲמִשִּׁים כָּתְנוֹת כֹּהֲנִים שְׁלֹשִׁים וַחֲמֵשׁ
ע מֵאוֹת׃ וּמֵרָאשֵׁי הָאָבוֹת נָתְנוּ

destroyed and was not restored during the times of the Second Temple (*Metzudos*, quoting *Sotah* 48b).[1] Clearly, then, the statement *until the Kohen of the Urim and Tumim arises* refers to the final redemption in Messianic times, when the Third Temple will be rebuilt, and the *Urim and Tumim* will be restored. The *Kohanim* who could not identify their ancestors were in effect told that their status would be clarified only at the time of the final redemption. [See ArtScroll *Ezra* 2:63.]

◆§ The Total

66. כָּל־הַקָּהָל כְּאֶחָד — *The entire congregation together* [lit. *as one*]. This refers to everyone — Israelites, *Kohanim*, Levites, Nethinites, and the children of Solomon's slaves (*Metzudos*).

אַרְבַּע רִבּוֹא אַלְפַּיִם שְׁלֹשׁ־מֵאוֹת וְשִׁשִּׁים — *Forty-two thousand three hundred and sixty*. The sum total of the family members enumerated in this chapter falls far short of this amount. *Metzudos*, quoting *Seder Olam* 29, explains that only the members of the tribes of Judah and Benjamin are listed by name. Thirteen thousand members of the other tribes also went up to the Holy Land with them, but are not named or enumerated. The thirteen thousand unlisted immigrants brought the total to 42,360. [See ArtScroll *Ezra* 2:64.]

Ralbag remarks that the total given here by Nehemiah coincides with the amount recorded in *Ezra* 2:64. This amount surely changed as a result of the births and deaths which took place from the days of the first immigration until the times of Nehemiah. This change is reflected in the statistics recorded here for individual families. However, the original total was retained here to conform with the opening phrase (v. 6) recorded by Nehemiah — *these are the children of the province ascending from the captivity of the exile*. Those who went up from

1. According to *Rambam, Beis HaBechirah* 4:1, the *Urim and Tumim* was actually worn by the *Kohen Gadol* during the Second Temple, but did not reply to his requests for Divine revelation. *Raavad* holds that there was no *Urim and Tumim* at all during the Second Temple. See Appendix to ArtScroll Mishnah *Yoma* for a fuller discussion of this.

[66] *The entire congregation together, forty-two thousand three hundred and sixty.* [67] *Besides their male and female slaves who numbered seven thousand three hundred and thirty-seven; they had two hundred and forty-five male and female singers.* [68] *The camels, four hundred thirty-five; the donkeys, six thousand seven hundred and twenty.*

[69] *A few of the family heads contributed for the labor; Hatirshatha contributed to the treasury one thousand golden darkemons, fifty basins, five-hundred and thirty priests' tunics.*

[70] *And some of the family heads contributed to the*

the Diaspora during the first immigration totaled 42,360.

⊲§ The Slaves and Beasts

67. מְשֹׁרְרִים וּמְשֹׁרְרוֹת — *Male and female singers.* The singers performed during the journey, which was conducted with great rejoicing (*Malbim*).

מָאתַיִם וְאַרְבָּעִים וַחֲמִשָּׁה — *Two hundred forty-five. Ezra* 2:65 lists 200 singers. The forty-five additional singers were children at the time of the immigration described in *Ezra* and were, therefore, included with the 200 adults. By Nehemiah's time, these children had grown to maturity and were counted separately (*Metzudos*).

⊲§ The Donations

70. וּמִקְצָת רָאשֵׁי הָאָבוֹת נָתְנוּ לַמְּלָאכָה — *A few of the family heads contributed for the labor. Metzudos* identifies the donations as those recorded in *Ezra* 2:6 — 61,000 golden *darkemons* and 5,000 silver *manehs* toward the cost of building the Temple, and 100 tunics for the *Kohanim.*

נָתַן לָאוֹצָר — *Contributed to the treasury.* Hatirshatha's donation is not mentioned in *Ezra* (ch. 2) because it was given now, during the period covered in the Book of *Nehemiah.* When Nehemiah (Hatirshatha) recounted his discovery of the Book of Lineage (v. 5), he recorded his donation together with the contributions made by the family heads during Ezra's time (*Metzudos*).

כָּתְנוֹת כֹּהֲנִים — *Priests' tunics.* The tunics were to be worn by the *Kohanim* during the Temple service (*Metzudos*).

71. וּמֵרָאשֵׁי הָאָבוֹת נָתְנוּ — *And some of the family heads contributed.* This verse refers to the family heads who made donations now, during the times of Nehemiah. The amount of their donations, specified at the end of this verse, differed greatly from those given by the family heads in *Ezra* 2:69 (*Metzudos*).

According to *Malbim*, the donations recorded in our verse were given by family heads who had not served during Cyrus' times. Or, alternatively, were a second donation from the family heads whose first contribution is recorded in *Ezra*.

לְאוֹצַ֣ר הַמְּלָאכָ֗ה זָהָ֞ב דַּרְכְּמוֹנִ֛ים שְׁתֵּ֥י רִבּ֖וֹת
עא וְכֶ֕סֶף מָנִ֖ים אַלְפַּ֥יִם וּמָאתָֽיִם׃ וַאֲשֶׁר֙ נָתְנוּ֙
שְׁאֵרִ֣ית הָעָ֔ם זָהָ֞ב דַּרְכְּמוֹנִ֛ים שְׁתֵּ֥י רִבּ֖וֹא
וְכֶ֕סֶף מָנִ֖ים אַלְפָּ֑יִם וְכָתְנֹ֥ת כֹּהֲנִ֖ים שִׁשִּׁ֥ים
עב וְשִׁבְעָֽה׃ וַיֵּשְׁב֣וּ הַכֹּהֲנִים֩ וְהַלְוִיִּ֨ם וְהַשּׁוֹעֲרִ֜ים
וְהַמְשֹׁרְרִ֨ים וּמִן־הָעָ֧ם וְהַנְּתִינִ֛ים וְכָל־
יִשְׂרָאֵ֖ל בְּעָרֵיהֶ֑ם וַיִּגַּע֙
הַחֹ֣דֶשׁ הַשְּׁבִיעִ֔י וּבְנֵ֥י יִשְׂרָאֵ֖ל בְּעָרֵיהֶֽם׃

לְאוֹצַר הַמְּלָאכָה — *To the work treasury.* This refers to the treasury set aside for the work of improving or adding to the Temple. It should not be confused with the treasury used for constructing the Temple, which already stood when the present donations were given (*Metzudos*).

72. וַאֲשֶׁר נָתְנוּ שְׁאֵרִית הָעָם — [Lit. *that which*] *the rest of the people gave.* This donation is not recorded in *Ezra* ch. 2. *Malbim* explains that when the family heads now made their second donation (comm., v. 71), the people added the gifts enumerated in our verse.

☙§ The People Settled

73. וּמִן־הָעָם — *Some of the people.* These were the constituents of the tribes of Judah and Benjamin (*Metzudos*).

וְכָל־יִשְׂרָאֵל — *And all of Israel.* These were the members of all the tribes other than Judah and Benjamin (*Metzudos*).

בְּעָרֵיהֶם — *In their cities.* The people settled in the cities which they had inhabited before the exile to Babylon (*Metzudos*; see comm. v. 6). [*Metzudos'* understanding is that our verse refers only to the first immigrants who went to Jerusalem during the days of Cyrus. The people then settled in the cities which they had inhabited before the exile.]

וַיִּגַּע הַחֹדֶשׁ הַשְּׁבִיעִי וּבְנֵי יִשְׂרָאֵל בְּעָרֵיהֶם — *The seventh month arrived, with the children of Israel in their cities.* The first portion of this verse, *and all of Israel settled in their cities,* is virtually identical with *Ezra* 2:70. It serves as the conclusion of the genealogical record of the original immigrants to the Land of Israel. The latter part of the verse — the mention of the arrival of the seventh month with the children of Israel in their cities — is identical with *Ezra* 3:1. After this, however, the two Books diverge. *Ezra* (3:2) describes the construction of the altar (3:23) whereas *Nehemiah* (8:1-8) portrays the reading of the Torah Scroll by Ezra the Scribe.

The commentaries offer two interpretations of the sequence of these events.

Rashi's approach is as follows: The document found by Nehemiah [v. 5], and quoted throughout our chapter [described as *the Book of Lineage of those who had first ascended* ... (v. 5)], extends through chapters 8, 9, and 10. Hence, all of the events described in those chapters took place during the period of the first immigration, in the reign of King Cyrus. This is the period covered in *Ezra* chapters 1-4.

In discussing *Rashi's* approach, *Malbim* notes that *Ezra the Scribe* figures prominently in chapter 8 (e.g., vs. 1, 2, 4-6). Since

work treasury, twenty thousand golden darkemons and
two thousand and two hundred silver manehs. 71 *The*
rest of the people gave twenty thousand golden
darkemons, two thousand silver manehs, and sixty-
seven priestly tunics. 72 *Then the Kohanim, Levites,*
gatekeepers, singers, some of the people, the Nethinites,
and all of Israel settled in their cities; the seventh month
arrived, with the children of Israel in their cities.

Rashi includes this in the Book of *those who had ascended first* (v. 5), it follows that Ezra ascended to Jerusalem with the first immigrants. Yet Ezra's name is not listed among the first immigrants in *Ezra* ch. 2; his arrival in the Holy Land a number of years later is recorded in *Ezra* 7:1 (see comm. 1:1). Evidently, Ezra went up with the first immigrants under Cyrus, returned to the Diaspora [presumably when Cyrus revoked his permission for the construction of the Temple; see *Ezra* 4:24], and then ascended again some years later. His activities in Jerusalem in Cyrus' times are described in *Nehemiah* (ch. 8). His *second* ascension, and his subsequent activities, are portrayed in *Ezra* (chs. 7-10).

Rashi's approach is supported by *Pirkei d' R' Eliezer* (ch. 38) and *Yalkut Shimoni* (*II Kings* 17) — both sources indicating that Ezra accompanied Zerubabel at the time of the original immigration to the Holy Land. This is clearly disputed, however, by the Talmud (*Megillah* 16b) and by *Midrash Shir HaShirim* (5:5), who maintain that Ezra did not leave Babylon until the year following the construction of the Temple, as recorded in *Ezra* 7:1-6. On this basis, *Ri Mitrani* disagrees with *Rashi*. His opinion is that our verse, *the seventh month arrived, with the children of Israel in their cities,* refers to events in two different time periods. It serves as the final quotation from this *Book of Lineage* (v. 5.) copied by Nehemiah, referring to the arrival of the seventh month during the times of Cyrus, when the first immigration had taken place. The verse is also the introduction to the events in chapter 8 of *Nehemiah*, which took place during the reign of King Darius. Then, too, the people gathered in the seventh month, as they had in the times of Cyrus. When the work of construction described in the preceding chapters of *Nehemiah* (1-7) was completed, the people settled in their cities, and when the seventh month arrived, the people gathered to hear Ezra read from the Torah Scroll.

Ri Mitrani assumes that Ezra remained in the Holy Land throughout Nehemiah's construction of the wall of Jerusalem in Darius' twentieth year (6:15). Since his name does not appear until chapter 8, when the work was already completed, it is evident that he took no part in this activity. Why did Ezra not take part in the construction?

Ri Mitrani answers that Ezra had been instructed by the king to organize the Jewish religious observance in the Holy Land and to support the Temple (*Ezra* 7:12-26), but only Nehemiah was appointed to fortify the city walls (2:5-8). Ezra feared that the enemies of the Jews would slander him before the king, accusing him of disobeying instructions by turning from his appointed tasks and assisting Nehemiah in the construction of the city's wall. He therefore refrained from any involvement in the construction. [See comm. 1:2.]

ח
א־ב

א וַיֵּאָסְפוּ כָל־הָעָם כְּאִישׁ אֶחָד אֶל־הָרְחוֹב
אֲשֶׁר לִפְנֵי שַׁעַר־הַמָּיִם וַיֹּאמְרוּ לְעֶזְרָא
הַסֹּפֵר לְהָבִיא אֶת־סֵפֶר תּוֹרַת מֹשֶׁה אֲשֶׁר־
ב צִוָּה יהוה אֶת־יִשְׂרָאֵל: וַיָּבִיא עֶזְרָא הַכֹּהֵן
אֶת־הַתּוֹרָה לִפְנֵי הַקָּהָל מֵאִישׁ וְעַד־אִשָּׁה
וְכֹל מֵבִין לִשְׁמֹעַ בְּיוֹם אֶחָד לַחֹדֶשׁ הַשְּׁבִיעִי:

VIII

Chapters 8, 9 and 10 describe a progression of inspirational experiences culminating in the signing of the בְּרִית אֱמָנָה, *Covenant of Faith.* This document formalized the people's renewal of their commitment to whole-hearted Torah observance, and served as the climactic event in the rejuvenation of the Jewish community centered around Jerusalem. Chapter 8 portrays the celebration of the Rosh Hashanah and Succos festivals. This was the catalyst for the repentance described in chapter 9, which, in turn, led to the declaration of the Covenant in chapter 10.

Rosh Hashanah is the first in a ten-day period of evaluation and spiritual renewal entitled יָמִים נוֹרָאִים, *days of awe.* This is followed by the Succos celebration, when the sense of inner satisfaction and fulfillment engendered by the renewal experience is epxressed in joyous festivity.

Against the backdrop of the events recounted here, these holidays took on even greater meaning. Rosh Hashanah assumed a uniquely communal significance, inasmuch as the people found themselves gathered together, *as one man* (v. 1) in their holy city. On this Day of Judgment, the community examined itself, and could find nothing but a pale reflection of its former greatness. The people wept (v. 9), but their leaders reinvigorated them with the reminder that Rosh Hashanah was a day for Jews to be confident in God's favorable judgment of them (see comm. v. 10).

Two weeks later, the Succos celebration began, with an added element of special joy. Jerusalem was, for the first time since its destruction, restored once again as the center of Jewish life. The Temple Mount again served as the focus of Jewish prayer and service. The words of the prophet Amos (9:11) held particular significance: *In that day I will raise the fallen Succah* [i.e., Temple] *of David*. Little wonder, then, that *from the days of Jeshua* (v. 17), the *mitzvah* of *succah* had not been fulfilled on a comparable level.

◆§ The People Request Torah

1. וַיֵּאָסְפוּ כָל־הָעָם — *Then all the people gathered.* According to *Rashi*, this chapter is part of the Book of Lineage (7:5) copied by Nehemiah. The events described took place during the first immigration from Babylon, under King Cyrus (*Ezra* 1-4). In *Ri Mitrani's* view, the Book of Lineage ended in chapter 7. Our chapter narrates events that occurred after the reconstruction of Jerusalem's walls (during Darius' twentieth year), described in the preceding chapter (see comm. 7:73).

כְּאִישׁ אֶחָד — *As one man.* They gathered quickly at the eastern side of the city, as if only one man were traveling to the plaza (*Metzudos*).

שַׁעַר־הַמָּיִם — *The Water Gate.* This gate stood at the eastern side of the city,

VIII 1-2

Then all the people gathered as one man at the plaza before the Water Gate; and told Ezra the Torah scholar to bring the scroll of the Torah of Moses, which Hashem commanded to Israel. [2] *So Ezra the Kohen brought the Torah before the congregation — men, women, and all who heard with understanding — on the first day of the seventh month.*

facing the Temple (*Malbim* 3:26; *Yoma* 69b; see comm. v. 3).

הַסֹּפֵר — *The Torah scholar.* The translation follows *Metzudos*, supported by *Chullin* 106a. [See also ArtScroll *Ezra* 7:6.]

תּוֹרַת מֹשֶׁה — *The Torah of Moses.* Because Moses minimized his own role, stating that he was unworthy of receiving God's Torah, the Torah was ascribed to him, as in the verse (*Malachi* 3:22): *Remember the Torah of My servant Moses* (*Shabbos* 89).

[In contrast to Moses, Nehemiah's name does not appear in the title of his Book in the order of Scriptures, because he requested that God credit him for his good deeds (see preface, ch. 1; comm. 5:19).]

☙ Ezra Brings the Torah

2. עֶזְרָא הַכֹּהֵן — *Ezra the Kohen.*

Ezra was the uncle of the *Kohen Gadol* Jeshua ben Jozadak (*Ezra* 3:2). According to *Rambam* (foreword to *Yad HaChazakah*), Ezra himself eventually served as a *Kohen Gadol*, just before Shimon HaTzadik. [See *Rashi*, *I Chronicles* 5:41; ArtScroll *Ezra* 7:1.]

אֶת־הַתּוֹרָה — *The Torah. Malbim* notes that our verse mentions *the Torah* whereas v. 8 states that they read from *the scroll* (בַּסֵּפֶר). The word *scroll* is deleted from our verse to suggest that Ezra also taught the people the Oral Law (תּוֹרָה שֶׁבְּעַל פֶּה) [which was not committed to writing until the Mishnah was compiled over a century after the Second Temple's destruction (*Rambam*, foreword to *Yad HaChazakah*)].

מֵאִישׁ וְעַד־אִשָּׁה — *Men, women* [lit. *from man until woman*]. This is a figure of speech meaning *all of the people* (*Metzudos*). In *Malbim's* opinion, this refers to those who were not well-educated. For them, the more easily understood written Torah was read.

וְכֹל מֵבִין לִשְׁמֹעַ — *And all who heard with understanding* [lit. *who understood to hear*]. This refers to those who understood more deeply (*Metzudos*). For the learned, the Oral Law (תּוֹרָה שֶׁבְּעַל פֶּה), with all its profundities, was recited (*Malbim*).

According to *Ralbag*, however, our phrase refers to the young children, who were also brought to listen to the reading of the Torah, provided they were mature enough to *hear with understanding.* Similarly, the Torah commands all the people to gather at the Temple every seventh year (הַקְהֵל), including the children, to listen to the words of Torah (*Deut.* 31:12). [*Gur Aryeh* (there) explains that the *mitzvah* was to bring those children old enough to understand.]

בְּיוֹם אֶחָד לַחֹדֶשׁ הַשְּׁבִיעִי — *On the first day of the seventh month*, the month of Tishrei. Rosh Hashanah falls on the first day of this month (*Rashi; Metzudos*). [Although it was the first day of Tishrei, it was the second day of Rosh Hashanah (*Beitzah* 6a, see *Rashi* ad loc. s.v. מימות עזרא ואילך; see comm. to 2:13).]

ח

ג־ה

ג וַיִּקְרָא־בוֹ לִפְנֵי הָרְחוֹב אֲשֶׁר ׀ לִפְנֵי שַֽׁעַר־
הַמַּיִם מִן־הָאוֹר עַד־מַחֲצִית הַיּוֹם נֶגֶד
הָאֲנָשִׁים וְהַנָּשִׁים וְהַמְּבִינִים וְאָזְנֵי כָל־
ד הָעָם אֶל־סֵפֶר הַתּוֹרָה׃ וַֽיַּעֲמֹד עֶזְרָא
הַסֹּפֵר עַל־מִגְדַּל־עֵץ אֲשֶׁר עָשׂוּ לַדָּבָר
וַיַּעֲמֹד אֶצְלוֹ מַתִּתְיָה וְשֶׁמַע וַעֲנָיָה וְאוּרִיָּה
וְחִלְקִיָּה וּמַעֲשֵׂיָה עַל־יְמִינוֹ וּמִשְּׂמֹאלוֹ פְּדָיָה
וּמִישָׁאֵל וּמַלְכִּיָּה וְחָשֻׁם וְחַשְׁבַּדָּנָה זְכַרְיָה
ה מְשֻׁלָּם׃ וַיִּפְתַּח
עֶזְרָא הַסֵּפֶר לְעֵינֵי כָל־הָעָם כִּי־מֵעַל
כָּל־הָעָם הָיָה וּכְפִתְחוֹ עָמְדוּ כָל־הָעָם׃

Ezra Reads

3. לִפְנֵי הָרְחוֹב אֲשֶׁר לִפְנֵי שַׁעַר־הַמַּיִם — *Before the plaza, which is before the Water Gate.* The Talmud (*Yoma* 69b, *Sotah* 40b) quotes two opinions concerning the site of the reading. One opinion identifies the site as the outer courtyard of the Temple [עֶזְרַת נָשִׁים, *Women's Courtyard*]. According to the second, the location was on the Temple Mount, but outside the Temple grounds.

מִן־הָאוֹר — *From the first light* [lit. *from the light*].

Ezra began his reading with the first light of day (*Rashi*; *Metzudos*).

עַד־מַחֲצִית הַיּוֹם — *Until midday.* The reading of the Torah on Rosh Hashanah (v. 2) from dawn until midday teaches that the first half of a festival day should be devoted to the spiritual fulfillment of Torah study (חֲצִי לַה׳).[1] The rest of the day should be set aside for the *mitzvah* of rejoicing and partaking of food and drink (see *Beitzah* 15b). It is also an obligation to supply the poor with food so that they, too, may rejoice (*Ralbag*, v. 10, see comm. there).

4. אֲשֶׁר־עָשׂוּ לַדָּבָר — *Made for the purpose.* The tower was erected especially for Ezra's Torah reading (*Rashi*; *Metzudos*).

וַיַּעֲמֹד אֶצְלוֹ — *Near him stood. Ralbag* points out that the public reading of the Torah may only take place before a quorum (*minyan*) of ten Jewish men (see *Shulchan Aruch, Orach Chaim* 55:3) standing in the area where the reading takes place. The raised platform upon which Ezra stood constituted a separate domain [רְשׁוּת] from the surrounding courtyard. Therefore, it was necessary for those listed in this verse to stand on the platform with Ezra, so that there might be a quorum in the immediate area of the Torah reading.

[*Orach Chaim* 55:20 asserts that when the reading takes place before a *minyan*, then all others listening, even those standing in a totally different domain, are credited with the *mitzvah* of having heard the reading. Thus, all of those standing in the courtyard

1. [*Mishnah Berurah* (529:1) explains that the first half of the day is spent in prayer as well as study. See comm. v. 10.]

[3] He read from it before the plaza, which is before the
Water Gate, from the first light until midday, opposite
the men, the women, and those who understood; and the
ears of all the people were towards the Torah scroll.
[4] Ezra the Torah scholar stood on a wooden tower made
for the purpose; near him stood Matethiah and Shema,
and Anaiah, and Uriah, and Helekiah, and Maaseiah, to
his right, and to his left, Pedaiah, and Mishael, and
Malekiah, and Hashum, and Hashebadanah, [and]
Zechariah Meshullam. [5] Ezra opened the scroll before
the eyes of all the people, for he was above all the people;
and when he opened it, all the people were still.

were credited with the reading, since a *minyan* stood with Ezra on the platform.][1]

זְכַרְיָה מְשֻׁלָּם — *Zechariah Meshullam.* The Talmud (*Megillah* 23a) asserts that both names refer to the same person. His name was actually *Zechariah*, but he was given the added name *Meshullam*, meaning *complete*, or *perfect*, because of his completeness and perfection in carrying out good deeds.

The Talmud's interpretation is evidently derived from the fact that the other names in the passage begin with the prefix *vav, and* — *Matethiah 'and' Shema 'and' Anaiah*, etc. However, there is no *'and'* between *Zechariah* and *Meshullam*. This indicates that Zechariah and Meshullam are the same person (*Maharsha*).

Based on this interpretation, the Talmud notes that Ezra was flanked by six men on each side, corresponding to the six men that the Rabbis required be called up to the Torah on Yom Kippur. [The connection with Yom Kippur is based, evidently, on the profound repentance experienced by the people as an outgrowth of the reading (v. 9), comparable to repentance on the Day of Atonement).]

Malbim questions the assumption that Zechariah and Meshullam are one and the same person, citing *Ezra* 8:16, *to Zechariah and to Meshullam*, as an indication that the names refer to different people.

[This may be answered with the assumption that the *Zechariah* and *Meshullam* mentioned in *Ezra* are not to be identified as the *Zechariah Meshullam* of our verse. This is particularly valid according to the commentators who assert that Ezra's reading here occurred after the twentieth year of Darius' reign, whereas the story in the Book of *Ezra* took place in the seventh year of his reign [see comm. 7:73, 8:1].

5. כִּי־מֵעַל כָּל־הָעָם הָיָה — *For he was above all the people.* Since he stood higher than the people, all were able to see him (*Rashi*; *Metzudos*).

עָמְדוּ כָל־הָעָם — *All the people were still* [lit. *stood*]. When Ezra opened the Torah scroll to begin reading, all were silent (*Rashi*; *Ibn Ezra; Metzudos;* see *Job* 32:16), or *stood* motionless (*Ralbag*).

According to one Talmudic opinion (*Sotah* 39a), this verse is the source for the requirement that the congregation remain silent during the Torah reading in the synagogue. [See *Shulchan Aruch, Orach Chaim* 146:2.]

1. *Orach Chaim* 55:19 rules that a raised platform within the synagogue does not constitute a separate domain, in conflict, apparently, with *Ralbag*. *Biur Halachah* there, however, cites differing opinions who require, like *Ralbag*, that the *minyan* stand on the platform.

ח ו ו וַיְבָ֣רֶךְ עֶזְרָ֔א אֶת־יהוָ֥ה הָאֱלֹהִ֖ים הַגָּד֑וֹל וַיַּעֲנ֨וּ
ו־ז כָל־הָעָ֜ם אָמֵ֤ן ׀ אָמֵן֙ בְּמֹ֣עַל יְדֵיהֶ֔ם וַיִּקְּד֛וּ
ז וַיִּֽשְׁתַּחֲוֻּ֥ לַֽיהוָ֖ה אַפַּ֥יִם אָֽרְצָה׃ וְיֵשׁ֡וּעַ וּבָנִ֡י
וְשֵׁרֵֽבְיָ֣ה ׀ יָמִ֡ין עַקּ֡וּב שַׁבְּתַ֣י ׀ הֽוֹדִיָּ֡ה מַֽעֲשֵׂיָ֡ה
קְלִיטָ֣א עֲזַרְיָה֩ יוֹזָבָ֨ד חָנָ֤ן פְּלָאיָה֙ וְהַלְוִיִּ֔ם
מְבִינִ֥ים אֶת־הָעָ֖ם לַתּוֹרָ֑ה וְהָעָ֖ם עַל־עָמְדָֽם׃

Ibn Ezra, in an alternate interpretation, translates *all the people stood*, explaining that they rose in honor of the Torah reading in accordance with the statement in the Talmud (*Megillah* 21a): 'From the days of Moses until Rabban Gamliel, Torah was studied only while standing.'

Orach Chaim 146:4 rules that the congregation is not required to stand during the reading of the Torah scroll. *Rama* there, however, cites a dissenting opinion requiring that the people stand. See *Mishnah Berurah* (19) there.

6. וַיְבָרֶךְ עֶזְרָא אֶת־ה׳ — *Ezra blessed* HASHEM.

Ralbag explains that Ezra recited the בִּרְכַּת הַתּוֹרָה, the blessing which is pronounced before studying Torah. Ezra must have uttered this blessing *before* the reading of the Torah described in verse 3, since the blessing over a *mitzvah* must always precede its performance. [See *Orach Chaim* 25:8.]

Indeed, the text of that entire blessing is ascribed to Ezra and his Rabbinical court (*Rambam*, *Hilchos Berachos* 1:3,5).[1]

הָאֱלֹהִים הַגָּדוֹל — *The great God*. The Talmud (*Yoma* 69b) quotes several interpretations of this phrase.

Rav's interpretation is that Ezra made *God's* name *great* by uttering, in his blessing, the Ineffable Name [שֵׁם הַמְּפֹרָשׁ]. Ordinarily, one is forbidden to pronounce this name,[2] except when the *Kohanim* recited a blessing on the Temple grounds. Ezra, however, uttered his blessing in the outer courtyard [see comm. v. 3]. He was permitted to do so at this time as a הוֹרָאַת שָׁעָה, *temporary ruling*, by which the Supreme Rabbinical Court may temporarily suspend Torah prohibitions when the overriding spiritual needs of the entire community make this necessary (*Rambam, Mamrim* 2:4).

Rav Gidal [in a second interpretation] said, 'Ezra made God great by instituting a special blessing to be recited at the Temple: *Blessed is* HASHEM, *God of Israel, from world to world* [see 9:5].' *Rashi* (on *Yoma*) explains that this blessing was to be included as the closing statement of each blessing recited at the Temple. [The words *from world to world* mean from the present world to the World to Come (see *Berachos* 54a).]

וַיַּעֲנוּ כָל־הָעָם — *And all the people answered*. This may also be rendered *and all the people exclaimed*. See *Deut*. 27:14, see also ArtScroll *Ezra* 3:11.

1. The blessings recited before the performance of *mitzvos* (בִּרְכַּת הַמִּצְוֹת) are not Biblically required, but were made binding by a Rabbinical decree (*Rambam, Hilchos Berachos* 1:3-5). *Mishnah Berurah* 47:1, however, cites a number of halachic authorities who rule that the blessing over Torah study is Biblically mandated.

2. The basis for this prohibition is the passage זֶה־שְּׁמִי לְעֹלָם, *This is My Name forever* (*Exodus* 3:15). The word לְעֹלָם, *forever*, is read לְעַלֵּם, *to conceal*. The verse now reads, *this is My Name to conceal*, referring to the Name of God which appears at the beginning of that verse (*Pesachim* 50a, *Rashi*).

VIII
6-7

6 *Ezra blessed HASHEM, the great God, and all the people answered, 'Amen, Amen,' with their hands upraised; then they bowed, and prostrated themselves before HASHEM, face to the ground.* 7 *And Jeshua, Bani, Shereviah, Yamin, Akkuv, Shabsai, Hodeiah, Maaseiah, Kelita, Azariah, Yozabad, Hanan, Pelaiah and the Levites taught the Torah to the people, while the people stood.*

אָמֵן אָמֵן — *Amen, Amen.* The word *Amen* was repeated for emphasis (*Metzudos*). When one hears a blessing, one must answer, 'Amen,' meaning, 'The blessing is true. I believe it' (*Orach Chaim* 124:6).

בְּמֹעַל יְדֵיהֶם — *With their hands upraised.* They raised their hands heavenward[1] as a symbol of thankfulness to God, as in the case of King Solomon, *And he spread his palms heavenward* [*I Kings* 8:22] (*Rashi*).

וַיִּקְּדוּ וַיִּשְׁתַּחֲוּוּ — *Then they bowed, and prostrated themselves.* The Gemara (*Berachos* 34b) defines קִדָּה as the bending of the body forward while kneeling until the face touches the ground,[2] and הִשְׁתַּחֲוָאָה as the prostration of the entire body on the ground, arms and legs outstretched. [See *Rambam, Hilchos Berachos* 5:13.]

◆§ The Torah Clarified

7. וְהַלְוִיִּם — *And the Levites.* The Levites were chosen as teachers of Torah because this was their traditional role. '[The Levite] was set apart to serve *Hashem*, and to teach proper ways and righteous laws to the multitudes, as it is written (*Deut.* 33:10), *Let them* [the Levites] *teach your laws to Jacob and your Torah to Israel*' (*Rambam, Shemittah* 13:12).

מְבִינִים אֶת־הָעָם לַתּוֹרָה — *Taught the Torah to the people.* The Levites and others translated the words of the Torah that Ezra had read (*Rashi*).

When the Torah was read in public, scholars would be present to help the people understand the reading, as well as the תֻּרְגְּמָן [*turgeman*], *translator*, who repeated the verse in Aramaic, the language understood by all the people (*Ri Mitrani*). According to *Rambam* (*Tefillah* 2:10), Ezra instituted the custom of using the *turgeman*.[3] [See comm. v. 8.]

וְהָעָם עַל־עָמְדָם — *While the people stood.* The people had risen and stood throughout the reading (*Rashi*; *Ri Mitrani*). [This is different from v. 5, where עָמְדוּ כָל־הָעָם

1. *Rabbi Akiva Eiger* (*Orach Chaim* 89:1) explains why we no longer follow the custom of praying with uplifted hands. When the gentiles adopted this as a form of prayer, it became unacceptable for Jews. This parallels the Torah's prohibition of the single-stone altar [מַצֵּבָה]. Although used by the Patriarchs for their sacrifices, it was later prohibited for use as an altar because it was adopted by the heathens for their idolatrous sacrifices. [See *Rashi*, *Deut.* 16:22; ArtScroll *Ezra* 9:5.]

2. The Talmud (*Succah* 53a) relates that Rabban Shimon ben Gamliel was the only person in his generation able to perform a more difficult form of קִדָּה. He could hold the entire length of his body parallel to the ground, supporting his weight only by his thumbs, and lower his face until it touched the ground.

3. This custom was abandoned when Aramaic fell into disuse (*Megillah* 23b, 24a; *Shulchan Aruch, Orach Chaim* 145:1,3). *Tur* (*Orach Chaim* 145) explains that it would not be proper for the *turgeman* to translate the reading into any language other than Aramaic. Only the Aramaic translation (*Targum*) of the Bible, which was written with Divine Inspiration (רוּחַ הַקֹּדֶשׁ), was acceptable to the Rabbis to be designated as part of the public Torah reading (see comm. v. 8).

ח ח־ט

ח וַיִּקְרְאוּ בַסֵּפֶר בְּתוֹרַת הָאֱלֹהִים מְפֹרָשׁ וְשׂוֹם
ט שֶׂכֶל וַיָּבִינוּ בַּמִּקְרָא׃ וַיֹּאמֶר נְחֶמְיָה
הוּא הַתִּרְשָׁתָא וְעֶזְרָא הַכֹּהֵן ׀ הַסֹּפֵר וְהַלְוִיִּם
הַמְּבִינִים אֶת־הָעָם לְכָל־הָעָם הַיּוֹם קָדֹשׁ־
הוּא לַיהוָה אֱלֹהֵיכֶם אַל־תִּתְאַבְּלוּ וְאַל־תִּבְכּוּ
כִּי בוֹכִים כָּל־הָעָם כְּשָׁמְעָם אֶת־דִּבְרֵי הַתּוֹרָה׃

is translated *all the people were still*; see comm. there.]

8. וַיִּקְרְאוּ — *They read*. The Levites read the Torah to the people, i.e., they translated the reading to enable them to comprehend it (*Ralbag*).

Metzudos, however, attributes the reading to the people. Although only Ezra actually read the scroll (v. 6), the people's listening is considered like reading. [This follows the well-known Talmudic dictum: שׁוֹמֵעַ כְּעוֹנֶה, *Listening is like reading* (*Succah* 38b). According to this rule, a person required to pronounce a prayer or blessing may discharge his obligation merely by listening to someone else's reading (see *Rambam, Hil. Berachos* 1:11).]

בַּסֵּפֶר בְּתוֹרַת הָאֱלֹהִים — *The scroll, God's Torah.* I.e., Scripture (*Ri Mitrani*; see *Megillah* 3a, *Nedarim* 37b).

In *Malbim's* opinion, the repetition of the prefix 'בְּ,' *in*, ('*in*' *the scroll*, '*in*' *God's Torah*) indicates that there are really two phrases, with distinct meanings. *The scroll* is the Written Torah, while *God's Torah* refers to the Oral Law. Both were now taught to the people.

מְפֹרָשׁ — *Clearly*. Following the Talmud (*Megillah* 3a; *Nedarim* 37b), *Ri Mitrani* and *Ralbag* explain מְפֹרָשׁ as a reference to *Targum*,[1] the Aramaic translation of the Pentateuch, which '*clarified*' the Scriptures to the people.

Rambam (*Tefillah* 12:10) states that Ezra instituted the custom, prevalent in Talmudic times, of reading the *Targum* in the synagogue along with the Torah. After the reader read each verse in Hebrew from the Torah scroll, the *turgeman* (*translator*) would recite the verse's Aramaic translation, so that all the people could understand. Our verse is the source for *Rambam's* assertion that the *turgeman* was instituted by Ezra (*Kesef Mishneh*).

וְשׂוֹם שֶׂכֶל וַיָּבִינוּ בַּמִּקְרָא — *With the application of wisdom, they clarified through the reading.* The Talmud (*Megillah* 3a; *Nedarim* 37b) identifies *the application of wisdom* as a reference to פְּסוּקִים, pauses indicating the end of a verse. *They clarified through the reading* refers to פִּסְקֵי טְעָמִים, the prescribed cantillation which divides the sentence into various parts; or, alternatively, to the מְסוֹרָה — the tradition detailing the proper spelling and pronunciation of each word. The Torah scroll has neither punctuation nor vowels. Once the Levites and other teachers taught the correct punctuation and pronunciation of the text, it could be understood with wisdom and clarity.

As noted above, *Malbim* understands *the scroll* as a reference to Scripture and *God's Torah* as referring to the Oral Torah tradition (see comm. to v. 2). In conjunction with this, he explains that the word *clearly*, referring to *Targum*, correlates to *the scroll*, i.e., Scripture. The phrases *the applica-*

1. The *Targum* to the Five Books of the Torah was subsequently forgotten, and then restored by Onkelos the Proselyte (see *Gittin* 66b), who heard it from the mouths of Rabbi Eliezer and Rabbi Yehoshua (*Megillah* 3a).

8 They read the scroll, God's Torah, clearly; with the application of wisdom, they clarified through the reading. 9 Nehemiah, who is Hatirshatha, Ezra the Kohen and Torah scholar, and the Levites who taught the people, said to all the people, 'This day is sacred to H*ASHEM your God; do not mourn or weep' — for all the people wept when they heard the words of the Torah.*

tion of wisdom, meaning the פְּסוּקִים and פִּסְקֵי טְעָמִים, and *the clarification of the text,* meaning the מְסוֹרוֹת, correlate to the Oral Torah.

Malbim explains: Proper pronunciation and sentence structure, as determined by the oral tradition, are the basic building blocks for understanding the Torah. The meaning of Scripture is dependent on the point at which each sentence and phrase ends. In addition, pronunciation is often critical in determining the *halachah* derived from Scripture. For example, the word חלב appears in the passage prohibiting cooking milk and meat together (*Exodus* 23:19). חלב can be pronounced חֵלֶב, *fat*, or חָלָב, *milk*. It is the oral tradition which teaches the proper pronunciation (the latter), and hence the proper *halachah.*

Thus, the Levites clarified the meaning of Scripture by use of the *Targum,* and revealed the sources for the oral tradition indicated by the proper reading of the Biblical verses. The phrase *with the application of wisdom, they clarified through the reading* alludes to both teachings.

9. נְחֶמְיָה הוּא הַתִּרְשָׁתָא — *Nehemiah, who is Hatirshatha*. Hatirshatha was another name for Nehemiah. See comm. to 7:65.

כִּי בוֹכִים כָּל־הָעָם כְּשָׁמְעָם אֶת־דִּבְרֵי הַתּוֹרָה — *For all the people wept when they heard the words of the Torah.* They wept because they had not carried out the Torah's laws properly (*Rashi; Metzudos*).

Ralbag conjectures that the people wept when the Levites explained that Rosh Hashanah was a day of judgment, and the portions of the Torah describing the terrible punishments which befall evildoers (*Lev.* 26:14-46, and *Deut.* 28:15-68) were read.

HaMoadim B'Halachah (see ArtScroll *The Festivals in Halachah*, pgs. 72-73) proposes a novel explanation for the weeping. The people knew that they had observed two days[1] of Rosh Hashanah in the Diaspora, but thought that only one day was required in the Holy Land. When they heard the Rosh Hashanah reading on the second day (v. 13), they concluded that God was not pleased with the Temple they had built, and they had been relegated to the status of exiles. Or, that their leaders had forseen the destruction of the Second Temple, and had retained the second day of the festival in anticipation of another exile. The people were overcome with despondence, and wept. But Nehemiah and Ezra ... informed them that their apprehensions were mistaken. They explained that the day was actually Rosh Hashanah, since no witnesses had appeared before the Supreme Rabbinical Court the previous day to attest to the sighting of the new moon. Their explanation: *This day is sacred to our Lord* — not because of doubt, nor because of decree, but because the day itself was actually Rosh Hashanah, with the result that the day was *sacred to* H*ASHEM.*

1. According to *Tosafos* (*Rosh Hashanah* 18a) and *Rambam* (*Kiddush HaChodesh* 5:7), the communities outside of *Eretz Yisrael* at this time observed a two-day Rosh Hashanah. *Rashi* (*Rosh Hashanah* 18a), however, maintains that only one day was observed. See also comm. to v. 13.

ח
י וַיֹּאמֶר לָהֶם לְכוּ אִכְלוּ מַשְׁמַנִּים וּשְׁתוּ
י־יב מַמְתַקִּים וְשִׁלְחוּ מָנוֹת לְאֵין נָכוֹן לוֹ כִּי־קָדוֹשׁ
הַיּוֹם לַאֲדֹנֵינוּ וְאַל־תֵּעָצֵבוּ כִּי־חֶדְוַת יהוה
יא הִיא מָעֻזְּכֶם׃ וְהַלְוִיִּם מַחְשִׁים לְכָל־הָעָם
יב לֵאמֹר הַסּוּ כִּי הַיּוֹם קָדֹשׁ וְאַל־תֵּעָצֵבוּ׃ וַיֵּלְכוּ

10. אִכְלוּ מַשְׁמַנִּים וּשְׁתוּ מַמְתַקִּים — *Eat rich foods, drink sweet beverages.* When the people were reminded that Rosh Hashanah was a time of judgment, they decided to fast. They were told, however, that fasting is not permitted on Rosh Hashanah — on the contrary, they were to eat and drink in honor of the day (*Malbim*).

Ralbag explains that our verse refers to the *mitzvah* of enjoying the festival by eating and drinking (*oneg Yom Tov*) during the second portion of the day (חֲצִי לָכֶם). The first half of the day is to be devoted to God (חֲצִי לַה׳) and spent in study and prayer (see v. 3) (see *Beitzah* 15b; *Orach Chaim* 529:1).

Shulchan Aruch (*Orach Chaim* 597:1) rules that eating and drinking are required on Rosh Hashanah, and fasting is forbidden. *Mishnah Berurah* cites our verse as proof, and explains that although Rosh Hashanah is a Day of Judgment, and thus deserving of great solemnity, it is also considered a festival (see *Psalms* 81:14; *Rosh Hashanah* 8a), and is subject to the *mitzvah* of וְשָׂמַחְתָּ בְּחַגֶּךָ, *rejoice on your festival* (*Deut*. 16:14).

Despite the awesomeness of the Day of Judgment, Jews rejoice on Rosh Hashanah and celebrate with food and drink, secure in the knowledge that the loving God will judge them favorably (*Tur Orach Chaim* 597,581). However, care should be taken not to fully content oneself with food, in order to preserve the solemnity of the day (*Beis Yosef* 597).

וְשִׁלְחוּ מָנוֹת לְאֵין נָכוֹן לוֹ — *And send portions to those unprepared.* Send gifts to the poor, who have no food of their own prepared (*Rashi; Metzudos*). Nehemiah instructed the people to fulfill the Torah's command to aid the poor during the festivals, so that they, too, might enjoy the *Yom Tov* (*Ralbag*; see *Deut*. 16:11,14; *Rambam, Hilchos Megillah* 2:17).

The Talmud (*Beitzah* 15b) interprets our verse as a reference to עֵרוּב תַּבְשִׁילִין, *eruv tavshilin*. When *Yom Tov* falls on Friday, preparing food during *Yom Tov* for the Sabbath is forbidden unless a token preparation for the Sabbath, consisting of some bread and a cooked dish, is set aside before the holiday. This token preparation is known as the *eruv tavshilin* [lit. *mixture of cooked dishes*] (*Orach Chaim* 527:1-3).[1]

The Rosh Hashanah festival described here fell on Friday. It was therefore necessary to prepare an *eruv tavshilin* on Thursday so that Sabbath preparations would be permitted during the festival. Nehemiah was concerned that some members of the community might have failed, through unavoidable circumstances, to prepare the *eruv*. He, therefore, instructed the others to *send portions to those unprepared*, i.e., to send Sabbath meals to those who were unable to prepare those meals on *Yom Tov* because they had failed to set aside the *eruv*.[2]

כִּי־קָדוֹשׁ הַיּוֹם — *For this day is sacred.* [*Leviticus* 23:2 describes the festivals as

1. Preparation of the Sabbath meals on *Yom Tov* which falls on Friday is Biblically permissible, but prohibited by Rabbinic decree. The Rabbis legislated a symbolic device — the *eruv tavshilin* — to be used in lifting the restriction. The rationale of the *eruv* is that the token Sabbath preparation set aside on Thursday is seen as the basic act of preparation, with the remaining cooking done on *Yom Tov* merely its completion (*Rama, Orach Chaim* 527:1).

2. The verse expresses this in terms of giving לְאֵין נָכוֹן לוֹ, *to those unprepared*, rather than לְאֵין לוֹ, *to those who don't have.* The Talmud (*Beitzah* 12b) deduces from this that the rules for

VIII
10-12

[10] *And he said to them, 'Go, eat rich foods, drink sweet*
beverages, and send portions to those unprepared, for
this day is sacred to our Lord; do not be melancholy, for
HASHEM's rejoicing is your strength.' [11] *The Levites*
[also] quieted all the people saying, 'Hush! For this day
is sacred; be not melancholy.' [12] *So all the people went*

מִקְרָאֵי קֹדֶשׁ, *holy convocations. Ramban* explains that the festivals are times when the people are called together to sanctify the day through prayer, festive garments, and joyous meals. The last requirement is derived from our verse: *Eat rich foods, drink sweet beverages ... for this day is sacred to our Lord.*]

וְאַל־תֵּעָצֵבוּ — *Do not be melancholy.* When the people wept (v. 9), Nehemiah instructed them not to be sad, but to rejoice, confident that God would judge the Jewish people favorably (*Malbim; Tur, Biur HaGra* 581:28).

כִּי־חֶדְוַת ה׳ הִיא מָעֻזְּכֶם — *For HASHEM's rejoicing is your strength. Hashem's* commandment to rejoice on *Yom Tov* [*Deut*. 16:14] will give you strength (*Ibn Ezra; Metzudos*).

Ralbag, however, translates *for HASHEM's rejoicing is your strength* [in him]. *Hashem's* commandment to rejoice on the festival brings strength of attachment to him. Closeness to God is best achieved through rejoicing. The commandment of rejoicing,[1] will bring you *strength in him.*

The Talmud (*Beitzah* 15b) derives from this passage that God repays those who must borrow in order to pay for *Yom Tov* food and drink. 'God says to Israel: *My children, borrow against Me, sanctify the day [Yom Tov], have faith in Me, and I shall repay you.' Rashi* explains how this is derived. *HASHEM's rejoicing,* referring to one's rejoicing for the sake of *Hashem's mitzvah, is your strength,* meaning the source of your strength in repaying the loans you took to buy the food and drink.

The Talmud adds that all of a person's income for the year is decided on Rosh Hashanah, except for the expenditures for the Sabbath and *Yom Tov,* and tuition for children's Torah education. Providence repays the funds expended for these needs without any deduction from the sum designated as the year's income.

11. וְהַלְוִיִּם מַחְשִׁים לְכָל־הָעָם — *The Levites [also] quieted all the people.* The Levites told the people to stop their weeping (*Rashi*).

כִּי־הַיּוֹם קֹדֶשׁ — *For this day is sacred. Malbim* explains that the two statements refer to the two parts of the *Yom Tov* day. The part devoted to *Hashem* through study and prayer is described as *sacred to Hashem*. The second portion, described

those who did not set aside the *eruv* out of negligence are different than for those who unavoidably failed to do so (see *Rosh* loc. cit.; *Orach Chaim* 527:7,20).

1. The prophets did not receive their prophecy at will, but prepared their minds and remained joyful, benevolent, and secluded; for prophecy is not visited upon the melancholy or the despondent, but upon the joyous. Therefore, those aspiring to prophecy had harps, drums, flutes, and violins played before them while striving for prophecy (*Rambam, Yesodei HaTorah* 7:4).

'A person's joy in performing a *mitzvah* ... is a great form of worship, and anyone avoiding this rejoicing deserves punishment. To rejoice before *Hashem* is to be great and glorious' (*Rambam, Lulav* 8:15).

כָּל־הָעָם לֶאֱכֹל וְלִשְׁתּוֹת וּלְשַׁלַּח מָנוֹת
וְלַעֲשׂוֹת שִׂמְחָה גְדוֹלָה כִּי הֵבִינוּ בַּדְּבָרִים
יג אֲשֶׁר הוֹדִיעוּ לָהֶם: וּבַיּוֹם הַשֵּׁנִי
נֶאֶסְפוּ רָאשֵׁי הָאָבוֹת לְכָל־הָעָם הַכֹּהֲנִים
וְהַלְוִיִּם אֶל־עֶזְרָא הַסֹּפֵר וּלְהַשְׂכִּיל אֶל־דִּבְרֵי
יד הַתּוֹרָה: וַיִּמְצְאוּ כָּתוּב בַּתּוֹרָה אֲשֶׁר צִוָּה יהוה
בְּיַד־מֹשֶׁה אֲשֶׁר יֵשְׁבוּ בְנֵי־יִשְׂרָאֵל בַּסֻּכּוֹת
טו בֶּחָג בַּחֹדֶשׁ הַשְּׁבִיעִי: וַאֲשֶׁר יַשְׁמִיעוּ וְיַעֲבִירוּ
קוֹל בְּכָל־עָרֵיהֶם וּבִירוּשָׁלִַם לֵאמֹר צְאוּ הָהָר

merely as *sacred*, is spent in eating and drinking (for the sake of the *mitzvah* of rejoicing on *Yom Tov*). This also contributes to the day's sanctification.

12. וּלְשַׁלַּח מָנוֹת — *Send portions.* They sent food to those who were unprepared [v. 10] (*Metzudos*).

וְלַעֲשׂוֹת שִׂמְחָה גְדוֹלָה כִּי הֵבִינוּ בַּדְּבָרִים אֲשֶׁר הוֹדִיעוּ לָהֶם — *And engage in great rejoicing, for they understood the matters of which they had been informed.* They rejoiced with their understanding of the Torah which they had been taught [vs. 7, 8] (*Metzudos*).

According to *Malbim*, the people now understood that they were commanded to rejoice, and to send gifts to the poor. They then proceeded to eat, drink, send gifts, and engage in great rejoicing.

◆§ The Second Day

13. וּבַיּוֹם הַשֵּׁנִי — *And on the second day.* This refers to the second day of Rosh Hashanah (*Rashi*). The Rabbis relate (*Beitzah* 6a; *Rosh Hashanah* 19b) that Rosh Hashanah that year was celebrated for two days (*Metzudos*).

The Torah designates one day only — the first of Tishrei — as Rosh Hashanah (*Leviticus* 23:24,25). In Biblical and Talmudic times (*Rambam, Kiddush HaChodesh* 5:3), the first day of the new month was fixed by the Supreme Court in Jerusalem, based on the testimony of witnesses who had sighted the new moon. Each month lasted at least twenty-nine days. However, when witnesses failed to appear on the thirtieth day, the day was incorporated into the old month, now swollen (מְעֻבָּר) with the extra day, and the new month began on the thirty-first day (*Rambam, Kiddush HaChodesh* 1:4-6; the subject is discussed in ArtScroll Mishnayos *Rosh Hashanah*, pgs. 14-17).

Since it was generally assumed that the witnesses would appear on the thirtieth day, Rosh Hashanah was celebrated after twenty-nine days of Elul had passed. During the period described here in Nehemiah, however, the witnesses did not appear on the thirtieth day. Thus, that day belonged to Elul, and the new year did not begin until the thirty-first day. The people gathered again on the *second day*, which was actually the first day of Tishrei, for a repetition of the Rosh Hashanah celebration (*Rashi, Beitzah* 6a, *Rosh Hashanah* 19b; see *Rambam, Kiddush HaChodesh* 5:7, 8; cf. *Haamek She'elah, Ki Savo, She'ilta* 158).

וּלְהַשְׂכִּיל אֶל־דִּבְרֵי הַתּוֹרָה — *To delve into the words of Torah.* They gathered together to learn with great concentration, so that they might understand fully the *mitzvos* written in the Torah (*Metzudos*).

14. וַיִּמְצְאוּ כָּתוּב בַּתּוֹרָה — *They found written in the Torah.* R' Yehudah HaLevi, author of the *Kuzari*, points out (through the voice of the Khazar king) that the verse apparently implies that the

to eat, drink, send portions, and engage in great rejoicing, for they understood the matters of which they had been informed.

13 *And on the second day, the family heads of all the people, the Kohanim, and the Levites gathered to Ezra the Torah scholar, to delve into the words of Torah.* 14 *They found written in the Torah that HASHEM had commanded through Moses, that the Children of Israel shall dwell in succos during the festival in the seventh month.* 15 *[Then they commanded] that it be made known, and a proclamation issued in all their cities and in Jerusalem saying: Go out to the hills and*

chain of Torah transmission from Sinai to Ezra had been broken. *They found*, i.e., rediscovered, the laws about the festival of Succos.

The Rabbi (in the dialogue of the *Kuzari*) informs the Khazar king that this is impossible (cf. 3:63). Ezra and the *Kohanim* and Levites (as well as the entire Babylonian community) had never lost touch with the details and principles of Jewish law given on Mount Sinai. They certainly knew about Succos. The people referred to in the verse, however, represented a segment of the post-destruction population living in *Eretz Yisrael*. Due to the oppression they had suffered in a land dominated by their enemies, many of these Jews were unlearned (commentary of *Otzar Nechmad*, ibid.). For them, the *mitzvah* of *succah* was a novel discovery. The *Kuzari* explains that Scripture often narrates from the perspective of the general populace. It is axiomatic, however, that, to Ezra and the Levites, and the general population, wherever isolation and persecution did not disrupt communal life, basic Torah awareness and practice were not in question.

יֵשְׁבוּ בְנֵי־יִשְׂרָאֵל בַּסֻּכּוֹת — *The Children of Israel shall dwell in succos.* [The *succah* is a temporary hut consisting of at least three walls (or two walls plus a partial, token third wall) covered with leaves, stalks, or branches which have been detached from the ground. During the seven-day Succos festival, which begins on the fifteenth day of the month of Tishrei, all male Jews are required to make the *succah* their principal dwelling place, from the passage, בַּסֻּכֹּת תֵּשְׁבוּ שִׁבְעַת יָמִים, *You shall dwell in succos for seven days* (*Leviticus* 23:42).]

בֶּחָג — *During the festival.* [The seven-day Succos holiday is referred to here merely as 'the festival' (חג), rather than 'the Succos festival.' This is based, evidently, on the Biblical passage, *celebrate it* (Succos) *as a festival* (חג) *to HASHEM for seven days* (*Leviticus* 23:41). *I Kings* 8:2 also describes the people's gathering on Succos as having taken place *during the festival* (בֶּחָג).]

◆§ Preparing the Succos

15. וַאֲשֶׁר יַשְׁמִיעוּ — *[Then they commanded] that it be made known.* The verse begins with the words *that it be made known.* The phrase *Then they commanded* is implied. For a comparable verse, see *I Samuel* 9:27 (*Rashi*).

וְיַעֲבִירוּ קוֹל — *And a proclamation issued.* The proclamation instructed the people to celebrate the festival of Succos (*Rashi*).

ח
טז־יז

וְהָבִיאוּ עֲלֵי־זַיִת וַעֲלֵי־עֵץ שֶׁמֶן וַעֲלֵי הֲדַס
וַעֲלֵי תְמָרִים וַעֲלֵי עֵץ עָבֹת לַעֲשֹׂת סֻכֹּת
טז כַּכָּתוּב: וַיֵּצְאוּ הָעָם וַיָּבִיאוּ וַיַּעֲשׂוּ לָהֶם
סֻכּוֹת אִישׁ עַל־גַּגּוֹ וּבְחַצְרֹתֵיהֶם וּבְחַצְרוֹת
בֵּית הָאֱלֹהִים וּבִרְחוֹב שַׁעַר הַמַּיִם
יז וּבִרְחוֹב שַׁעַר אֶפְרָיִם: וַיַּעֲשׂוּ כָל־הַקָּהָל
הַשָּׁבִים מִן־הַשְּׁבִי | סֻכּוֹת וַיֵּשְׁבוּ בַסֻּכּוֹת כִּי

[Presumably, this proclamation was issued after sundown, when the Rosh Hashanah holiday concluded. The people were then permitted to collect materials necessary for Succos.]

עֲלֵי־זַיִת ... — *Olive leaves ...* The people were instructed to gather leaf-covered branches for use in building the roofs of their *succos*.

Our verse is cited by the Talmud to demonstrate the basic requirements for the covering of the *succah*. All of the objects listed here to be used for the *succah's* roof — *olive leaves, leaves of the oil tree, leaves of the hadas, and leaves of the date trees, and leaves of the braided tree* — grow from the ground and are not eligible to become *tamei* (ritually impure). These attributes, the Talmud teaches, are requirements for a *succah's* covering (*Succah* 11b, 12a).

In a dissenting opinion, Rabbi Yehudah (*Succah* 36b, 37a) contends that the *succah* roof must consist of the leaves and branches of only four particular species — the citron (*esrog*), the palm (*lulav*), the braided tree (*hadas*), and the myrtle (*aravah*) — the Four Species which must be taken in the hands during Succos (*Leviticus* 23:40). Accordingly, Rabbi Yehudah maintains that the leaves of the olive and oil trees mentioned in our passage were not gathered for the *succah* roofs, but for their walls, which may be constructed of any material.

The prevailing opinion is that the *succah's* roof need not be made of the Four Species, but may be constructed from any growing thing (see *Rambam*, *Hilchos Succah* 5:1; *Orach Chaim* 629:1).

וַעֲלֵי הֲדַס — *Or leaves of the hadas.* Both the *hadas* and the *braided tree* mentioned later in the passage are types of the myrtle branch. On the *hadas*, two leaves sprout from the branch at the same level around its circumference, followed by a single leaf sprouting at a different level. These myrtle branches are known as the *hadas shoteh* (lit. *foolish hadas*, i.e., the irregular *hadas*), and they are disqualified from use with the *esrog*, *lulav* and *aravos*. The braided tree is a type of myrtle in which groups of three leaves sprout from the branch at the same level around the circumference of the stalk; this is the type which must be used as one of the Four Species. The *hadas shoteh*, however, may be used for covering the *succah*, and was, therefore, mentioned in our verse among the branches the people were to gather for use (*Rashi*; *Succah* 12a; see further *Rama*, *Orach Chaim* 641:3; see also ArtScroll Mishnayos *Succah* 3:2).

וַעֲלֵי תְמָרִים וַעֲלֵי עֵץ עָבֹת — *And leaves of the date trees and leaves of the braided tree.* These are the *lulav* and the *hadas* (*Rashi*). [They are referred to, respectively, in *Leviticus* 23:40 as כַּפֹּת תְּמָרִים, *date tree palms*, and עֲנַף עֵץ־עָבֹת, *the branch of the braided tree.*]

Besides collecting branches of the olive, oil tree, or *hadas shoteh* for the *succah* covering, the people were also to gather *lulavim* and *hadasim* to be taken on Succos as part of the Four Species. Obviously, the people were also com-

bring olive leaves, or leaves of the oil tree, or leaves of the hadas, and leaves of the date trees and leaves of the braided tree, to make succos, as it is written.
16 *So the people went out and brought, and made themselves succos, each on his roof, in their courtyards, in the courtyards of God's Temple, in the plaza of the Water Gate, and in the plaza of the Gate of Ephraim.*
17 *The entire congregation of returnees from the captivity made succos and dwelt in the succos; for the*

manded to gather *esrogim* and *aravos* to complete the Four Species. For the sake of brevity, this command is not recorded in the text (*Metzudos*).

According to *Ralbag*, however, all the objects enumerated were to be used as *succah* covering. Although any object which grows from the earth may be used, these were chosen for their decorative value or for their pleasant aroma.

לַעֲשֹׂת סֻכֹּת — *To make succos.* This phrase is related only to the command for the people to gather *olive leaves, leaves of the oil tree,* and *leaves of the hadas,* which were intended for use as covering for the *succos*. However, the two other objects gathered by the people — *leaves of the date trees* and *leaves of the braided tree* — were used as two of the Four Species (*Metzudos* from *Succah* 12a; see *Ralbag* above).

כַּכָּתוּב — *As it is written* in *Leviticus* 23:42: *You shall dwell in succos for seven days.*

Alternatively, this refers to the Torah's command (*Deuteronomy* 16:13): *You shall make the festival of Succos for yourself.*[1]

◆§ The Succos

16. וַיָּבִיאוּ — *And brought.* [They brought the branches and leaves, as instructed in v. 15.

The events in this verse, gathering the materials and building the *succos*, could have occurred any time (excluding Yom Kippur) between the conclusion of Rosh Hashanah but before the beginning of Succos, i.e., between 1 Tishrei and 15 Tishrei.]

עַל־גַּגּוֹ וּבְחַצְרֹתֵיהֶם — *On his roof, in their courtyards. Ralbag* notes that the *succos* were placed in open places, in conjunction with the Talmud's ruling that a *succah* underneath a roof or tree may not be used for the *mitzvah* [Mishnah, *Succah* 1:2].

וּבְחַצְרוֹת בֵּית הָאֱלֹהִים וּבִרְחוֹב שַׁעַר הַמַּיִם — *In the courtyards of God's Temple, in the plaza of the Water Gate.*

It is not generally permissible to build a *succah* in the public domain [and thereby deprive the public of their use of the area] (*Rama, Orach Chaim* 637:2). However, Ezra's *Beis Din*, acting as the representatives of the general interest (לֵב בֵּית דִּין מַתְנֶה), decreed that the public domain be opened for the use of *succos* (*Malbim*; see *Tosefta, Bava Kama* 6:13 with comm. of *Magen Avraham*).

17. וַיֵּשְׁבוּ בַסֻּכּוֹת — *And dwelt in the succos.* They made the *succah* their principal dwelling place, as required by

1. Based on this verse, *Avnei Nezer* (*Orach Chaim* 459) rules that building a *succah* for the holiday is not merely a preparation for the *mitzvah* of dwelling in the *succah* on *Yom Tov*, but is in itself a *mitzvah*. [Thus, according to *Avnei Nezer's* ruling, the command *to make succos as it is written* may be interpreted as a reference to the special *mitzvah* of making the *succah*.]

ח לֹא־עָשׂוּ מִימֵי יֵשׁוּעַ בִּן־נוּן כֵּן בְּנֵי יִשְׂרָאֵל
יח עַד הַיּוֹם הַהוּא וַתְּהִי שִׂמְחָה גְּדוֹלָה מְאֹד:
יח וַיִּקְרָא בְּסֵפֶר תּוֹרַת הָאֱלֹהִים יוֹם | בְּיוֹם מִן־
הַיּוֹם הָרִאשׁוֹן עַד הַיּוֹם הָאַחֲרוֹן וַיַּעֲשׂוּ־חָג
שִׁבְעַת יָמִים וּבַיּוֹם הַשְּׁמִינִי עֲצֶרֶת כַּמִּשְׁפָּט:

the *mitzvah* (*Metzudos*). 'We eat and drink and dwell in the *succah* all seven days, day and night, in the same way that we dwell at home; all seven days the home should be a temporary place and the *succah* a permanent one' (*Orach Chaim* 639:1).

כִּי לֹא־עָשׂוּ מִימֵי יֵשׁוּעַ בִּן־נוּן כֵּן בְּנֵי יִשְׂרָאֵל עַד הַיּוֹם הַהוּא — *For the Children of Israel had not done this from the days of Jeshua bin Nun until that day.* This verse presents an obvious difficulty. How is it possible that the *mitzvah* of *succah* was never fulfilled throughout the nine centuries which had elapsed from the days of Joshua until the times of Ezra? Evidently, the verse must be interpreted on another level:

According to *Ralbag*, the people now excelled in the love of God with which they fulfilled the *mitzvah* of *succah*, as expressed in their daily reading of the Torah (v. 18). Although the people had fulfilled the *mitzvah* of *succah* throughout their history, they had not achieved this closeness to *Hashem* since the days of Joshua, when the Torah was also read daily during the festival.

Ri Mitrani's interpretation is that the great level of rejoicing in the *mitzvah* of the *succah* had not been experienced since the days of Joshua.

Metzudos comments that the people now made the *succah* their *sole* dwelling place throughout the festival, although the law requires only that the *succah* be the *principal* dwelling place. Thus, they observed the *mitzvah* in its most exalted form (מִצְוָה מִן הַמֻּבְחָר) [see *Orach Chaim* 639]. This had not been done since the days of Joshua.

The Talmud (*Arachin* 32b) presents two interpretations of our verse.

One opinion is that the sanctity of *Eretz Yisrael*[1] that was first instituted when Joshua and the Israelites conquered the Promised Land had expired with the destruction of the First Temple and the exile of the nation [קְדֻשָּׁה רִאשׁוֹנָה קִדְּשָׁה לְשַׁעְתָּהּ וְלֹא קִדְּשָׁה לֶעָתִיד לָבֹא]. The sanctity of the Land was now reestablished by Ezra and his followers, when they resettled the Holy Land. It is this reactivation of the sanctity of the Land which is referred to by the passage, *the Children of Israel had not done . . . from the days of Jeshua until that day.*

Malbim wonders how our verse, which clearly describes only the unprecedented fulfillment of the *mitzvah* of *succah*, is interpreted as referring to the sanctification of the Land. He answers that the inference is based on the action of Ezra and his court in opening the public domain for the building of *succos*. The power to establish this new ruling concerning the use of public property was derived from their capacity as rededicators of the Land. This ruling meant that even those who did not own private property were able to build *succos*. In the past, however, only property owners could perform the *mitzvah*. Thus, the *mitzvah* of *succah* was now observed as never before because of the new conditions set forth by Ezra when he

1. *Kaftor Vaferach* (ch. 10) maintains that *Eretz Yisrael* was invested with its special sanctity as a place set aside for devotion to *mitzvos*, and for communion with the Divine Presence, when God promised it to the Patriarchs (*Genesis* 13:14-17, 28:4,13). Hence this special status of the Holy Land was not created by Joshua's conquest, nor did it expire with the destruction of

VIII
18
Children of Israel had not done this from the days of Jeshua bin Nun until that day; there was extremely great rejoicing. 18 *He read from the scroll of God's Torah daily, from the first day until the last; they performed the festival for seven days, and on the eighth day, the Assembly, as prescribed.*

resanctified the Land.

A second opinion in the Talmud holds that the original sanctification of *Eretz Yisrael* at the time of Joshua's conquest is eternal, and remained in place despite the destruction of the Temple and the exile [קְדֻשָּׁה רִאשׁוֹנָה קִדְּשָׁה לְשַׁעְתָּהּ וְקִדְּשָׁה לֶעָתִיד לָבֹא]. Accordingly, there was no resanctification during the time of Ezra.

Our phrase, therefore, is interpreted differently. It alludes to an unprecedented act performed by Ezra and his followers: Through their prayer they abolished the passion for idol worship (see comm. to 9:4). [The statement in the text that they made *succos* and dwelt in them is understood allegorically as referring to the great merit of Ezra (*Rashi*), which protected them during their prayer from the arguments of the accusing spirit (שָׂטָן), just as the *succah* protects those who dwell in it.] The Israelites had not prayed for the abolition of this evil passion *even in the days of Joshua*, who could have ended the lust for idolatry through prayer. Joshua failed to offer these prayers, and it was left to Ezra and his followers (who were, like Joshua, supported by the great merit of resettling the Land) to destroy the passion for idol worship.

The Talmud adds that Joshua's name, which is generally spelled יְהוֹשֻׁעַ, is spelled here יֵשׁוּעַ [Jeshua], with the letter ה missing. The deletion symbolizes Joshua's failure to bring about the demise of the desire for idolatry.

וַתְּהִי שִׂמְחָה גְּדוֹלָה מְאֹד — *There was extremely great rejoicing.* Because they had so fully performed the *mitzvah*, they rejoiced greatly (*Metzudos*).

18. וַיִּקְרָא בְּסֵפֶר תּוֹרַת הָאֱלֹהִים — *He read from the scroll of God's Torah.* Ezra read the Torah before the people (*Metzudos*).

יוֹם בְּיוֹם — *Daily* [lit. *day in the day*]. The translation follows *Rashi* and *Metzudos*.

Ibn Ezra, however, interprets *He read daily what was fitting for the day.* Each day he read the portion of the Torah suitable for that day. [*Megillah* 31a specifies the proper reading for each day of the festival. See *Orach Chaim* 659.]

מִן־הַיּוֹם הָרִאשׁוֹן עַד הַיּוֹם הָאַחֲרוֹן — *From the first day until the last.* From the first until the last day of the festival (*Metzudos*).

וַיַּעֲשׂוּ־חָג שִׁבְעַת יָמִים — *They performed the festival for seven days.* They offered the special sacrifices prescribed for the holiday [see *Numbers* 29:12-34] (*Metzudos*).

וּבַיּוֹם הַשְּׁמִינִי עֲצֶרֶת — *And on the eighth day, the Assembly.* On the eighth day, they kept the festival of *Assembly*, Shemini Atzeres (שְׁמִינִי עֲצֶרֶת), and brought the proper sacrifices (*Metzudos*).

כַּמִּשְׁפָּט — *As prescribed.* As prescribed in the Torah [*Numbers* 29:35-38] (*Metzudos*).

the Temple and the banishment of the people to exile. Yet the Talmud links the sanctity of the land with Joshua's conquest and occupation. *Kaftor Vaferach* explains that this refers only to an *additional* level of sanctity invested in the Land, which is the basis for the special *mitzvos* related to the land (מִצְוֹת הַתְּלוּיוֹת בָּאָרֶץ), i.e., tithing, *Shemittah*, etc. (see *Rambam*, *Terumos*

ט
א־ד

א וּבְיוֹם עֶשְׂרִים וְאַרְבָּעָה לַחֹדֶשׁ הַזֶּה נֶאֶסְפוּ
בְנֵי־יִשְׂרָאֵל בְּצוֹם וּבְשַׂקִּים וַאֲדָמָה עֲלֵיהֶם:
ב וַיִּבָּדְלוּ זֶרַע יִשְׂרָאֵל מִכֹּל בְּנֵי נֵכָר וַיַּעַמְדוּ
וַיִּתְוַדּוּ עַל־חַטֹּאתֵיהֶם וַעֲוֹנוֹת אֲבֹתֵיהֶם:
ג וַיָּקוּמוּ עַל־עָמְדָם וַיִּקְרְאוּ בְּסֵפֶר תּוֹרַת יהוה
אֱלֹהֵיהֶם רְבִעִית הַיּוֹם וּרְבִעִית מִתְוַדִּים
ד וּמִשְׁתַּחֲוִים לַיהוה אֱלֹהֵיהֶם: וַיָּקָם

IX

The fasting and repentance recounted in this chapter flow naturally from the experience of the High Holidays which preceded it. [See preface to chapter 8.] In essence, chapter 9 (from verse 6 till the end, verse 37) is a record of the passionate homily of repentance and confession which the Levites delivered before a subdued, receptive audience. [See prefatory remarks to verse 6 for *Malbim's* overview of the speech.] It represents the Scriptural view of human events, presenting God as the moving force of Jewish history, and, indeed, of all of the myriad events in the human experience. In addition, the speech contains a passage incorporated into the morning prayer service as well as numerous other inspirational and poetic segments.

1. וּבְיוֹם עֶשְׂרִים וְאַרְבָּעָה לַחֹדֶשׁ הַזֶּה — *On the twenty-fourth day of this month.* The preceding chapter concludes by describing the celebration of the festival of Succos, and then Shemini Atzeres, on 22 Tishrei. On the twenty-fourth day of *this month*, i.e., of Tishrei, the people gathered to fast and repent. Since fasting is forbidden on festivals and the day after a festival (*isru chag*), the people waited until 24 Tishrei to gather (*Yerushalmi, Avodah Zarah* 1:1; *Malbim*, see *Orach Chaim* 494:3, *Mishnah Berurah* 6).

Tosafos (*Rosh Hashanah* 19b), however, assert that the communal repentance was not delayed by even one day. According to *Tosafos*, the *twenty-fourth day* refers to the twenty-third of the month of Tishrei, the day following the close of the festival. Although this was, indeed, the twenty-fourth day following the appearance of the new moon, as indicated in the text, the witnesses to the moon's appearance did not appear before the Rabbinical court until the following day, which was declared the first of the calendar month of Tishrei (see comm. to 8:13). Since the first of Tishrei was actually the second day of the new moon, the twenty-third day of the month is referred to as the twenty-fourth. [See *Maharsha* to *Tosafos*; *Tzion Yerushalayim, Yerushalmi.*]

נֶאֶסְפוּ בְנֵי־יִשְׂרָאֵל — *The Children of Israel gathered.* They gathered in Jerusalem to repent their sins (*Metzudos*); specifically, for the sin of intermarriage with non-Jews [see v. 2] (*Ralbag*).

בְּצוֹם — *Fasting.* Fasting is an act of repentance, as it is written *return to me with all your hearts; with fasting, weeping, and lamenting* (*Joel* 2:12). Fasting and lamenting represent the denial of one's desires and the bitterness of one's heart, as opposed to the indulgence of one's desires

1:1-7). Thus, the frequent reference in our commentary to the expiration of the sanctity of the Land is valid only in relation to the additional sanctity generating the *Shemittah* and tithe obligations. The basic sanctity of *Eretz Yisrael*, however, remains immutable under all circumstances (cf. *Tosafos* to *Yevamos* 82b, s.v. ירושה ראשונה; also ArtScroll *Sheviis* intro. to ch. 6; ArtScroll *Ezra* 2:63 footnote 2).

On the twenty-fourth day of this month the Children of Israel gathered, fasting with sackcloth and dust over them. 2 *Israel's seed separated from all of the aliens, and then rose and confessed their sins and the transgressions of their fathers.* 3 *They remained standing in place and read from the scroll of the Torah of HASHEM, their God, one quarter of the day; [another] quarter they confessed and prostrated themselves before HASHEM their God.*

and one's pleasure while sinning (*Shaarei Teshuvah* 1:15).

The Talmud (*Berachos* 17a) states that the fast is a substitute for the offering of a sacrifice. The loss of body fat and blood by the fast is accepted in place of the burning of the sacrificial animal's fats and the sprinkling of its blood on the altar. [See *Orach Chaim* 565:4.]

וּבְשַׂקִּים וַאֲדָמָה עֲלֵיהֶם — *With sackcloth and dust over them.* The penitents wore sackcloth and placed dust on their heads as an expression of humility (*Metzudos*). Humility is part of penitence, since the repentant sinner should be aware of his lowliness which resulted from the transgression (*Shaarei Teshuvah* 1:23).

2. וַיִּבָּדְלוּ זֶרַע יִשְׂרָאֵל מִכֹּל בְּנֵי נֵכָר — *Israel's seed separated from all of the aliens.* The Israelites now separated themselves from their non-Jewish wives and children (*Rashi*; *Metzudos*). [For a discussion of the problems of intermarriage in Ezra's time and the severity of the transgression, see ArtScroll *Ezra* 9:10.]

Malbim notes that *Rashi* and *Metzudos* place the events of our chapter in the time period of the first return in the days of Cyrus (see comm. to 7:73). Accordingly, the problem of widespread intermarriage must have surfaced again some time after the repentance related here. It was Ezra's return in the seventh year of King Darius which finally resolved this matter (*Ezra* 7:8).

According to the other commentators, the events of our chapter occurred after Darius' twentieth year (2:1, see comm. to 7:73, 8:1). Presumably, although Ezra succeeded in expelling the gentile wives in the earlier period, as described in the Book of *Ezra*, later immigrants repeated the transgression of intermarriage, and the process of expulsion and repentance was reenacted after the twentieth year of Darius, as described in our chapter.

וַיַּעַמְדוּ וַיִּתְוַדּוּ — *And then rose and confessed.* Confession, *vidui*, is an essential component of repentance. In addition, remorse and resolution never to repeat the transgression are required (*Rambam*, *Teshuvah* 1:1).

Confession must be recited while standing (*Orach Chaim* 607:3, based on *Yoma* 87b). *Mishnah Berurah* explains that the standing position is indicative of humility, and hence of a whole-hearted confession.

חַטֹּאתֵיהֶם וַעֲוֹנוֹת — *Their sins and the transgressions.* *Yoma* (36b) defines חֵטְא as negligent sin, and עָוֹן as deliberate transgression.

אֲבֹתֵיהֶם — *Of their fathers*. The Talmud asserts (*Sanhedrin* 27b) that those who repeat the sins of their fathers are punished for their fathers' sins as well as their own. By continuing the practices of their sinful parents, the children express their own approval of the earlier sins, and thus render themselves equally culpable.

3. וַיָּקוּמוּ עַל־עָמְדָם — *They remained standing in place.* [See comm. to 8:7.]

וַיִּקְרְאוּ בְּסֵפֶר תּוֹרַת ה׳ אֱלֹהֵיהֶם רְבִעִית הַיּוֹם וּרְבִעִית מִתְוַדִּים וּמִשְׁתַּחֲוִים לַה׳ אֱלֹהֵיהֶם — *And read from the scroll of the Torah of HASHEM, their God, one quarter of the*

עַל־מַעֲלֵה הַלְוִיִּם יֵשׁוּעַ וּבָנִי קַדְמִיאֵל שְׁבַנְיָה ט
בֻּנִּי שֵׁרֵבְיָה בָּנִי כְנָנִי וַיִּזְעֲקוּ בְּקוֹל גָּדוֹל אֶל־ ה
יהוה אֱלֹהֵיהֶם: ה וַיֹּאמְרוּ הַלְוִיִּם יֵשׁוּעַ
וְקַדְמִיאֵל בָּנִי חֲשַׁבְנְיָה שֵׁרֵבְיָה הוֹדִיָּה שְׁבַנְיָה
פְתַחְיָה קוּמוּ בָּרְכוּ אֶת־יהוה אֱלֹהֵיכֶם מִן־
הָעוֹלָם עַד־הָעוֹלָם וִיבָרְכוּ שֵׁם כְּבֹדֶךָ וּמְרוֹמַם

day; [another] quarter they confessed and prostrated themselves before H*ASHEM their God.* The Talmud (*Megillah* 30b) explains that reading from the scroll and the confession took place during the second half of the day, i.e., during the afternoon hours, so that each event took a quarter of the day. The first half of the day, morning until midday, was spent in examining the people's actions for any evidence of misdeeds. This is derived from the description of the fast day in *Ezra* 9:4, when the people gathered with Ezra *concerning the transgression of the exile* until midday. Accordingly, *Orach Chaim* (576:16) writes: 'On every communal fast day decreed because of public affliction, the Rabbinical court and the elders would sit in the synagogue and examine the people's deeds until midday; they would eliminate the pitfalls leading to sin, admonish and investigate the robbers and remove them, subdue those who rule by force, etc. From midday until evening, one quarter of the day is spent in reading from the Torah and the Prophets, and the final quarter of the day in afternoon prayer (*Minchah*), in supplication, confession, and in crying out according to one's capacity.'

Ralbag explains that the end of the day, when the weakness and discomfort of the fast are most keenly felt, the people are most brokenhearted, and their prayers are, therefore, most likely to be accepted. Also, *Ralbag* remarks, the rectification of the people's sins by the court and the elders precedes the prayers, so that the prayers might be more readily accepted.

This follows the example of Moses, who first punished those who worshiped the golden calf, and only then prayed for forgiveness (*Exodus* 32:26-31).

☙ The Levites Cry Out

4. וַיָּקָם ... יֵשׁוּעַ וּבָנִי קַדְמִיאֵל שְׁבַנְיָה בֻּנִּי שֵׁרֵבְיָה בָּנִי כְנָנִי — *Then Jeshua, Bani, Kadmiel, Shebaniah, Buni, Sherebiah, Bani, and Chenani rose up.* The word וַיָּקָם, *rose up*, is singular, referring in particular to Jeshua. The phrase is understood, 'Jeshua rose up; similarly, Bani, Kadmiel . . . and Henani rose' (*Metzudos*).

עַל־מַעֲלֵה הַלְוִיִּם — *On the step of the Levites.* מַעֲלֵה [from עלה, to *ascend*] is translated as *step* by *Rashi* and *Metzudos*.

The Levites now stood on the steps at the Temple where they customarily stood when they sang during Temple services.

Middos 2:6 relates that three steps leading to a platform separated the Israelites' courtyard from the *Kohanim's* courtyard (*Ezras Kohanim*). The Levites stood on this platform when they sang during the daily Temple services, and it was here that they now stood to address the people (*Rashi*).

וַיִּזְעֲקוּ בְּקוֹל גָּדוֹל — *And cried out in a loud voice.* The purpose of the loud voice was to arouse wholehearted concentration on the words of prayer which follow (*Metzudos*). [*Orach Chaim* 61:4 cites the custom of reading the first passage of the *Shema* (*Hear O Israel,* H*ASHEM is our God,* H*ASHEM is One*) in a loud voice, in order to arouse the reader's wholehearted concentration.]

IX
4-5

[4] *Then Jeshua, Bani, Kadmiel, Shebaniah, Buni, Shere-
bah, Bani, and Chenani rose up on the step of the Levites,
and cried out in a loud voice to HASHEM their God.*
[5] *The Levites—Jeshua, Kadmiel, Bani, Hashabeniah, She-
rebiah, Hodeiah, Shebaniah, and Pethahiah — said, Rise
up and bless HASHEM your God, from the world until the
world; let them bless the name of Your glory, exalted*

According to the Talmud (*Yoma* 69b, *Sanhedrin* 64a), the crying out denotes an additional prayer, aside from the prayer recorded in the following passages (vs. 5-37). This prayer was specifically for the abolition of the passion for idolatry. This desire had caused the destruction of the First Temple and the death of many righteous [who were punished for the sins of their generation; see *Shabbos* 33b]. The Levites prayed that the passion be destroyed, and their prayer was granted.[1]

According to *Bach* (*Yoma* 69b), two other Talmudic interpretations apply to the crying out described in our verse. One interpretation is that the Levites pronounced the Ineffable Name of God, which ordinarily may not be uttered outside the confines of the Temple. Another interpretation is that the Levites praised God by referring to Him as *the great, powerful and awe-inspiring God* [see comm. v. 32. For a detailed explanation of both interpretations, see comm. to 8:6].

◆§ The Blessing

5. קוּמוּ בָּרְכוּ אֶת־ה׳ אֱלֹהֵיכֶם מִן־הָעוֹלָם עַד־הָעוֹלָם — *Rise up and bless HASHEM your God, from the world until the world.* The Levites addressed the people, telling them to rise up and bless *Hashem*, Who is their God from the beginning of the world until its end, i.e., whose Presence is immutable, since It has always existed and will always exist (*Ralbag*); Who rules from one end of the world to the other (*Metzudos*).

The Talmud (*Berachos* 63a; *Taanis* 16b) understands our verse as a reference to the World to Come. The people blessed *Hashem* their God from this world to the World to Come. This blessing, the Talmud explains, was inserted at the Temple prayer services into each of the eighteen blessings of the daily (*Shemoneh Esrei*) prayers. For example, the first blessing of the *Shemoneh Esrei*, which ends *Blessed are You, HASHEM, the Shield of Abraham,* was read in the Temple: *Blessed are You, HASHEM, God of Israel, from the world until the world; Blessed is the Shield of Abraham.* Similarly, the phrase *HASHEM, God of Israel, from the world until the world* was added to each blessing of the *Shemoneh Esrei*.

The Gemara states that the phrase *from the world until the world* was innovated by Ezra for use during the Second Temple. During the First Temple era only the words *from the world* were added to the Temple prayers, e.g., *may You be blessed, HASHEM, God of Israel, from the world; blessed is the shield of Abraham.* Ezra initiated the phrase *until the world,* referring to the World to Come, to controvert the denial of the existence of the next world which had arisen in his times (*Berachos* 63a).

וִיבָרְכוּ — *Let them bless.* The first part of this sentence was spoken to the people. The Levites now addressed themselves directly to God, saying that the people would *bless the name of His glory* (*Rashi*; *Metzudos*).

שֵׁם כְּבֹדֶךָ — *The name of Your glory.* God,

1. [This does not mean that all idolatry was eradicated, since idol worship is practiced even in modern times, particularly in Eastern countries. What was eradicated in Ezra's time was the passion for idolatry. *Chazon Ish* (*Letters*, 209) notes that Scripture is replete with warnings

ט עַל־כָּל־בְּרָכָה וּתְהִלָּה׃ ו אַתָּה־הוּא יהוה
ו לְבַדֶּךָ אַתָּ עָשִׂיתָ אֶת־הַשָּׁמַיִם שְׁמֵי הַשָּׁמַיִם
וְכָל־צְבָאָם הָאָרֶץ וְכָל־אֲשֶׁר עָלֶיהָ הַיַּמִּים
וְכָל־אֲשֶׁר בָּהֶם וְאַתָּה מְחַיֶּה אֶת־כֻּלָּם

in His essence, is beyond the grasp of human comprehension; consequently, our praises or blessings may not be directed towards the essence of God. We bless[1] *the name of His glory,* i.e., the name which describes His activities as Creator and Master of the universe. He makes His glory known through three things: a) His creation of the universe; b) His continual maintenance of the universe; c) His special relationship and supra-natural interaction with the righteous [see v. 7, 8] (*Malbim*).

The Talmud (*Taanis* 16b) asserts that in the Temple the people did not answer, 'Amen,' as is customary when hearing a blessing; they answered, 'May the name of the glory of His kingdom be blessed forever' (בָּרוּךְ שֵׁם כְּבוֹד מַלְכוּתוֹ לְעוֹלָם וָעֶד). This is derived from our passage, wherein the Levites stated that the people would *bless the name of Your glory*.

וּמְרוֹמַם עַל־כָּל־בְּרָכָה וּתְהִלָּה — *Exalted above every blessing and praise.* God's greatness surpasses all praises and blessings uttered by mortals, and even by the angels. His greatness is ineffable (*Ralbag*).[2] [See *Rashi* to *Exodus* 15:11.]

In *Malbim*'s opinion, the phrase *exalted above every blessing and praise* refers to the essence of God's being, which is absolutely unfathomable and beyond praise. Accordingly, *Malbim* connects this phrase with the opening words of the following verse: *You are* H*ASHEM, alone.* This refers to *Hashem*'s essence, alone and exalted, unfathomable and unreachable: *Exalted above every blessing and praise, You are* H*ASHEM alone.*

against idolatry, and with references to the Jewish people's repeated lapses into this abomination. He explains that in Biblical times, people actually lusted after idol worship. Modern man, however, cannot conceive of this passion, since it disappeared in Ezra's times.]

1. All of the blessings to be recited before performing a *mitzvah*, as composed by Ezra and his Rabbinical court (*Rambam*, *Berachos* 1:5), are grammatically inconsistent. They begin by addressing God directly, *May 'You' be blessed,* H*ASHEM*, בָּרוּךְ אַתָּה ה׳, but end by referring to God in the third person — *Who has sanctified us* (אֲשֶׁר קִדְּשָׁנוּ) *and commanded us* (וְצִוָּנוּ). This inconsistency was deliberate. The blessing is directed to God in His capacity as Creator and Master of the universe. In this sense, God is comprehensible (albeit marginally), and may be addressed directly — 'You' — as one addresses a person in direct conversation. This accounts for the opening phrase of the blessing, *May You be blessed,* H*ASHEM*. The end of the blessing, however, refers to God in His essence, the source of sanctity and of the commandments. In this sense, God is incomprehensible and unapproachable. Thus, the description of Him must be made in the third person, as one refers to a person who is not present and not seen. This accounts for the ending of the blessing — *Who has sanctified us and commanded us* (*Nefesh HaChaim* 2:3).

2. *Berachos* 33b relates that a person once recited a long list of God's praises. When he had finished, Rav Chanina admonished him: 'Have you completed all of your Master's praises? Even the three praises which we recite ("The great, powerful and awe-inspiring God") are permitted only because Moses stated them in the Torah (*Deut.* 10:17), and the Men of the Great Assembly [Ezra and his colleagues] decreed that they be recited in the prayers (9:32). Yet you pronounced all those praises? This is comparable to a mortal king who possessed a million golden dinars but was praised for having silver — is this not an insult?'

IX
6

above every blessing and praise. [6] *You are* HASHEM, *You alone; You made the heavens, the heavens of the heavens, and all their hosts, the earth and everything upon it, the seas and everything in them; You give them all life;*

⸎ The Levite's Prayer; God as the Creator

6-37. Verse 6 begins the prayer recited by the Levites. *Malbim* presents the general themes for the following verses: verses 7-8 discuss how *Hashem* especially chose Abraham and his descendants, and made a covenant to give them the Chosen Land; Verses 9-15 describe how God kept the covenant by taking them out of Egypt and leading them out of the desert; verses 15-25 tell how He brought them into the land although they turned from His word; verses 26-30 describe how the descendants of Abraham sinned in the land, angering Him; and how God nevertheless saved them repeatedly, until finally He allowed them to fall into the hands of the inhabitants of the land; verses 31-37 discuss how, despite all this, He did not abandon them or remove His special providence. Finally, the Levites beseeched God to remember their suffering and their efforts to correct their wrongdoings by initiating their own covenant [enumerated in chapter 10] to keep God's Torah.

6. אַתָּה־הוּא ה׳ לְבַדֶּךָ — *You are* HASHEM, *You alone.* This verse is the beginning of the prayer recited by the Levites (*Ralbag*; *Malbim*).

Rashi (*Bava Basra* 25a) asserts that this verse was authored by the Men of the Great Assembly (אַנְשֵׁי כְּנֶסֶת הַגְּדוֹלָה) [see footnote to v. 32]. Apparently, the Men of the Great Assembly composed the words of the prayer for the Levites. [See comm. to v. 7.]

[The daily morning prayers (פְּסוּקֵי דְזִמְרָה) include this verse through verse 11. According to some texts, the closing clause of the previous verse, וִיבָרְכוּ שֵׁם כְּבֹדֶךָ וּמְרוֹמַם עַל־כָּל־בְּרָכָה וּתְהִלָּה, is also included. The Yemenite text (תכלאל) includes this last phrase but deletes verses 6-11. [See *Siddur Tzelusa D'Avraham*, p. 225.]

The word י־ה־ו־ה used here to represent *Hashem* is derived from הֲוָיָה, denoting creativity. Only God himself can truly create: *You alone are Yud-Keh-Vav-Keh* (*Ralbag*).

אַתָּ עָשִׂיתָ אֶת הַשָּׁמַיִם — *You made the heavens. Malbim* explains that our verse shows how the universe proclaims God's glory — *You made the heavens* — their existence is evidence of Your creative act, and thus proclaims Your glory.

שְׁמֵי הַשָּׁמַיִם — *The heavens of the heavens. Ramban* (*Genesis* 1:8) interprets שָׁמַיִם, *heavens*, as the stars and heavenly bodies in the lower portion of heaven, and שְׁמֵי הַשָּׁמַיִם, *the heavens of the heavens,* as the outer reaches of space surrounding the heavens where no stars are found.

וְכָל־צְבָאָם — *And all their hosts.* This refers to the stars (*Ralbag*) and planets (*Metzudos*).

Ramban (*Genesis* 2:1) explains that the hosts of heaven are the sun, moon, and stars, as well as the angels and the souls of human beings.

וְאַתָּה מְחַיֶּה אֶת־כֻּלָּם — *You give them all life.* Mortals can only make inanimate objects which require no sustenance. God, however, sustains the universe constantly. Without him, everything would cease to exist (*Ralbag*). [See *Rambam, Yesodai HaTorah* 1:3.]

Nefesh HaChaim (1:2) cites the words of the morning prayer: *[God] in His goodness, renews the act of creation every day, constantly ...*

Ramban (preface to *Job*) also notes that

ט ז וּצְבָא הַשָּׁמַיִם לְךָ מִשְׁתַּחֲוִים׃ אַתָּה הוּא יהוה
ז־ח הָאֱלֹהִים אֲשֶׁר בָּחַרְתָּ בְּאַבְרָם וְהוֹצֵאתוֹ
ח מֵאוּר כַּשְׂדִּים וְשַׂמְתָּ שְׁמוֹ אַבְרָהָם׃ וּמָצָאתָ
אֶת־לְבָבוֹ נֶאֱמָן לְפָנֶיךָ וְכָרוֹת עִמּוֹ הַבְּרִית

the Torah's assurance of worldly satisfaction for the righteous and death and destruction for the wicked presumes God's control of nature at all times. Goodness and evil can only cause physical change through God's intervention.

וּצְבָא הַשָּׁמַיִם לְךָ מִשְׁתַּחֲוִים — *And the hosts of heaven bow to You.*[1] *Malbim* explains that this statement was intended to refute the idea that the planets are empowered to control events on earth independently of God's will. You have not abandoned earthly creatures to the dictates of the planets, for *the hosts of heaven bow to you.*

God Chose Abraham

7. אֲשֶׁר בָּחַרְתָּ בְּאַבְרָם — *You chose Abram.* The Talmud (*Berachos* 13a) asserts that this passage was stated by one of the prophets. [The text (v. 5) specifies that the Levites (who are not counted among Israel's forty-eight prophets) recited this prayer. Evidently, one of the prophets composed the prayer for them. See *R' Zvi Hirsch Chiyus*.]

Malbim explains this verse as an elaboration of the statement (v. 5) *let them bless the name of Your glory*, which refers to God's glory emanating from the universe. Our verse adds that God's glory emanates, also, from His miraculous protection of the righteous. This miraculous providence was first directed towards Abram, whom God chose as the first recipient of the providential care which supersedes the laws of nature.

וְהוֹצֵאתוֹ מֵאוּר כַּשְׂדִּים — *And brought him out of Ur Kasdim. Ur Kasdim* was the city of Abraham's youth. The name, which means the *inferno of Kasdim*, reflects the flaming kiln into which Abram was thrown by Nimrod (*Metzudos*), for destroying his father's idols (*Rashi, Genesis* 11:28).

God's miraculous rescue of Abram from the flames marked the beginning of the designation of Abram as the recipient of God's miraculous providence (*Malbim*).

וְשַׂמְתָּ שְׁמוֹ אַבְרָהָם — *And designated his name Abraham. Genesis* (17:4-5) relates that God told Abram that his name would be changed to Abraham, for he would be the father of a multitude of nations. The Talmud (*Berachos* 13a) explains that the original name אַבְרָם, *Abram*, is derived from the words אַב אֲרָם, *father of Aram*. Abram was the father, or leader, of Aram, the country of his birth. Later he was named אַבְרָהָם, *Abraham*, which is derived from the words אַב הֲמוֹן, *father of multitudes*. This refers to Abraham's status as the father of a *multitude of nations*, i.e., the Jewish people, consisting of twelve tribes, each

1. Based on different interpretations of our verse, the Talmud (*Bava Basra* 25a) debates whether the Divine Presence is found equally in all places.

One opinion is that the heavens bow to Him wherever they are. Mortal messengers, the Talmud explains, must return to the one who sent them after completing their task. However, the hosts of heaven need not do this, but may bow in whichever place they may be, since the *Shechinah* (the manifestation of God's presence) is omnipresent.

A second Talmudic opinion disagrees, contending that the *Shechinah* resides in the west. *The hosts of heaven bow to You* alludes to the sun and the moon, which rise from the east, and then descend, as if bowing, towards the west, indicating that the *Shechinah* resides there.

and the hosts of heaven bow to You. [7] *You are* HASHEM *the God, You chose Abram and brought him out of Ur Kasdim, and designated his name Abraham.* [8] *You found his heart faithful before You, and made a covenant with*

of which is considered a nation (*Maharasha*).

The Talmud (*Nedarim* 33b) points out that the name אַבְרָם is numerically equivalent to 243, while אַבְרָהָם equals 248. At first Abram was master over 243 of the 248 organs of his body — he had not yet mastered his two eyes, his two ears, and his reproductive organ. With the change to the name Abraham (when he was circumcised [see comm. to v. 8]), he was made master of all 248 organs. *Ran* explains that all of Abraham's senses, as well as the limbs of his body, were placed completely under his control. His senses of sight, hearing and touch could be activated or deactivated at will. Thus Abraham functioned only for *mitzvos*[1] (see *Rashi*, *Genesis* 17:1).

The Talmud in *Berachos* adds that anyone calling Abraham by his earlier name Abram transgresses the positive commandment *Let your name be Abraham*, or the negative commandment, *Your name shall no longer be called Abram* (*Genesis* 17:5).[2] Despite this prohibition, our passage describes Abraham with the original name Abram because its purpose is to recount the praises of God (Who chose him when he was still called Abram and designated his name to Abraham — *Rashi* ibid.).

◆§ The Covenant

8. וּמָצָאתָ אֶת־לְבָבוֹ נֶאֱמָן לְפָנֶיךָ — *You found his heart faithful before You.* This refers to the ten tests which Abraham withstood, attesting to his faithful heart (*Malbim*; see *Avos* 5:3). [The word נֶאֱמָן also alludes to the concept of *constant* or *unchanging*; see 10:1; *Ramban*, *Exodus* 17:12. Abraham's heart was unchanging in his absolute devotion to God.]

Yalkut explains the significance of God's *finding* Abraham's heart faithful, by comparing the matter to a king who lost one of the crown jewels. His entire court began sweeping the area. The first attempts failed to locate the jewel, but finally, after much searching, it was found. Similarly, the Torah lists the descendants of Noah until Abraham (*Genesis* 11:10-26). It was necessary to list these names to teach that God searched in every generation for a devoted heart, until He found it in Abraham.

וְכָרוֹת עִמּוֹ הַבְּרִית — *And made a covenant with him.* Although the text here discusses only the covenant concerning the Holy Land, *Yalkut* interprets the phrase *covenant with him* as an allusion to the covenant of circumcision. Because of his advanced age [99 years (*Genesis* 17:1)], Abraham was unable to

1. In relating the story of Abraham's binding up of Isaac and his preparation to slaughter him, *Akeidas Yitzchak* (*Genesis* ch. 22) describes Abraham's grasping of the slaughtering knife: *And Abraham sent forth his hand, and took the knife to slaughter his son.* Why is Abraham's grasping of the knife described as *sending forth* his hand? It was God's will that Abraham indicate his readiness to sacrifice Isaac by placing him on the Altar. However, it was not the will of God that Abraham actually perform the slaughter (see *Rashi* to *Genesis* 22:12). Thus, Abraham's hand, conditioned to operate only for a *mitzvah*, would not move. It took an extraordinary exertion of will on Abraham's part to force the unwilling hand into action — *he sent forth his hand*, literally forced it into action.

2. *Pri Chadash* (*Orach Chaim* 67) maintains that the transgression is of Rabbinic origin. The Biblical passage cited by the Talmud is not the actual source for the prohibition, but is merely the allusion (אַסְמַכְתָּא) upon which the rabbis based their opinion (cf. *Tzlach*; *Dagul Merevavah* to *Orach Chaim* 156).

לָתֵת אֶת־אֶרֶץ הַכְּנַעֲנִי הַחִתִּי הָאֱמֹרִי וְהַפְּרִזִּי
וְהַיְבוּסִי וְהַגִּרְגָּשִׁי לָתֵת לְזַרְעוֹ וַתָּקֶם אֶת־
ט דְּבָרֶיךָ כִּי צַדִּיק אָתָּה׃ וַתֵּרֶא אֶת־עֳנִי אֲבֹתֵינוּ
בְּמִצְרָיִם וְאֶת־זַעֲקָתָם שָׁמַעְתָּ עַל־יַם־סוּף׃
י וַתִּתֵּן אֹתֹת וּמֹפְתִים בְּפַרְעֹה וּבְכָל־עֲבָדָיו

perform the circumcision on himself. God then aided Abraham and together they performed the circumcision. Thus, God literally made the covenant with him (*Rashi, Genesis* 17:25).

[The allusion to the *bris milah*, covenant of circumcision, is appropriate here, since this verse follows the change to the name Abraham (v. 7). This change was made when God commanded Abraham to circumcise himself (*Genesis* 17:4-5). *Ramban* explains that Abraham's elevation through the circumcision covenant made him worthy of fathering Isaac, and through him the Jewish nation. Since the name אַבְרָהָם signifies אַב הֲמוֹן, *the father of multitudes*, or the father of the Jewish people (see comm. to v. 7), it follows that the new name was based on the circumcision.]

לָתֵת אֶת־אֶרֶץ — *To give the land.* This refers to בְּרִית בֵּין הַבְּתָרִים, the *Covenant between the Sections* (*Genesis* 15), when God promised to give *Eretz Yisrael*, the Land of Israel, to Abraham's descendants (*Ralbag*).[1]

Malbim explains that *Eretz Yisrael* is the place where God provides miraculous providential aid to the Jewish people. Thus, the covenant promising Abraham's descendants the Holy Land follows God's miraculous rescue of Abraham from Ur Kasdim (v. 7).

הַכְּנַעֲנִי הַחִתִּי הָאֱמֹרִי וְהַפְּרִזִּי וְהַיְבוּסִי וְהַגִּרְגָּשִׁי — *The Canaanite, the Hitite, the Emorite, the Perizite, the Jebusite, and the Girgashite.* This verse mentions only six of the ten pagan nations mentioned in God's promise to Abraham [the others are Kenites, the Kenizites, the Kadmonites, and the Rephaim (*Genesis* 15:19, 20)], because only their land was given to the Jewish people who followed Joshua into the Holy Land. The land of the other four will be given to the Jews only during the final redemption, with the coming of the Messiah (*Ralbag*). [See *Rashi* to *Genesis* 15:19.]

[In addition to the six nations recorded here (and in *Genesis* 15:20, 21), a seventh people — the Hivites — is mentioned in the Torah (*Deut*. 7:1). Perhaps the names Rephaim and Hivites can be used interchangeably (see further, ArtScroll *Genesis* 15:20).]

לָתֵת לְזַרְעוֹ — [Lit. *to give*] *to his descendants.* The text repeats the words *to give*, reading literally: [*You*] *made a covenant 'to give' the land of the Canaanite, the Hitite . . . and the Girgashite, 'to give' to his descendants.* The repetition is necessary because of the lengthy list of names inserted after the first word *to give*; the words are repeated to clarify that the verse means *to give to his descendants* (*Metzudos*).

Malbim interprets the repetition as two distinct references. It was given to Abraham in the sense that he had God's guarantee. It was furthermore given to his descendants in the literal sense, when they conquered the land (*Malbim*).

וַתָּקֶם אֶת־דְּבָרֶיךָ — *And You upheld Your word.* God carried out His word (the

1. It was customary for the parties establishing a covenant to dissect an animal and walk between its sections (to signify that, like the sections of the animal, the two parties now became parts of a whole) [*Rashi, Genesis* 15:10].

him to give the land of the Canaanite, the Hitite, the Emorite, the Perizite, the Jebusite, and the Girgashite to his descendants; and You upheld Your word, for You are righteous. 9 *You observed the affliction of our forefathers in Egypt, and You heard their cries at the Sea of Reeds.* 10 *You performed omens and wonders against Pharaoh and all his servants, and*

covenant) by giving Abraham's children the Land, and by elevating them spiritually so that they might deserve the Land (*Ralbag*).

כִּי צַדִּיק אָתָּה׃ — *For You are righteous.* God was righteous by fulfilling His promise (*Ralbag*). In *Malbim's* view, He was righteous in ejecting the pagan peoples[1] from the Holy Land and giving it to the Israelites.

The Redemption from Egypt

9. וַתֵּרֶא אֶת־עֳנִי אֲבֹתֵינוּ — *You observed the affliction of our forefathers.* This verse alludes to *Exodus* 3:7, where God appeared to Moses and said to him, *'I have observed the affliction of My people in Egypt . . .'*

The affliction in Egypt is related to the promise that Abraham's descendants would be given the Land of Israel (v. 8), since God stipulated in the Covenant between the Parts (*Genesis* 15; see comm., v. 8) that Abraham's children would endure the Egyptian bondage before inheriting the Land. The Egyptian bondage was a necessary preparation for the entrance into *Eretz Yisrael*. Egypt was the crucible which shaped a nation worthy of God's miraculous, providential care (*Malbim*; see comm. to v. 7).

וְאֶת־זַעֲקָתָם שָׁמַעְתָּ עַל־יַם־סוּף — *And You heard their cries at the Sea of Reeds.* [The reference is to the Biblical passage: *And Pharaoh came close; the Children of Israel lifted their eyes, and lo! Egypt was traveling after them! They were extremely afraid, and the Children of Israel cried out to Hashem* (*Exodus* 14:10).]

When the Jewish people were trapped with the Sea of Reeds before them and Pharaoh's army in pursuit, God heard their cries and provided His special providence to rescue them. Although the Israelites were not worthy of being rescued, God heard their cries because He had promised their forefathers that He would redeem them (*Ralbag*).[1]

10. וַתִּתֵּן אֹתֹת וּמֹפְתִים — *You performed omens and wonders.* [This refers to the Biblical passage: *HASHEM took us out of Egypt . . . with omens and wonders* (*Deut*. 26:8).]

Ramban (*Deut*. 13:2) explains the meaning of *omens* and *wonders*. The אוֹת, *omen*, refers to any occurrence foretold through prophecy. The word אוֹת is derived from אָתָא — to *come* [as *Deut*. 33:2] (*Ramban*; see *Chavel*)], indicating that it was predicted that the occurrence *would come*. In Egypt the punishment of עָרוֹב (mixture of wild

1. The Torah itself testifies that these people forfeited their right to the Land because of their evil actions (see ArtScroll *Genesis* 15:16; *Rashi* to *Genesis* 1:1).

2. *Rashi* in *Exodus* 14:10 comments that the people, at this moment, followed a trait they had learned from their forefathers — that of crying out in prayer. Thus, it was appropriate that they were saved through the merit of the forefathers. By adopting the saintly activity of the Patriarchs, they proved themselves worthy of benefiting from God's promise to redeem their descendants.

ט
יא־יב

וּבְכָל־עַם אַרְצוֹ כִּי יָדַעְתָּ כִּי הֵזִידוּ עֲלֵיהֶם
יא וַתַּעַשׂ־לְךָ שֵׁם כְּהַיּוֹם הַזֶּה: וְהַיָּם בָּקַעְתָּ
לִפְנֵיהֶם וַיַּעַבְרוּ בְתוֹךְ־הַיָּם בַּיַּבָּשָׁה וְאֶת־
רֹדְפֵיהֶם הִשְׁלַכְתָּ בִמְצוֹלֹת כְּמוֹ־אֶבֶן בְּמַיִם
יב עַזִּים: וּבְעַמּוּד עָנָן הִנְחִיתָם יוֹמָם וּבְעַמּוּד

animals which attacked the Egyptians) was predicted beforehand, when God said: מָחָר יִהְיֶה הָאֹת הַזֶּה, *Tomorrow this omen shall occur* (*Exodus* 8:19). The מוֹפֵת, *wonder*, refers to the occurrence openly transcending laws of nature, although not necessarily foretold in advance. The word מוֹפֵת is a shortened form of מוּפְלָאת, *marvelous* or *wonderful*. The wonders in Egypt were God's miraculous deeds, performed without previous predictions, such as the changing of Moses' staff into a snake before Pharaoh. This was described by God as מֹפֵת (*Exodus* 4:21).

Our verse, which describes the omens and wonders in the land of Egypt, corresponds with the previous statement (v. 9), *You observed the affliction of our forefathers in Egypt*. The following verse, which portrays the splitting of the Sea of Reeds, corresponds with the statement (v. 9), *And you heard their cries at the Sea of Reeds* (*Malbim*).

כִּי יָדַעְתָּ כִּי הֵזִידוּ עֲלֵיהֶם — *For You knew that they did evil against them.* No injustice was done when the Egyptians were punished, for *You knew that they did evil against them*. Pharaoh and the Egyptians had persecuted the Jews dreadfully. They intended, finally, to destroy them completely, as Pharaoh commanded, *'Let every [Jewish] son born be cast into the river'* (*Exodus* 1:22). Thus, the Egyptians clearly deserved God's punishment.

Similarly, God was justified in hardening Pharaoh's heart and denying him the choice to free the Jews (*Exodus* 10:1). He punished Pharaoh for his evil wickedness against the Israelites *before*, when he was free to choose between good and evil. The hardening of the heart was done later, to permit God to reveal His wonders to the Jewish people, so that they might be aware of His greatness (*Ralbag*).

Rambam (*Genesis* 15:14), too, interprets our phrase as a justification of God's punishment against the entire Egyptian people. Why were they punished, *Ramban* asks, when God had already said to Abraham: *Your descendants shall be strangers in a land not their own, and shall be enslaved to them, and they shall afflict them* (*Genesis* 15:13)? Were the Egyptians not performing a *mitzvah* in fulfilling God's will that the Jews be enslaved? *Ramban* answers that the Egyptians oppressed the Jews far in excess of God's statement to Abraham. God had said only that Abraham's children would be *enslaved* and *afflicted*, but the Egyptians tried to limit the Jewish population, embittered their lives with hard labor, and cast their sons into the river (*Exodus* 1). It was for these excesses that the Egyptians were punished.

Furthermore, the excessive persecution inflicted by the Egyptians indicated that their intentions generally were not to fulfill God's will, but were hateful and destructive. Thus, they were punished not only for the excessive affliction over and above God's statement to Abraham, but for all of their persecution of the Jews. Although God had willed some persecution, the Egyptians were judged by their hateful intent, and were punished as if there had been no heavenly decree of enslavement (see *Chavel*, notes to *Ramban*; *Kedushas HaLevi*).

all the people of his land, for You knew that they did evil
against them; and You made a name for Yourself, as this
day. 11 *You split the sea before them, and they crossed*
through the sea on dry land; but their pursuers You cast
into the depths like a stone in mighty waters. 12 *You led*
them daily with a pillar of cloud and with a pillar of

וַתַּעַשׂ־לְךָ שֵׁם — *And You made a name for Yourself.* Through the omens and wonders mentioned at the beginning of the verse, *You made a name for Yourself* (*Ralbag*).

The omens and wonders in Egypt were intended to make God's name renowned, as the Torah says (*Exodus* 10:1-2): *I have hardened his* [*Pharaoh's*] *heart, and the heart of his servants, that I might place these omens within him; so that you should retell, in the ears of your son and your son's son, how I toyed with Egypt, and My omens which I placed in them; then you will know that I am* HASHEM (*Malbim*). This is realized each year on the night of Passover when every Jew is commanded to relate to his children the story of the Exodus from Egypt. [See *Rambam, Chametz U'Matzah* 7:1.]

כְּהַיּוֹם הַזֶּה — *As this day.* Your fame spread then, and became as great as it is now, when everyone recognizes You (*Metzudos*).

11. וְהַיָּם בָּקַעְתָּ לִפְנֵיהֶם — *You split the sea before them.* The splitting of the sea is yet another of God's miracles through which He revealed His greatness to the Israelites (*Ralbag*).

וַיַּעַבְרוּ בְתוֹךְ־הַיָּם בַּיַּבָּשָׁה — *And they crossed through the sea on dry land.* When the Israelites went into the sea it had not yet divided; they actually went into the water. They kept marching into the water until it reached their noses. At that moment, the sea split and they found themselves on dry land. Thus, the verse says, *and they crossed through the sea — on dry land.* They crossed the sea before it became dry land (*Shemos Rabbah*).

וְאֶת־רֹדְפֵיהֶם הִשְׁלַכְתָּ בִמְצוֹלֹת כְּמוֹ־אֶבֶן בְּמַיִם עַזִּים — *But their pursuers You cast into the depths like a stone in mighty waters.* [This verse is based on *Exodus* 15:5: *They* [the Egyptian pursuers] *sank into the depths like a stone.*] You cast the Egyptian pursuers into the depths so forcefully that they plunged to the bottom like a stone (*Ralbag*), which sinks rapidly to the bottom even in mighty, rushing water (*Metzudos*).

After splitting the upper part of the sea, God made the crossing easy by turning the lower waters into dry land. When they finished crossing, the dry land returned to its original liquid state, and the Egyptians were cast into its depths. *The depths*, then, refers to the very same waters over which the Israelites had passed (*Siddur HaGra, Avnei Eliyahu*).

12. וּבְעַמּוּד עָנָן הִנְחִיתָם יוֹמָם — *You led them daily with a pillar of cloud.* [This verse is based on *Exodus* 13:21: HASHEM *went before them daily in a pillar of cloud to lead them on the way, and at night in a pillar of fire to illuminate for them.*] The Israelites were accompanied throughout their wanderings in the desert by clouds of glory which hovered over them and protected them. The *succah* in which the Jews of all generations are commanded to live during the Succos festival commemorates those clouds. (See *Succah* 11b; *Rosh Hashanah* 3a; *Rashi*, *Leviticus* 23:43.)

The pillar of cloud showed that God's presence rested among the Jewish people,

אֵשׁ לַיְלָה לְהָאִיר לָהֶם אֶת־הַדֶּרֶךְ אֲשֶׁר יֵלְכוּ־
יג בָהּ: וְעַל הַר־סִינַי יָרַדְתָּ וְדַבֵּר עִמָּהֶם מִשָּׁמָיִם
וַתִּתֵּן לָהֶם מִשְׁפָּטִים יְשָׁרִים וְתוֹרוֹת אֱמֶת
יד חֻקִּים וּמִצְוֹת טוֹבִים: וְאֶת־שַׁבַּת קָדְשְׁךָ
הוֹדַעְתָּ לָהֶם וּמִצְווֹת וְחֻקִּים וְתוֹרָה צִוִּיתָ לָהֶם
טו בְּיַד מֹשֶׁה עַבְדֶּךָ: וְלֶחֶם מִשָּׁמַיִם נָתַתָּ לָהֶם
לִרְעָבָם וּמַיִם מִסֶּלַע הוֹצֵאתָ לָהֶם לִצְמָאָם
וַתֹּאמֶר לָהֶם לָבוֹא לָרֶשֶׁת אֶת־הָאָרֶץ אֲשֶׁר־

as stated in *Numbers* 14:14 — *That You, HASHEM, are seen eye to eye, with Your cloud standing over them; You go before them daily with the pillar of cloud, and with the pillar of fire at night* (*Malbim*).

13. וְעַל הַר־סִינַי יָרַדְתָּ וְדַבֵּר עִמָּהֶם — *You descended on Mount Sinai and spoke to them.* [This refers to the Biblical passages describing God's appearance at Sinai to give the Torah: *HASHEM descended on Mount Sinai* (*Exodus* 19:20); *Face to face, HASHEM spoke with you on the mountain, from within the fire* (*Deut.* 5:4).]

Rambam (*Yesodei HaTorah* 8:1) describes the revelation at Sinai: 'Our eyes, not those of strangers, saw; and our ears, not those of others, heard the fire and the sounds and the flames when he [Moses] approached the blackness, with the voice speaking to him while we heard: "*Moses, Moses, go and say to them . . .*" '

You lowered the heavens and spread them over Mount Sinai (*Metzudos*). One might think that God literally descended on Mount Sinai — but the passage states, *I spoke to you from Heaven* (*Exodus* 20:19). This teaches that He [God] lowered the upper and lower heavens, and spread them over the mountain like a sheet over a bed. Then the throne of glory descended upon them (*Rashi*, *Exodus* 20:19).

Ralbag remarks that God spoke from heaven in a wondrous way, with miraculous voices and sounds which the people actually *saw and heard*. [See *Rashi*, *Exodus* 20:15.]

וַתִּתֵּן לָהֶם מִשְׁפָּטִים יְשָׁרִים — *You gave them righteous laws.* This refers to the laws in the Ten Commandments governing one's conduct towards one's fellows: — *Do not desire your fellow's home, Do not bear false witness, Do not commit adultery, Do not steal, Do not commit murder, and Honor your father and your mother* (*Ralbag*).

Malbim, however, interprets *righteous laws* as referring to the laws governing relations with one's fellow enumerated in the portion of *Mishpatim* (*Exodus* 21-24). All of these laws were given by God to Moses while the people stood at Mount Sinai. [See *Ramban*, *Exodus* 24:1.]

וְתוֹרוֹת אֱמֶת — *And true teachings. Malbim* explains that this phrase refers to teachings concerning faith and belief, i.e., *teachings of truth. Ralbag* specifies that the reference is to the first two of the Ten Commandments [which refer to faith and belief]: *I am HASHEM your God*, and *Do not have any false gods* (*Ralbag*).

חֻקִּים וּמִצְוֹת טוֹבִים — *Statutes and commandments [for] good. Statutes* [חֻקִּים] refers to the *mitzvos* given with no explanation of their reason, such as *Do not cook a kid in its mother's milk* [*Exodus* 23:19] (*Rashi*, *Numbers* 19:2; *Malbim*). [See also comm. to 10:30.]

According to *Malbim*, the phrase

fire at night to illuminate for them the way they were to
travel. 13 *You descended on Mount Sinai and spoke to*
them from heaven; You gave them righteous laws and
true teachings, and statutes and commandments [for]
good. 14 *You made Your sacred Sabbath known to*
them, and commanded them commandments, statutes,
and teachings through Your servant Moses. 15 *You gave*
them bread from heaven for their hunger, and ex-
tracted for them water from the rock for their thirst;
and You told them to come and inherit the Land which

commandments for good refers to the commandments to be good to others, such as *to lend people money* (*Exodus* 22:24).

14. וְאֶת־שַׁבַּת קָדְשְׁךָ הוֹדַעְתָּ לָהֶם — *You made Your sacred Sabbath known to them.* Even before the Israelites in the desert reached Mount Sinai, God made the Sabbath known to them through the *manna* (מן). By doubling the portion of *manna* which fell each Friday, and withholding the *manna* on the Sabbath, God made known the special sanctity of the Sabbath (*Ralbag*).

Malbim, however, comments that the reference is to the *mitzvah*: *Remember the Sabbath day to sanctify it* (*Exodus* 20:8) stated in the Ten Commandments, and *On the seventh day you shall rest* (*Exodus* 23:12), repeated in the portion of *Mishpatim*. *God made the Sabbath known to them*, i.e., made known to them the articles of faith represented by Sabbath observance — (1) faith in the truth of God's act of creation, when He rested on the seventh day, and (2) faith in God's continuous providential ordering of world events [הַשְׁגָּחָה].

The Sabbath is singled out from all the other Ten Commandments because it is a day honored by physical rest and intellectual edification (*Ibn Ezra*).

וּמִצְווֹת וְחֻקִּים וְתוֹרָה צִוִּיתָ לָהֶם בְּיַד מֹשֶׁה עַבְדֶּךָ — *And commanded them commandments, statutes, and teachings through Your servant Moses.* After hearing the Commandments from God, the Israelites feared they would expire if He continued to speak to them. They, therefore, requested that Moses speak to them in the future [*Exodus* 20:16]. Henceforth, God gave the commandments, statutes, and teachings through Moses (*Ralbag*).

Malbim asserts that the reference here is to the commandments, statutes, and teachings given to the Israelites through Moses while they camped in the desert around Mount Sinai. This includes all of the commandments in the books of *Exodus*, *Leviticus*, and *Numbers* until *Numbers* 12:16.

15. וְלֶחֶם מִשָּׁמַיִם נָתַתָּ לָהֶם לִרְעָבָם — *You gave them bread from heaven for their hunger.* The phenomenon of *manna*, bread from heaven, was another example by which God used miracles to bring the Jewish people closer to Him (*Ralbag*).

וּמַיִם מִסֶּלַע הוֹצֵאתָ לָהֶם לִצְמָאָם — *And extracted for them water from the rock for their thirst.* On two occasions [*Exodus* 16:6, *Numbers* 20:11], God extracted water from the rock for the Israelites (*Ralbag*).

וַתֹּאמֶר לָהֶם לָבוֹא לָרֶשֶׁת אֶת־הָאָרֶץ — *And You told them to come and inherit the Land.* God's promise that the Israelites would inherit the Land was stated in Moses' remarks to the people (*Deut.* 1:21):

טז נָשָׂאתָ אֶת־יָדְךָ לָתֵת לָהֶם: וְהֵם וַאֲבֹתֵינוּ
הֵזִידוּ וַיַּקְשׁוּ אֶת־עָרְפָּם וְלֹא שָׁמְעוּ אֶל־
יז מִצְוֹתֶיךָ: וַיְמָאֲנוּ לִשְׁמֹעַ וְלֹא־זָכְרוּ נִפְלְאֹתֶיךָ
אֲשֶׁר עָשִׂיתָ עִמָּהֶם וַיַּקְשׁוּ אֶת־עָרְפָּם וַיִּתְּנוּ־
רֹאשׁ לָשׁוּב לְעַבְדֻתָם בְּמִרְיָם וְאַתָּה אֱלוֹהַּ
°חֶסֶד ק׳ סְלִיחוֹת חַנּוּן וְרַחוּם אֶרֶךְ־אַפַּיִם וְרַב־°וחסד
יח וְלֹא עֲזַבְתָּם: אַף כִּי־עָשׂוּ לָהֶם עֵגֶל מַסֵּכָה
וַיֹּאמְרוּ זֶה אֱלֹהֶיךָ אֲשֶׁר הֶעֶלְךָ מִמִּצְרָיִם

See, HASHEM your God placed the Land before you, go up and inherit ... (*Malbim*). According to *Ralbag*, our passage refers to God's instructions to the Israelites in the desert to send spies to the land of Canaan (*Numbers* 13:2) so that they might capture the land more easily. [See *Ramban*, *Rashi* to *Numbers* 13:2.]

אֲשֶׁר נָשָׂאתָ אֶת־יָדְךָ לָתֵת לָהֶם — *Which You raised up Your hand.* This refers to *Exodus* 6:8 — *And I shall bring you to the Land which I raised My hand to give to Abraham, Isaac, and Jacob ...* (*Rashi*; *Metzudos*). [God's promise to the Patriarchs is stated in *Genesis* 12:7, 15:18, 17:18,19, 26:3, 28:4.]

The raising of God's hand denotes His oath (*Ralbag*).

16. וְהֵם וַאֲבֹתֵינוּ הֵזִידוּ — *But they and our ancestors were wicked. They* — the twelve spies who spied out the land of Canaan — *and our ancestors* — the rest of the people — were wicked (*Ralbag*). *Metzudos*, however, translates *They — our ancestors — were wicked.*

The wickedness refers to the people's desire to send spies (*Malbim*). *Rashi* (*Numbers* 13:2) explains that the people sinned in requesting spies to ascertain whether the land was good. Since God had already informed them of the excellence of *Eretz Yisrael* (*Exodus* 3:17), they should have depended on His word. According to *Ramban* (*Numbers* 13:2), the sin lay in the people's unwillingness to unquestioningly follow God's cloud wherever it would lead them. They should have depended upon His power to conquer the land.

וַיַּקְשׁוּ אֶת־עָרְפָּם — *They stiffened their necks.*[1] This is a figurative way of depicting the people's unwillingness to follow Hashem. It was as if their necks were stiff, and could not be turned towards God (*Metzudos*).

17. וַיְמָאֲנוּ לִשְׁמֹעַ — *They refused to listen.* When the spies delivered their malicious report about the Holy Land, the people refused to listen to Joshua and Caleb, who said to them (*Numbers* 14:7-8): *'The Land which we passed through ... is extremely good. If God*

1. *Maharal* (*Netzach Yisrael* 25) asserts that even the wickedness of the Jewish people is rooted in goodness. The very stiff-neckedness (קְשֵׁה עֹרֶף) which caused the people's sinfulness (*Exodus* 33:5) is a quality of spirituality. Physical beings are easily swayed, being drawn from one passion to the next. More exalted spiritual beings, however, tend naturally towards constancy and continuity, and will not easily change. Thus, the Israelites, who are naturally spiritual and intellectual, tend to persist in their attitudes and activities; even when these activities are wicked, the Jewish personality follows its instinctive spiritual tendencies, and clings stiff-neckedly to the sinfulness.

You raised up Your hand to give them. [16] *But they and*
our ancestors were wicked; they stiffened their necks,
and did not listen to Your commandments. [17] *They*
refused to listen, and did not remember Your marvels
which You performed with them; they stiffened their
necks and, in their rebelliousness, appointed a leader to
return to their bondage. But You are the God of forgive-
ness, benevolent and compassionate, slow to anger and
abundantly kind, and You did not forsake them.
[18] *Although they had made themselves a molten calf and*
said, 'This is your god who brought you up from Egypt,'

desires us, He will bring us to this Land and give it to us — a land flowing with milk and honey' (*Ralbag*).

The people also refused to heed Moses' words (*Deut*. 1:29-30): *Do not be broken, do not fear them. HASHEM, your God who goes before you, will do battle for you, like all that He did for you in Egypt before your eyes* (*Malbim*).

וְלֹא־זָכְרוּ נִפְלְאֹתֶיךָ אֲשֶׁר עָשִׂיתָ עִמָּהֶם — *And did not remember Your marvels which You performed with them.* They did not remember the marvels God had wrought previously, which should have caused them to have absolute faith in His ability to perform any miracle He wished (*Ralbag*).

וַיַּקְשׁוּ אֶת־עָרְפָּם — *They stiffened their necks.* They did not have the required faith in God (*Ralbag*).

וַיִּתְּנוּ־רֹאשׁ לָשׁוּב לְעַבְדֻתָם — *And ... appointed a leader to return to their bondage.* They never actually appointed a leader, but wished to do so, when they said (*Numbers* 14:4) ... *Let us appoint a leader and return to Egypt* (*Ralbag; Metzudos*). *Rashi* (ibid.) comments that they actually meant: 'Let us appoint a false god.'

בְּמִרְיָם — *In their rebelliousness.* Their wish to return to Egypt stemmed from their great rebelliousness (*Metzudos*). [This verse coincides with the verse (מְרַגְּלִים) in *Deut.* 1:26: *You did not desire to go up; you rebelled against the words of HASHEM your God.*]

אֶרֶךְ־אַפַּיִם — *Slow to anger.* You did not punish them immediately but allowed them to wander in the desert for forty years [*Numbers* 14:34] (*Ralbag*).

וְלֹא עֲזַבְתָּם — *And You did not forsake them.* During the forty years of wandering in the desert, God did not forsake them, but provided His miraculous providential aid [see v. 19] so that they might become more devoted to Him. This came as a result of God's covenant with the Patriarchs (*Ralbag*; see comm. to vs. 7, 8).

18. אַף כִּי־עָשׂוּ לָהֶם עֵגֶל מַסֵּכָה — *Although they had made themselves a molten calf.* Their refusal of the Land (v. 16,17) was not their first sin — they had previously worshiped the golden calf. For the transgression alone they deserved destruction (*Exodus* 32:8-10). Yet, in Your great compassion, You did not forsake them (*Malbim*).

וַיֹּאמְרוּ זֶה אֱלֹהֶיךָ אֲשֶׁר הֶעֶלְךָ מִמִּצְרָיִם — *And said, 'This is your god who brought you up from Egypt.'* (This corresponds with *Exodus* 32:4 — *He [Aaron] made it into a molten calf, and they said, 'These*

יט וַֽיַּעֲשׂוּ נֶאָצוֹת גְּדֹלוֹת: וְאַתָּה בְּרַחֲמֶיךָ הָרַבִּים
לֹא עֲזַבְתָּם בַּמִּדְבָּר אֶת־עַמּוּד הֶעָנָן לֹא־סָר
מֵעֲלֵיהֶם בְּיוֹמָם לְהַנְחֹתָם בְּהַדֶּרֶךְ וְאֶת־עַמּוּד
הָאֵשׁ בְּלַיְלָה לְהָאִיר לָהֶם וְאֶת־הַדֶּרֶךְ אֲשֶׁר
כ יֵלְכוּ־בָהּ: וְרוּחֲךָ הַטּוֹבָה נָתַתָּ לְהַשְׂכִּילָם
וּמַנְךָ לֹא־מָנַעְתָּ מִפִּיהֶם וּמַיִם נָתַתָּה לָהֶם
כא לִצְמָאָם: וְאַרְבָּעִים שָׁנָה כִּלְכַּלְתָּם בַּמִּדְבָּר
לֹא חָסֵרוּ שַׂלְמֹתֵיהֶם לֹא בָלוּ וְרַגְלֵיהֶם
כב לֹא בָצֵקוּ: וַתִּתֵּן לָהֶם מַמְלָכוֹת וַעֲמָמִים

are your gods, Israel, who brought you up from the land of Egypt.')

וַיַּעֲשׂוּ נֶאָצוֹת גְּדֹלוֹת — *And they performed deeds that were greatly maddening. Ralbag* understands this as a modifying clause to the statements immediately preceding it. Making the calf and saying, 'This is your god,' were greatly maddening.

19. וְאַתָּה בְּרַחֲמֶיךָ הָרַבִּים לֹא עֲזַבְתָּם — *But You, in Your great compassion, did not forsake them.* Because of the maddening sins [v. 18], they deserved to be forsaken — but you did not do so (*Metzudos; Ralbag*). Although the Israelites were condemned to wander in the desert, God's miraculous providential care remained with them throughout (*Ralbag; Malbim*).

וְאֶת־הַדֶּרֶךְ אֲשֶׁר יֵלְכוּ־בָהּ — *And [to lead them on] the way they were to travel.* The pillar of fire had led them when they traveled at night. The purpose of the cloud and the fire was to instill faith in God in the Israelites, as well as to lead them on the way and illuminate the night (*Ralbag*).

20. וְרוּחֲךָ הַטּוֹבָה נָתַתָּ לְהַשְׂכִּילָם — *You gave Your good spirit to make them understand.* God extended the Divine spirit of wisdom and understanding from Moses to the seventy elders of Israel [*Numbers* 11:17] (*Ibn Ezra*). This enabled the elders to teach the Israelites, and *make them understand* the Torah (*Ralbag*).

Malbim interprets the *good spirit* as the spirit of prophecy which rested on Moses, enabling him to receive the Torah and teach the Israelites to understand it.

According to *Metzudos*, the reference here is to a general spirit of understanding which God bestowed on the Israelites so that they would better understand the Torah.

וּמַנְךָ לֹא־מָנַעְתָּ מִפִּיהֶם — *You did not withhold Your manna from their mouths.* The manna fell from heaven throughout the forty years that the Israelites wandered in the desert (*Ralbag*). [As stated in the Torah, *The Children of Israel ate the manna for forty years, until they came to settled land* (*Exodus* 16:35).]

וּמַיִם נָתַתָּה לָהֶם לִצְמָאָם — *And You gave them water for their thirst.* This refers to the well which accompanied the Israelites miraculously throughout the forty years in the desert and supplied them with water (*Malbim*). *Taanis* 9a states that the well was given to the people of Israel because of Miriam's merit. When she died, it disappeared, but returned in the

and they performed deeds that were greatly maddening. [19] *But You, in Your great compassion, did not forsake them in the desert; the pillar of cloud did not turn away from them by day to lead them on the way, and the pillar of fire at night to illuminate for them, and [to lead them on] the way they were to travel.* [20] *You gave Your good spirit to make them understand; You did not withhold Your manna from their mouths, and You gave them water for their thirst.* [21] *For forty years You supported them in the desert, they did not lack; their clothing did not wear out, and their feet did not swell.* [22] *Then You gave them kingdoms and nations,*

merit of Moses and Aaron. [See *Rashi, Numbers* 20:3.]

21. וְאַרְבָּעִים שָׁנָה כִּלְכַּלְתָּם בַּמִּדְבָּר — *For forty years You supported them in the desert.* [*Exodus* 16:35; see comm. to previous verse.]

שַׂלְמֹתֵיהֶם לֹא בָלוּ — *Their clothing did not wear out.* [This coincides with *Your clothing did not decay* (*Deut*. 8:4).]

Rashi (*Deut*. 8:4) explains that the clouds of glory (עַנְנֵי כָבוֹד) which protected the Israelites in the desert (see comm. to v. 12) rubbed against their clothing, and cleaned and ironed them. In addition, the children's clothing grew along with their bodies, so that it was never necessary for the children to change to a larger size.

וְרַגְלֵיהֶם לֹא בָצֵקוּ — *And their feet did not swell.* The word בָּצֵק usually refers to leavened dough, which rises and swells. Here, the reference is to the swelling of the feet from excessive walking. Although the Israelites wandered throughout the desert, their feet did not swell (*Metzudos; Rashi, Deut*. 8:4). *Ralbag's* interpretation is that the shoes on the Israelites' feet did not swell and crack.

22. וַתִּתֵּן לָהֶם מַמְלָכוֹת וַעֲמָמִים — *Then You gave them kingdoms and nations.* This refers to the land of Sihon and Og mentioned at the end of our verse (*Metzudos*). This land lay east of the river Jordan, and was apportioned to the tribes of Reuben, Gad, and half of Menasseh upon their request. The remaining tribes settled the land of Canaan, west of the Jordan.

Malbim states that God gave the lands of Sihon and Og to the Israelites although they were not included in His promise to the Patriarchs.

Malbim refers to God's promise to Abraham (*Genesis* 15:18-21), in which all of the nations occupying the territory of the Holy Land are listed. In *Malbim's* opinion the lands of Sihon and Og were not included in the list. This is supported by our text, which mentions in this verse that God gave them the land of Sihon and Og, and in the next passage that God brought them to the land which He had promised to their forefathers.

Ramban (*Numbers* 21:21), however, notes that *Numbers* 21:21 refers to Sihon as *the king of the Emorites*. Thus, he asserts that the countries occupied by Sihon and Og were included in God's promise that Abraham's descendants would receive the land of the *Emorites* (*Genesis* 15:21). Why, then, are the lands of Sihon and Og mentioned here separately? Although the lands of Sihon and Og were promised to Abraham, they were not meant to be occupied by the Israelites until the final redemption (see *Rashi, Genesis*

וַתַּחְלְקֵם לְפֵאָה וַיִּירְשׁוּ אֶת־אֶרֶץ סִיחוֹן וְאֶת־
אֶרֶץ מֶלֶךְ חֶשְׁבּוֹן וְאֶת־אֶרֶץ עוֹג מֶלֶךְ־הַבָּשָׁן:
כג וּבְנֵיהֶם הִרְבִּיתָ כְּכֹכְבֵי הַשָּׁמָיִם וַתְּבִיאֵם אֶל־
הָאָרֶץ אֲשֶׁר־אָמַרְתָּ לַאֲבֹתֵיהֶם לָבוֹא לָרָשֶׁת:
כד וַיָּבֹאוּ הַבָּנִים וַיִּירְשׁוּ אֶת־הָאָרֶץ וַתַּכְנַע
לִפְנֵיהֶם אֶת־יֹשְׁבֵי הָאָרֶץ הַכְּנַעֲנִים וַתִּתְּנֵם
בְּיָדָם וְאֶת־מַלְכֵיהֶם וְאֶת־עַמְמֵי הָאָרֶץ
לַעֲשׂוֹת בָּהֶם כִּרְצוֹנָם: כה וַיִּלְכְּדוּ עָרִים בְּצֻרוֹת

15:19). Thus, they are not included here with the other promised lands intended for occupation by Joshua and his followers [v. 23].

וַתַּחְלְקֵם לְפֵאָה — *And separated them into a corner.* The Jews were set aside in a corner of their own, separated from the gentiles in the surrounding countries (*Rashi*). *Malbim* interprets: *You separated* those Israelite tribes who settled in the land of Sihon and Og *into a corner* of their own — they settled on the eastern side of the Jordan, while the other tribes settled in the land of Canaan, on the western side.

Ralbag, however, translates *and apportioned them to the beginning edge.* God apportioned the land of Sihon and Og to the beginning edge of the Israelite nation, i.e., the firstborn among the twelve tribes — Reuben was Jacob's firstborn; Gad was Zilpah's firstborn; and Menasseh was the firstborn of Joseph, who was, himself, Rachel's firstborn. In another interpretation, *Ralbag* renders *You apportioned them to the edge*, referring to the least populous of the tribes, those who stood at the bottom edge of the population list. *Metzudos'* translation is *and You dispersed them to the edge* — You dispersed the idolatrous nations to the edge of the earth when they fled before the Israelites.

אֶרֶץ סִיחוֹן וְאֶת־אֶרֶץ מֶלֶךְ חֶשְׁבּוֹן — *The land of Sihon, the land of the king of Heshbon*. Sihon first conquered the city of Heshbon and the entire Moabite territory from the Moabite nation (*Numbers* 21:26). Then the Israelites conquered this land from Sihon [21:24] (*Ralbag*). [The Torah forbids the Israelites to attack the Moabite nation (*Deut.* 2:19). Thus, they were only permitted to conquer the Moabite territory after it had been taken by Sihon. Sihon "purified" Moab for Israel (*Rashi, Numbers* 21:26).]

וְאֶת־אֶרֶץ עוֹג מֶלֶךְ־הַבָּשָׁן — *And the land of Og, king of Bashan.* Og, a giant who was already living during the days of the Patriarch Abraham, was slain by Moses himself during the conquest of his land (*Rashi*, *Numbers* 21:34, 35).

23. וּבְנֵיהֶם הִרְבִּיתָ — *You multiplied their children*. Because of the great number of Israelite children, You broadened the boundaries of the Holy Land (*Malbim*).

כְּכֹכְבֵי הַשָּׁמָיִם — *Like the stars of the heavens.* [This alludes to God's blessing to Abraham (*Genesis* 15:5), *'Look at the heavens and count the stars, if you can count them.' Then He* [God] *said to him, 'So shall your descendants be.'*]

וַתְּבִיאֵם אֶל־הָאָרֶץ אֲשֶׁר־אָמַרְתָּ לַאֲבֹתֵיהֶם לָבוֹא לָרָשֶׁת — *And brought them to come and inherit the Land of which You spoke and separated them into a corner; they inherited the land of Sihon, the land of the king of Heshbon, and the land of Og, king of the Bashan.* 23 *You multiplied their children like the stars of the heavens, and brought them to come and inherit the Land of which You spoke to their forefathers.* 24 *The children came and inherited the Land. You subdued, before them, the Canaanite inhabitants of the land, and gave them over, with their kings and the peoples of the land, to do with them as they pleased.* 25 *They captured fortified cities*

to their forefathers. Ralbag explains that *the land* mentioned in this verse refers to the land of Canaan, which lay west of the territories of Sihon and Og, across the Jordan River. Its borders are outlined in the Torah (*Numbers* 34:3-12) as beginning from the river Jordan and reaching westward until the Mediterranean Sea.

This was the Land promised to Abraham. The text now describes how God fulfilled His covenant with Abraham [v. 8] (*Malbim*).

24. וַתַּכְנַע לִפְנֵיהֶם אֶת־יֹשְׁבֵי הָאָרֶץ הַכְּנַעֲנִים — *You subdued, before them, the Canaanite inhabitants of the land.* This refers to those inhabitants of the land who did not offer resistance to the Israelites — the Girgashites and the Hivites. The Girgashites fled before the Jewish nation, and the Hivites made peace with the Jews (*Malbim*).

[*Malbim's* source is *Midrash Rabbah* (*Leviticus* 17:6) which states that Joshua first informed the nations inhabiting *Eretz Yisrael* that they could either leave the Land, remain and make peace, or failing these choices, engage in battle. The Girgashites fled, and settled in Africa; the Gibeonites (Hivites) made peace (*Joshua* 10:1); and the remaining 31 kings made war and were defeated (*Joshua* 12:7-24).]

Rambam (*Melachim* 6:1-4) states that in all wars, even those with the seven Canaanite nations and Amalek, an offer of peace is first made. It is only if the offer is spurned that the nations are to be attacked. This is derived from the passage (*Joshua* 11:19): *There was no city which made peace with the children of Israel except the Hivite, the inhabitants of Gibeon,* which indicates that all the others spurned Joshua's peace offer.

וַתִּתְּנֵם בְּיָדָם וְאֶת־מַלְכֵיהֶם וְאֶת־עַמְמֵי הָאָרֶץ לַעֲשׂוֹת בָּהֶם כִּרְצוֹנָם — *And gave them over, with their kings and the peoples of the land, to do with them as they pleased.* This part of the verse refers to all the inhabitants of the Holy Land (besides the Hivites and Girgashites) who battled the Israelites. God gave them over to the Israelites to destroy them (*Malbim*).

These nations refused to accept Joshua's offer of peace. *Joshua* 11:20 tells why: *for this was from HASHEM, to strengthen their hearts to wage war with Israel, so that they might be destroyed* (*Rambam, Melachim* 6:4). [See footnote to v. 8.]

25. וַיִּלְכְּדוּ עָרִים בְּצֻרוֹת — *They captured fortified cities.* This corresponds with (*Deut.* 6:10): *When HASHEM your God shall bring you to the Land ... to give to you great, good cities which you did not build* (*Malbim*).

ט וְאֲדָמָה שְׁמֵנָה וַיִּירְשׁוּ בָּתִּים מְלֵאִים־כָּל־
כו־כז טוּב בֹּרוֹת חֲצוּבִים כְּרָמִים וְזֵיתִים וְעֵץ
מַאֲכָל לָרֹב וַיֹּאכְלוּ וַיִּשְׂבְּעוּ וַיַּשְׁמִינוּ
כו וַיִּתְעַדְּנוּ בְּטוּבְךָ הַגָּדוֹל: וַיַּמְרוּ וַיִּמְרְדוּ בָּךְ
וַיַּשְׁלִכוּ אֶת־תּוֹרָתְךָ אַחֲרֵי גַוָּם וְאֶת־
נְבִיאֶיךָ הָרָגוּ אֲשֶׁר־הֵעִידוּ בָם לַהֲשִׁיבָם
כז אֵלֶיךָ וַיַּעֲשׂוּ נֶאָצוֹת גְּדוֹלֹת: וַתִּתְּנֵם בְּיַד

בָּתִּים מְלֵאִים־כָּל־טוּב — *Houses filled with everything good.* This corresponds with the Biblical passage describing what the Israelites would find when they reached the Holy Land (*Deut.* 6:11): *Houses filled with everything good,*[1] *which you did not fill* (*Malbim*).

בֹּרוֹת חֲצוּבִים כְּרָמִים וְזֵיתִים — *Hewn pits, vineyards, olive orchards. Hewn pits* refers to [storage] pits hewn into solid rock (*Metzudos*).

This verse coincides with *Deuteronomy* 6:11 — *Hewn pits which you did not hew, vineyards and olive orchards which you did not plant* (*Malbim*).

וַיֹּאכְלוּ וַיִּשְׂבְּעוּ — *So they ate, became satiated.* This corresponds with *Deuteronomy* 6:11: *and you shall eat and become satiated* (*Malbim*).

וַיַּשְׁמִינוּ — *And fattened.* Their bodies became fat, fleshy (*Metzudos*).

According to *Ibn Ezra*, their *hearts* fattened. [I.e., they become unresponsive to experiences which should have generated feelings of devotion to God and love for their fellows. It was as if their ears were blocked and insulated with fat. *Ibn Ezra's* interpretation is based on Isaiah's admonition (*Isaiah* 6:10): *Fatten the heart of this people, harden his ears ... lest he sees with his eyes and hears with his ears, and his heart understands and repents and is cured.*]

וַיִּתְעַדְּנוּ בְּטוּבְךָ הַגָּדוֹל — *And delighted in Your great goodness.* The overindulgence described in this passage caused

1. *Ramban* (*Deut.* 6:10, citing *Chullin* 17a) explains that this Biblical verse permitted the soldiers involved in battle to eat whatever food they found in the conquered Canaanite houses or fields, even if not kosher (provided the food had not been used for idolatry). This special permit applied only during the battle for the conquest of the Land.

Midrash Rabbah (*Leviticus* 17:6) states that the phrase *houses filled with everything good* suggests hidden treasures which awaited the Israelites who entered the Holy Land. This is based on *Leviticus* 14:33-57, which outlines the procedure to be followed when a leprous growth (צָרַעַת) is found on the walls of a house in the land of Canaan. The Torah states that the infected stones must first be removed and replaced; then, if the growth reappears, the entire structure is to be razed. The opening passage of this chapter seems to be introducing a fortunate occurrence. *When you come to the land of Canaan which I give you as an inheritance, then I shall place a leprous blight in the house of the Land of your inheritance.* 'Is this good news?' asks the Midrash. Evidently, the Rabbis answer, it alludes to the hidden treasures of the Canaanites which awaited those who entered the Holy Land. When the Canaanites heard that the Israelites would invade the Land, they buried their treasure in the walls of their houses and in their fields. After the Israelites occupied the Land, God caused leprous blights to appear on the walls of the houses where the treasures were buried. The inhabitants of the houses had the walls razed, and found the treasures. This is the meaning of *houses filled with everything good* — filled with the treasures buried there by the Canaanites (see Talmud *Horios* 10a).

IX
26-27

and a fat land, and inherited houses filled with everything good; hewn pits, vineyards, olive orchards, and abundant food trees. So they ate, became satiated and fattened, and delighted in Your great goodness. [26] *Then they were recalcitrant and rebellious against You, cast off Your Torah behind themselves, murdered Your prophets who warned them in order to cause them to return to You, and performed deeds that were greatly maddening.* [27] *So You gave them over into the hands of*

the rebelliousness described in the following passage (*Ralbag*).

After describing the pleasures the people would enjoy upon settling in the Holy Land, *Deuteronomy* (6:12) warns against this: *Watch yourself, lest you forget HASHEM who took you out of the land of Egypt* (*Malbim*).

26. וַיַּמְרוּ וַיִּמְרְדוּ בָּךְ — *Then they were recalcitrant and rebellious against You.* The repetition — *recalcitrant and rebellious* — indicates the severity of the rebelliousness (*Metzudos*).

According to *Malbim*, וַיַּמְרוּ refers to a milder form of rebelliousness. וַיִּמְרְדוּ indicates total deterioration — complete abandoning of the Torah, as explained by the following clause, [*They*] *cast off Your Torah.*

וַיַּשְׁלִכוּ אֶת־תּוֹרָתְךָ — [*And they*] *cast off Your Torah.* They followed the nations in the practice of idolatry (*Ralbag*). The Talmud (*Horios* 8a) equates idolatry with transgressing the entire Torah.

אַחֲרֵי גַוָּם — *Behind themselves.* גַוָּם is translated literally *their bodies*, as in *I Samuel* 31:12 (*Metzudos*). [See *I Kings* 14:9.]

וְאֶת־נְבִיאֶיךָ הָרָגוּ — [*They*] *murdered Your prophets.* Jezebel, the Zidonian wife of Ahab, King of Israel, murdered all the prophets of Israel except for 100 who were hidden by Obadiah (*I Kings* 18:4). The Judean king Joash ordered the murder of the prophet Zechariah ben Jehoiada (*II Chronicles* 24:21); and the Judean king Menasseh murdered the prophet Isaiah (*II Kings* 21:16; *Sanhedrin* 103b) (*Ralbag*).

אֲשֶׁר־הֵעִידוּ בָם — *Who warned them.* הֵעִידוּ literally means *testified*. It can also mean *warned* since warnings are usually given before witnesses who can later testify that the warning took place (*Metzudos*). [Corporeal punishment is only meted out if the transgressor was warned immediately before the act. See *Rambam, Sanhedrin* 16:4.]

Another translation is *who bore witness against them*. The prophets bore witness to the punishment which they saw would befall those failing to repent (*Ralbag*).

לַהֲשִׁיבָם אֵלֶיךָ — *In order to cause them to return to You.* 'The prophets ... spoke constantly about repentance' (*Shaarei Teshuvah* 1:1).

[The description of the task of the murdered prophets in our passage coincides with *II Chronicles* 24:19-21, which portrays the activities of the prophet Zechariah ben Jehoiada the *Kohen,* who was murdered by Joash: *He* [*God*] *sent them prophets to cause them to return to HASHEM; they warned them but they did not listen.* The text relates that Zechariah spoke to the people about their sins, and how he was murdered by the king.]

צָרֵיהֶם וַיָּצֵרוּ לָהֶם וּבְעֵת צָרָתָם יִצְעֲקוּ אֵלֶיךָ
וְאַתָּה מִשָּׁמַיִם תִּשְׁמָע וּכְרַחֲמֶיךָ הָרַבִּים תִּתֵּן
כח לָהֶם מוֹשִׁיעִים וְיוֹשִׁיעוּם מִיַּד צָרֵיהֶם: וּכְנוֹחַ
לָהֶם יָשׁוּבוּ לַעֲשׂוֹת רַע לְפָנֶיךָ וַתַּעַזְבֵם בְּיַד
אֹיְבֵיהֶם וַיִּרְדּוּ בָהֶם וַיָּשׁוּבוּ וַיִּזְעָקוּךָ וְאַתָּה
מִשָּׁמַיִם תִּשְׁמַע וְתַצִּילֵם כְּרַחֲמֶיךָ רַבּוֹת
כט עִתִּים: וַתָּעַד בָּהֶם לַהֲשִׁיבָם אֶל־תּוֹרָתֶךָ

27. וַתִּתְּנֵם בְּיַד צָרֵיהֶם — *So You gave them over into the hands of their enemies.* This refers to the days of the Judges[1] when the people worshiped idols and were given over to their enemies. This is stated in *Judges* 2:14: *God was angered by Israel, and He gave them over to oppressors who oppressed them* (*Ralbag; Malbim*).

The period of the Judges followed the death of Joshua and the entire generation which had witnessed the miraculous conquest of the land. The people began to follow idols and were given over to their enemies. Periodically, God sent the people judges who rescued them, but when the judges died, the people reverted to their idolatry (*Judges* 2:7-19). The period lasted some four hundred years, and is covered by the Book of *Judges.* It is described by the mishnah (*Avos* 1:1) as the period of the elders (זְקֵנִים). The last of the elders was Eli who taught Samuel, the first of the era of Prophets (*Rashi, I Samuel* 1:1; *Avos* 1:1; however, *Rav, Avos* 1:1, considers Eli and Samuel both the first of the Prophets).

וּבְעֵת צָרָתָם יִצְעֲקוּ אֵלֶיךָ — *But at the time of their affliction, they would cry out to You.* [See *Judges* 3:9, 15; 4:3; 6:7.]

Shaarei Teshuvah (citing *Deut.* 4:34) asserts that God accepts repentance even when it is brought about by the sinner's great suffering, i.e., even when the motivation is not purely for the sake of God, but in order to alleviate the suffering.

וְאַתָּה מִשָּׁמַיִם תִּשְׁמָע — *And You would hear from heaven.*

Although the verb תִּשְׁמָע, *you will hear,* is in the future tense, in this verse it is translated: *You would hear* (*Rashi*). *Rashi* (*Job* 1:5) establishes the rule that in cases of constant action, the future tense may be used to denote constancy. Applying the rule here, we may conclude that the future *will hear* is used in our verse in the sense of *would hear*, to indicate that God always heard their prayers when they repented.

תִּתֵּן לָהֶם מוֹשִׁיעִים וְיוֹשִׁיעוּם מִיַּד צָרֵיהֶם — *Would give them deliverers who would deliver them from the hands of their enemies.* [This follows *Judges* 2:16: *HASHEM established judges who delivered them from their oppressors.*

The verb תִּתֵּן, in the future tense, is used to indicate that God always gave them deliverers. See above.]

28. וּכְנוֹחַ לָהֶם — *But when it would ease for them. Metzudos* explains: when they were able to rest from the persecution of the nations [i.e., when the persecution stopped].

יָשׁוּבוּ לַעֲשׂוֹת רַע לְפָנֶיךָ — *They would revert to doing evil before You.* [The process of reverting to evil after being saved is repeated throughout the Book of

1. *Ralbag* makes this point because the previous verse mentions the murder of the prophets, which took place after the days of the Judges had concluded.

their enemies, who afflicted them; but at the time of their affliction, they would cry out to You. And You would hear from heaven, and in Your abundant compassion, would give them deliverers who would deliver them from the hands of their enemies.
28 *But when it would ease for them, they would revert to doing evil before You; and You would abandon them into the hands of their enemies, who oppressed them; then they again repented and cried out to You, and You would hear from heaven and, in Your compassion, would rescue them numerous times.*
29 *You warned them in order to return to Your Torah,*

Judges. See *Judges* 2:19; 3:12; 4:1; 6:1; 8:33.]

וַתַּעַזְבֵם בְּיַד אֹיְבֵיהֶם — *And You would abandon them into the hands of their enemies.* In the preceding passage, the word צָרֵיהֶם refers to the enemy who oppresses for his own personal gain, but not out of hatred; אֹיְבֵיהֶם refers to the pathological enemy, who oppresses from hatred. Verse 27, describing the time when the Israelites first sinned in the times of the Judges, relates that God merely gave them into the hands of צָרֵיהֶם, *enemies* who oppressed them for personal gain, but who would not attack when their desires were satisfied. Our verse, however, describes the Israelites' repetition of sin after the oppression was eased. Now God gave them over to אֹיְבֵיהֶם, *enemies* who hated them, and oppressed them even without personal gain (*Malbim*).

וַיִּרְדּוּ בָהֶם — *Who oppressed them.* The preceding verse states that the enemies *afflicted them* (וַיָּצֵרוּ לָהֶם). Our verse states that the enemies *oppressed them,* indicating a more pervasive enemy presence. In verse 27, when the people began to sin, the enemies did no more than afflict them. In our verse, when the sins were repeated, God allowed the enemies to oppress them (*Malbim*).

וְתַצִּילֵם כְּרַחֲמֶיךָ — *And, in Your compassion, would rescue them.* The preceding verse states: *[You] in Your abundant compassion ... would deliver them,* whereas our verse states: *[You] in Your compassion, would rescue them. Deliverance* (יְשׁוּעָה) denotes complete conquest of the enemy. Verse 27 portrays the deliverance of the people when they repented after having begun to sin. This took place in the early years of the Judges, such as in the days of Ehud. This complete deliverance from their enemies came about through God's *abundant compassion. Rescue* (הַצָּלָה) means only the prevention of destruction by the oppressor, but does not signify conquest of the enemy. Our verse tells of the *rescue* of the people when they repented after repeated reversion to sinning. This occurred in the days of the later Judges. Then they were saved from destruction, but did not conquer their enemies. This *rescue* came about through God's *compassion* but not His *abundant compassion* (*Malbim*).

רַבּוֹת עִתִּים — *Numerous times.* The cycle of sin and downfall followed by repentance and rescue was repeated many times, throughout the era of the Judges (*Metzudos; Malbim*).

29. וַתָּעַד בָּהֶם — *You warned them.* This verse refers to the era of the kings of both Judah and Israel, when the prophets warned the people that punishment awaited them for their sins (*Ralbag*).

ט
ל-לא

וְהֵמָּה הֵזִידוּ וְלֹא־שָׁמְעוּ לְמִצְוֺתֶיךָ
וּבְמִשְׁפָּטֶיךָ חָטְאוּ־בָם אֲשֶׁר־יַעֲשֶׂה אָדָם
וְחָיָה בָהֶם וַיִּתְּנוּ כָתֵף סוֹרֶרֶת וְעָרְפָּם הִקְשׁוּ
ל וְלֹא שָׁמֵעוּ׃ וַתִּמְשֹׁךְ עֲלֵיהֶם שָׁנִים רַבּוֹת
וַתָּעַד בָּם בְּרוּחֲךָ בְּיַד־נְבִיאֶיךָ וְלֹא הֶאֱזִינוּ
לא וַתִּתְּנֵם בְּיַד עַמֵּי הָאֲרָצֹת׃ וּבְרַחֲמֶיךָ הָרַבִּים

[Jewish dynastic monarchy began with King David, anointed by the prophet Samuel soon after the close of the era of the Judges (*I Samuel* 16:13). His descendants sat on the throne of the kingdom of Judah in Jerusalem until the destruction of the First Temple. During the reign of David's grandson, Rehoboam, all the tribes besides Judah and Benjamin chose Jeroboam ben Nebat as their king (*I Kings* 12:20). This marked the beginning of the divided nation, with the northern kingdom called Israel, and the southern one, Judah.

Jeroboam, king of the northern tribes, set up two temples to rival the Temple in Jerusalem, and they were sinfully accepted by the people (*I Kings* 12:30). He was followed on the throne by a series of evil monarchs, until the Assyrians exiled the ten tribes (*II Kings* 17:6) and ended the Israelite monarchy about one hundred and thirty years before the destruction of the First Temple.]

The warnings mentioned here began in the days of the first Israelite king, Jeroboam ben Nebat, when the people began sinning constantly (*Malbim*).

[From the days of Jeroboam until the ten tribes were exiled, Scripture lists the constant grievous sins of the Israelites, and the unsuccessful warnings of the prophets Iddo, Ahijah, Jehu, Michaiahu, Elijah, and Elisha. Similarly, beginning with the period of the Judean king, Rehoboam (*I Kings* 14:22), Scripture recounts the constant transgressions of the members of the Judean kingdom, even during the reigns of the virtuous kings, Asa, Jehoshaphat, Joash, Amaziah, and Uziah. Only the Judean kings Hezekiah and Josiah rid the land of idolatry. During the reigns of all the other kings, the people sinned (See *I Kings* 12; *II Kings* 18.)]

וְלֹא־שָׁמְעוּ לְמִצְוֺתֶיךָ — *And did not listen to Your commandments.* This refers to the commandments involving the relationship between man and God (בֵּין אָדָם לַמָּקוֹם) [e.g., idolatry, Sabbath observance, etc.] (*Malbim*).

וּבְמִשְׁפָּטֶיךָ חָטְאוּ־בָם — *They transgressed through Your laws.* They transgressed by improperly carrying out Your laws. The laws and commandments should be fulfilled purely for the sake of the *mitzvah* (לִשְׁמָהּ). Even when carrying out the laws, however, the people acted with selfish intentions (שֶׁלֹּא לִשְׁמָהּ). Furthermore, their self-serving intentions in some cases actually transformed the *mitzvos* into transgressions, as when they took the lives of egregious evildoers for the purpose of revenge. In this case the *mitzvah* of destroying the wicked becomes murder. Thus, *they transgressed through Your laws,* i.e., committed transgressions by carrying out Your laws self-servingly (*Metzudos*).

[*Metzudos'* point is based on the Scriptural narrative concerning the extermination of the House of Jeroboam. The prophet Ahijah foretold the annihilation of the house of Jeroboam because of his sins (*I Kings* 15:29). This was accomplished by Baasa. Later, Baasa himself continued Jeroboam's evil deeds. He was

but they were evil, and did not listen to Your commandments; they transgressed through Your laws which a man should do in order that he might live by them; they turned their backs, stiffened their necks, and did not listen. [30] *But You extended [a period of grace] to them for many years, and warned them, with Your spirit, through Your prophets — however, they did not listen, so You gave them into the hands of the peoples of the lands.* [31] *In Your abundant compassion You did not*

then told by the prophet Jehu (*I Kings* 16:7) that he would be punished because he angered *God like the house of Jeroboam, and because he smote him. Metzudos* there explains that Baasa's attack upon the descendants of Jeroboam could not have been for the sake of the *mitzvah* of destroying evildoers, since he was himself guilty of the same evil. Obviously, his intentions were to consolidate his own regime by destroying the remnant of Jeroboam's dynasty. Thus, his extermination of Jeroboam's family, although it fulfilled prophecy, was considered murder.]

אֲשֶׁר־יַעֲשֶׂה אָדָם וְחָיָה בָהֶם — *Which a man should do in order that he might live by them.* [This is based on *Leviticus* 18:5.]

In contrast to other religious orders, which required that their followers sacrifice their children to their gods (see *Ramban, Leviticus* 18:21), the Torah requires the people to follow laws which bring their practitioners life, i.e., both spiritual and physical perfection (*Ralbag*).

Ramban (*Leviticus* 18:4; *Malbim* here) asserts that the phrase *laws which a man should do in order that he might live by them* refers to the *mitzvos* governing relationships between man and his fellow (בֵּין אָדָם לַחֲבֵרוֹ). These laws guarantee a peaceful, cooperative society. Their purpose is that *a man might live by them* tranquilly and without fear of harm.

Metzudos translates: *laws which a man should do in order that he might live 'through' them*. Through *mitzvos*, a man is rewarded with life.

וַיִּתְּנוּ כָתֵף סוֹרֶרֶת — *They turned their backs* [lit. *gave a turning shoulder*]. Despite the value of Your laws, which bring life, they turned their backs on the path of Your commandments (*Ralbag*); they ignored the admonitions (*Malbim*).

וְעָרְפָּם הִקְשׁוּ — *Stiffened their necks.* Even when punished, they stiffened their necks (*Malbim*).

30. וַתִּמְשֹׁךְ עֲלֵיהֶם שָׁנִים רַבּוֹת — *But You extended [a period of grace] to them for many years.* Our translation follows *Ralbag*. Although they deserved punishment immediately, you delayed punishment for many years.

וַתָּעַד בָּם בְּרוּחֲךָ בְּיַד־נְבִיאֶיךָ — *And warned them, with Your spirit, through Your prophets.* You warned them with the spirit of prophecy which emanates from You and rests on Your prophets (*Metzudos*; *Ralbag*). From the time of King Uziah of Judah until the destruction of the Temple, all of the prophets foretold the coming exile (*Malbim*).

וַתִּתְּנֵם בְּיַד עַמֵּי הָאֲרָצֹת — *So You gave them into the hands of the peoples of the lands.* Because they did not listen, you gave them over to *the peoples of the lands*, i.e., the Assyrians, who exiled the

לֹא־עֲשִׂיתָם כָּלָה וְלֹא עֲזַבְתָּם כִּי אֵל־
לב חַנּוּן וְרַחוּם אָתָּה׃ וְעַתָּה אֱלֹהֵינוּ הָאֵל
הַגָּדוֹל הַגִּבּוֹר וְהַנּוֹרָא שׁוֹמֵר הַבְּרִית וְהַחֶסֶד
אַל־יִמְעַט לְפָנֶיךָ אֵת כָּל־הַתְּלָאָה אֲשֶׁר־
מְצָאַתְנוּ לִמְלָכֵינוּ לְשָׂרֵינוּ וּלְכֹהֲנֵינוּ
וְלִנְבִיאֵינוּ וְלַאֲבֹתֵינוּ וּלְכָל־עַמֶּךָ מִימֵי
לג מַלְכֵי אַשּׁוּר עַד הַיּוֹם הַזֶּה׃ וְאַתָּה צַדִּיק

ten tribes (*II Kings* 17:6), and the Babylonians, who destroyed the Temple and exiled the members of the Judean kingdom (*II Kings* 25:11) (*Ralbag; Malbim*).

31. וּבְרַחֲמֶיךָ הָרַבִּים לֹא־עֲשִׂיתָם כָּלָה — *In Your abundant compassion You did not annihilate them.* They deserved annihilation because of the sins, but in Your abundant compassion You did not destroy them completely (*Ralbag; Malbim*).

וְלֹא עֲזַבְתָּם — *And did not abandon them.* You did not abandon them in the land of their captivity, but continued Your special providential care over them even there (*Ralbag*).

Malbim cites *Leviticus* 26:44: *Even with ... their being in the land of their enemies, I did not loathe them nor cast them out to annihilate them and destroy My covenant with them, for I am HASHEM their God.* God still fulfills his covenant with the Patriarchs, as stated in *Leviticus* 26:42: *I shall remember My covenant with Jacob, also My covenant with Isaac, and also My covenant with Abraham ...*

32. הַגָּדוֹל הַגִּבּוֹר וְהַנּוֹרָא — *The great, powerful, and awe-inspiring God.* The Talmud (*Yoma* 69b) states that this phrase was pronounced by the Men of the Great Assembly (אַנְשֵׁי כְּנֶסֶת הַגְּדוֹלָה).[1] [Although the phrase is part of the prayer spoken by the Levites (v. 5), they chose the words *great, powerful and awe-inspiring* by instruction of the Men of the Great Assembly.]

The group was entitled the Great Assembly because they reinstituted this phrase, which was first uttered by Moses (*Deut*. 10:17). After the destruction of the Temple, Jeremiah used the words *great and powerful God* (*Jeremiah* 32:18), but deleted the word *awe-inspiring* (נוֹרָא), since God had not exercised His awesomeness, but had allowed the Babylonians to desecrate the Temple. And Daniel, after the seventy-year subjugation of the Jews to the Babylonians, used the phrase *great and awe-inspiring God* (*Daniel* 9:4), but omitted the word גִּבּוֹר, *powerful*, since God had not used His power, but had permitted the subjugation of His people.

The Men of the Great Assembly, however, *restored the crown to its an-*

1. The Men of the Great Assembly consisted of one hundred and twenty Sages, among them the last of the prophets. The leader of the Assembly was Ezra, and its members included Haggai, Zechariah, Malachi, Daniel, Hananiah, Mishael, Azariah, Nehemiah, Mordechai, and Zerubabel (*Megillah* 17b; *Rambam*, preface to *Yad HaChazakah*). They were the last single group with whom the entire body of undisputed Oral Tradition was deposited (*Tos. Yom Tov, Avos* 1:1). They composed the authorized Jewish prayer book (*Megillah* 17b; *Rambam, Hilchos Tefillah* ch. 1), wrote a number of Books of Scripture (*Bava Basra* 15a), and instituted many Rabbinical injunctions designed to preserve Torah observance among the people (*Tiferes Yisrael, Avos* 1:1,5).

annihilate them and did not abandon them, for You are a benevolent, compassionate God. [32] *And now, our God — the great, powerful, and awe-inspiring God Who keeps the covenant and the kindness — let not all the suffering which has befallen us be belittled before You; to our kings, lords, Kohanim, prophets, forefathers and all Your people; from the days of the kings of Assyria until this day.* [33] *You are just*

cient glory (הֶחְזִירוּ עֲטָרָה לְיֹשְׁנָהּ) by pronouncing Moses' original phrase in its entirety, *the great, powerful, and awe-inspiring God.* 'On the contrary,' they declared, 'God contains His anger and permits the wicked nations to afflict the Jewish people [so that the Jews might atone for their sins] — therein lies His power! God prevents the nations from destroying His people, preserving one nation among many — therein lies His awesomeness!'

שׁוֹמֵר הַבְּרִית וְהַחֶסֶד — *Who keeps the covenant and the kindness.* The keeping of the covenant with the Patriarchs is related to the preceding phrase, *the great, powerful, and awe-inspiring God.* God's power and awesomeness are expressed through His protection of the Jewish people among the nations. This protection is based on his fulfillment of *the covenant* with the Patriarchs, when He promised to protect and reward their descendants (*Malbim*). Also God extends *the kindness* He exhibited towards the Patriarchs by bestowing it on their descendants (*Ralbag*).[1]

אַל־יִמְעַט לְפָנֶיךָ אֵת כָּל־הַתְּלָאָה אֲשֶׁר־מְצָאַתְנוּ — *Let not all the suffering which has befallen us be belittled before You.* Consider the extent of the people's suffering as sufficient for atonement (*Metzudos*). [*Shaarei Teshuvah* 4:13 explains that the suffering which God visits on transgressors is always less than what they deserve (based on *Deut.* 8:5; *Ezra* 9:13, see ArtScroll *Ezra*).]

Since the covenant is still in effect, the exile is only temporary — a means of expiating our sins. So accept our suffering as atonement (*Malbim*).

[*Yoma* 86a states that suffering is a means of expiating sins, based on *Psalms* 89:33 — *I shall remember their transgressions with the* [*afflicting*] *staff, their sins with wounds.*]

מִימֵי מַלְכֵי אַשּׁוּר — *From the days of the kings of Assyria.* This refers to the Assyrian king who exiled the ten tribes (*II Kings* 17:6) and attacked the territory of Judah, conquering all of the Judean fortified cities except Jerusalem (*II Kings* 18:13). Subsequently, it was an easier matter for the Babylonians to exile those Jews who remained [*II Kings* 25:11] (*Ralbag*). Thus, it was the Assyrian assault which marked the beginning of the Exile (*Malbim*).

33. וְאַתָּה צַדִּיק — *You are just.* צַדִּיק, *tzaddik*, indicates one who acts justly, with proper judgment (*Ramban, Genesis* 6:9).

1. The first blessing recited in the *Shemoneh Esrei* prayer is *May You be blessed,* HASHEM, *the Shield of Abraham* (מָגֵן אַבְרָהָם). *Chiddushei HaRim* (cited by *Sfas Emes, Lech Lecha* 651) explains that the Patriarch Abraham implanted, through his life of complete devotion to *Hashem*, the intuitive love of God which marks the Jewish personality throughout the ages. God is the *shield of Abraham*, i.e., He shields the spirit of Abraham which lives in all His descendants.

עַל כָּל־הַבָּא עָלֵינוּ כִּי־אֱמֶת עָשִׂיתָ וַאֲנַחְנוּ
לד הִרְשָׁעְנוּ: וְאֶת־מְלָכֵינוּ שָׂרֵינוּ כֹּהֲנֵינוּ
וַאֲבֹתֵינוּ לֹא עָשׂוּ תּוֹרָתֶךָ וְלֹא הִקְשִׁיבוּ
אֶל־מִצְוֹתֶיךָ וּלְעֵדְוֹתֶיךָ אֲשֶׁר הַעִידֹתָ בָּהֶם:
לה וְהֵם בְּמַלְכוּתָם וּבְטוּבְךָ הָרָב אֲשֶׁר־נָתַתָּ
לָהֶם וּבְאֶרֶץ הָרְחָבָה וְהַשְּׁמֵנָה אֲשֶׁר־נָתַתָּ
לִפְנֵיהֶם לֹא עֲבָדוּךָ וְלֹא־שָׁבוּ מִמַּעַלְלֵיהֶם
לו הָרָעִים: הִנֵּה אֲנַחְנוּ הַיּוֹם עֲבָדִים וְהָאָרֶץ
אֲשֶׁר־נָתַתָּה לַאֲבֹתֵינוּ לֶאֱכֹל אֶת־פִּרְיָהּ

עַל כָּל־הַבָּא עָלֵינוּ — *Concerning all that has befallen us.* You are justified in punishing us with all the suffering that has befallen us (*Rashi*).

כִּי־אֱמֶת עָשִׂיתָ — *For You have acted truthfully.* You fulfilled Your promises (*Metzudos*). However, according to *Ralbag*, the truthfulness refers to God's judgment in punishing the Jewish people. You meted out Your punishment with truth and righteousness, as well as compassion.

וַאֲנַחְנוּ הִרְשָׁעְנוּ — *But we have been wicked.* This wickedness does not refer to the original sins which caused the punishment, but to the wickedness of the people afterward, in exile. Although You were just and truthful in judging us, we ignored the lesson of Your judgment, and continued to act wickedly (*Malbim*).

The chapter in *Leviticus* 26:14-46, entitled as the תּוֹכָחָה, *admonition*, lists the punishments awaiting those who sin, and then states *and if, with these* [punishments], *you do not hear Me, then I shall add to your suffering sevenfold for your sins.* After listing further punishments, it states: *And if, with these, you do not in your suffering* [turn] *to Me, but go with Me casually; then I, too, shall go with you casually; I, too, shall smite you sevenfold for your sins.*

Shaarei Teshuvah 2:2 explains that failure to accept God's punishment as an indication of one's sinfulness is, in itself, a grave transgression. When the sinner assumes that the suffering is casual and coincidental, God withdraws His special providential care. God, too, treats the sinner *casually* [leaving him open to further suffering and privation].

34. וְאֶת־מְלָכֵינוּ שָׂרֵינוּ כֹּהֲנֵינוּ וַאֲבֹתֵינוּ לֹא עָשׂוּ תּוֹרָתֶךָ — *With our kings, lords, Kohanim, and forefathers who did not fulfill Your Torah.* In *Malbim's* view, our phrase is related to the words *You are just* in the preceding verse: *You are just with our kings, lords, Kohanim, and forefathers*, i.e., You were just in punishing them, for they were sinful. According to *Metzudos*, our passage continues the closing statement of the preceding verse: *We have been wicked* [together] *with our kings, lords, Kohanim, and forefathers.*

Ramban (*Leviticus* 26:16) understands the confession in our verse as a fulfillment of the verse in *Leviticus* 26:40, *They shall confess their sins and the sins of their fathers.* That passage is one of the closing verses of the *admonition* (תּוֹכָחָה) in *Leviticus* 26:14-46 (see comm. v. 33) which alludes to the destruction of the First Temple and the Babylonian Exile. Like our verse, it mentions only the people's confession, but not their complete repentance. [Confession is only part of repentance. See *Rambam*, *Teshuvah*

concerning all that has befallen us, for You have acted
truthfully, but we have been wicked, [34] *with our kings,*
lords, Kohanim, and forefathers who did not fulfill Your
Torah, nor did they heed Your commandments and
warnings with which You warned them. [35] *Even in their*
kingdom with Your abundant goodness which You gave
them, and in the broad, fat land which You placed
before them, they did not serve You, and did not repent
of their wicked deeds. [36] *But today we are slaves; the*
land which You gave to our forefathers to eat of its fruit

1:1; *Shaarei Teshuvah* 1.] The confession was not accompanied by complete, whole-hearted *teshuvah* (repentance). Thus, the redemption, at this time, was also not complete. Only a fraction of the nation returned to the Holy Land; although the Second Temple was rebuilt, the people remained subjugated to the Persian kings. In contrast, the admonition in *Deuteronomy* 28:15-69 refers to the destruction of the Second Temple and the ensuing diaspora. The words of comfort which follow this admonition (*Deut.* 30:1-10) describe the final, complete redemption which will follow our present exile. There, Scripture describes the whole-hearted *teshuvah* of the Jewish people [see 1:6,7; *Ezra* 9:7].

וּלְעֵדוֹתֶיךָ — *And warnings.* This refers to the warnings in the Torah and the Prophets (*Ralbag*).

35. וְהֵם בְּמַלְכוּתָם ... לֹא עֲבָדוּךָ — *Even* [lit. *and*] *in their kingdom ... they did not serve You.* Verses 33-35 show that the people were wicked in times of suffering and in times of plenty. In verse 33, *We have been wicked* refers to the continued wickedness of the people after they were exiled [see comm. there]. Our verse describes the wickedness during times of plenty (*Malbim*; *Metzudos*).

וּבְאֶרֶץ הָרְחָבָה — *And in the broad ... land.* [This coincides with God's description of the Holy Land during Moses' vision of the burning bush (*Exodus* 3:8): *I shall descend to rescue* (My nation) *and bring it up from* [Egypt] *to a good, broad land.*]

36. הִנֵּה אֲנַחְנוּ הַיּוֹם עֲבָדִים — *But today we are slaves.* We are slaves of the Persian kings (*Metzudos*).

[Verse 35 states that our forefathers, in their own kingdom of plenty, *did not serve You*. This is followed by the statement in our verse, *today we are slaves*. This sequence coincides with the Biblical admonition (*Deut.* 28:47,48) warning of God's punishment of the people's sins: *Because you did not serve* HASHEM, *your God, with joy and a good heart, with an abundance of everything, you shall serve your enemy.* In our passage, too, the sequence may be understood: 'Because we did not serve You, we must serve our enemies.'

Rambam (*Teshuvah* 9:1) explains that this Biblical admonition serves as the rationale for all of God's punishment meted out in this world [in contrast to the punishment reserved for the World to Come; see *Hilchos Teshuvah* 8]. The comforts and riches of this world are intended to facilitate the performance of *mitzvos*. When the *mitzvos* are ignored, the riches are withdrawn, and replaced by poverty and persecution, which impede the performance of *mitzvos*. In

ט וְאֶת־טוּבָהּ הִנֵּה אֲנַחְנוּ עֲבָדִים עָלֶיהָ׃
לז לז וּתְבוּאָתָהּ מַרְבָּה לַמְּלָכִים אֲשֶׁר־נָתַתָּה עָלֵינוּ
בְּחַטֹּאותֵינוּ וְעַל־גְּוִיֹּתֵינוּ מֹשְׁלִים וּבִבְהֶמְתֵּנוּ
כִּרְצוֹנָם וּבְצָרָה גְדוֹלָה אֲנָחְנוּ׃
י א וּבְכָל־זֹאת אֲנַחְנוּ כֹּרְתִים אֲמָנָה וְכֹתְבִים
א־ב ב וְעַל הֶחָתוּם שָׂרֵינוּ לְוִיֵּנוּ כֹּהֲנֵינוּ׃ וְעַל

effect, God is saying, 'You could have performed the *mitzvos* during your time of wealth. Since you chose not to fulfill them, I shall prevent you from performing them by afflicting you with poverty and persecution.' [*Because you did not serve* HASHEM *... with an abundance, you shall serve your enemy.*]

Malbim interprets our verse as an expression of intent to atone for the wrongs committed by the forefathers. They did not serve You, although they had great riches (v. 35). *We are slaves, suffering*, yet we shall serve You, despite our suffering and enslavement, and sign a declaration of faithfulness to God (10:1).

אֲנַחְנוּ עֲבָדִים עָלֶיהָ — *We are slaves upon it.* We are slaves upon the Land, for we must pay taxes to the gentiles for living in our own country (*Rashi*). *Ibn Ezra*, however, translates *We are slaves* for *it*. [We are slaves *for the sake of the Land*. If we did not wish to settle the Holy Land, we could live a wealthy, comfortable life in Babylon.]

37. וּתְבוּאָתָהּ — *Its fruits.* This refers to the fruits of *Eretz Yisrael* (*Rashi*).

מַרְבָּה לַמְּלָכִים — *Are delicacies for the kings.* This is *Rashi's* translation. *Metzudos*, however, translates: Its fruits *being 'profit' to the kings*. The Persian kings collect taxes from the fruits of the Land, and confiscate its finest, most desirable products. According to *Malbim*, the translation is: *Its fruits bring usury to the kings*. In order to finance the working of the land, money was borrowed from the kings at usurious rates of interest.

וּבְצָרָה גְּדֹלָה אֲנָחְנוּ — *We are under great affliction. Ramban* (*Leviticus* 26:41) notes that the prediction in *Leviticus* (see comm. v. 33), that the people, after great suffering, would confess their sins, is followed by the statement that God would bring them into the land of their enemies. Why should confession be followed by bringing the people to the land of their enemies? *Ramban* answers that *Leviticus'* confession of sin alludes to the confession in our chapter, and the phrase that follows, 'the land of their enemies' refers to *Eretz Yisrael* under enemy control. Because the confession was not accompanied by complete *teshuvah* [see comm. v. 34], the people who were brought back to the Holy Land were subject to the rule of the Persian monarchs, as it is written, *today we are slaves ... we are under great affliction.*

X

Chapter 10 is the culmination of the events of chapters 8 and 9 (see respective prefaces). It records the *Bris Amanah (Covenant of Faith)*, the document which expressed the voluntary commitment of the people to uphold the entire Torah, particularly, the laws they had previously neglected (see pref. remarks to vs. 31-40). The spirit of *teshuvah* (chapters 8 and 9) prevailed, and the people resolved to change old ways and renew their spiritual lives in the Holy Land.

IX 37 *and goodness — we are slaves upon it.* [37] *Its fruits are delicacies for the kings whom You placed over us for our transgressions; they rule over our bodies and our animals at their pleasure — we are under great affliction.*

X 1 *But, despite all this, we establish a lasting covenant in writing, signed by our lords, our Levites, and Kohanim.*

◆§ The Lasting Covenant

1. וּבְכָל־זֹאת — *But, despite all this.* Despite our suffering [9:36, 37] (*Rashi*). Also, to atone for the sins of the forefathers, who did not serve God in their prosperity [9:35] (*Malbim*), we establish a covenant with God.

אֲנַחְנוּ כֹּרְתִים אֲמָנָה — *We establish a lasting covenant* [lit. *we cut lastingly*].

The verb כֹּרֵת, literally *cut*, means to *establish a* covenant (*Metzudos*). [Establishing a covenant is scripturally described as כְּרִיתַת בְּרִית, literally *cutting a covenant*, after the custom of cutting an animal into two parts. The participants in the covenant would then walk between the parts. See 9:8; *Rashi*, to *Genesis* 15:10.]

The word אֲמָנָה from the word אמן, literally *trustworthy*, includes the connotation *lasting* (*Metzudos; Malbim;* see comm. to 9:8). We are establishing a *Bris Amanah*, a lasting covenant with God for the purpose of deepening our faith in Him (*Rashi*). As a part of the covenant, we swear to follow God's Torah by fulfilling the *mitzvos* [v. 30] and refraining from intermarriage [v. 31] (*Ralbag; Ibn Ezra*).

וְעַל הֶחָתוּם — *Signed by* [lit. *and on the signed*]. The translation follows *Rashi*. *Ri Mitrani* leaves the word וְעַל untranslated.

Midrash Tanchuma (*Vayechi* 8) notes that the text does not state *signing*, but *on the signed*. This alludes to a miraculous occurrence. The document was left inside the Temple. The following day it was found signed by God, indicating His acceptance of the covenant. Therefore, the text does not state that the people wrote and signed the document, but that they wrote it and it was signed, i.e., by God.

שָׂרֵינוּ לְוִיֵּנוּ כֹּהֲנֵינוּ — *Our lords, our Levites, and Kohanim.* Most of the distinguished men among us signed our covenant as witnesses (*Rashi*). The covenant was signed by all of our leaders (*Ralbag*).

Malbim comments that the description of the signers here is surprising. The *Kohanim*, most distinguished of the signers, should have been mentioned first, followed by Levites, and finally by the lords. Indeed, the actual list of signers (vs. 2-28) follows the order of *Kohanim*, Levites, lords. Why, then, has the order in our verse been reversed? *Malbim* conjectures that it was customary to execute two forms of each document. One was the *open* document, read from top to bottom. On this document, the order of signatures was *Kohanim*, Levites, lords. The second was the *closed* document, which was written, signed, and then rolled up and sealed (see *Jeremiah* 32:14). Here, the lower portion, which carried the signatures of the witnesses, was doubled back and left as an outside flap. When read, this revealed *first* the names of those who had signed *last*. Our verse, which refers to this *closed* document, reads, *on the sealed one, our lords, Levites, and Kohanim* — in reverse order of distinction. The actual list of signers (vs. 2-28) refers to the *open* document, and therefore follows the order: *Kohanim*, Levites, lords.

הַחֲתוּמִים נְחֶמְיָה הַתִּרְשָׁתָא בֶּן־חֲכַלְיָה
ג־ד וְצִדְקִיָּה׃ שְׂרָיָה עֲזַרְיָה יִרְמְיָה׃ פַּשְׁחוּר
ה־ו אֲמַרְיָה מַלְכִּיָּה׃ חַטּוּשׁ שְׁבַנְיָה מַלּוּךְ׃ חָרִם
ז־ח מְרֵמוֹת עֹבַדְיָה׃ דָּנִיֵּאל גִּנְּתוֹן בָּרוּךְ׃ מְשֻׁלָּם
ט אֲבִיָּה מִיָּמִן׃ מַעַזְיָה בִלְגַּי שְׁמַעְיָה אֵלֶּה
י הַכֹּהֲנִים׃ וְהַלְוִיִּם וְיֵשׁוּעַ בֶּן־אֲזַנְיָה בִּנּוּי מִבְּנֵי
יא חֵנָדָד קַדְמִיאֵל׃ וַאֲחֵיהֶם שְׁבַנְיָה הוֹדִיָּה
יב קְלִיטָא פְלָאיָה חָנָן׃ מִיכָא רְחוֹב חֲשַׁבְיָה׃
יג־יד זַכּוּר שֵׁרֵבְיָה שְׁבַנְיָה׃ הוֹדִיָּה בָנִי בְּנִינוּ׃
טו רָאשֵׁי הָעָם פַּרְעֹשׁ פַּחַת מוֹאָב עֵילָם
טז־יז זַתּוּא בָּנִי׃ בֻּנִּי עַזְגָּד בֵּבָי׃ אֲדֹנִיָּה בִגְוַי עָדִין׃
יח־כ אָטֵר חִזְקִיָּה עַזּוּר׃ הוֹדִיָּה חָשֻׁם בֵּצָי׃ חָרִיף
כא עֲנָתוֹת °נובי׃ מַגְפִּיעָשׁ מְשֻׁלָּם חֵזִיר׃ °נֵיבָי ק׳
כב־כג מְשֵׁיזַבְאֵל צָדוֹק יַדּוּעַ׃ פְּלַטְיָה חָנָן עֲנָיָה׃
כד־כה הוֹשֵׁעַ חֲנַנְיָה חַשּׁוּב׃ הַלּוֹחֵשׁ פִּלְחָא שׁוֹבֵק׃
כו־כז רְחוּם חֲשַׁבְנָה מַעֲשֵׂיָה׃ וַאֲחִיָּה חָנָן עָנָן׃
כח־כט מַלּוּךְ חָרִם בַּעֲנָה׃ וּשְׁאָר הָעָם הַכֹּהֲנִים
הַלְוִיִּם הַשּׁוֹעֲרִים הַמְשֹׁרְרִים הַנְּתִינִים וְכָל־
הַנִּבְדָּל מֵעַמֵּי הָאֲרָצוֹת אֶל־תּוֹרַת הָאֱלֹהִים
נְשֵׁיהֶם בְּנֵיהֶם וּבְנֹתֵיהֶם כֹּל יוֹדֵעַ מֵבִין׃

2. וְעַל הַחֲתוּמִים — *Those who signed.* The text (vs. 2-28) now enumerates all those who signed the document.

Malbim observes that eighty-three signatories are listed. This corresponds with the seventy members of the Sanhedrin [the supreme judicial and legislative body] and the thirteen administrative appointees to the Temple: the assistant *Kohen Gadol* (סְגַן) and his two aides, seven caretakers, and three treasurers (see *Rambam*, *Klei HaMikdash*, 4:16-18).

10. וְיֵשׁוּעַ — *Jeshua*. According to *Metzudos*, the name is Vejushua. The *vav* at the beginning of the word is not the prefix *and*, but is part of his name. However, *Ralbag* (and others) elsewhere notes that Scripture occasionally adds an irregular *vav* to the beginning of a name, although no prefix is called for in the context of that phrase [see ArtScroll comm. to *I Chronicles* 4:15 and 27:4].

11. וַאֲחֵיהֶם — *Their brethren*. This refers to the companions of the aforementioned [v. 10] Levites (*Metzudos*).

2 *Those who signed: Nehemiah Hatirshatha son of*
Hachaliah, and Zedekiah, 3 *Seraiah, Azariah, Jeremiah,*
4 *Pashhur, Amariah, Malchijah,* 5 *Hattush, Shebaniah,*
Malluch, 6 *Harim, Meremoth, Obadiah,* 7 *Daniel, Gin-*
nthon, Baruch, 8 *Meshullam, Abijah, Mijamin,* 9 *Maa-*
ziah, Bilgai, Shemaiah; these are the Kohanim. 10 *The*
Levites: Jeshua son of Azaniah, Binui of the sons of
Henadad Kadmiel. 11 *Their brethren: Shebaniah,*
Hodeiah, Kelita, Pelaiah, Hanan, 12 *Micha, Rehob,*
Hashabiah, 13 *Zaccur, Sherebiah, Shebaniah,* 14 *Hodeiah,*
Bani, Beninu. 15 *The leaders of the people: Parosh, the*
governor of Moab, Eilam, Zattu, Bani, 16 *Buni, Azgad,*
Bevai, 17 *Adoniah, Bigvai, Adin,* 18 *Atar, Hezekiah, Azur,*
19 *Hodeiah, Hashum, Betzai,* 20 *Hariph, Anathoth, Nevai,*
21 *Magpiash, Meshullam, Hazir,* 22 *Meshezabel, Zadok,*
Jaddua, 23 *Pelatiah, Hanan, Anaiah,* 24 *Hoshea, Hana-*
niah, Hashub, 25 *Halohesh, Pilha, Shobek,* 26 *Rehum,*
Hashabenah, Maaseiah, 27 *Vaahiah, Hanan, Anan,*
28 *Malluch, Harim, Baanah.* 29 *The remainder of the*
people — the Kohanim, Levites, gatekeepers, singers,
Nethinites, all those who had separated themselves from
the nations of the lands to God's Torah, their wives,
sons, and daughters; all who knew how to understand.

15. פַּחַת מוֹאָב — *The governor of Moab.* The translation follows *Metzudos* (see ArtScroll *Ezra* 2:6).

29. וּשְׁאָר הָעָם — *The remainder of the people.* This refers to the remaining people, who did not actually sign the document of the covenant [v. 1] (*Metzudos; Malbim*), but joined in swearing to uphold the Torah (v. 30).

הַשּׁוֹעֲרִים הַמְשֹׁרְרִים — *Gatekeepers, singers.* [This also refers to the Levites, some of whom were gatekeepers and some singers. See comm. 7:44,45.]

הַנְּתִינִים — *Nethinites.* [The Nethinites were descendants of a group of Gibeonites who had made peace with the Israelites during the times of Joshua. See comm. 7:46.]

וְכָל־הַנִּבְדָּל מֵעַמֵּי הָאֲרָצוֹת אֶל־תּוֹרַת הָאֱלֹהִים — *All those who had separated themselves from the nations of the lands to God's Torah.* This refers to the proselytes (גֵּרִים), who had disengaged themselves from the beliefs of the gentiles and attached themselves to God's Torah and to the fulfillment of *mitzvos* (*Rashi*).

כֹּל יוֹדֵעַ מֵבִין — *All who knew how to understand. Ralbag* and *Malbim* attach our phrase to the phrase, *their wives, sons, and daughters.* Those among the

ל מַחֲזִיקִים עַל־אֲחֵיהֶם אַדִּירֵיהֶם וּבָאִים בְּאָלָה
וּבִשְׁבוּעָה לָלֶכֶת בְּתוֹרַת הָאֱלֹהִים אֲשֶׁר
נִתְּנָה בְּיַד מֹשֶׁה עֶבֶד־הָאֱלֹהִים וְלִשְׁמוֹר
וְלַעֲשׂוֹת אֶת־כָּל־מִצְוֹת יְהוָה אֲדֹנֵינוּ
לא וּמִשְׁפָּטָיו וְחֻקָּיו: וַאֲשֶׁר לֹא־נִתֵּן בְּנֹתֵינוּ לְעַמֵּי
לב הָאָרֶץ וְאֶת־בְּנֹתֵיהֶם לֹא נִקַּח לְבָנֵינוּ: וְעַמֵּי
הָאָרֶץ הַמְבִיאִים אֶת־הַמַּקָּחוֹת וְכָל־שֶׁבֶר
בְּיוֹם הַשַּׁבָּת לִמְכּוֹר לֹא־נִקַּח מֵהֶם בַּשַּׁבָּת
וּבְיוֹם קֹדֶשׁ וְנִטֹּשׁ אֶת־הַשָּׁנָה הַשְּׁבִיעִית

wives, sons, and daughters [of the proselytes (see above)] — who were learned enough to understand took the oath to follow God (as explained in verse 30).

◆§ The Oath

30. מַחֲזִיקִים עַל־אֲחֵיהֶם אַדִּירֵיהֶם — *They held with their great brethren.* All those mentioned in the preceding verse held with their great brethren, i.e., they joined (agreed with) the great men who had signed the covenant (*Metzudos; Malbim*).

Ri Mitrani renders: *They pressed upon their powerful brethren,* i.e., the righteous among the people *pressed upon their powerful brethren* who were wicked, and forced them to enter into the oath to fulfill the Torah.

According to *Ralbag*, our verse is translated as if the order of the words were reversed, reading אַדִּירֵיהֶם מַחֲזִיקִים עַל אֲחֵיהֶם, *the powerful pressed upon their brethren,* meaning that the powerful in the community pressured the others to take an oath to fulfill the Torah.

בְּאָלָה — *Into a curse.* אָלָה is defined as an oath accompanied by a curse, as in *Numbers* 5:21 — *Then the Kohen shall adjure the woman* [suspected of adultery] *to swear with the oath of the curse* (*Metzudos*). The sense of the oath of the curse is that the one taking the oath declares, 'May God visit a curse upon me if I do not fulfill the following ...' See *Rambam, Shevous* 2:2.

וּבִשְׁבוּעָה לָלֶכֶת בְּתוֹרַת הָאֱלֹהִים — *And an oath to walk in God's Torah.* The Talmud (*Nedarim* 8a) states that it is permitted to strengthen one's resolve to perform a *mitzvah* by swearing to fulfill it. Although an unnecessary oath is forbidden, this is not considered a redundant *shevuah*, since it provides him with the resolve necessary to fulfill the *mitzvah*, whereas, with the first, Sinaitic oath, he might have failed to perform the *mitzvah.* The Talmud (there) cites *Psalms* 119:106: *'I swore — and carried it out — to observe Your commandments.'*

וְלִשְׁמוֹר וְלַעֲשׂוֹת — *And to observe and fulfill.* [לִשְׁמוֹר, *to observe*, refers to the observance of the negative commandments (לֹא תַעֲשֶׂה), i.e., refraining from what is prohibited. לַעֲשׂוֹת, *to fulfill*, refers to the fulfillment of the positive commandments (עֲשֵׂה), i.e., performing what is required. See *Ramban, Exodus* 20:8. In the בְּרִית אֲמָנָה, *Bris Amanah*, the Jews swore to observe all the *mitzvos*, positive and negative.]

וּמִשְׁפָּטָיו וְחֻקָּיו — *And His laws and statutes.* [מִשְׁפָּט, *law*, refers to those Torah laws which are understood with human logic, such as the prohibitions against

30 *They held with their great brethren, and entered into
a curse and an oath to walk in God's Torah which was
given through Moses, the servant of God, and to observe
and fulfill all the commandments of* HASHEM *our Lord,
and His laws and statutes;* 31 *and not to give our daugh-
ters to the peoples of the land or take their daughters for
our sons.* 32 *Also, the peoples of the land who bring
merchandise and all produce to sell on the Sabbath
day — let us not buy from them on the Sabbath and
holidays, and let us relinquish during the seventh year,*

murder and robbery. חֹק, *statute*, refers to those commandments beyond human comprehension such as *shaatnez* (the prohibition against wearing clothing made of wool and linen), and *parah adumah* (the special purification laws associated with the red cow). See comm. 9:13.]

31-40. The particular observances enumerated in the ensuing verses — intermarriage [v. 31], Sabbath observance [v. 32], and contributions to the Temple [vs. 33-35] and the *Kohanim* [vs. 36-40] — were those which the people had failed to keep properly. The oath was specifically intended to strengthen these observances as well as other *mitzvos* (*Ralbag*).

◆§ Intermarriage

31. וַאֲשֶׁר לֹא־נִתֵּן בְּנֹתֵינוּ לְעַמֵּי הָאָרֶץ — *And not to give our daughters to the peoples of the land.* This refers to the grave transgression of intermarriage with the peoples living in the Land, i.e., *any* non-Jews, not just with the members of the seven nations indigenous to the Holy Land (*Malbim*). [See comm. to 9:2.]

◆§ The Sabbath

32. שֶׁבֶר — *Produce.* The translation follows *Rashi* and *Metzudos*. (See *Genesis* 47:14.)

לֹא־נִקַּח מֵהֶם בַּשַּׁבָּת וּבְיוֹם קֹדֶשׁ — *Let us not buy from them on the Sabbath and holidays.* The prohibition against doing business on the Sabbath and holidays is not a Biblical one (מִדְאוֹרַיְתָא) but was legislated by the Rabbis (מִדְרַבָּנָן). The purpose was to avoid the Biblical transgression of *writing* (receipts, accounts, etc.) on the Sabbath, which would result from engaging in commerce (*Ralbag*; *Rashi* in *Beitzah* 37a; see also 13:15-18).

The Rabbinical prohibition against doing business on the Sabbath was actually in effect long before this time. However, now the people accepted upon themselves an additional stringency: not to purchase any produce which the gentiles had brought to the market in Jerusalem on the Sabbath (*Doros HaRishonim*, vol. I, section 3, ch. 32,35 quoted in *Toldos Am Olam*).

וְנִטֹּשׁ אֶת־הַשָּׁנָה הַשְּׁבִיעִית — *And let us relinquish during the seventh year. Let us relinquish* 'the working of the land' *during the seventh year* (*Metzudos*; see *Rashi*, *Exodus* 23:11). Let the owners relinquish their rights to gather in its fruits during the seventh (*Shemittah*) year. During that year, landowners in *Eretz Yisrael* must allow free access to all produce growing on their property (*Ralbag*; *Ramban*, *Exodus* 23:11).

[The Torah (*Exodus* 23:10,11; *Leviticus* 25:1-7) requires that all fields in *Eretz Yisrael* be left fallow every seventh year. In addition, ownership rights over the produce growing there spontaneously must be relinquished. This period of rest

לג וּמַשָּׁא כָל־יָד: וְהֶעֱמַדְנוּ עָלֵינוּ מִצְוֺת לָתֵת
עָלֵינוּ שְׁלִישִׁית הַשֶּׁקֶל בַּשָּׁנָה לַעֲבֹדַת בֵּית
לד אֱלֹהֵינוּ: לְלֶחֶם הַמַּעֲרֶכֶת וּמִנְחַת הַתָּמִיד
וּלְעוֹלַת הַתָּמִיד הַשַּׁבָּתוֹת הֶחֳדָשִׁים לַמּוֹעֲדִים

for the land is entitled the *Shemittah* year (*Deut*. 15:1).]

וּמַשָּׁא כָל־יָד — *And loans given by every hand.* This refers to all monetary loans, which must be relinquished once the seventh year of *Shemittah* has passed, as stated in *Deuteronomy* (15:1-6) (*Rashi*).

The people now felt it necessary to take an oath [v. 30] to strengthen the *Shemittah* observance because the Jews had not previously kept *Shemittah* properly, as stated by the prophet Jeremiah [see *II Chronicles* 36:21] (*Ralbag*).[1]

Malbim asserts that the people now voluntarily assumed the obligation of observing *Shemittah*. This was necessary because the obligation of keeping *Shemittah* during the Second Temple era was under dispute. This dispute centered on whether there is a full Scriptural connection between *Shemittah* and *Yovel*.[2]

Yovel is observed only when all of the Jewish nation is settled in *Eretz Yisrael* (*Arachin* 32b). Since the majority of the Jewish people did not return to the Holy Land when the Second Temple was rebuilt (see ArtScroll *Ezra* 2:64), *Yovel* was not celebrated. According to the opinion linking *Shemittah* with *Yovel*, *Shemittah*, too, was not obligatory during the Second Temple. *Malbim* explains that the people now swore to uphold the *Shemittah* restrictions to refute this possibility, and affirm that *Shemittah* does not depend on *Yovel* (see further *Tosafos, Arachin* 32b; see fn. to ArtScroll *Sheviis* 6:1).

⸎ One Third of a Shekel

33. וְהֶעֱמַדְנוּ עָלֵינוּ מִצְוֺת — *And we took upon ourselves commandments.* Although they took upon themselves only one commandment (to donate one third of a shekel), our verse uses the plural *commandments*. Based on this, the Talmud (*Bava Basra* 9a) notes that the *mitzvah* of charity is equal to all the *mitzvos* combined.

Tosafos (ibid.) notes that our verse does not refer to donations for the poor, but to the upkeep of the Temple, as stated at the end of the verse — *for the service of our God's Temple.* Since supporting the needy is more commendable than donating to the Temple, it follows that charity to the poor is certainly equal to all the *mitzvos*.

לָתֵת עָלֵינוּ שְׁלִישִׁית הַשֶּׁקֶל — *To give one third of a shekel yearly.* The Torah requires that each person give half a shekel yearly for the Temple needs [*Exodus* 30:13]. The amount here was a third of a shekel, because that amount, in the days of Nehemiah, was equal to half a shekel during the time of the Torah (*Ralbag*; *Malbim*; see *Shekalim* 2:4).

According to *Ibn Ezra* and *Metzudos*, the donation of one third of a shekel was made in *addition* to the half shekel which the people were already obligated to pay by Biblical command.

The Talmud (*Bava Basra* 8b) interprets this verse as an allusion to the amount of charity to be given yearly: 'Every man

1. The destruction of the First Temple was a punishment for the transgression of the *Shemittah* laws. Indeed, the seventy years of Babylonian exile corresponded with seventy *Shemittah* years which the people had desecrated [*Leviticus* 26:34,35. See *Rashi* there].

2. *Yovel* [Jubilee] is celebrated after the passage of fifty years, i.e., after seven *Shemittah* cycles. During the *Yovel* year, the restrictions against cultivating the land and withholding its fruits must be observed. In addition, all ancestral landed property is returned to its original owners, and slaves are freed. (See *Leviticus* 25:8-13.)

X
33-34

and loans given by every hand. [33] *And we took upon ourselves commandments to give one third of a shekel yearly for the service of our God's Temple.* [34] *For the arranged bread, the meal-offering of the continual-offering, the continual burnt-offering, the Sabbaths, New Moons and*

should give at least one third of a shekel yearly.' [This applies even when no needy person appears; one must seek out the needy to give one third of a shekel. When an indigent person requests charity, however, he should be helped according to his needs. See *Yoreh Deah*, 249:1,2.]

Yerushalmi (*Shekalim* 2:3) interprets שְׁלִישִׁית as שְׁלֹשֶׁת, *three*: The people were not called upon to donate to the Temple more than *three times* during the year.

לַעֲבֹדַת בֵּית אֱלֹהֵינוּ — *For the service of our God's Temple.* The original half shekels given by the Israelites in the desert [*Exodus* 30:13] were used for the purchase of communal sacrifices and for the construction of the supports (אֲדָנִים) for the Tabernacle (*Rashi, Exodus* 30:15). The shekels given in later times were also used for sacrifices and repairs of the Temple buildings (בֶּדֶק הַבַּיִת). This is evident from our verse and from *II Chronicles* 24:6, when King Joash asked that the people give the half shekel for the Temple upkeep (*Ramban, Exodus* 30:12).

34. לְלֶחֶם הַמַּעֲרֶכֶת — *For the arranged bread.* This refers to the *lechem hapanim, the show bread* (*Metzudos*). [On the Sabbath, the *Kohanim* placed the *show bread* (לֶחֶם הַפָּנִים) on the Table (שֻׁלְחָן) in the Temple, to be left there until the following Sabbath. *Lechem hapanim* consisted of twelve u-shaped loaves, *arranged* in two rows, each consisting of six loaves. Because the u-shape left the two ends, or faces, of the bread open, the bread was entitled *lechem hapanim* [literally *bread of faces*] (see *Rashi, Exodus* 25:29,30; *Leviticus* 24:5-9). The use of the phrase *arranged bread* (לֶחֶם הַמַּעֲרֶכֶת) in our verse follows *Leviticus* 24:6, *you shall place them in two arrangements, six to the array . . .*]

וּמִנְחַת הַתָּמִיד — *The meal-offering of the continual-offering.*

This refers to the מִנְחַת נְסָכִים, *libation meal-offering*, which accompanied the continual-offering. [The *tamid, continual-offering*, was an offering of two lambs made each day in the Temple, one in the morning and one in the afternoon (see below). Along with these lambs, a *minchah*-offering (meal-offering) consisting of flour mixed with olive oil was brought. This was burnt on the altar. A libation of wine (נְסָכִים) accompanied the *minchah* and was poured on the altar; hence the name *libation meal-offering*. See *Numbers* 15:1-13; *Rambam, Maaseh Hakorbanos* 2:1-7.]

Ralbag, however, translates מִנְחַת הַתָּמִיד as *the continual-offering*, referring to the incense (קְטֹרֶת) which was burnt on the golden altar twice daily. [See *Exodus* 30.]

וּלְעוֹלַת הַתָּמִיד — *The continual burnt-offering.* [This *offering* (קָרְבַּן תָּמִיד) was a communal sacrifice offered twice daily, morning and evening, every day of the year. It consisted of one lamb on each occasion offered as an עוֹלָה, *burnt-offering*; i.e., an offering totally consumed on the altar. See *Numbers* 28:1-8.]

הַשַּׁבָּתוֹת — *The Sabbaths.* This refers to the additional (מוּסָף, *mussaf*) sacrifices brought on the Sabbath (*Metzudos*; see *Numbers* 28:9,10).

הֶחֳדָשִׁים — *New Moons.* This refers to the special additional sacrifices brought on the first of each month (*Malbim*; see *Numbers* 28:11-14).

לַמּוֹעֲדִים — *And festivals.* As on the Sabbath and New Moon, additional com-

וְלַקֳּדָשִׁים וְלַחַטָּאוֹת לְכַפֵּר עַל־יִשְׂרָאֵל וְכֹל
לה מְלֶאכֶת בֵּית־אֱלֹהֵינוּ׃ וְהַגּוֹרָלוֹת
הִפַּלְנוּ עַל־קֻרְבַּן הָעֵצִים הַכֹּהֲנִים הַלְוִיִּם
וְהָעָם לְהָבִיא לְבֵית אֱלֹהֵינוּ לְבֵית־אֲבֹתֵינוּ
לְעִתִּים מְזֻמָּנִים שָׁנָה בְשָׁנָה לְבַעֵר עַל־
לו מִזְבַּח יְהוָה אֱלֹהֵינוּ כַּכָּתוּב בַּתּוֹרָה׃ וּלְהָבִיא

munal offerings were brought on the festivals (*Malbim*). [See *Numbers* chs. 28,29.]

וְלַקֳּדָשִׁים — *The holy things.* The reference here is to the special sheep (כִּבְשֵׂי עֲצֶרֶת) brought as communal *peace-offerings*, and the two breads (שְׁתֵּי הַלֶּחֶם) offered on the festival of Shavuos [*Leviticus* 23:17]; also the *omer*-offering brought on the second day of Passover (see *Rashi*, *Leviticus* 23:11) (*Metzudos; Malbim*).

וְכֹל מְלֶאכֶת בֵּית־אֱלֹהֵינוּ — *And all the work of our God's Temple.* According to *Metzudos*, this refers to the repairs of Temple buildings. According to *Ralbag*, it refers to a number of communal offerings not specified in the text, such as olive oil to be used as fuel for the Menorah, flour and oil for the *minchah* offerings, wine for the libations, and the red cow (פָּרָה אֲדֻמָּה) [see *Numbers* 19].

☙ The Wood Offering

35. וְהַגּוֹרָלוֹת הִפַּלְנוּ עַל־קֻרְבַּן הָעֵצִים — *Then we cast lots for the wood-offering.* The wood-offering consisted of firewood donated to the altar as fuel for burning the sacrifices. The fuel itself was also considered an offering (see *Taanis* 26a; *Rashi*, *Menachos* 20b, 106b).

The lots were to determine the amount of wood to be brought by each donor (*Rashi*), or the date that each donor was to present the wood (*Metzudos*).

The people [v. 30] swore to bring this donation to insure an adequate supply of firewood. This had previously been neglected. [See pref. remarks to vs. 31-40.]

הַכֹּהֲנִים הַלְוִיִּם וְהָעָם — *The Kohanim, Levites, and the people.* All of these — *Kohanim*, Levites, and the rest of the people — cast lots (*Metzudos*).

לְעִתִּים מְזֻמָּנִים — *At appointed times.* Those selected to bring the wood for the Altar at a certain date supplied enough to last until the next date, when the next family brought their donation (*Rashi; Taanis* 26a). There were nine appointed times: 1 Nissan; 20 Tammuz; 5, 7, 10, 15, and 20 Av; 20 Elul; and 1 Teves (*Taanis* 26a).

שָׁנָה בְשָׁנָה — *Yearly.* The Talmud (*Taanis* 28a) explains: When the exiles first ascended, they could find no wood in the wood chamber; these [families] arose and volunteered their own. In recognition of their generosity, the prophets among them stipulated that these families would be privileged to bring their annual firewood donation, even if the chamber were already filled with wood, as it is written: *Then we cast lots for the wood-offering . . . at appointed times yearly.*

כַּכָּתוּב בַּתּוֹרָה — *As it is written in the Torah, 'Let the sons of Aaron place fire on the altar, and arrange wood on the fire. Then let the sons of Aaron, the Kohanim, arrange the pieces (of the sacrifice) . . . on the wood which is on the fire'* (*Leviticus* 1:7,8).]

☙ Mitzvos

36-38. These verses list *mitzvos* dealing with first fruits (v. 36), redemption of the firstborn sons (v. 37), and various tithes that must be taken before the produce of the Holy Land may be eaten (v. 38).

The Talmud records a wide-ranging dis-

festivals, the holy things, the sin-offerings to atone for Israel, and all the work of our God's Temple.

35 *Then we cast lots for the wood-offering — the Kohanim, Levites, and the people — to bring to our God's Temple, the Temple of our forefathers, at appointed times, yearly, to burn on the altar of* HASHEM *our God, as it is written in the Torah.* 36 *And to bring*

pute concerning the sanctity of the Holy Land. One view is that the sanctification of *Eretz Yisrael* instituted through Joshua's conquest of the Land remains eternally effective, regardless of whether the Jewish people inhabit the Land or are exiled, קְדֻשָּׁה רִאשׁוֹנָה קִדְּשָׁה לִשְׁעָתָהּ וְקִדְּשָׁה לֶעָתִיד לָבֹא. Another opinion is that Joshua's sanctification was effective only so long as the people inhabited the Land, but expired with the destruction of the First Temple and the exile of the people to Babylon, קְדֻשָּׁה רִאשׁוֹנָה קִדְּשָׁה לִשְׁעָתָהּ וְלֹא קִדְּשָׁה לֶעָתִיד לָבֹא (see *Chagigah* 3b, *Chullin* 7a, et al.). According to the latter view, the observance of the Land-related *mitzvos* [such as *terumah*, *maaser* (tithes), and *bikkurim* (first fruits)], was no longer required after the exile (*Rambam, Hil. Terumos* 1:5).

The status of these Land-related *mitzvos* when the exiles returned during the times of Ezra and Nehemiah and resanctified the Land is a matter of dispute (*Yerushalmi, Sheviis* 6:1). R' Elazar's opinion is that there was no Biblical requirement for performing these commandments during the days of the Second Temple.[1] Thus, verses 36 and 38 list Land-related commandments among the *mitzvos* which the people *voluntarily accepted* with the self-imposed *Bris Amanah* (v. 1). Although the covenant also included non-Land-related commandments, which are Biblically required even in the diaspora — such as giving the firstborn animals to the *Kohanim* — the *Bris Amanah* was basically formulated for *mitzvos* which were not Biblically incumbent but were now voluntarily accepted. Because the people willingly accepted upon themselves these voluntary commandments, they were credited with having performed even the obligatory *mitzvos* voluntarily.

R' Yose, however, holds that once Ezra and Nehemiah resanctified the Land, the people were Biblically obliged to perform the Land-related commandments.[2] Why, then, are the Land-related *mitzvos* included among the voluntary obligations of the covenant? R' Yose answers that since the people accepted the obligations of Land-related *mitzvos* joyfully, Scripture credits them as having performed them voluntarily.

36. **וּלְהָבִיא** — *And to bring . . .* The people vowed to bring the first fruits (*bikkurim*) of the Holy Land to the Temple, as stated

1. *Rambam* (*Hil. Terumos* 1:26) explains that the Biblical obligation is in effect only when all [or at least the majority] of Jews reside in the Holy Land. Therefore, Ezra's resanctification of the Land did not reinstitute the Biblical obligation for *terumah* and *maaser* (see *Aruch HaShulchan HaAsid* 52:6), since the majority of the nation remained in exile.

Another interpretation of *Yerushalmi* is as follows: In R' Elazar's opinion, the people were not obligated to sanctify the Land in the days of Ezra, and in fact left certain parts unsanctified. In those parts of *Eretz Yisrael* which they did choose to sanctify, however, they were indeed Biblically obligated to observe the Land-related *mitzvos*. Thus, their decision to sanctify certain sections of the Land constituted a voluntary acceptance of the Land-related *mitzvos* for those areas (*Rash, Sheviis* 6:1).

2. According to the alternative explanation of *Yerushalmi* cited in the previous footnote, R' Yose's view is that Ezra and his followers were obligated to sanctify all of *Eretz Yisrael*, so that the Land-related *mitzvos* were Biblically mandated throughout the country. Since they were obligated to do so, the reinstatement of these *mitzvos* was in no sense voluntary. According to this interpretation, R' Elazar and R' Yose both agree that once the Land was sanctified by Ezra and his followers, all of Land-related *mitzvos* were Biblically mandated (see *Rash, Ridvaz, Sheviis* 6:1; *Tos.* to *Yevamos* 82b, s.v. ירושה ראשונה).

י
לז-לח

אֶת־בִּכּוּרֵי אַדְמָתֵנוּ וּבִכּוּרֵי כָּל־פְּרִי כָל־
לז עֵץ שָׁנָה בְשָׁנָה לְבֵית יהוה׃ וְאֶת־בְּכֹרוֹת
בָּנֵינוּ וּבְהֶמְתֵּנוּ כַּכָּתוּב בַּתּוֹרָה וְאֶת־בְּכוֹרֵי
בְקָרֵינוּ וְצֹאנֵינוּ לְהָבִיא לְבֵית אֱלֹהֵינוּ
לח לַכֹּהֲנִים הַמְשָׁרְתִים בְּבֵית אֱלֹהֵינוּ׃ וְאֶת־
רֵאשִׁית עֲרִיסֹתֵינוּ וּתְרוּמֹתֵינוּ וּפְרִי כָל־
עֵץ תִּירוֹשׁ וְיִצְהָר נָבִיא לַכֹּהֲנִים אֶל־
לִשְׁכוֹת בֵּית־אֱלֹהֵינוּ וּמַעְשַׂר אַדְמָתֵנוּ לַלְוִיִּם

in *Deuteronomy* 26:2: *Take from the first of all the fruits of the Land ...* (*Metzudos*).

The farmer would designate the first fruits to ripen as *bikkurim* by attaching an identifying tag to them while they grew. After the harvest, he brought them to the Temple and gave them to the *Kohen*, who, after the proper ceremony, would eat them within the confines of the city of Jerusalem (*Deut*. 26:1-12; *Rambam, Hil. Bikkurim* 1:5, 2:19).

The Mishnah (*Bikkurim* 1:3) states that the Torah requires *bikkurim* to be brought only from the seven species mentioned in describing the goodness of Eretz Yisrael: *a good land ... a land of wheat, barley, grapes, figs, pomegranates, a land of oil-producing olives and* [*date*] *honey* (*Deut*. 8:7, 8).

אֶת־בִּכּוּרֵי אַדְמָתֵנוּ וּבִכּוּרֵי כָּל־פְּרִי כָל־עֵץ — *The first fruits of our land, and the first fruits of all the fruits of all the trees.* The opening phrase, *the first fruits of our land,* refers to the *bikkurim* brought from wheat and barley, which grow directly from the land (*Ralbag*; *Malbim*). The next phrase, *and the first fruits of all the fruits of all the trees,* refers to *bikkurim* brought from trees.

According to *Rashi*, this means the fruit of all trees. Although Scripture requires only that *bikkurim* be brought from the seven species (see above), Rabbinical legislation mandates that they be brought from *all fruit. Ralbag* and *Malbim,* however, maintain that *fruits of all the trees* refer only to the fruits of the seven species.

Malbim asserts that the people voluntarily accepted upon themselves to bring more *bikkurim* than Biblically required. Biblically, even a single first ripening grain of fruit may be brought as *bikkurim* (*Rambam, Bikkurim* 2:17). The people now obligated themselves to bring a sixtieth of the crop, thus fulfilling the Rabbinical requirement.

According to *Ibn Ezra*, the second phrase refers to *bikkurim*, but the first phrase — *the first fruits of our land* — refers to two communal meal-offerings: the *omer* and the Two Loaves of Shavuos. [The *omer* is an offering of barley. It is cut the evening of the second day of Passover and offered at the Temple the next day. No grain growing in the Holy Land may be cut before the reaping of the *omer;* no grain planted after the past year's *omer* may be eaten until the *omer* is offered on the altar (*Leviticus* 23:14; *Rambam, Temidin U'Musafin* 7:2-17). Hence the *omer* is described as *the first fruits of our land* — first to be reaped, and first before grain is eaten.

The Two Loaves are made of wheat. No grain of the present year's crop may be brought on the altar until the Two Loaves are offered on Shavuos (*Leviticus* 23:17; *Rambam, Temidin U'Musafin* 8). Hence the Two Loaves are described as *the first fruits of our land*, first to be brought on the altar.]

The Firstborn

37. וְאֶת־בְּכֹרוֹת בָּנֵינוּ — *And the firstborn*

yearly, the first fruits of our land, and the first fruits of all the fruits of all the trees to HASHEM's Temple. [37] *And the firstborn of our sons and animals, as it is written in the Torah; and the firstborn of our cattle and sheep — to bring to our God's Temple to the Kohanim who serve at our God's Temple.* [38] *The first of our dough, our separated portions, and the fruits of all the trees of grapes and olives we shall bring to the Kohanim, to the chambers of our God's Temple; and the tithe of our land to the Levites,*

of our sons. This refers to the *mitzvah* of redeeming the firstborn son [פִּדְיוֹן הַבֵּן] by giving the *Kohen* five shekels [*Exodus* 13:13] (*Metzudos*).

וּבְהֶמְתֵּנוּ — *And animals.* This refers to the *mitzvah* of redeeming the firstborn donkey by giving the *Kohen* a sheep in its place [*Exodus* 13:13] (*Ibn Ezra; Metzudos*).

כַּכָּתוּב בַּתּוֹרָה — *As it is written in the Torah.* [The source is *Exodus* 13:13.]

The commandments to redeem the firstborn son and the firstborn donkey are listed together. This is followed by the *mitzvah* to give the firstborn kosher animal, which may not be redeemed (*Ralbag*).

וְאֶת־בְּכוֹרֵי בְקָרֵינוּ וְצֹאנֵינוּ לְהָבִיא לְבֵית אֱלֹהֵינוּ לַכֹּהֲנִים —*And the firstborn of our cattle and sheep — to bring to our God's Temple to the Kohanim.* The firstborn male offspring of kosher cattle or sheep must be presented by its owner to the *Kohen*, who brings it as a sacrifice [*Exodus* 13:12] (*Malbim*).

◆§ Challah and Terumah

38. וְאֶת־רֵאשִׁית עֲרִיסֹתֵינוּ — *The first of our dough.* This refers to the *mitzvah* of separating a piece of dough (*challah*) from the loaf or loaves to be baked, and giving it to the *Kohen*. (*Malbim*; see *Numbers* 15:20, where this piece is described as *the first of your dough*.)

וּתְרוּמֹתֵינוּ וּפְרִי כָל־עֵץ תִּירוֹשׁ וְיִצְהָר — *Our separated portions, and the fruits of all the trees of grapes and olives.*

[This refers to the *mitzvah* of *terumah*. When the produce of the Land of Israel is harvested, a portion is *separated* and given to the *Kohen*. This is known as *terumah*, literally 'raised' (*Numbers* 18:26-29).]

Our separated portions refers to the *terumah* taken from the grains. *The fruits of all the trees of grapes and olives* refers to the *terumah* taken from grapes and olives (*Metzudos*). *Ralbag* includes the fruits of all other trees.

According to *Malbim*, the people now voluntarily accepted upon themselves to take *terumah* from the *fruits of all the trees*, in addition to taking *terumah* from grains, wine, and olive oil, as Biblically required.

נָבִיא לַכֹּהֲנִים אֶל־לִשְׁכוֹת בֵּית־אֱלֹהֵינוּ — *We shall bring to the Kohanim, to the chambers of our God's Temple.* The *terumah* did not have to be brought to the Temple; it could be given to the *Kohanim* at any place. However, it was customary at that time to bring the *terumah* to the Temple chambers, where the *Kohanim* could generally be found (*Rashi*).

וּמַעְשַׂר אַדְמָתֵנוּ לַלְוִיִּם — *And the tithe of our land to the Levites.* This refers to the tithes [*maaser rishon*] of the produce of

וְהֵם הַלְוִיִּם הַמְעַשְּׂרִים בְּכֹל עָרֵי עֲבֹדָתֵנוּ׃
לט וְהָיָה הַכֹּהֵן בֶּן־אַהֲרֹן עִם־הַלְוִיִּם בַּעְשֵׂר
הַלְוִיִּם וְהַלְוִיִּם יַעֲלוּ אֶת־מַעֲשַׂר הַמַּעֲשֵׂר
לְבֵית אֱלֹהֵינוּ אֶל־הַלְּשָׁכוֹת לְבֵית הָאוֹצָר׃ כִּי
מ אֶל־הַלְּשָׁכוֹת יָבִיאוּ בְנֵי־יִשְׂרָאֵל וּבְנֵי הַלֵּוִי
אֶת־תְּרוּמַת הַדָּגָן הַתִּירוֹשׁ וְהַיִּצְהָר וְשָׁם כְּלֵי
הַמִּקְדָּשׁ וְהַכֹּהֲנִים הַמְשָׁרְתִים וְהַשּׁוֹעֲרִים
וְהַמְשֹׁרְרִים וְלֹא נַעֲזֹב אֶת־בֵּית אֱלֹהֵינוּ׃

the land which were given to the Levites (*Malbim*) [as it is written (*Numbers* 18:21) — *and to the sons of Levi I have given all the tithes in Israel as an inheritance*].

וְהֵם הַלְוִיִּם הַמְעַשְּׂרִים בְּכֹל עָרֵי עֲבֹדָתֵנוּ — *For they, the Levites, take tithes in all the cities of our toil.* The Levites take the tithes from us in all the cities where we toil in activating the soil (*Malbim*).

The toil of working the soil is mentioned here to emphasize that although the people worked hard for their produce, they gladly gave of it to the Levites, who had not labored in the fields (*Ralbag*).

◆§ The Levites Give Terumah

39. הַכֹּהֵן בֶּן־אַהֲרֹן — *The Kohen, son of Aaron.* [All the *Kohanim* are descended from Aaron, brother of Moses. Aaron himself served as the first *Kohen Gadol* at the Tabernacle when the Israelites wandered in the desert after the Exodus from Egypt. See *Exodus* 28:38-43; *Numbers* 25:10-13.]

עִם־הַלְוִיִּם בַּעְשֵׂר הַלְוִיִּם — *With the Levites at the Levites' tithing.* The tithe given to the Levite contained a portion for the *Kohen* [see following comm.]. Therefore, the Levite received his tithe in the presence of the *Kohen* (*Ri Mitrani*; *Metzudos*), to ensure that he would not withhold the portion he was obligated to set aside for the *Kohen* (*Ralbag*).

Malbim's interpretation is that our verse refers to the penalty imposed upon the Levites who failed to accompany Ezra in his ascent from the exile to the Holy Land (see ArtScroll *Ezra* 8:15). The Talmud (*Yevamos* 86b) relates that Ezra and his court decreed that the tithe regularly given to the Levite would now be shared by the *Kohanim*, who were also from the Levite family. [See *Rambam*, *Hil. Maaser* 1:4, *Kesef Mishneh*.] Thus, Scripture now states: *The Kohen ... shall be with the Levites at the Levites' tithing*, i.e., let the *Kohen* share in the tithe originally intended for the Levite.

וְהַלְוִיִּם יַעֲלוּ אֶת־מַעֲשַׂר הַמַּעֲשֵׂר — *And the Levites shall bring up the tithe of the tithe.* The Israelite was required to set aside one tenth of his produce (מַעֲשֵׂר) for the Levite. When the Levite received this tithe, he was obligated, in turn, to set aside one tenth of *his* fruits for the *Kohen* (*Numbers* 18:26-29). *The tithe of the tithe* (מַעֲשֵׂר מִן הַמַּעֲשֵׂר) refers to the tenth which the Levite took from his own portion and gave to the *Kohen* (*Rashi*; *Metzudos*).

לְבֵית אֱלֹהֵינוּ — *To our God's Temple.* The Levites brought the tithe up to the

X
39-40

for they, the Levites, take tithes in all the cities of our toil.
39 *The Kohen, son of Aaron, shall be with the Levites at the Levites' tithing, and the Levites shall bring up the tithe of the tithe to our God's Temple, to the chambers of the storage house.*
40 *For the Children of Israel and the sons of the Levites brought the separated portions of grain, wine, and oil to the chambers, wherein were the Temple vessels with the Kohanim who served, the gatekeepers, and the singers, so as not to abandon our God's Temple.*

Temple to the *Kohanim*, who remained [at that time] at the Temple (*Rashi*).

אֶל־הַלְּשָׁכוֹת לְבֵית הָאוֹצָר — *To the chambers of the storage house.* This refers to the storage house used for *terumah* (*Metzudos*).

40. יָבִיאוּ בְנֵי־יִשְׂרָאֵל וּבְנֵי הַלֵּוִי אֶת־תְּרוּמַת הַדָּגָן הַתִּירוֹשׁ וְהַיִּצְהָר — *The Children of Israel and the sons of the Levites brought the separated portions of grain, wine, and oil.* [The Israelites brought their *terumah* (v. 38), and the Levites their tithe of the tithe (v. 39).]

וְשָׁם כְּלֵי הַמִּקְדָּשׁ וְהַכֹּהֲנִים הַמְשָׁרְתִים וְהַשּׁוֹעֲרִים וְהַמְשֹׁרְרִים — *Wherein were the Temple vessels with the Kohanim who served, the gatekeepers, and the singers.* The Temple vessels were stored in the chambers, so the *Kohanim* and Levite gatekeepers and singers [7:73] remained there to guard them (*Metzudos*).

וְלֹא נַעֲזֹב אֶת בֵּית אֱלֹהֵינוּ — *So as not to abandon our God's Temple.* The *terumah* was brought to the *Kohanim* at the Temple so that they would not have to abandon their watch over the vessels at the Temple (*Metzudos*).

According to *Rashi*, chapters 7-10 were part of the book of ancestral records of the *first immigrants* (7:5) found by Nehemiah. The list of immigrants (ch. 7), and the narration of events following (ch. 8-10) were copied by Nehemiah from that book and inserted into the Book of *Nehemiah*. Our verse concludes the section copied from that book. The following chapters [11-13] return to the narrative of the first section of the Book of *Nehemiah*, which portrays Nehemiah's efforts to strengthen the city of Jerusalem.

XI

This chapter resumes the narrative of 7:4 which related that Jerusalem had been settled only sparsely by the returned exiles. It was natural for the leaders of the people to make their houses in Jerusalem, but for ordinary citizens a move from the comfort of the countryside to the more congested condition of city life (see comm. to v. 2) constituted a sacrifice. Thus, in order to fully reinhabit the city, a lottery was cast. The names of those families who moved into Jerusalem are explicitly mentioned and comprise the greater portion of this chapter. The chapter concludes with a general listing of the places in the surrounding countryside where the remainder of the people settled.

יא
א־ד

א וַיֵּשְׁבוּ שָׂרֵי־הָעָם בִּירוּשָׁלָ͏ִם וּשְׁאָר הָעָם
הִפִּילוּ גוֹרָלוֹת לְהָבִיא ׀ אֶחָד מִן־הָעֲשָׂרָה
לָשֶׁבֶת בִּירוּשָׁלַ͏ִם עִיר הַקֹּדֶשׁ וְתֵשַׁע הַיָּדוֹת
ב בֶּעָרִים׃ וַיְבָרְכוּ הָעָם לְכֹל הָאֲנָשִׁים
ג הַמִּתְנַדְּבִים לָשֶׁבֶת בִּירוּשָׁלָ͏ִם׃ וְאֵלֶּה
רָאשֵׁי הַמְּדִינָה אֲשֶׁר יָשְׁבוּ בִּירוּשָׁלָ͏ִם וּבְעָרֵי
יְהוּדָה יָשְׁבוּ אִישׁ בַּאֲחֻזָּתוֹ בְּעָרֵיהֶם יִשְׂרָאֵל
הַכֹּהֲנִים וְהַלְוִיִּם וְהַנְּתִינִים וּבְנֵי עַבְדֵי שְׁלֹמֹה׃
ד וּבִירוּשָׁלַ͏ִם יָשְׁבוּ מִבְּנֵי יְהוּדָה וּמִבְּנֵי בִנְיָמִן
מִבְּנֵי יְהוּדָה עֲתָיָה בֶן־עֻזִּיָּה בֶּן־זְכַרְיָה בֶן־

◆§ The Lottery

1. וַיֵּשְׁבוּ שָׂרֵי־הָעָם בִּירוּשָׁלַם וּשְׁאָר הָעָם הִפִּילוּ גוֹרָלוֹת — *Now, the lords of the people settled in Jerusalem, while the remainder of the people cast lots.* Nehemiah paved the way for the full rehabitation of the city by strengthening the people's support of the *Kohanim* and the Temple service (10:33-40), essentials for making Jerusalem a viable center for the people's religious experience. All that remained was to actually move a part of the population back within its walls. Accordingly, the lords returned to settle the city. However, since so much of the city was in ruins, many others of lesser means found it a hardship to move there. It was therefore necessary to set up a system of lots that would bring the general populace back to Jerusalem to rebuild its ruins (*Malbim* here and 7:4; *Ralbag*).

לְהָבִיא אֶחָד מִן־הָעֲשָׂרָה לָשֶׁבֶת בִּירוּשָׁלַם עִיר הַקֹּדֶשׁ — *To bring one-tenth to settle in the Holy City of Jerusalem.* The settlers were brought in to protect the city (*Rashi*), and rebuild it (*Ralbag*).

The tenth of the people settling in the Holy City corresponded to the tithe (*maaser*) given to the Levites [10:38] and the *Kohanim* [10:39] (*Malbim*).

2. וַיְבָרְכוּ הָעָם לְכֹל הָאֲנָשִׁים הַמִּתְנַדְּבִים — *And the people blessed all the men who volunteered.* In addition to those chosen by lot to live in Jerusalem, other people volunteered to settle it (*Rashi*).

Since the people blessed those who volunteered to settle in Jerusalem, it is apparent that dwelling in Jerusalem constituted a sacrifice. The Talmud (*Kesubos* 110b) derives that living in a large city is less desirable than living in a small town.[1] *Rashi* (ibid.) explains that large cities are crowded and airless; small towns offer fresh air and gardens. *Metzudos* explains that living costs are higher in heavily populated areas.

3-23. The genealogies listed from verse 3 onward parallel those listed in *I Chronicles* 9:3-17, with some differences. The dissimilarities are more pronounced than the variations between the genealogical lists of *Ezra*, chapter 2 and *Nehemiah*, chapter 7. Perhaps it is because of this that *Malbim* (here and in *I Chronicles*) main-

1. Based on this derivation, the Talmud rules that when a couple marries in a small town, the husband may not require his wife to follow him to a large city (see *Rambam*, *Ishus* 13:17; *Even HaEzer* 75a).

*Now, the lords of the people settled in Jerusalem,
while the remainder of the people cast lots to bring
one-tenth to settle in the Holy City of Jerusalem, with
nine-tenths in cities.* 2 *And the people blessed all the men
who volunteered to settle in Jerusalem.*
3 *The following are the heads of the territory who
settled in Jerusalem; in the cities of Judah, each man
settled on his ancestral territory, in their cities —
Israelites, Kohanim, Levites, Nethinites, and sons of
Solomon's slaves.* 4 *[Some] of the sons of Judah and
Benjamin settled in Jerusalem; of the sons of Judah.
Athaiah the son of Uziah, the son of Zechariah, the son*

tains that our two lists merely augment each other, but are not different versions of the same list. According to *Malbim*, the list in *Nehemiah* was recorded in order to supply details which are missing from *Chronicles* (cf. ArtScroll *I Chronicles*, chapter 9).

3. וְאֵלֶּה רָאשֵׁי הַמְּדִינָה אֲשֶׁר יָשְׁבוּ בִּירוּשָׁלָם — *The following* [lit. *these*] *are the heads of the territory who settled in Jerusalem.* The heads of the territory are listed below, beginning with verse 4 (*Rashi*; *Metzudos*).

Ralbag, however, translates: *These* [volunteers of the preceding verse] *were the heads of the territory, who settled in Jerusalem.* Our verse explains that those volunteers were the heads of the territory.

בַּאֲחֻזָּתוֹ בְּעָרֵיהֶם — *On his ancestral territory, in their cities.* The people now settled in *their* cities, i.e., those cities which had been theirs [or their ancestors'] before the First Temple's destruction and the Babylonian exile (*Metzudos*).

◆§ The Sons of Judah and Benjamin

4. מִבְּנֵי יְהוּדָה וּמִבְּנֵי בִנְיָמִן — [*Some*] *of the sons of Judah and Benjamin. I Chronicles* 9 also lists those who settled at this time in Jerusalem, but adds some members of tribes other than Judah and Benjamin. Since those settlers were few in number, *Nehemiah* deletes them (*Metzudos*).

Malbim offers a different explanation: *Chronicles* precedes the book of *Ezra-Nehemiah*. In composing his book, Nehemiah quoted from *I Chronicles* 9:3 the phrase *some of the sons of Judah and Benjamin settled in Jerusalem*, to indicate that his list refers to the same settlers as that of *Chronicles*. Having established that the subject of both lists are the same, Nehemiah avoided repetition by omitting the members of other tribes included in the *Chronicles* list, and supplemented the *Chronicles* list with additions contained in the following verses.

עֲתָיָה — *Athaiah.* Only the most distinguished of the settlers are enumerated here (*Rashi*).

Athaiah and Maasaiah the son of Baruch (v. 5) were the leaders of the 468 *sons of Perez* listed in verse 6 (*Ri Mitrani*). *I Chronicles* (9:4) refers to Athaiah as *Uthai*. This is not unusual; *Chronicles* often lists names slightly changed from other books of Scripture (*Ramban*, *Sefer HaGeulah I*).

בֶּן־עֻזִּיָּה בֶּן־זְכַרְיָה — *The son of Uziah, the son of Zechariah.* The names of Uziah and Zechariah do not appear in *I Chronicles* 9:4 as the ancestors of *Uthai* [*Athaiah*].

אֲמַרְיָה בֶּן־שְׁפַטְיָה בֶּן־מַהֲלַלְאֵל מִבְּנֵי־פָרֶץ׃
ה וּמַעֲשֵׂיָה בֶן־בָּרוּךְ בֶּן־כָּל־חֹזֶה בֶּן־חֲזָיָה בֶּן־
ו עֲדָיָה בֶן־יוֹיָרִיב בֶּן־זְכַרְיָה בֶּן־הַשִּׁלֹנִי׃ כָּל־
בְּנֵי־פֶרֶץ הַיֹּשְׁבִים בִּירוּשָׁלָם אַרְבַּע מֵאוֹת
ז שִׁשִּׁים וּשְׁמֹנָה אַנְשֵׁי־חָיִל׃ וְאֵלֶּה
בְּנֵי בִנְיָמִן סַלֻּא בֶּן־מְשֻׁלָּם בֶּן־יוֹעֵד בֶּן־פְּדָיָה
בֶּן־קוֹלָיָה בֶּן־מַעֲשֵׂיָה בֶּן־אִיתִיאֵל בֶּן־
ח יְשַׁעְיָה׃ וְאַחֲרָיו גַּבַּי סַלָּי תְּשַׁע מֵאוֹת עֶשְׂרִים
ט וּשְׁמֹנָה׃ וְיוֹאֵל בֶּן־זִכְרִי פָּקִיד עֲלֵיהֶם וִיהוּדָה
י בֶן־הַסְּנוּאָה עַל־הָעִיר מִשְׁנֶה׃ מִן־
יא הַכֹּהֲנִים יְדַעְיָה בֶן־יוֹיָרִיב יָכִין׃ שְׂרָיָה
בֶן־חִלְקִיָּה בֶּן־מְשֻׁלָּם בֶּן־צָדוֹק בֶּן־
מְרָיוֹת בֶּן־אֲחִיטוּב נְגִד בֵּית הָאֱלֹהִים׃

אֲמַרְיָה — *Amariah.* Amariah is referred to in *I Chronicles* (9:4) as *Imri* (*Malbim*).

בֶּן־שְׁפַטְיָה בֶּן־מַהֲלַלְאֵל — *The son of Shephatiah, the son of Mahalalel.* These names, too, do not appear in *Chronicles*, but were added by Nehemiah (*Malbim*).

מִבְּנֵי פָרֶץ — *Of the sons of Perez.* [*I Chronicles* 9:4 identifies Perez as the son of Judah, founder of his tribe. See *Genesis* 38:29.]

5. וּמַעֲשֵׂיָה בֶן־בָּרוּךְ בֶּן־כָּל־חֹזֶה... בֶּן־הַשִּׁלֹנִי — *Maasaiah the son of Baruch, the son of Kal Hozeh ... the son of Hashiloni. Hashiloni* is a reference to Judah's son Shelah [see *Genesis* 38:5] (*Metzudos*).

I Chronicles (9:5) lists *from Shiloni, Asaiah the firstborn and his sons. Asaiah* refers to Maasaiah. Nehemiah traces six generations of Maasaiah's ancestors missing from *Chronicles* (*Malbim*).

6. כָּל־בְּנֵי־פֶרֶץ הַיֹּשְׁבִים בִּירוּשָׁלָם — *All of the sons of Perez who settled in Jerusalem.* Athaiah (v. 4) and Maasaiah (v. 5) were the leaders of the sons of Perez (*Ri Mitrani*).

אַרְבַּע מֵאוֹת שִׁשִּׁים וּשְׁמֹנָה — *Four hundred sixty-eight.* Our text numbers the sons of Perez, but not the sons of Hashiloni [v. 5]. *I Chronicles* (9:5, 6) lists the sons of Hashiloni, and also the sons of Zerah [another son of Judah; see *Genesis* 38:30]. The number 690 given there includes the sons of Hashiloni and of Zerah (*Metzudos*).

Malbim explains that Nehemiah did not list the sons of Zerah since they are already listed in *Chronicles*. Furthermore, according to *Malbim*, the number 690 given there includes the sons of Zerah but not of Hashiloni. Since our verse gives the numbers of the sons of Perez as 468, and *Chronicles* numbers the sons of Perez and of Zerah as 690, it follows that the sons of Zerah numbered 222.

7. סַלֻּא בֶּן־מְשֻׁלָּם בֶּן־יוֹעֵד בֶּן־פְּדָיָה — *Salu the son of Meshullam, the son of Joed, the son of Pedaiah. I Chronicles* (9:7) lists *Salu the son of Meshullam, the son of Hodaviah, the son of Hassenuah.* Nehemiah added the names of Salu's ancestors missing from *Chronicles*, and deleted those already mentioned there (*Malbim*).

8. וְאַחֲרָיו גַּבַּי סַלָּי — *After him: Gabai*

XI
5-11

of Amariah, the son of Shephatiah, the son of Mahalalel,
of the sons of Perez. 5 *And Maasaiah the son of Baruch,*
the son of Kal Hozeh, the son of Hazaiah, the son of
Adaiah, the son of Joiarib, the son of Zechariah, the son
of Hashiloni. 6 *All of the sons of Perez who settled in*
Jerusalem — four hundred sixty-eight warriors.
7 *The following are the sons of Benjamin. Salu the son*
of Meshullam, the son of Joed, the son of Pedaiah, the son
of Kolaiah, the son of Maaseiah, the son of Ithiel, the son
of Isaiah. 8 *After him: Gabai Salai, nine hundred twenty-*
eight. 9 *Joel the son of Zichri was appointed over them,*
and Judah the son of Hassenuah was assistant over the
city.
10 *Of the Kohanim: Jedaiah the son of Joiarib,*
Jachin. 11 *Seraiah the son of Hilkiah the son of*
Meshullam the son of Zadok, the son of Meraioth, the
son of Ahitub, the supervisor over God's Temple.

Salai. After Salu, i.e., lower than Salu in distinction, came Gabai Salai (*Metzudos*).

תְּשַׁע מֵאוֹת עֶשְׂרִים וּשְׁמֹנָה — *Nine hundred twenty-eight.* The 928 were the followers of Salu and Gabai Salai (*Ri Mitrani*). According to *Metzudos*, the 928 accompanied Gabai Salai.

The name Gabai Salai does not appear in *Chronicles*, while three other names, Ibneiah, Eilah, and Meshullam the son of Shephatiah — which appear among the sons of Benjamin — are not mentioned here in *Nehemiah*. Moreover, the total for the sons of Benjamin given there [v. 9] is 956 rather than 928. *Ri Mitrani* and *Malbim* explain that the total of 928 here refers to the families of both Salu (v. 7) and Gabai Salai.

The three additional families mentioned in *Chronicles* must have numbered only 28, producing the total of 956 mentioned here.

9. וְיוֹאֵל בֶּן־זִכְרִי — *Joel the son of Zichri.* The information in this verse does not appear in *Chronicles*, and was therefore added here by Nehemiah (*Malbim*).

עַל־הָעִיר מִשְׁנֶה — *Was assistant over the city.* He was the assistant mayor (*Metzudos*). Alternatively, he was assistant to the official, Joel (*Ralbag*).

◈ The Kohanim

10. מִן־הַכֹּהֲנִים — *Of the Kohanim.* This refers to the *Kohanim* who settled in Jerusalem (*Metzudos*).

יְדַעְיָה בֶן־יוֹיָרִיב — *Jedaiah the son of Joiarib. I Chronicles* [9:10] lists Jedaiah *and* Jehoiarib. Nehemiah mentions the two names to indicate that Jedaiah was actually Joiarib's son (*Malbim*).

יָכִין — *Jachin.* [*I Chronicles* (9:10) writes *and Jachin,* making it clear that he was another person.]

11. שְׂרָיָה בֶן־חִלְקִיָּה . . . נְגִד בֵּית הָאֱלֹהִים — *Seraiah the son of Hilkiah, the supervisor over God's Temple. I Chronicles* (9:11) lists *Azariah the son of Hilkiah.* In our verse, Azariah is referred to as Seraiah to teach that he was also known by the latter name.

יב וַאֲחֵיהֶם עֹשֵׂה הַמְּלָאכָה לַבַּיִת שְׁמֹנֶה מֵאוֹת
עֶשְׂרִים וּשְׁנָיִם וַעֲדָיָה בֶּן־יְרֹחָם בֶּן־פְּלַלְיָה
בֶּן־אַמְצִי בֶן־זְכַרְיָה בֶּן־פַּשְׁחוּר בֶּן־מַלְכִּיָּה:
יג וְאֶחָיו רָאשִׁים לְאָבוֹת מָאתַיִם אַרְבָּעִים
וּשְׁנָיִם וַעֲמַשְׁסַי בֶּן־עֲזַרְאֵל בֶּן־אַחְזַי בֶּן־
יד מְשִׁלֵּמוֹת בֶּן־אִמֵּר: וַאֲחֵיהֶם גִּבֹּרֵי חַיִל מֵאָה
עֶשְׂרִים וּשְׁמֹנָה וּפָקִיד עֲלֵיהֶם זַבְדִּיאֵל בֶּן־
טו הַגְּדוֹלִים: וּמִן־הַלְוִיִּם שְׁמַעְיָה בֶן־חַשּׁוּב
טז בֶּן־עַזְרִיקָם בֶּן־חֲשַׁבְיָה בֶּן־בּוּנִּי: וְשַׁבְּתַי
וְיוֹזָבָד עַל־הַמְּלָאכָה הַחִיצֹנָה לְבֵית הָאֱלֹהִים
יז מֵרָאשֵׁי הַלְוִיִּם: וּמַתַּנְיָה בֶן־מִיכָא בֶּן־זַבְדִּי
בֶּן־אָסָף רֹאשׁ הַתְּחִלָּה יְהוֹדֶה לַתְּפִלָּה

Seraiah son of Hilkiah served as supervisor (not *Kohen Gadol*) of the Second Temple during the times of Nehemiah. He should not be confused with the *Kohen Gadol* Seraiah, son of Hilkiah, who was killed by Nebuchadnezzar at the time of the destruction of the First Temple (*II Kings* 25:8-21). The latter Seraiah was the grandfather of Jeshua the son of Jozadak, the first *Kohen Gadol* to officiate at the Second Temple [see *I Chronicles* 5:39-41, *Ezra* 3:2] (*Malbim*).

12. וַאֲחֵיהֶם עֹשֵׂה הַמְּלָאכָה לַבַּיִת — *With their brethren who performed the Temple service.* These were Jedaiah's [v. 10] and Seraiah's [v. 11] fellow *Kohanim*, who performed the sacrificial and other services at the Temple (*Rashi*; *Metzudos*).

The families of the *Kohanim*, but not their tasks, are enumerated in *I Chronicles* (9:10-13). Our passage adds the information that Jedaiah and his colleagues (vs. 10-12) performed the Temple services (*Malbim*).

שְׁמֹנֶה מֵאוֹת עֶשְׂרִים וּשְׁנָיִם — *Eight hundred twenty-two.*

The enumeration of the families of Jedaiah, Jachin [v. 10], Seraiah [v. 11], and their companions does not appear in *Chronicles* (*Malbim*).

בֶּן־פְּלַלְיָה בֶּן־אַמְצִי בֶן־זְכַרְיָה — *The son of Pelaliah, the son of Amzi, the son of Zechariah. Nehemiah* added these names, which do not appear in *I Chronicles* (9:12) among Adaiah's ancestors (*Malbim*).

13. וְאֶחָיו — *With his brethren.* With Adaiah's colleagues (*Malbim*).

מָאתַיִם אַרְבָּעִים וּשְׁנָיִם — *Two hundred forty-two.* This count of Adaiah [v. 12] and his companions does not appear in *I Chronicles* (*Malbim*).

וַעֲמַשְׁסַי — *And Amashesai.* This name, too, does not appear among the *Kohanim* listed in *Chronicles*, but was added by Nehemiah (*Malbim*).

14. מֵאָה עֶשְׂרִים וּשְׁמֹנָה — *One hundred twenty-eight.* This number, added to 242 [v. 13], and 822 [v .12], produces a total of 1,192. *I Chronicles* (9:13) lists 1,760 *Kohanim*.

I Chronicles (9:12,13) mentions Maasai

[12] *With their brethren who performed the Temple*
service — eight hundred twenty-two; and Adaiah the
son of Jeroham, the son of Pelaliah, the son of Amzi, the
son of Zechariah, the son of Pashhur, the son of
Malechiah. [13] *With his brethren, family heads — two*
hundred forty-two; and Amashesai the son of Azarel,
the son of Ahezai, the son of Meshilemoth, the son of
Immer. [14] *With their brethren, the warriors — one*
hundred twenty-eight; Zabdiel, son of the great, was
appointed over them.

[15] *Of the Levites: Shemaiah the son of Hashub, the*
son of Azrikam, the son of Hashabiah, the son of
Buni. [16] *With Shabethai and Jozabad over the outer*
work of God's Temple — of the Levite heads.
[17] *Mattaniah the son of Micha, the son of Zabdi, the son*
of Asaph, was head of beginning the praise at prayer,

the son of Adiel and his companions, whose names do not appear in *Nehemiah*. Evidently, Maasaiah's group totaled 568. This number, added to Nehemiah's total of 1192, equals *Chronicles'* total of 1760 (*Malbim*).

◆§ The Levites

15. בֶּן־חֲשַׁבְיָה בֶּן־בּוּנִּי — *The son of Hashabiah, the son of Buni. I Chronicles* (9:14) traces Shemaiah's ancestry to Hashabiah, of the family of Merari (son of Levi; see *Genesis* 46:11). Nehemiah added Hashabiah's great-great-grandfather Buni [*I Chronicles* 6:30, 31], who was a well-known personage (*Malbim*).

16. וְשַׁבְּתַי וְיוֹזָבָד — *With Shabethai and Jozabad.* Shemaiah, Shabethai, and Jozabad supervised the outer work (*Malbim*). *Chronicles* does not mention Shabethai and Jozabad.

עַל־הַמְּלָאכָה הַחִיצֹנָה לְבֵית הָאֱלֹהִים — *Over the outer work of God's Temple. Chronicles,* in listing the Levites, does not relate what their tasks were. Therefore, Nehemiah added here that Shemaiah, Shabethai, and Jozabad were supervisors of the outer work (*Malbim*).

They were approved supervisors of the Temple's outside work [i.e., Temple needs brought from outside the Temple (*Ralbag*)], such as bringing building materials to repair the Temple walls, and wood to be burned on the Altar (*Rashi; Metzudos*).

Ri Mitrani's explanation is that the Levites aided the *Kohanim* in all their work [*outside* the sacrificial services, which could only be performed by the *Kohanim*].

מֵרָאשֵׁי הַלְוִיִּם — *Of the Levite heads.* Shemaiah, Shabethai, and Jozabad were among the chiefs of the Levites (*Metzudos*).

17. רֹאשׁ הַתְּחִלָּה יְהוֹדֶה לַתְּפִלָּה — *Was head of beginning the praise at prayer.* Mattaniah was head of the Levite singers; he was appointed to be the first to sing the praises beginning the prayer (*Rashi; Metzudos*). According to *Ibn Ezra*, it was Mattaniah's ancestor Asaph who began the praise.

The word יְהוֹדֶה is understood as יוֹדֶה, meaning *will praise*. The letter ה is addi-

יא
יח־כב
°יְדוּתוּן ק׳

וּבַקְבֻּקְיָה מִשְׁנֶה מֵאֶחָיו וְעַבְדָּא בֶּן־שַׁמּוּעַ
יח בֶּן־גָּלָל בֶּן־°ידיתוּן: כָּל־הַלְוִיִּם בְּעִיר הַקֹּדֶשׁ
יט מָאתַיִם שְׁמֹנִים וְאַרְבָּעָה: וְהַשּׁוֹעֲרִים
עַקּוּב טַלְמוֹן וַאֲחֵיהֶם הַשֹּׁמְרִים בַּשְּׁעָרִים
כ מֵאָה שִׁבְעִים וּשְׁנָיִם: וּשְׁאָר יִשְׂרָאֵל הַכֹּהֲנִים
הַלְוִיִּם בְּכָל־עָרֵי יְהוּדָה אִישׁ בְּנַחֲלָתוֹ:
כא וְהַנְּתִינִים יֹשְׁבִים בָּעֹפֶל וְצִיחָא וְגִשְׁפָּא עַל־
כב הַנְּתִינִים: וּפְקִיד הַלְוִיִּם בִּירוּשָׁלַםִ עֻזִּי
בֶּן־בָּנִי בֶּן־חֲשַׁבְיָה בֶּן־מַתַּנְיָה בֶּן־מִיכָא מִבְּנֵי
אָסָף הַמְשֹׁרְרִים לְנֶגֶד מְלֶאכֶת בֵּית־הָאֱלֹהִים:

tional, as in יְהוֹסֵף (*Psalms* 81:6) for יוֹסֵף (*Rashi; Ibn Ezra*).

Ri Mitrani divides the phrase into two sections. Mattaniah was רֹאשׁ הַתְּחִלָּה, *head of the beginning*, i.e., head of the first *mishmar*, or group of Levites, to begin the service at the Temple. In addition, יְהוֹדֶה לַתְּפִלָּה, *he praised at prayer*. Mattaniah, who had reached old age, had fasted and prayed that the Temple construction be completed during his lifetime.

Malbim, too, separates the two phrases. רֹאשׁ הַתְּחִלָּה, Mattaniah was *the head and beginning*, i.e., the greatest, of all the other Levites. *I Chronicles* (9:15) lists Mattaniah after Bakbakar (named here Bakbukiah), Heresh and Galal, seeming to imply that Mattaniah was less distinguished than the others. To dispel this impression, Nehemiah states that Mattaniah was, in fact, *the head and beginning*, greater than the others. The second phrase, יְהוֹדֶה לַתְּפִלָּה, states that Mattaniah *praised at prayer*.

An alternative interpretation is that יְהוֹדֶה לַתְּפִלָּה is a double name, or perhaps two names, as in *I Chronicles* (25:4) where words which seem to convey meaning are actually names (*Malbim*).

וּבַקְבֻּקְיָה מִשְׁנֶה מֵאֶחָיו — *And Bakbukiah was second among his brethren.* Bakbukiah was second to open the praise and prayer (*Ibn Ezra; Metzudos*).

Ri Mitrani renders *Bakbukiah was in the house of study among his brothers*, as in *II Kings* 22:14, where *Targum* relates מִשְׁנֶה to וְשִׁנַּנְתָּם, *You shall teach them* (*Deut*. 6:7).

וְעַבְדָּא בֶּן־שַׁמּוּעַ — *Also Abda the son of Shamua.* He also settled in Jerusalem (*Metzudos*). Abda is referred to in *I Chronicles* (9:16) as Obadiah the son of Shemaiah (*Malbim*).

18. בְּעִיר הַקֹּדֶשׁ מָאתַיִם שְׁמֹנִים וְאַרְבָּעָה — *In the Holy City — two hundred eighty-four. I Chronicles* lists the names of the Levites but not their number. Nehemiah lists their number, and adds that the Levites dwelt *in the Holy City*. He therefore excluded Berechiah the son of Asa, who dwelt in the town of the Netophathites (*I Chronicles* 9:16), outside Jerusalem (*Malbim*).

19. עַקּוּב טַלְמוֹן וַאֲחֵיהֶם — *Akkub, Talmon, and their brethren. I Chronicles* (9:17) lists four leading gatekeepers — Shallum, Akkub, Talmon, and Ahiman. The words *their brethren* in our verse refer to Shallum and Ahiman (*Malbim*).

מֵאָה שִׁבְעִים וּשְׁנָיִם — *One hundred seventy-two.* Since *Chronicles* does not number the gatekeepers, *Nehemiah* gives

and Bakbukiah was second among his brethren; also
Abda the son of Shamua, the son of Galal, the son of
Jeduthun. 18 *All the Levites in the Holy City — two*
hundred eighty-four. 19 *The gatekeepers: Akkub, Tal-*
mon, and their brethren, who stood guard at the gates:
one hundred seventy-two.
20 *The remainder of Israelites, Kohanim, and*
Levites [settled] in all the cities of Judah, each in his
ancestral property. 21 *The Nethinites settled in*
Ophel, and Ziha and Gishpa were over the
Nethinites. 22 *The appointee over the Levites in*
Jerusalem — Uzi the son of Bani, the son of Hashabiah,
the son of Mattaniah, the son of Micha, of the sons
of Asaph — the singers — over the work of God's House.

their number (*Malbim*).

The sum of 172 may be explained as follows: The prophet Samuel and King David divided the Levites into 24 groups, each entitled a *mishmar* [*watch*] (*Rambam, Klei HaMikdash* 3:9; see also comm. to 12:7). Each *mishmar* of gatekeepers consisted of seven members, one to work each day of the week. Thus, the total of Levite gatekeepers was 168. With their four leaders — Shallum, Akkub, Talmon, and Ahiman — they totaled 172 (*Malbim*).

◆§ The Remaining Jews

20. בְּכָל־עָרֵי יְהוּדָה — *In all the cities of Judah.* The remaining Jews settled in all the cities of Judah (*Metzudos*).

21. וְהַנְּתִינִים — *The Nethinites.* See comm. to 7:46.

בָּעֹפֶל — *In Ophel.* Ophel was the name of a place in Jerusalem (*Rashi*).

Ralbag renders עֹפֶל, *a high place.* The Nethinites dwelt in a high part of the city near the Temple, so that they would be at hand to serve its needs. *Metzudos* translates *Ophel* as *tower.* [See comm. 3:26; *Metzudos, Isaiah* 32:14.]

וְצִיחָא וְגִשְׁפָּא עַל־הַנְּתִינִים — *And Ziha and Gishpa were over the Nethinites.* Ziha and Gishpa were appointed overseers for the Nethinites (*Rashi; Metzudos*).

22. וּפְקִיד הַלְוִיִּם — *The appointee over the Levites.* The appointees over the Levites, Judeans, and Benjaminites [v. 9] and the *Kohanim* [v. 14] are listed in here, but not in *Chronicles.*

מִבְּנֵי אָסָף הַמְשֹׁרְרִים — *Of the sons of Asaph — the singers.* Asaph was a Levite singer who attained prophecy under the tutelage of King David (*I Chronicles* 25:1,2). Paradoxically, he was a descendant of Korah who led a rebellion against Moses (*Numbers* ch. 16). Although the earth opened and swallowed up Korah and his followers, his sons were miraculously given refuge within the chasm. From there, at the very edge of the abyss, they sang exquisite songs expressing their yearning for God (see *Rashi* to *Psalms* 42:12). Ultimately, Korah's progeny — Asaph, Heman, and Jeduthun — were appointed by David as leaders of song in the Temple service (see further ArtScroll *I Chronicles* 6:16-17).

לְנֶגֶד מְלֶאכֶת בֵּית־הָאֱלֹהִים — *Over the work of God's house.* Uzi, of the sons of

כג כִּֽי־מִצְוַ֥ת הַמֶּ֖לֶךְ עֲלֵיהֶ֑ם וַאֲמָנָ֥ה עַל־
כד הַמְשֹׁרְרִ֖ים דְּבַר־י֥וֹם בְּיוֹמֽוֹ׃ וּפְתַֽחְיָ֗ה
בֶּן־מְשֵׁיזַבְאֵ֞ל מִבְּנֵֽי־זֶ֤רַח בֶּן־יְהוּדָה֙ לְיַ֣ד הַמֶּ֔לֶךְ
כה לְכָל־דָּבָ֖ר לָעָֽם׃ וְאֶל־הַחֲצֵרִ֖ים בִּשְׂדֹתָ֑ם מִבְּנֵ֣י
יְהוּדָ֗ה יָשְׁבוּ֙ בְּקִרְיַ֤ת הָֽאַרְבַּע֙ וּבְנֹתֶ֔יהָ וּבְדִיבֹן֙
כו וּבְנֹתֶ֔יהָ וּבִֽיקַבְצְאֵ֖ל וַחֲצֵרֶֽיהָ׃ וּבְיֵשׁ֥וּעַ וּבְמֹלָדָ֖ה
כז וּבְבֵ֥ית פָּֽלֶט׃ וּבַחֲצַ֣ר שׁוּעָ֗ל וּבִבְאֵ֛ר שֶׁ֖בַע
כח-כט וּבְנֹתֶֽיהָ׃ וּבְצִֽקְלַ֔ג וּבִמְכֹנָ֖ה וּבִבְנֹתֶֽיהָ׃ וּבְעֵ֥ין
ל רִמּ֛וֹן וּבְצָרְעָ֖ה וּבְיַרְמֽוּת׃ זָנֹ֤חַ עֲדֻלָּם֙ וְחַצְרֵיהֶ֔ם
לָכִישׁ֙ וּשְׂדֹתֶ֔יהָ עֲזֵקָ֖ה וּבְנֹתֶ֑יהָ וַֽיַּחֲנ֥וּ מִבְּאֵֽר־
לא שֶׁ֖בַע עַד־גֵּֽיא־הִנֹּֽם׃ וּבְנֵ֥י בִנְיָמִ֖ן מִגָּ֑בַע מִכְמָ֥שׂ
לב וְעַיָּ֖ה וּבֵֽית־אֵ֥ל וּבְנֹתֶֽיהָ׃ עֲנָת֥וֹת נֹ֖ב עֲנָֽנְיָֽה׃
לג-לד חָצ֣וֹר ׀ רָמָ֣ה גִּתָּֽיִם׃ חָדִ֥יד צְבֹעִ֖ים נְבַלָּֽט׃

Asaph, was appointed to oversee the Temple repairs, and all expenditures for the Temple repairs, together with Shabethai and Jozabad [v. 16] (*Rashi*). This was done under the auspices of the king, as explained in the following verse (*Ralbag*).

Malbim translates לְנֶגֶד, as *a supervisor*, from נָגִיד, *ruler*. He observes that members of Asaph's family were traditionally appointed as Temple overseers since the days of King David (who had organized the Levites into separate groups. See *I Chronicles* 24-26).

Ri Mitrani, however, translates הַמְשֹׁרְרִים לְנֶגֶד מְלֶאכֶת בֵּית־הָאֱלֹהִים, *who sang at God's Temple*. The sons of Asaph sang during the service, i.e., the offering of the Temple sacrifices.

23. כִּי־מִצְוַת הַמֶּלֶךְ עֲלֵיהֶם וַאֲמָנָה עַל־הַמְשֹׁרְרִים — *For the king commanded and entrusted the singers.* The Persian king Artahshast—Darius (see 2:1) — who financed the Temple expenditures (see 2:8) — appointed the Levites who were to handle those expenditures, and entrusted them with the funds (*Rashi*; *Ralbag*).

Malbim suggests that *the king* refers to King David, who decreed that the Levite singers of the children of Asaph always be entrusted with the supervision of the Temple expenditures. Alternatively, *the king* refers to King Darius, who followed the tradition established by King David, and appointed members of the family of Asaph as Temple supervisors. *Malbim* translates וַאֲמָנָה עַל־הַמְשֹׁרְרִים, *he was the skilled artist over the singers*. Uzi was the skilled musician appointed to instruct the others in the art of choral singing.

דְּבַר־יוֹם בְּיוֹמוֹ — *With the daily affairs.* The singers were entrusted with expending funds for the Temple's daily needs (*Rashi*; *Ralbag*).

Malbim translates *for each day*. The appointee, Uzi, instructed the singers (see above) *each day*; he chose which praise to sing and taught them how to sing it.

[23] *For the king commanded and entrusted the singers with the daily affairs.*

[24] *Pethahiah the son of Mesheizabel, of the sons of Zerah, son of Judah, at the king's hand for all matters of the people.* [25] *To the towns in their fields — of the sons of Judah settled in Kiriath HaArba and its villages, Dibon and its villages, and in Jekabzel and its outskirts.* [26] *In Jeshua, in Moladah, and in Beith Palet;* [27] *In Hazar Shual, and in Beer Sheba and its villages;* [28] *In Ziklag, in Mechonah and its villages;* [29] *In Ein Rimon, in Zarah, and in Jarmuth;* [30] *Zanoah, Adullam, and their outskirts, Lachish and its fields, Azekah and its villages; they encamped from Beer Sheba until the Valley of Hinom.*

[31] *The sons of Benjamin, from Gaba; Michmas, Aijah, Beth El, and its villages.* [32] *Anathoth, Nob, Ananiah,* [33] *Hazor, Ramah, Gittaim.* [34] *Hadid, Zeboim, Nebalat,*

24. לְיַד הַמֶּלֶךְ לְכָל־דָּבָר לָעָם — *At the king's hand for all matters of the people.* Pethahiah was the adviser concerning all that the people requested from the king. As the king's counselor, Pethahiah had ready access to him (*Rashi; Metzudos*).

Ralbag, however, understands that Pethahiah collected taxes and supervised the royal income. According to *Malbim*, Pethahiah was the king's appointee for matters concerning the Temple [which were already discussed in vs. 21-22].

⸎ The Towns

25. וְאֶל־הַחֲצֵרִים — *To the towns.* The list now turns to those who settled in open, unwalled towns (*Metzudos*). Our verse elaborates on a previous passage (v. 3) which states that some settled in Jerusalem, while others resided in their ancestral lands in the cities of Judah (*Malbim*).

Leviticus 25:31 defines חָצֵר as an unwalled town (*Ralbag*).

בִּשְׂדֹתָם — *In their fields.* The unwalled towns contained many fields (*Metzudos*).

בְּקִרְיַת הָאַרְבַּע — *In Kiriath HaArba.* [The city of Hebron was also known as *Kiriath Arba*. See *Genesis* 23:2, *Rashi*.]

וּבְנֹתֶיהָ — *And its villages* [lit. *daughters*]. This refers to the villages adjacent to the town (*Metzudos*). [See *Numbers* 21:25, *Rashi*.]

וַחֲצֵרֶיהָ — *And its outskirts,* i.e., small nearby areas (*Metzudos*).

30. גֵּיא־הִנֹּם — *The Valley of Hinom.* See 12:13.

⸎ The Benjaminites

31. וּבְנֵי בִנְיָמִן — *The sons of Benjamin.* The preceding verses (25-30) listed the Judeans who settled in the city of Judah; our verse lists Benjaminites who settled in the cities of Benjamin (*Malbim*).

מִגָּבַע — *From Gaba.* Their settlement began from the city of Gaba (*Metzudos*).

לה־לו לֹד וְאוֹנוֹ גֵּי הַחֲרָשִׁים: וּמִן־הַלְוִיִּם מַחְלְקוֹת
א יְהוּדָה לְבִנְיָמִין: וְאֵלֶּה
הַכֹּהֲנִים וְהַלְוִיִּם אֲשֶׁר עָלוּ עִם־זְרֻבָּבֶל
בֶּן־שְׁאַלְתִּיאֵל וְיֵשׁוּעַ שְׂרָיָה יִרְמְיָה עֶזְרָא:
ב־ג אֲמַרְיָה מַלּוּךְ חַטּוּשׁ: שְׁכַנְיָה רְחֻם
ד־ה מְרֵמֹת: עִדּוֹא גִנְּתוֹי אֲבִיָּה: מִיָּמִין מַעַדְיָה
ו־ז בִּלְגָּה: שְׁמַעְיָה וְיוֹיָרִיב יְדַעְיָה: סַלּוּ עָמוֹק
חִלְקִיָּה יְדַעְיָה אֵלֶּה רָאשֵׁי הַכֹּהֲנִים וַאֲחֵיהֶם
ח בִּימֵי יֵשׁוּעַ: וְהַלְוִיִּם יֵשׁוּעַ בִּנּוּי קַדְמִיאֵל
שֵׁרֵבְיָה יְהוּדָה מַתַּנְיָה עַל־הֻיְּדוֹת הוּא וְאֶחָיו:

36. מַחְלְקוֹת יְהוּדָה לְבִנְיָמִין — *Divisions to Judah and to Benjamin.* The Levites were divided into groups which settled in different cities throughout the lands of Judah and Benjamin (*Rashi*; *Metzudos*).

When the Holy Land was first apportioned in the times of Joshua, the *Kohanim* settled in the territories of Judah and Benjamin while the Levites were given cities among the other tribes (*Joshua* 21:4-8). Now, however, the Levites could not settle in their original cities, which were too distant from Jerusalem. They therefore settled near Jerusalem in the areas of Judah and Benjamin [see 12:29].

XII

Jerusalem is the center of Jewish spiritual life. Accordingly, before describing the dedication of the city's walls, chapter 12 (vs. 1-26) begins by detailing the generations of leaders among those who maintained the Temple and its sacrificial services — the *Kohanim* and Levites. The climax of the chapter is the description of the sanctification of the city's walls (vs. 27-43). This reinstated Jerusalem as the functional center of Judaism, just as it had been in the days before the destruction of the First Temple.

☙ The Kohanim and Levites with Zerubabel

1. אֲשֶׁר עָלוּ עִם־זְרֻבָּבֶל — *Who ascended with Zerubabel.* The narrative in *Nehemiah* takes place a number of years after Zerubabel led the first group of immigrants from Babylon, during the days of the Persian king Cyrus [*Ezra* 2:1]. At this point, continuing from the conclusion of chapter 10, the narrative reverts to the days of Cyrus, and lists the *Kohanim* and Levites who ascended then (*Malbim*).

וְיֵשׁוּעַ שְׂרָיָה יִרְמְיָה — *And Jeshua: Seraiah, Jeremiah.* Jeshua is the *Kohen Gadol* Jeshua ben Jozadak, who led the immigration together with Zerubabel (*Rashi*; *Metzudos*; see *Ezra* 3:2).

Zerubabel and Jeshua led the people; Seraiah, Jeremiah and the others listed through v. 7 led the *Kohanim* (*Metzudos*).

עֶזְרָא — *Ezra*. This cannot be the Ezra of the Book of *Ezra*, since the latter did not ascend originally with Zerubabel (*Ri Mitrani*; see, however, comm. to 7:73).

XI 35-36 [35] *Lod, Ono, Gai Haharashim.* [36] *Of the Levites, there*
were divisions to Judah and to Benjamin.

XII 1-8 *The following are the Kohanim and Levites who*
ascended with Zerubabel the son of Shealtiel, and
Jeshua: Seraiah, Jeremiah, Ezra; [2] *Amariah, Maluch,*
Hatush; [3] *Shechaniah, Rehum, Meremoth;* [4] *Ido,*
Ginnthoi, Abijah; [5] *Mijamin, Maadiah, Bilgah;*
[6] *Shemaiah and Joiarib, Jedaiah;* [7] *Sallu, Amok, Hilkiah,*
Jedaiah; these were the heads of the Kohanim with
their brethren in the days of Jeshua. [8] *The Levites:*
Jeshua, Binui, Kadmiel, Sherebiah, Judah, Mattaniah,
who was over the huyedoth, he and his brethren;

6. שְׁמַעְיָה וְיוֹיָרִיב — *Shemaiah and Joiarib.* *Malbim* notes that the first sixteen leaders of the *Kohanim* (vs. 1-6, until Shemaiah), who had emigrated with Zerubabel and Jeshua, later signed the *Bris Amanah* in the days of Nehemiah (see 10:2-9). The next six, beginning with Joiarib, are not named in the *Bris Amanah;* six others were named instead (10:2-8). Evidently, the six on our list, who led the *Kohanim* in Zerubabel's time, were later replaced by six greater leaders who emigrated after them (*Malbim*).

7. רָאשֵׁי הַכֹּהֲנִים — *The heads of the Kohanim.* The *Kohanim* had been divided by King David into twenty-four groups known as *mishmaros* (lit. *watches*), each performing the Temple services during its designated week (*Taanis* 27a; *Rambam*, *Klei HaMikdash* 4:3; see further ArtScroll *I Chronicles*, Appendix V). Each *head of the Kohanim* was the leader of his *mishmar* (*Ri Mitrani; Malbim*).

Although King David had set up twenty-four *mishmaros*, only twenty-two names are mentioned here. Apparently two families of *Kohanim* disappeared during the Babylonian exile (*Ri Mitrani*). Alternatively, the leaders of the two unnamed *mishmaros* are not mentioned in their own right because they were sons of the *Kohen Gadol* Jeshua, or of the leaders already listed here (*Malbim*).

◆§ The Levites

8. וְהַלְוִיִּם — *The Levites.* Like the *Kohanim*, the Levites too were divided by King David into *mishmaros*, each *mishmar* serving at the Temple during its assigned week (*Ralbag*; see *Rambam, Klei HaMikdash* 3:9). Accordingly, the Levites named here ascended with Zerubabel, and were among the leaders of the Levitical *mishmaros* (*Ralbag*).

יֵשׁוּעַ — *Jeshua.* This Jeshua is not the same as the one mentioned in verse 1. The Jeshua here was a Levite, not a *Kohen* (see 10:10).

מַתַּנְיָה עַל־הֻיְּדוֹת — *Mattaniah, who was over the huyedoth.* Mattaniah was in charge of playing the musical instrument known as *huyedoth* (*Rashi*).

Ibn Ezra and *Metzudos* translate הֻיְּדוֹת as הוֹדוֹת, *praise*, i.e., he led the Levite singers, who sang God's praises while the sacrifices were offered, as it is written (11:17), *Mattaniah . . . was head of beginning the praise at prayer.* According to *Malbim*, עַל הֻיְּדוֹת, *Al Huyedoth*, was the name of a Levite. The word preceding

יב
ט־יד

°וְעֻנִּי ק׳ ט וּבַקְבֻּקְיָה °וענו אֲחֵיהֶם לְנֶגְדָּם לְמִשְׁמָרוֹת׃
י וְיֵשׁוּעַ הוֹלִיד אֶת־יוֹיָקִים וְיוֹיָקִים הוֹלִיד אֶת־
יא אֶלְיָשִׁיב וְאֶלְיָשִׁיב אֶת־יוֹיָדָע׃ וְיוֹיָדָע הוֹלִיד
יב אֶת־יוֹנָתָן וְיוֹנָתָן הוֹלִיד אֶת־יַדּוּעַ׃ וּבִימֵי
יוֹיָקִים הָיוּ כֹהֲנִים רָאשֵׁי הָאָבוֹת לִשְׂרָיָה מְרָיָה
יג לְיִרְמְיָה חֲנַנְיָה׃ לְעֶזְרָא מְשֻׁלָּם לַאֲמַרְיָה
°לִמְלִיכוּ ק׳ יד יְהוֹחָנָן׃ °למלוכי יוֹנָתָן לִשְׁבַנְיָה יוֹסֵף׃

עַל הַיְּדוֹת is punctuated with an *esnachta*, which signifies the end of a phrase. This indicates that עַל הַיְּדוֹת does not modify *Mattaniah*, but is an independent statement.

9. וּבַקְבֻּקְיָה — *And Bakbukiah.* [See 11:17 *and Bakbukiah was second among his brethren.*]

אֲחֵיהֶם — *Their brethren.* The brethren of Mattaniah and his men (*Metzudos*). According to *Malbim*, the reference is to Bakbukiah's brothers, Galal and Heresh, mentioned in *I Chronicles* [9:15].

לְנֶגְדָּם — *Were equal to them.* The rest of the Levites were divided into *mishmaros* like the Levites already mentioned (*Metzudos*).

לְמִשְׁמָרוֹת — *In the watches.* [See comm. to v. 7.]

☙ The High Priests

10. וְיֵשׁוּעַ הוֹלִיד . . . — *Jeshua begot . . .* Jeshua is the *Kohen Gadol* (High Priest) mentioned in verse 1 (*Ri Mitrani*; *Metzudos*). Each of the men listed in verses 10-11 were *Kohanim Gedolim* (*Rashi*). Each succeeded his father as *Kohen Gadol* (*Metzudos*).

11. יַדּוּעַ — *Jadua.* The Talmud records that Alexander the Great conquered the Persian empire thirty-four years after the Second Temple was built (*Avodah Zarah* 9a). When Alexander invaded the Holy Land, Shimon HaTzaddik [the Righteous] appeared before him (*Yoma* 69a).[1] Shimon was a grandchild of Jadua [*Yuchasin*; see *Tzemach David*, 4:445]. He in turn was the sixth-generation descendant of Jeshua [v. 10], the *Kohen Gadol* who served when the Second Temple was built. Thus, Shimon HaTzaddik, who was seven generations removed from Jeshua, served as a *Kohen Gadol* thirty-four years after him. How could eight generations have passed within a span of thirty-four years?

If we postulate that Jeshua was over one hundred years old when the Temple was rebuilt, and each of his descendants became a father at the age of fifteen, it was possible for eight generations to live and serve within thirty-four years. The first three may have been quite old at the time of their appointment, and may have died soon after assuming office. Then, because of Shimon's great personal merit, he was chosen, over his father and grandfather, to succeed Eliashib as *Kohen Gadol*.

Alternatively, *all* of Shimon's ancestors served as *Kohanim Gedolim*. However, his more immediate forebears had been

1. Alexander marched towards Jerusalem with the intention of destroying the Temple. Shimon HaTzaddik donned the vestments of the *Kohen Gadol*, and, accompanied by attendants bearing flaming torches, rode to meet the Greek conqueror. When Alexander saw the face of the *Kohen Gadol*, he fell to the ground and prostrated himself. "It is this face," Alexander explained, "which always appears before me in battle and brings me victory" (*Yoma* 69a).

XII 9-14

[9] *Bakbukiah and Uni; their brethren were equal to them in the watches.* [10] *Jeshua begot Joiakim, Joiakim begot Eliashib, and Eliashib begot Joiada.* [11] *Joiada begot Jonathan, and Jonathan begot Jadua.* [12] *In the days of Joiakim, the Kohanim who were family heads were: over Seraiah, Meraiah; over Jeremiah, Hananiah;* [13] *Over Ezra, Meshullam; over Amariah, Jehohanan;* [14] *Over Melichu, Jonathan; over Shebaniah, Joseph;*

disqualified after a short period upon becoming *tamei* [ritually unclean] (*Yoma* 2:1), whereupon Shimon was chosen (*Malbim*).[1]

12. וּבִימֵי יוֹיָקִים — *In the days of Joiakim.* Joiakim was a *Kohen Gadol* [mentioned in v. 10] (*Rashi*).

Verses 1-7 list the names of the heads of the families of *Kohanim* during the times of Jeshua the son of Jehozadak [v. 1]. Our verse begins a list of the heads of the *Kohanim* during the tenure of Jeshua's son, the *Kohen Gadol* Joiakim (*Ralbag*).

Malbim raises a problem. Chapter 3 [v. 1] records the construction of the city walls by the *Kohen Gadol* Eliashib, son and successor of Joiakim [v. 10]. Yet chapter 10 [v. 10] in recording the signers of the *Bris Amanah*, lists the names of all the *Kohanim* who had served under the *Kohen Gadol* Jeshua, Eliashib's grandfather, who officiated as *Kohen Gadol* during the first immigration, in the days of Zerubabel [12:1].

Malbim offers two solutions:

(1) The signing of the *Bris Amanah* took place during Jeshua's tenure, in the times of Zerubabel, *before* the construction of the city walls [see comm. 7:73].

(2) All of the leading *Kohanim* who served as heads of the *mishmaros* under Jeshua were still alive during the period of his grandson Eliashib. They were replaced by the other leaders because of their old age, but were still recognized as the leading *Kohanim* of the day, and were therefore chosen to sign the *Bris Amanah*.

הָיוּ כֹהֲנִים רָאשֵׁי הָאָבוֹת — *The Kohanim who were family heads were.* Each *mishmar* (see comm. to v. 7) was composed of a different family. The text now lists the heads of each *mishmar* (*Rashi*).

לִשְׂרָיָה מְרָיָה לְיִרְמְיָה חֲנַנְיָה — *Over Seraiah, Meraiah; over Jeremiah, Hananiah.* The *Kohen* Meraiah was the leader of the *mishmar* of the family of Seraiah; Hananiah was the leader of the *mishmar* of the family of Jeremiah (*Rashi*; *Ralbag*).

Ibn Ezra offers an alternate translation: *Seraiah was over Meraiah; Jeremiah, over Hananiah.* After the death of Seraiah [listed in v. 1], Meraiah became family head in his place. After Jeremiah's death, Hananiah was appointed family head in his place.

14. לִמְלִיכוּ . . . לִשְׁבַנְיָה — *Over Melichu . . . over Shebaniah.* Melichu is called Maluch in verse 2 (*Ri Mitrani*).

Hatush, listed between Maluch and Shechaniah [vs. 2-3] among the *Kohanim* during the times of the *Kohen Gadol* Jeshua, does not appear in our list of those in the times of Joiakim [v. 12-21]. Perhaps his family was included in one of the other families listed (*Metzudos*).

According to *Malbim*, only the leaders who did *not* serve as heads of *mishmaros* in Jeshua's time are listed here under the *Kohen Gadol* Joiakim. Therefore, Hatush, who was leader under Jeshua as well as Joiakim, is not listed here. Similarly, the leader of Miniamin [v. 17] is not listed

1. R' Yitzchak Isaac HaLevi (*Doros HaRishonim*, Vol. 1, pg. 196ff) conjectures that Shimon was not *Kohen Gadol* at the time he met Alexander. His grandfather was. However, due to his advanced age and Shimon's great personal stature, Shimon was chosen to greet Alexander.

יב טו־טז לְחָרִם עַדְנָא לִמְרָיוֹת חֶלְקָי: °לַעֲדָיא זְכַרְיָה
טו־כד °לעדוא ק׳
יז לְגִנְּתוֹן מְשֻׁלָּם: לַאֲבִיָּה זִכְרִי לְמִנְיָמִין
יח לְמוֹעַדְיָה פִּלְטָי: לְבִלְגָּה שַׁמּוּעַ לִשְׁמַעְיָה
יט־כ יְהוֹנָתָן: וּלְיוֹיָרִיב מַתְּנַי לִידַעְיָה עֻזִּי: לְסַלַּי קַלָּי
כא לְעָמוֹק עֵבֶר: לְחִלְקִיָּה חֲשַׁבְיָה לִידַעְיָה
כב נְתַנְאֵל: הַלְוִיִּם בִּימֵי אֶלְיָשִׁיב יוֹיָדָע וְיוֹחָנָן
וְיַדּוּעַ כְּתוּבִים רָאשֵׁי אָבוֹת וְהַכֹּהֲנִים עַל־
כג מַלְכוּת דָּרְיָוֶשׁ הַפָּרְסִי: בְּנֵי לֵוִי רָאשֵׁי
הָאָבוֹת כְּתוּבִים עַל־סֵפֶר דִּבְרֵי הַיָּמִים וְעַד־
כד יְמֵי יוֹחָנָן בֶּן־אֶלְיָשִׁיב: וְרָאשֵׁי הַלְוִיִּם חֲשַׁבְיָה
שֵׁרֵבְיָה וְיֵשׁוּעַ בֶּן־קַדְמִיאֵל וַאֲחֵיהֶם לְנֶגְדָּם

because he, too, served under Jeshua.

15. לְחָרִים — *Over Harim.* Harim is called Rehum in verse 3 (*Ri Mitrani*).

16. לְגִנְּתוֹן — *Over Ginnthon.* Ginnthon is Ginnthoi of verse 4 (*Ri Mitrani*).

17. לְמִנְיָמִין לְמוֹעַדְיָה פִּלְטָי — *Over Miniamin and Moadiah, Piltoi.* Piltoi headed two groups — the *mishmar* of Miniamin, and the *mishmar* of Moadiah. An alternative explanation is *Over Aveiah, Zichri, over Miniamin;* Zichri was the leader of Abijah and Miniamin, while Piltoi was the leader of only Moadiah (*Ralbag*).

According to *Metzudos*, Piltoi was the leader of a single *mishmar* called by two names — Miniamin and Moadiah.

20. לְסַלַּי — *Over Sallai.* Sallai is Sallu of verse 7 (*Ri Mitrani*).

21. לִידַעְיָה נְתַנְאֵל — *Over Jedaiah, Nethanel.* Twenty-two leaders of the *mishmaros* of the *Kohanim* in Joiakim's time [vs. 12-21] are named although there were twenty-four *mishmaros* [see *Malbim* v. 7]. The text does not list all the names (*Rashi*).

◆§ The Days of Eliashib

22. The chapter opens with the lists of the leading *Kohanim* and Levites in the times of the *Kohen Gadol* Jeshua before the reconstruction of the Temple [v. 1-7 for *Kohanim*; v. 8-9 for Levites]. Then the chapter lists the new leaders of the *Kohanim* in the days of Jeshua's son Joiakim [v. 12-21]. However, no mention is made of new Levite leaders during Joiakim's reign. *Malbim* notes that most of the Levites ascended to the Holy Land only *after* the Temple was rebuilt [see *Ezra* 8:15]. Thus, they retained their leadership when Joiakim succeeded Jeshua a short time later. Afterward, when Eliashib was appointed *Kohen Gadol*, the Levites appointed new leaders. Our verse mentions *The Levites in the days of Eliashib*, i.e., the new Levite leaders (*Malbim*).

הַלְוִיִּם בִּימֵי אֶלְיָשִׁיב יוֹיָדָע וְיוֹחָנָן וְיַדּוּעַ — *The Levites in the days of Eliashib: Joiada, Johanan, and Jadua.* The Levite leaders in the days of the *Kohen Gadol* Eliashib son of Joiakim [v. 10] were Joiada, Johanan, and Jadua (*Rashi*).

Joiada, Johanan, and Jadua were Levites, as distinguished from the *Kohanim* Joiada, Jonathan, and Jadua of v. 11 (*Ri Mitrani*).

Metzudos translates *The Levites in the*

15 *Over Harim, Adna; over Meraioth, Helkoi;* 16 *Over*
Ido, Zechariah; over Ginnthon, Meshullam; 17 *Over*
Abijah, Zichri; over Miniamin and Moadiah, Piltoi;
18 *Over Bilgah, Shamua; over Shemaiah, Jonathan;*
19 *Over Joiarib, Matenai; over Jedaiah, Uzi;* 20 *Over*
Sallai, Kallai; over Amok, Eber; 21 *Over Hilkiah, Hasha-*
biah; over Jedaiah, Nethanel; 22 *The Levites in the days*
of Eliashib: Joiada, Johanan, and Jadua, recorded as
family heads, and the Kohanim [as well,] during the
reign of Darius the Persian.
23 *The sons of Levi who were heads of families*
were recorded in the book of chronicles, until the days
of Johanan the son of Eliashib. 24 *The heads of*
the Levites: Hashabiah, Sherebiah, and Jeshua son of
Kadmiel, with their brethren opposite them, praising

days of Eliashib, [as well as] Joiada, Johanan, and Jadua. The Levites as well as the successive *Kohanim Gedolim* Joiada, Johanan, and Jadua (vs. 9-10) were recorded as family heads.

וְהַכֹּהֲנִים — *And the Kohanim* [as well]. This refers to the leaders of the *Kohanim* during the times of Joiakim [vs. 12-21]. These leaders retained their positions during the days of Eliashib (*Rashi*). Their names were recorded in the chronicles of the time (*Metzudos*).

עַל־מַלְכוּת דָּרְיָוֶשׁ הַפָּרְסִי — *During the reign of Darius the Persian.* The names of the Levites and *Kohanim* mentioned in this verse were recorded during the reign of the Persian king Darius (*Rashi*).

Metzudos' translation is *and the Kohanim — through the monarchy of Darius the Persian.* The leaders of the *Kohanim* in Darius' time did not rise to their positions solely by their own merit. They received their appointments through the king.

23. בְּנֵי לֵוִי — *The sons of Levi. The sons of Levi* includes all leaders from the times of King David, when they were divided into *mishmaros* (*Ri Mitrani*).

כְּתוּבִים עַל־סֵפֶר דִּבְרֵי הַיָּמִים — *Were recorded in the book of chronicles.* The names of the Levites were recorded in a book of chronicles in which all of the events of the times were recorded (*Malbim*). This book has not been preserved (*Ralbag*). The book of chronicles mentioned in *I Kings* 14:19 was also lost (*Ri Mitrani*).

24. וְרָאשֵׁי הַלְוִיִּם — *The heads of the Levites.* Verses 24-25 list the Levites' leaders during the days of Joiakim (*Metzudos*). *Malbim* supports *Metzudos* by citing v. 26: *These [the Levites] were in the days of Joiakim. Ri Mitrani*, however, holds that the Levites listed here lived in the times of the *Kohen Gadol* Eliashib [v. 22].

חֲשַׁבְיָה — *Hashabiah.* Hashabiah was one of the Levites who had signed the *Bris Amanah* (*Malbim*; see 10:12).

שֵׁרֵבְיָה וְיֵשׁוּעַ בֶּן־קַדְמִיאֵל — *Sherebiah, and Jeshua son of Kadmiel.* These Levites had ascended with Zerubabel [v. 8]. They remained as leaders through the days of Joiakim, when the Levites of vs. 24-25 were listed (*Malbim*).

וַאֲחֵיהֶם לְנֶגְדָּם — *With their brethren opposite them.* Those listed here were the

לְהַלֵּל לְהוֹדוֹת בְּמִצְוַת דָּוִיד אִישׁ־הָאֱלֹהִים
כה מִשְׁמָר לְעֻמַּת מִשְׁמָר׃ מַתַּנְיָה וּבַקְבֻּקְיָה
עֹבַדְיָה מְשֻׁלָּם טַלְמוֹן עַקּוּב שֹׁמְרִים שׁוֹעֲרִים
כו מִשְׁמָר בַּאֲסֻפֵּי הַשְּׁעָרִים׃ אֵלֶּה בִּימֵי יוֹיָקִים
בֶּן־יֵשׁוּעַ בֶּן־יוֹצָדָק וּבִימֵי נְחֶמְיָה הַפֶּחָה
כז וְעֶזְרָא הַכֹּהֵן הַסּוֹפֵר׃ וּבַחֲנֻכַּת חוֹמַת
יְרוּשָׁלַםִ בִּקְשׁוּ אֶת־הַלְוִיִּם מִכָּל־מְקוֹמֹתָם
לַהֲבִיאָם לִירוּשָׁלָםִ לַעֲשֹׂת חֲנֻכָּה וְשִׂמְחָה
וּבְתוֹדוֹת וּבְשִׁיר מְצִלְתַּיִם נְבָלִים וּבְכִנֹּרוֹת׃

leaders of the Levite singers. Their brethren — the other leaders of the Levites — were opposite them, i.e., were equivalent and also led their Levite groups in singing (*Metzudos*).

לְהַלֵּל לְהוֹדוֹת — *Praising and thanking.* Hashabiah, Sherebiah, and Jeshua led the Levites in singing praises during the Temple services (*Malbim*).

Ri Mitrani, who places Hashabiah and his companions in the time of Eliashib, explains that there were two groups of Levites: Those listed above [v. 22] assisted the *Kohanim*, while the Levites listed in our passage were in charge of the singing at the Temple.

בְּמִצְוַת דָּוִיד אִישׁ־הָאֱלֹהִים — *By command of David, the man of God.* [King David had divided the Levites into twenty-four *mishmaros* or *watches* (see comm. v. 7).]

מִשְׁמָר לְעֻמַּת מִשְׁמָר — *Watch opposite watch.* No *mishmar* was accorded higher standing than any other. They were equal. This is a reiteration of the phrase above לְנֶגְדָּם, *opposite them* (*Metzudos*).

25. מַתַּנְיָה וּבַקְבֻּקְיָה — *Mattaniah, Bakbukiah.* These Levites, too, had accompanied Zerubabel [vs. 8,9], and remained leaders until the times of Joiakim (*Malbim*).

שֹׁמְרִים שׁוֹעֲרִים — *Guardians, gatekeepers.* Both words refer to the same assignment. *Gatekeepers* was added for clarification (*Metzudos*).

בַּאֲסֻפֵּי הַשְּׁעָרִים — *At the gateposts.* Our translation follows *Rashi*.

Ralbag traces אֲסֻפֵּי to the root אסף, *to gather*. Mattaniah, Bakbukiah ... and Akkub were leaders of the Levite gatekeepers who *gathered at the gates.* According to *Metzudos*, אֲסֻפֵּי הַשְּׁעָרִים, *Asuphei Hashearim*, is the name of the place where this particular *mishmar* stood watch.

26. אֵלֶּה — *These.* The gatekeepers named above [v. 25] served in the days of Joiakim (*Rashi*). *Metzudos* expands the context of the verse to include the leaders of the *Kohanim* and Levites as well as gatekeepers listed above [vs. 12-21, 24,25]. They all served in Joiakim's time.

בִּימֵי יוֹיָקִים ... וּבִימֵי נְחֶמְיָה ... וְעֶזְרָא — *In the days of Joiakim ... and in the days of Nehemiah ... and Ezra.* Our verse places Ezra and Nehemiah in *Eretz Yisrael* in Joiakim's time. Now Joiakim's son Eliashib served as *Kohen Gadol* during the reign of the Persian king, Darius; hence Joiakim, Ezra, and Nehemiah must have arrived in the Holy Land *before* Darius' reign. *Nehemiah* 2:1, however, places Nehemiah's ascent to the Holy Land in the twentieth year of

and thanking by command of David, the man of God, watch opposite watch; 25 *Mattaniah, Bakbukiah, Obadiah, Meshullam, Talmon, and Akkub — guardians, gatekeepers at their watch at the gateposts.* 26 *These were in the days of Joiakim the son of Jeshua the son of Jozadak, and in the days of Nehemiah the ruler and Ezra the Kohen and scholar.*

27 *At the dedication of the wall of Jerusalem, the Levites were sought from all their places to be brought to Jerusalem to perform the dedication with rejoicing, with thanksgiving, and with the playing of cymbals, nevels,*

Artahshast (2:1), who is identified as Darius' son [or as Darius]. Evidently, Nehemiah had previously been in the Land of Israel at a much earlier date (*Ralbag*).

[Similarly, *Ezra* 7:1 describes Ezra's ascent to the Holy Land at the time of Artahshast. Evidently, both Ezra and Nehemiah had ascended to the Land during Cyrus' reign, but then returned to Babylon, perhaps when the Temple construction was halted. Later, they ascended again. Mordechai, too, left the Holy Land and returned to Babylon. See ArtScroll *Ezra* 2:2.]

Malbim remarks that Nehemiah and Ezra survived Joiakim and died during the lifetime of his son Eliashib. Thus, *the heads of the Levites who were in the days of Joiakim ... Nehemiah ... and Ezra ...* served in their positions for an extended period.

◆§ The Dedication of the City

27-43. The following verses describe the sanctification of the city of Jerusalem. Sanctification has legal ramifications. For example, sacrifices classified as קָדָשִׁים קַלִּים, *offerings of lesser holiness,* may be eaten anywhere inside the sacred walls of Jerusalem. Jerusalem had originally been sanctified by King Solomon when he built the First Temple. Why did Nehemiah consecrate the city a second time?

According to one Talmudic opinion (*Shevuos* 16a), Solomon's original sanctification expired when the Babylonians destroyed the First Temple and the city. Nehemiah now resanctified it.

However, another view is that Solomon's sanctification is effective eternally. Accordingly, Nehemiah's sanctification ritual was a symbolic act, commemorating the rejuvenation of the sacred city. [See *Rambam, Beis HaBechirah* 6:14.]

27. וּבַחֲנֻכַּת חוֹמַת יְרוּשָׁלַם — *At the dedication of the wall of Jerusalem.* With the completion of the city walls, the city itself was ready for sanctification through the dedication ceremony (*Rashi*). The city, its walls, and the Temple Courtyard [עֲזָרָה] were now sanctified (*Ri Mitrani*).

הַלְוִיִּם מִכָּל־מְקוֹמֹתָם — *The Levites ... from all their places.* The Levites who dwelt outside the city of Jerusalem were brought to the city (*Malbim*).

וּבְתוֹדוֹת — *With thanksgiving.* Our translation follows *Rashi. Ralbag* and *Malbim*, however, render *with the thanksgiving offering bread* used in the sanctification ritual (v. 31).

וּבְשִׁיר מְצִלְתַּיִם נְבָלִים וּבְכִנֹּרוֹת — *And with the playing of cymbals, nevels, and harps.* The Talmud (*Shevuos* 15b) asserts that these musical instruments were

כח וַיֵּאָסְפוּ בְּנֵי הַמְשֹׁרְרִים וּמִן־הַכִּכָּר סְבִיבוֹת
כט יְרוּשָׁלַם וּמִן־חַצְרֵי נְטֹפָתִי: וּמִבֵּית הַגִּלְגָּל
וּמִשְּׂדוֹת גֶּבַע וְעַזְמָוֶת כִּי חֲצֵרִים בָּנוּ לָהֶם
ל הַמְשֹׁרְרִים סְבִיבוֹת יְרוּשָׁלָם: וַיִּטַּהֲרוּ הַכֹּהֲנִים
וְהַלְוִיִּם וַיְטַהֲרוּ אֶת־הָעָם וְאֶת־הַשְּׁעָרִים
לא וְאֶת־הַחוֹמָה: וָאַעֲלֶה אֶת־שָׂרֵי יְהוּדָה
מֵעַל לַחוֹמָה וָאַעֲמִידָה שְׁתֵּי תוֹדֹת גְּדוֹלֹת
וְתַהֲלֻכֹת לַיָּמִין מֵעַל לַחוֹמָה לְשַׁעַר הָאַשְׁפֹּת:

played throughout the streets of Jerusalem during the sanctification ceremony, and certain psalms were sung. *Tosafos* explain that the psalms were chosen for their references to God's protection from enemies. They were intended as a prayer for God's help in resisting the enemies who had attempted to disrupt the construction of the city walls[1] (2:10, 3:33-35). According to *Rashi*, some psalms were chosen for their reference to the Temple dedication. Also the Hymn of Thanksgiving [מִזְמוֹר לְתוֹדָה (Psalm 100)] was sung (to give thanks for the reconstruction of the city). [See *Mishneh LaMelech, Beis HaBechirah* 6:12.]

28. וַיֵּאָסְפוּ בְּנֵי הַמְשֹׁרְרִים וּמִן־הַכִּכָּר — *The sons of the singers also gathered, and from the plain.* Those who dwelt in the city of Jerusalem and those who lived in the plain near Jerusalem, gathered (*Metzudos*).

30. וַיִּטַּהֲרוּ הַכֹּהֲנִים וְהַלְוִיִּם — *Then the Kohanim and Levites purified themselves.* The *Kohanim* and Levites who were *tamei* [ritually unclean] purified themselves by immersing in a *mikveh* (*Metzudos*).

וַיְטַהֲרוּ אֶת־הָעָם — *Afterward they purified the people.* First they purified themselves; then they purified the people (*Rashi*). They urged the people to purify themselves (*Metzudos*).

וְאֶת־הַשְּׁעָרִים וְאֶת־הַחוֹמָה — *The gates and the wall.* They removed all objects causing *tumah* [such as the carcasses of rodents and animals], throughout the city (*Rashi*). They also removed any repulsive, disgusting objects (*Metzudos*).

◆§ The March Begins

31. אֶת־שָׂרֵי יְהוּדָה — *The lords of Judah.* All the lords of Judah were gathered near Nehemiah's home (*Malbim*).

מֵעַל לַחוֹמָה — *Near the wall.* מֵעַל is translated *near* as in *Numbers* 2:20 (*Malbim*). The members of the procession stood adjacent to the wall and marched around it. *Rashi* (*Shevuos* 15a) is of the opinion that the procession marched *outside* the city wall. *Tosafos* (*Shevuos* 15b) maintain that they marched within the city walls.

An alternative translation is *on top of the wall*. The lords were brought up to the top of the wall, where the march around the city took place (*Ralbag; Malbim; Ritva*).

1. When Ezra sanctified Jerusalem they marched around the city and recited Psalm 91 to rid themselves of harmful, destructive elements (this chapter praises God for his protective power during times of great danger). The chanting was joyful, accompanied by musical instruments (*Rabbeinu Yonah* on *Rif, Berachos* 1:3).

and harps. 28 *The sons of the singers also gathered, and
from the plain around Jerusalem, and from Hatzrei Ne-
tophathi.* 29 *Also from Beth Hagilgal and from the fields
of Geba and Azmaveth; for the singers had constructed
open cities for themselves around Jerusalem.* 30 *Then the
Kohanim and Levites purified themselves; afterward
they purified the people, the gates and the wall.* 31 *I
brought the lords of Judah up near the wall, and I placed
standing two large thanksgiving loaves; then the march
towards the right near the wall to the Refuse Gate.*

וָאַעֲמִידָה — *And I placed standing.* Nehemiah brought the thanksgiving loaves to the wall where he and the others stood (*Metzudos; Malbim*).

שְׁתֵּי תוֹדֹת גְּדוֹלֹת — *Two large thanksgiving loaves.* Although the term תּוֹדָה generally refers to the animal component of the thanksgiving offering, the Talmud (*Shevuos* 14a) demonstrates that תּוֹדָה גְּדוֹלָה refers to the *loaves* accompanying the thanksgiving offering.

The thanksgiving loaves [לַחְמֵי תוֹדָה] were leavened loaves such as those brought as part of all thanksgiving offerings (תּוֹדָה). [This offering consisted of a sheep, goat, or ox (*Rambam, Maaseh HaKorbanos* 1:11), thirty unleavened loaves (*matzah*), and ten leavened loaves (*chametz*). Each leavened loaf was as large as three unleavened loaves (*Maaseh HaKorbanos* 9:17,18), and was therefore called a *large thanksgiving loaf.* Two large thanksgiving loaves were carried around the city of Jerusalem in the ritual of sanctification (*Rashi, Shevuos* 14a).]

Malbim translates: *two thanksgiving offerings.* Five leavened loaves from each of two thanksgiving offerings were carried around one side of the city, and the remaining loaves from each of the two offerings around the other side. [See comm. to v. 38.]

Ri Mitrani and *Ibn Ezra* translate שְׁתֵּי תוֹדֹת, *two thanksgiving groups.* Two groups of Levites singing songs of thanksgiving marched around the city to sanctify it. [See *Midrash Shocher Tov* 56.]

וְתַהֲלֻכֹת — *Then the march.* Then the march around the city began (*Rashi; Metzudos*).

Malbim translates *then the marches.* Two separate marches began from the same point and moved around the city walls, one towards the south and the other towards the north. Both finally met, thus completing the march around the wall.

A different translation is *and the pathways* built atop the wall (*Malbim*).

לַיָּמִין — *Towards the right.* They left the confines of the city in order to march around it, and turned to the right side to begin the march (*Rashi*). This refers to the right side of a person facing the city (*Rashi, Shevuos* 15a).

According to *Malbim*, one of the two processions began from a point near Nehemiah's home at the center of the city's western wall, at the Gate of the Valley [שַׁעַר הַגַּיְא; see 2:13]. From there it proceeded towards the south [to the right of a person facing the city].

מֵעַל לַחוֹמָה — *Near the wall.* According to *Metzudos*, the lords of Judah first climbed atop the wall, then, when the march began, descended and walked to the wall to the Refuse Gate.

לְשַׁעַר הָאַשְׁפֹּת — *To the Refuse Gate.* From its starting point at the center of the

לב וַיֵּלֶךְ אַחֲרֵיהֶם הוֹשַׁעְיָה וַחֲצִי שָׂרֵי יְהוּדָה:
לג-לד וַעֲזַרְיָה עֶזְרָא וּמְשֻׁלָּם: יְהוּדָה וּבִנְיָמִן
וּשְׁמַעְיָה וְיִרְמְיָה:
לה וּמִבְּנֵי הַכֹּהֲנִים בַּחֲצֹצְרוֹת זְכַרְיָה בֶן־יוֹנָתָן
בֶּן־שְׁמַעְיָה בֶּן־מַתַּנְיָה בֶּן־מִיכָיָה בֶּן־זַכּוּר
לו בֶּן־אָסָף: וְאֶחָיו שְׁמַעְיָה וַעֲזַרְאֵל מִלֲלַי
גִּלֲלַי מָעַי נְתַנְאֵל וִיהוּדָה חֲנָנִי בִּכְלֵי־
שִׁיר דָּוִיד אִישׁ הָאֱלֹהִים וְעֶזְרָא הַסּוֹפֵר
לז לִפְנֵיהֶם: וְעַל שַׁעַר הָעַיִן וְנֶגְדָּם עָלוּ עַל־
מַעֲלוֹת עִיר דָּוִיד בַּמַּעֲלֶה לַחוֹמָה מֵעַל
לְבֵית דָּוִיד וְעַד שַׁעַר הַמַּיִם מִזְרָח:
לח וְהַתּוֹדָה הַשֵּׁנִית הַהוֹלֶכֶת לְמוֹאל וַאֲנִי

32. וַיֵּלֶךְ אַחֲרֵיהֶם הוֹשַׁעְיָה — *Hoshaiah . . . walked after them.* Hoshaiah walked after those who carried the thanksgiving loaves (*Metuzdos*).

The Talmud (*Shevuos* 15b) explains that the two thanksgiving loaves [v. 31] were carried at the head of the procession. [According to *Tiferes Yisrael* (*Shevuos* 2:2:14), the musicians with their instruments preceded the loaves.] The members of the Sanhedrin followed, then the rest of the people.

According to *Malbim*, *after them* means after the loaves of the *two* thanksgiving sacrifices (see comm., v. 31).

33. וַעֲזַרְיָה. . . . — *With* [lit. *and*] *Azariah . . .* These marchers are singled out because they were the most distinguished (*Metzudos*).

34. יְהוּדָה וּבִנְיָמִן — *Judah, Benjamin.* These were lords (*Rashi*).

◆§ The Kohanim

35. וּמִבְּנֵי הַכֹּהֲנִים בַּחֲצֹצְרוֹת — *Of the sons of the Kohanim, with trumpets.* The *Kohanim* are commanded [*Numbers* 10:10] to sound the trumpets at the Temple on days of rejoicing, during the bringing of the *shelamim* (peace) offerings. The thanksgiving loaves here were part of a thanksgiving-*shelamim* offering [see *Rambam, Maaseh HaKorbanos* 1:6]; and the day of the city's sanctification was one of rejoicing. Therefore, the *Kohanim* sounded the trumpets (*Ralbag*).

[The *mitzvah* of sounding the trumpets applies only when the *shelamim* must be brought at a specified date, e.g., the *shelamim* brought during the Shavuos festival (see *Arachin* 11b; *Rambam, Maaseh HaKorbanos* 1:4). The thanksgiving offering brought at the sanctification ceremony does not fit into this category, since it was not restricted to a specific date. Evidently, *Ralbag's* intention is not that the *Kohanim* were Biblically commanded to sound the trumpets during the sanctification processions, but that the process of sanctification paralleled the conditions under which the command applies.

36. וְאֶחָיו — *And his brethren.* The colleagues of Zechariah [v. 35] played the music (*Rashi*; *Metzudos*).

בִּכְלֵי־שִׁיר דָּוִיד — *With instruments of the songs of David.* The *Kohanim* played King David's songs of God's praise on

XII 32-38

[32] *Hoshaiah and half of the lords of Judah walked after
them;* [33] *With Azariah, Ezra, and Meshullam,* [34] *Judah,
Benjamin, Shemaiah, and Jeremiah.*
[35] *Of the sons of the Kohanim, with trumpets: Ze-
chariah the son of Jonathan, the son of Shemaiah, the son
of Mattaniah, the son of Michaiah, the son of Zaccur, the
son of Asaph.* [36] *And his brethren: Shemaiah, Azarel,
Milalai, Gilalai, Maai, Nethanel, Judah, and Hanani,
with instruments of the songs of David, the man of God:
Ezra the scholar was before them.* [37] *Then, before the
Gate of the Spring; they ascended further to the steps of
the City of David, the steps of the wall; then from before
the house of David until the Water Gate to the east.*
[38] *Now the second thanksgiving went alongside, and I*

their instrument (*Ralbag*).

Metzudos translates *with the musical instruments* of David. The *Kohanim* used King David's own instruments.

וְעֶזְרָא הַסּוֹפֵר לִפְנֵיהֶם — *Ezra the scholar was before them.* Ezra marched before the *Kohanim* (*Malbim*).

☙ The Procession Continues

37. וְעַל שַׁעַר הָעַיִן — *Then, before the Gate of the Spring.* The procession then continued around the city from the Refuse Gate [v. 31] until it reached the area before the Gate of the Spring (*Rashi; Metzudos*).

עַל־מַעֲלוֹת עִיר דָּוִיד — *To* [lit. *over*] *the steps of the City of David.* [See 3:15, where it is stated that these steps *descended* from the City of David.]

בַּמַּעֲלֶה לַחוֹמָה — *The steps of the wall.* The steps of the City of David themselves formed the wall (*Rashi; Ibn Ezra*). *Metzudos*, however, renders *the steps to the wall: The steps of the City of David* [leading] *to the wall.*

מֵעַל לְבֵית דָּוִיד — *Then from before the house of David.* Then they proceeded from the area before the house of David (*Metzudos*) to the southwestern corner of the city (*Malbim*; see 3:19).

וְעַד שַׁעַר הַמַּיִם מִזְרָח — *Until the Water Gate to the east.* They then marched eastward until the Water Gate (*Metzudos*), in the southeastern corner of the city (*Malbim*).

38. וְהַתּוֹדָה הַשֵּׁנִית — *Now the second thanksgiving.* A second loaf, belonging to another thanksgiving sacrifice, was carried around the wall of the city alongside the loaf from the first thanksgiving offering (*Rashi; Metzudos*).

According to *Malbim*, *five* leavened loaves from a second thanksgiving sacrifice were carried alongside *five* loaves from the first sacrifice [see comm. v. 31].

לְמוֹאל — *Alongside.* This is *Rashi's* translation, following one opinion in *Shevuos* 15b. *Malbim* cites *Yerushalmi Sanhedrin* 1:3, which bases the translation of מוּל, *alongside*, on the passage [*Numbers* 22:5] וְהוּא יֹשֵׁב מִמֻּלִי, *he sits alongside me.*

Malbim also quotes a second opinion in *Shevuos*, translating *Now the second thanksgiving sacrifice went below*, i.e., the bread of the second thanksgiving sacrifice was carried immediately behind the bread of the first. *Yerushalmi's* source

יב
לט־מג

אַחֲרֶיהָ וַחֲצִי הָעָם מֵעַל לְהַחוֹמָה מֵעַל
לט לְמִגְדַּל הַתַּנּוּרִים וְעַד הַחוֹמָה הָרְחָבָה׃ וּמֵעַל
לְשַׁעַר־אֶפְרַיִם וְעַל־שַׁעַר הַיְשָׁנָה וְעַל־שַׁעַר
הַדָּגִים וּמִגְדַּל חֲנַנְאֵל וּמִגְדַּל הַמֵּאָה וְעַד
שַׁעַר הַצֹּאן וְעָמְדוּ בְּשַׁעַר הַמַּטָּרָה׃
מ וַתַּעֲמֹדְנָה שְׁתֵּי הַתּוֹדֹת בְּבֵית הָאֱלֹהִים וַאֲנִי
מא וַחֲצִי הַסְּגָנִים עִמִּי׃ וְהַכֹּהֲנִים אֶלְיָקִים מַעֲשֵׂיָה
מִנְיָמִין מִיכָיָה אֶלְיוֹעֵינַי זְכַרְיָה חֲנַנְיָה
מב בַּחֲצֹצְרוֹת׃ וּמַעֲשֵׂיָה וּשְׁמַעְיָה וְאֶלְעָזָר וְעֻזִּי
וִיהוֹחָנָן וּמַלְכִּיָּה וְעֵילָם וָעָזֶר וַיַּשְׁמִיעוּ
מג הַמְשֹׁרְרִים וְיִזְרַחְיָה הַפָּקִיד׃ וַיִּזְבְּחוּ בַיּוֹם־
הַהוּא זְבָחִים גְּדוֹלִים וַיִּשְׂמָחוּ כִּי הָאֱלֹהִים
שִׂמְּחָם שִׂמְחָה גְדוֹלָה וְגַם הַנָּשִׁים וְהַיְלָדִים
שָׂמֵחוּ וַתִּשָּׁמַע שִׂמְחַת יְרוּשָׁלַםִ מֵרָחוֹק׃

for the translation of מול, *below*, is from the passage (*Leviticus* 5:8) מִמּוּל עָרְפּוֹ, *below the neck of its head.*

Ri Mitrani understands לְמוּאל as *to the left.* A second group of marchers circled the city towards *the left side*, while the first group marched towards the *right* [v. 31], until they met halfway around the city.

וַאֲנִי אַחֲרֶיהָ — *And I followed.* I, Nehemiah, followed the bread of the second thanksgiving offering.

Nehemiah followed the second thanksgiving bread. The lords marched after him, followed by Ezra and then the *Kohanim* (*Malbim*).

וַחֲצִי הָעָם מֵעַל לְהַחוֹמָה מֵעַל לְמִגְדַּל הַתַּנּוּרִים — *With half the people near the wall, until the Tower of the Ovens.* Half of the people who stood near the wall accompanied me, Nehemiah, from the Water Gate [v. 37] to the Tower of the Ovens (*Metzudos*).

Malbim asserts that *half the people* refers to a procession towards the *left*, which took place simultaneously with the procession towards the right. Verse 32 states that *half the lords of Judah* marched towards the right. The remaining *half of the people* marched from the wall to the left, to the Tower of the Ovens.

וְעַד הַחוֹמָה הָרְחָבָה — *And until the Broad Wall.* The procession to the left moved from west to east along the northern wall until the place known as the Broad Wall (*Malbim*).

39. וְעָמְדוּ בְּשַׁעַר הַמַּטָּרָה — *And they stood at the Prison Gate.* This was the gate leading to the prison courtyard (*Ralbag*).

Both processions met finally at the Prison Gate, thus completing the circling of the city (*Malbim*).

40. וַתַּעֲמֹדְנָה שְׁתֵּי הַתּוֹדֹת בְּבֵית הָאֱלֹהִים — *Then the two thanksgivings stood at the Temple of God.* The two thanks-

followed with half the people near the wall, until
the Tower of the Ovens and until the Broad Wall.
39 *Then from the Gate of Ephraim until the Old Gate*
to the Gate of the Fish, then the Tower of Hananel to
the Tower of Hameiah until the Sheep Gate; and
they stood at the Prison Gate. 40 *Then the two thanks-*
givings stood at the Temple of God, and I with half
the leaders with me. 41 *And the Kohanim: Eliakim,*
Maaseiah, Miniamin, Michaiah, Elioeinai, Zechariah,
and Hananiah, with trumpets. 42 *Also Maasiah,*
Shemaiah, Elazar, Uzi, Jehohanan, Malchiah, Eilam,
Azer, and Jashmeiu — the singers, with Jezrahiah, who
officiated. 43 *On that day they offered up a great number*
of sacrifices and rejoiced, for God caused them to
rejoice greatly; the women and children also rejoiced,
and the rejoicing of Jerusalem was heard from afar.

giving breads [or groups of breads (*Malbim*)] which had been at the fore of the procession around the city [v. 30-31] were now brought to the Temple (*Rashi*).

וַאֲנִי וַחֲצִי הַסְּגָנִים עִמִּי — *And I with half the leaders with me.* I, Nehemiah, followed the loaves, and half the leaders accompanied me (*Metzudos*).

According to *Malbim*, Nehemiah and the leaders who accompanied him had circled half the city towards the right [v. 31] and now moved northward to the Temple (*Malbim*).

41. וְהַכֹּהֲנִים — *And the Kohanim.* In *Malbim's* opinion, the *Kohanim* enumerated in this passage had circled half of the city to the left, and now marched southward to the Temple.

42. וּמַעֲשֵׂיָה וּשְׁמַעְיָה — *Also Maasiah, Shemaiah.* Maasiah and the others were the singers who now came to the Temple to sing (*Metzudos*).

According to *Malbim*, Maasiah and Shemaiah were also members of the group which had marched to the left and now walked southward to the Temple.

וַיַּשְׁמִיעוּ הַמְשֹׁרְרִים — *And Jashmeiu — the singers.* The translation follows *Metzudos*. However, *Malbim* renders וַיַּשְׁמִיעוּ הַמְשֹׁרְרִים, *and the singers made* [their voices] *heard.*

וְיִזְרַחְיָה הַפָּקִיד — *With Jezrahiah, who officiated.* Jezrahiah, who was appointed supervisor of the singers, also came to the Temple (*Metzudos*), where he taught the songs for this occasion (*Malbim*).

43. זְבָחִים גְּדוֹלִים — *A great number of sacrifices.* Our translation follows *Metzudos*.

Malbim renders *large sacrifices*. Large, fattened animals were chosen for the offerings.

כִּי הָאֱלֹהִים שִׂמְּחָם שִׂמְחָה גְדוֹלָה — *For God caused them to rejoice greatly. God* made their hearts joyful (*Metzudos*). They did not rejoice because of feasting; their rejoicing was spiritual, caused by God (*Malbim*).

מד וַיִּפָּקְדוּ בַיּוֹם הַהוּא אֲנָשִׁים עַל־הַנְּשָׁכוֹת
לָאוֹצָרוֹת | לַתְּרוּמוֹת לָרֵאשִׁית וְלַמַּעַשְׂרוֹת
לִכְנוֹס בָּהֶם לִשְׂדֵי הֶעָרִים מְנָאוֹת הַתּוֹרָה
לַכֹּהֲנִים וְלַלְוִיִּם כִּי שִׂמְחַת יְהוּדָה עַל־
מה הַכֹּהֲנִים וְעַל־הַלְוִיִּם הָעֹמְדִים: וַיִּשְׁמְרוּ
מִשְׁמֶרֶת אֱלֹהֵיהֶם וּמִשְׁמֶרֶת הַטָּהֳרָה
וְהַמְשֹׁרְרִים וְהַשֹּׁעֲרִים כְּמִצְוַת דָּוִיד שְׁלֹמֹה
מו בְנוֹ: כִּי־בִימֵי דָוִיד וְאָסָף מִקֶּדֶם °ראש
הַמְשֹׁרְרִים וְשִׁיר־תְּהִלָּה וְהֹדוֹת לֵאלֹהִים:
מז וְכָל־יִשְׂרָאֵל בִּימֵי זְרֻבָּבֶל וּבִימֵי נְחֶמְיָה
נֹתְנִים מְנָיוֹת הַמְשֹׁרְרִים וְהַשֹּׁעֲרִים דְּבַר־

°רָאשֵׁי ק׳

◆§ Portions of the Kohanim and Levites

44. וַיִּפָּקְדוּ ... אֲנָשִׁים — *Men were appointed.* Treasurers were appointed over the storage places (*Metzudos*).

עַל־הַנְּשָׁכוֹת — *Over the chambers.* These chambers were in the Temple (*Rashi*).

The word נְשָׁכוֹת is the equivalent of לְשָׁכוֹת, *chambers*. The letters נ and ל are sometimes interchangeable (*Rashi; Ibn Ezra; Metzudos; Ramban, Genesis* 25:3).

לָאוֹצָרוֹת — *For the storage places.* The Temple chambers were used as storage places (*Metzudos; Malbim*).

לַתְּרוּמוֹת — *Of the terumah.* [*Terumah* refers to the portion *raised up* (separated) from the produce of the Holy Land and given to a *Kohen*. See 10:38.]

לָרֵאשִׁית — *The first gift.* This refers to *challah*, a portion of bread broken off and given to the *Kohen 'first'* — before the remainder of the bread is eaten (*Metzudos*; see 10:38).

According to *Malbim*, *the first gift* refers to *bikkurim*, the *first fruits* of the land to ripen, which are brought to the Temple and given to the *Kohen*. [See 10:38.]

וְלַמַּעַשְׂרוֹת — *And the tithe.* This tithe is one tenth of the land's produce, given to the Levites (*Metzudos*; see 10:38).

מְנָאוֹת הַתּוֹרָה — *The portions ordained by the Law.* The *terumah* tithe, the first gift, and the tenth tithe are Biblically required (*Metzudos*).

לַכֹּהֲנִים וְלַלְוִיִּם — *For the Kohanim and Levites.* The *Kohanim* and Levites came to the Temple chambers to receive their portions (*Rashi*).

לִכְנוֹס בָּהֶם — *To be gathered.* Until this time, the Levites traveled to the fields for their tithes [10:38, 39]. Now, however, Nehemiah made arrangements for the Israelites to bring the tithes to the chambers of the Temple (*Malbim*). The new arrangement freed the Levites to devote themselves completely to their tasks at the Temple (*Ralbag*).

45. וַיִּשְׁמְרוּ מִשְׁמֶרֶת אֱלֹהֵיהֶם — *And kept the watch of their God.* Any obligatory task which a person has been appointed to perform is described in Scripture as מִשְׁמֶרֶת, literally *watch* (*Rashi; Numbers* 3:7).

The Kohanim and Levites stood and

44 *And on that day men were appointed over the chambers for the storage places of the terumah, the first gift, and the tithe, in which the portions ordained by the Law for the Kohanim and Levites were to be gathered from the fields of the cities; for there was rejoicing in Judah over the Kohanim and Levites who stood.* 45 *And kept the watch of their God and the watch of purity; also the singers and the gatekeepers, as commanded by David [to] his son Solomon.* 46 *For in the days of David and Asaph, the heads of the singers in earlier times, and the songs of praise and thanks to God.* 47 *And all of Israel, in the days of Zerubabel and the days of Nehemiah, gave portions to the singers and the gatekeepers, each in*

kept the watch of their God by carrying out their tasks in the Temple (*Metzudos*). According to *Ralbag*, the *Kohanim* and Levites guarded the Temple. *Rambam* explains that the guards were not exclusively for protection; they were a mark of respect and honor for the Temple, even when there was no possibility of enemy attack. [See *Ramban*, preface to *Numbers*.]

וּמִשְׁמֶרֶת הַטָּהֳרָה — *And the watch of purity.* The *Kohanim* and Levites also kept watch to make sure that nothing impure (טָמֵא) entered the Temple (*Metzudos; Ralbag;* see *Rambam, Beis HaMikdash* 3).

וְהַמְשֹׁרְרִים וְהַשֹּׁעֲרִים — *Also the singers and the gatekeepers.* The singers and gatekeepers followed King David's system of division into *mishmaros*, watches (*Metzudos*; see comm. v. 7).

The people arranged for the storage of the tithes (see ahead v. 47) at the Temple for the benefit of those Levites who took part in their *mishmar's* service at the Temple (*Malbim*).

כְּמִצְוַת דָּוִיד שְׁלֹמֹה בְנוֹ — *As commanded by David* [*to*] *his son Solomon.* Our translation follows *Metzudos. Ri Mitrani*, however, translates, *as made customary by David and his son Solomon.*

I Chronicles (ch. 23) records that David established Solomon as king of Israel, then assembled the *Kohanim* and Levites and divided them into groups. *Metzudos'* interpretation is that David made the divisions, and then commanded Solomon to follow them when the Temple would be built. According to *Ri Mitrani*, both David and Solomon established the custom of the *mishmaros*.

46. כִּי־בִימֵי דָוִיד וְאָסָף — *For in the days of David and Asaph.* Asaph was a Levite. Under King David's tutelage, he attained the level of prophecy (*I Chronicles* 25:2; see 11:21).

מִקֶּדֶם רָאשֵׁי הַמְשֹׁרְרִים — *The heads of the singers in earlier times.* David and Asaph were the heads of the singers in ancient times (*Metzudos; Ri Mitrani*).

Malbim's understanding is that in the days of David, Asaph and his descendants were designated to serve perpetually as singers.

וְשִׁיר־תְּהִלָּה וְהוֹדוֹת לֵאלֹהִים — *And the songs of praise and thanks to God.* David and Asaph designated the songs of praise and thanks (*Metzudos*).

Malbim's interpretation is that in the

יג
א־ב

יוֹם בְּיוֹמוֹ וּמַקְדִּשִׁים לַלְוִיִּם וְהַלְוִיִּם מַקְדִּשִׁים
א לִבְנֵי אַהֲרֹן: בַּיּוֹם הַהוּא נִקְרָא
בְּסֵפֶר מֹשֶׁה בְּאָזְנֵי הָעָם וְנִמְצָא כָּתוּב בּוֹ
אֲשֶׁר לֹא־יָבוֹא עַמֹּנִי וּמֹאָבִי בִּקְהַל הָאֱלֹהִים
ב עַד־עוֹלָם: כִּי לֹא קִדְּמוּ אֶת־בְּנֵי יִשְׂרָאֵל
בַּלֶּחֶם וּבַמָּיִם וַיִּשְׂכֹּר עָלָיו אֶת־בִּלְעָם לְקַלְלוֹ

days of David, when Asaph was designated as chief singer, the songs of praise and thanks were also chosen.

Ibn Ezra's interpretation of this passage is *for in the ancient days of David and Asaph* certain songs of praise and thanks were designated; similarly, in the present day, *the heads of the singers sang the same songs of praise and thanks to Hashem.*

47. דְּבַר־יוֹם בְּיוֹמוֹ — *Each in its proper day.* The gifts for the sustenance of the Levites were presented daily, so that the Levites could devote themselves to the Temple services (*Ralbag*; see comm. v. 44).

וּמַקְדִּשִׁים לַלְוִיִּם וְהַלְוִיִּם מַקְדִּשִׁים לִבְנֵי אַהֲרֹן — *And consecrated for the Levites, and the Levites consecrated for the sons of Aaron.* The Israelites consecrated the first tithe (*maaser rishon*) for the Levites, who, in turn, gave a tenth to the sons of Aaron, i.e., the *Kohanim* (*Rashi*). Alternatively, the Israelites gave money and food to the Levites, who gave some of it to the *Kohanim* (*Ralbag*).

Malbim understands this passage as a description of the *past* practice. The Israelites merely consecrated the tithe for the Levites, but did not provide for its delivery — the Levites had to come to the fields for it. Similarly, the Levites consecrated *terumah* for the *Kohanim*, but the latter were obliged to approach the Levites for it. Now, however, the tithes and the *terumah* were deposited at the Temple, where they were easily available for the Levites and *Kohanim* [v. 44] (*Malbim*).

XIII

The people had entered the *Bris Amanah, Covenant of Faith* (ch. 10) (during the reign of Cyrus, or years later, during the reign of Darius — see comm. 7:73), and vowed to refrain from intermarriage, observe the Sabbath and bring the tithes and donations to the Temple. With the passage of time, howerver, intermarriage and Sabbath desecration resurfaced, and the people were remiss in bringing their tithes. Chapter 13 portrays Nehemiah's efforts in dealing with these problems.

1. בַּיּוֹם הַהוּא — *On that day. Metzudos* understands *that day* as a reference to the day the wall was consecrated [12:27].

According to *Malbim, that day* is the day Nehemiah removed the possessions of Tobiah the Ammonite from the Temple chamber (see below, v. 8). Because Tobiah had intermarried into the Jewish community (6:18), *on that day* the Biblical admonition against marrying Ammonites was read publicly.

בְּסֵפֶר מֹשֶׁה — *[In] the Book of Moses.* This term refers to the Book of *Deuteronomy* [see *Deut.* 23:4] which was spoken by Moses (*Malbim*).

[The first four Books of the Bible do not appear as statements made by Moses, but

XIII 1-2

its proper day; and consecrated for the Levites, and the Levites consecrated for the sons of Aaron.

O*n that day the Book of Moses was read in the ears of the people, and in it was found written that an Ammonite or Moabite may never enter into God's congregation.* 2 *Because they did not come forward to the Children of Israel with bread and water, and he hired Balaam against him to curse him,*

as third-person narratives: *In the beginning, God created* ... (*Genesis* 1:1), *He called to Moses* (*Leviticus* 1:1), *God spoke to Moses in the desert* (*Numbers* 1:1), etc. The Book of *Deuteronomy*, however, is written for the most part in the first person: It begins by stating *These are the words which Moses spoke to all Israel*, and continues from Moshe's personal perspective. *You answered and spoke to me* (1:41), *Then HASHEM said to me* (1:42), etc. (until 31:1, when the form reverts to the third person narrative). *Deuteronomy* is, therefore, called the Book of Moses. It should be noted, however, that the entire Torah was dictated by God (*Menachos* 30a). See *Ramban's* opening statement in the preface to his Commentary on the Bible.]

אֲשֶׁר לֹא־יָבוֹא עַמֹּנִי וּמֹאָבִי בִּקְהַל הָאֱלֹהִים עַד־עוֹלָם — *That an Ammonite or Moabite may never enter into God's congregation.* [*Deuteronomy* 23:4 reads: *No Ammonite or Moabite may enter into God's congregation; even the tenth generation may not enter God's congregation, forever.*]

The Bible prohibits intermarriage with Ammonite or Moabite men (but not women) even after they convert (*Metzudos*; see *Rambam, Isurei Biah* 12:17, 18). [Later (v. 23), Nehemiah had to contend with the problem of intermarriage. The concern was with foreign wives. Here, the concern was with foreign men.]

2. כִּי לֹא קִדְּמוּ אֶת־בְּנֵי יִשְׂרָאֵל בַּלֶּחֶם וּבַמָּיִם — *Because they did not come forward to the Children of Israel with bread and water.* [This follows *Deuteronomy* 23:5: *Because they did not come forward to you with bread and water on the way, when you went out of Egypt* ...] *Ramban* (*Deut.* 23:5) explains that this accusation is leveled principally against the Ammonites (*Deut.* 2:19). *Malbim*, however, includes the Moabites as well in conjunction with their sin in hiring Balaam to curse the Jews (see comm. following). This misdeed might have been condoned, had it been motivated by fear of the Jewish military power. However, their failure to bring any tribute (in the form of food and drink) to the Israelites proved that the Moabites did not really fear them. The deciding factor in hiring Balaam, then, was not fear, but hatred. Thus, it is the Moabite's failure to bring out food and water which indicates that they are fully culpable for the sin of hiring Balaam.

וַיִּשְׂכֹּר עָלָיו אֶת־בִּלְעָם לְקַלְלוֹ — *And he hired Balaam against him to curse him.* [*Deuteronomy* 23:5 continues: *and that he hired against you Balaam the son of Beor from* ... *Aram Neharaiim to curse you*. The Moabite king hired the sorcerer Balaam to destroy the Jews by cursing them (see *Numbers* 21-24).

Ramban (*Deut*. 23:5) explains that the Ammonites and Moabites owed a debt of gratitude to the Jewish people. The patriarch Abraham had rescued Lot and his daughters, the ancestors of the Am-

ג וַיַּהֲפֹךְ אֱלֹהֵינוּ הַקְּלָלָה לִבְרָכָה׃ וַיְהִי כְּשָׁמְעָם
אֶת־הַתּוֹרָה וַיַּבְדִּילוּ כָל־עֵרֶב מִיִּשְׂרָאֵל׃
ד וְלִפְנֵי מִזֶּה אֶלְיָשִׁיב הַכֹּהֵן נָתוּן בְּלִשְׁכַּת
ה בֵּית־אֱלֹהֵינוּ קָרוֹב לְטוֹבִיָּה׃ וַיַּעַשׂ לוֹ לִשְׁכָּה
גְדוֹלָה וְשָׁם הָיוּ לְפָנִים נֹתְנִים אֶת־הַמִּנְחָה
הַלְּבוֹנָה וְהַכֵּלִים וּמַעְשַׂר הַדָּגָן הַתִּירוֹשׁ
וְהַיִּצְהָר מִצְוַת הַלְוִיִּם וְהַמְשֹׁרְרִים וְהַשֹּׁעֲרִים
ו וּתְרוּמַת הַכֹּהֲנִים׃ וּבְכָל־זֶה לֹא הָיִיתִי

monite and Moabite peoples (see *Genesis* 19:30-38), from captivity and death (*Genesis* 14:16). In addition, Lot and his daughters were spared from the destruction of Sodom and Gemorrah through the merit of Abraham (*Genesis* 19:24).

While the Ammonites sinned by not bringing out food and water, the Moabites sinned by hiring Balaam. Male Ammonites are forbidden to Jews in marriage because the men would normally greet passers-by with food. The Torah forbids male Moabites to marry Jews because the male is involved in hiring (*Ramban, Deut.* 23:5 from *Yevamos* 76:3, *Midrash Ruth* 4:8, *Yerushalmi, Yevamos* 8).

וַיַּהֲפֹךְ אֱלֹהֵינוּ הַקְּלָלָה לִבְרָכָה — *But our God transformed the curse into a blessing.* This phrase is not relevant to the sin of the hiring of Balaam, but it was added to avoid ending the Torah reading (v. 1) with an act of evil (*Metzudos*; see *Orach Chaim* 138, *Mishnah Berurah* 6).

Malbim, however, finds this phrase relevant to the sin. Perhaps the Moabites should be pardoned for hiring Balaam, since he did not, in the end, curse the Jews. This verse explains that the curse was thwarted only by God's intervention. Since their intentions were deadly, they are not to be pardoned.

☙ The People Obey

3. כָּל־עֵרֶב — *All who had assimilated.* The word עֵרֶב comes from תערובת, *mixture*. It refers to gentiles who had mixed with the Jewish people, as in עֵרֶב רַב, *a large mixture of peoples* [*Exodus* 12:38] (*Rashi*). Our verse refers to the many Ammonites and Moabites who had converted to Judaism and assimilated into the Jewish people (*Ralbag, Metzudos*).

מִיִּשְׂרָאֵל — *From Israel.* The Ammonites and Moabites were separated from Israel — i.e., it was decided that no Jew would marry them (*Ralbag*).

Sennacherib had exiled all of the peoples of the Biblical world [including the Ten Tribes of Israel] into foreign lands, making it impossible to identify any of the nations by their land of origin. Thus, those emanating from the lands of Ammon and Moab are now permitted to intermarry into the Jewish community, since their true national identity is unknown [see *Yadayim* 4:4; *Berachos* 28a; *Rambam, Isurei Biah* 12:25]. Why then were the Ammonites and Moabites separated? Apparently these were Ammonites and Moabites who had preserved their ethnic identity and were known not to have been among those transferred from some other land (*Malbim*).

☙ Eliashib and Tobiah

4. וְלִפְנֵי מִזֶּה — *Before this.* Before the separation just described (*Metzudos; Ibn Ezra*; *Malbim*). *Ri Mitrani*, however, interprets: before the completion of the city's walls and the settling of its inhabitants. (See comm. v. 6.)

אֶלְיָשִׁיב ... נָתוּן בְּלִשְׁכַּת בֵּית־אֱלֹהֵינוּ קָרוֹב לְטוֹבִיָּה — *Eliashib . . . had placed . . in the*

XIII
3-6

but our God transformed the curse into a blessing. [3] *So it*
came to pass that, when they heard the Torah, all who
had assimilated from Israel separated.

[4] *Before this, Eliashib the Kohen had placed*
[Tobiah's articles] in the chamber of our God's Temple,
[he was] close to Tobiah. [5] *He prepared for him a large*
chamber, wherein there was formerly placed the
meal offerings, the frankincense, the vessels, the tithe
of the grain, wine, and oil commanded for the Levites —
the singers and the gatekeepers — and the separated
portion for the Kohanim. [6] *Now during all this I was not*

chamber of our God's Temple ; [he was] close to Tobiah. Eliashib, who was a close friend of Tobiah, had placed Tobiah's household effects (v. 8) in the chamber of the Temple (*Rashi*).

Ri Mitrani's translation is: *Eliashib . . . was placed in a chamber of our God's Temple close to Tobiah.* Tobiah used a chamber at the Temple for himself and his family as a dwelling place. Eliashab followed suit, and occupied an adjoining chamber. According to *Malbim*, it was Eliashib who first used one of the Temple chambers. A nearby chamber was used for storing the tithes. When the people stopped giving tithes, the chamber remained empty, and Eliashib gave it to Tobiah for his personal use (*Malbim*).

Metzudos renders *Eliashib, Tobiah's close friend, who was placed* in the chamber of our God's Temple, i.e., who officiated in the Temple, prepared a large chamber for Tobiah.

Tobiah was a companion of Sanballat (*Rashi; Metzudos*). [Sanballat and Tobiah ridiculed the Jewish attempt to reconstruct the city walls (2:10.19; 3:35), and attempted to ambush the builders (ch. 4). He and his son had married into prominent Jewish families, and he was a powerful, influential person (6:17, 18).]

5. וַיַּעַשׂ לוֹ — *He prepared for him*. The translation follows *Rashi*. Eliashav prepared the chamber for Tobiah (*Rashi*) by emptying it for Tobiah's use (*Metzudos*). According to *Ri Mitrani*, Eliashib prepared a chamber for himself, adjacent to Tobiah's chamber (see above).

וְשָׁם הָיוּ לְפָנִים נֹתְנִים — *Wherein there was formerly placed.* This chamber had been used for the storage of Temple objects before Nehemiah came to Jerusalem (*Rashi*); or before Eliashib emptied space for Tobiah's use (*Metzudos*).

הַמִּנְחָה — *The meal offerings.* This refers to the flour for the meal offerings (*Metzudos*).

הַלְּבוֹנָה — *The frankincense.* This was offered up with the meal offering [*Leviticus* 2:1] and with the show bread (לֶחֶם הַפָּנִים) [*Leviticus* 24:7] (*Metzudos*).

מִצְוַת הַלְוִיִּם — *Commanded for the Levites.* The tithes which the people were commanded to give to the Levites had been stored in the chamber (*Metzudos*).

וְהַמְשֹׁרְרִים וְהַשּׁוֹעֲרִים — *The singers and the gatekeepers.* The functions of the Levites are specified here to stress the gravity of Eliashib's transgression. He emptied the chamber of the food needed to support the servants of God, i.e., *the singers and the gatekeepers*, in favor of Tobiah the Ammonite (*Metzudos*).

☙ Nehemiah's Reaction

6. וּבְכָל־זֶה — *Now during all this.* While the sacrificial materials and the

בִּירוּשָׁלָ͏ִם כִּי בִּשְׁנַת שְׁלֹשִׁים וּשְׁתַּיִם
לְאַרְתַּחְשַׁסְתְּא מֶלֶךְ־בָּבֶל בָּאתִי אֶל־הַמֶּלֶךְ
ז וּלְקֵץ יָמִים נִשְׁאַלְתִּי מִן־הַמֶּלֶךְ׃ וָאָבוֹא
לִירוּשָׁלָ͏ִם וָאָבִינָה בָרָעָה אֲשֶׁר עָשָׂה אֶלְיָשִׁיב
לְטוֹבִיָּה לַעֲשׂוֹת לוֹ נִשְׁכָּה בְּחַצְרֵי בֵּית
ח הָאֱלֹהִים׃ וַיֵּרַע לִי מְאֹד וָאַשְׁלִיכָה אֶת־
כָּל־כְּלֵי בֵית־טוֹבִיָּה הַחוּץ מִן־הַלִּשְׁכָּה׃
ט וָאֹמְרָה וַיְטַהֲרוּ הַלְּשָׁכוֹת וָאָשִׁיבָה שָּׁם
כְּלֵי בֵּית הָאֱלֹהִים אֶת־הַמִּנְחָה וְהַלְּבוֹנָה׃
י וָאֵדְעָה כִּי־מְנָיוֹת הַלְוִיִּם לֹא נִתָּנָה וַיִּבְרְחוּ
אִישׁ־לְשָׂדֵהוּ הַלְוִיִּם וְהַמְשֹׁרְרִים עֹשֵׂי
יא הַמְּלָאכָה׃ וָאָרִיבָה אֶת־הַסְּגָנִים וָאֹמְרָה
מַדּוּעַ נֶעֱזַב בֵּית־הָאֱלֹהִים וָאֶקְבְּצֵם וָאַעֲמִדֵם

tithes were being emptied by Eliashib in favor of Tobiah, I was away from Jerusalem (*Rashi; Metzudos*).

כִּי בִּשְׁנַת שְׁלֹשִׁים וּשְׁתַּיִם לְאַרְתַּחְשַׁסְתְּא מֶלֶךְ־בָּבֶל בָּאתִי אֶל הַמֶּלֶךְ — *For in the thirty-second year of Artahshast, king of Babylon, I came to the king.* In the king's thirty-second year I returned to him in Babylon (*Metzudos; Ri Mitrani*).

7. בְּחַצְרֵי בֵּית הָאֱלֹהִים — *In the courtyards of God's Temple.* This was a desecration of the sanctity of the Temple (*Malbim*; see *Rambam, Beis HaBechirah* 7).

8. וָאַשְׁלִיכָה אֶת־כָּל־כְּלֵי בֵית־טוֹבִיָּה — *So I cast out all of Tobiah's household articles.* According to *Ri Mitrani*, Tobiah and Eliashib had transgressed by taking one of the Temple chambers for their own use. Since Tobiah had been the first to transgress, he was punished first. [Evidently, *Ri Mitrani's* interpretation is that Nehemiah later expelled Eliashib from his chamber, although this is not mentioned clearly in the text. See comm. to v. 9 s.v. *the chambers*.]

Sanballat, although not mentioned by name in this verse, was a member of Tobiah's household, and was also expelled from the Temple by Nehemiah. Sanballat and Tobiah had previously been punished for scorning those rebuilding the sacred city [see 2:19]. Although they had lost their wealth and great power [ch. 6], they were still influential enough to gain the use of the Temple chamber, until Nehemiah returned to Jerusalem and had them expelled (*Wertheimer, notes to Ri Mitrani* 68; *Mishnas R' Eliezer*).

Malbim conjectures that it was to support his action against the criticism of Tobiah's relatives and defenders that Nehemiah arranged (v. 1) for the public reading of the portion of the Torah which stated that Tobiah, as an Ammonite, could not be accepted into the community (*Malbim*; see comm. v. 4).

9. וָאֹמְרָה וַיְטַהֲרוּ — *I gave the command* [lit. *And I said*], *and they purified.* They removed from the chambers anything *tamei* or repulsive (*Metzudos*).

in Jerusalem, for in the thirty-second year of Ar-
tahshast, king of Babylon, I came to the king, and at the
end of some days, requested leave of the king. 7 *Then I*
came to Jerusalem and thought into the evil that
Eliashib had done concerning Tobiah, to prepare a
chamber for him in the courtyards of God's Temple.
8 *This was extremely distressing to me, so I cast out all*
of Tobiah's household articles from the chamber. 9 *I*
gave the command, and they purified the chambers; I
returned there the vessels of God's Temple, the meal
offering, and the frankincense. 10 *Then I became aware*
that the Levites' portions had not been given, and the
Levites — the singers, those who performed the services
— had escaped, each to his field. 11 *So I battled the*
nobles, and said, 'Why is the Temple of God forsaken?'
Then I gathered them together and established them

הַלְּשָׁכוֹת — *The chambers.* They purified two chambers, one which had been occupied by Eliashib, and one by Tobiah (*Ralbag*; see comm. to vs. 4,8).

⟡ The Levites' Portions

10. וָאֵדְעָה — *Then I became aware.* I now turned my attention to a new problem (*Ri Mitrani*). According to *Malbim*, however, Nehemiah *became aware* of this new problem as a result of the Temple cleanup (vs. 8-9). The Temple chambers had originally held the Temple vessels, the meal offerings, and the tithes for the Levites (v. 5). Nehemiah expelled Tobiah and his household goods, and restored the original contents to the chamber (v. 9). When he sought to restore the Levites' portions, he realized that none had been brought to the Temple.

מְנָיוֹת הַלְוִיִּם לֹא נִתָּנָה — *The Levites' portions had not been given.* The tithes had not been brought to the Temple to support the Levites serving there (see 12:44).

The verb נִתָּנָה, *given*, is singular, while the subject of the sentence — מְנָיוֹת, *portions* — is plural. Not even one of the portions was given (*Ibn Ezra*). Alternatively, many portions are given at once by one person. The singular נִתָּנָה, *given*, refers to the single act of giving (*Malbim*).

וַיִּבְרְחוּ אִישׁ־לְשָׂדֵהוּ — *Each to his field.* In order to find sustenance, the Levites were forced to leave the Temple and travel to the fields to collect their portions (*Rashi; Ralbag*); alternatively: to cultivate their own fields to support themselves (*Metzudos; Malbim*).

עֹשֵׂי הַמְּלָאכָה — *Those who performed the services.* This refers to the Temple services, and includes the gatekeepers (12:47) (*Metzudos*).

11. מַדּוּעַ נֶעֱזַב בֵּית־הָאֱלֹהִים — *Why is the Temple of God forsaken?* Why is the Temple forsaken by the Levites, who are supposed to serve at the Temple (*Metzudos*)?

וָאֶקְבְּצֵם — *Then I gathered them together.* I gathered the *Kohanim* and the Levites together (*Rashi*).

יג
יב־טז

יב עַל־עָמְדָם׃ וְכָל־יְהוּדָה הֵבִיאוּ מַעְשַׂר
יג הַדָּגָן וְהַתִּירוֹשׁ וְהַיִּצְהָר לָאוֹצָרוֹת׃ וָאוֹצְרָה
עַל־אוֹצָרוֹת שֶׁלֶמְיָה הַכֹּהֵן וְצָדוֹק הַסּוֹפֵר
וּפְדָיָה מִן־הַלְוִיִּם וְעַל־יָדָם חָנָן בֶּן־זַכּוּר
בֶּן־מַתַּנְיָה כִּי נֶאֱמָנִים נֶחְשָׁבוּ וַעֲלֵיהֶם לַחֲלֹק
יד לַאֲחֵיהֶם׃ זָכְרָה־לִּי אֱלֹהַי
עַל־זֹאת וְאַל־תֶּמַח חֲסָדַי אֲשֶׁר עָשִׂיתִי
טו בְּבֵית אֱלֹהַי וּבְמִשְׁמָרָיו׃ בַּיָּמִים הָהֵמָּה
בִיהוּדָה | דֹרְכִים־גִּתּוֹת | בַּשַּׁבָּת וּמְבִיאִים
הָעֲרֵמוֹת וְעֹמְסִים עַל־הַחֲמֹרִים וְאַף־יַיִן
עֲנָבִים וּתְאֵנִים וְכָל־מַשָּׂא וּמְבִיאִים יְרוּשָׁלִַם
טז בְּיוֹם הַשַּׁבָּת וָאָעִיד בְּיוֹם מִכְרָם צָיִד׃ וְהַצֹּרִים

וַאַעֲמִדֵם עַל־עָמְדָם — *And established them on their place*, i.e., at their *mishmaros* [see 12:7].

12. וְכָל־יְהוּדָה הֵבִיאוּ — *And all Judah brought*. With the Levites reestablished at the Temple, the people were persuaded to bring the tithes to the Temple storehouses (*Rashi; Metzudos*). This enabled the Levites to remain at the Temple and perform its services (*Ralbag*).

13. וָאוֹצְרָה — *I appointed as treasurers* [lit. *I treasured*]. The translation follows *Ibn Ezra*.

וַעֲלֵיהֶם — *And it was for* [lit. *upon*] *them*. I made it incumbent on the treasurers to apportion the tithes to their brethren (*Metzudos*).

◆§ Nehemiah Requests Remembrance

14. זָכְרָה־לִּי — *Remember me* [lit. *for me*]. Remember me favorably, i.e., credit me (*Metzudos*). [This is the first of three places (vs. 14, 22, 31) where Nehemiah beseeched God to remember him favorably.]

Because Nehemiah requested that God credit him for his good deeds, he was punished with the deletion of his name from his book. The Rabbinic literature incorporates the Book of *Nehemiah* into the Book of *Ezra* [see 5:19] (*Sanhedrin* 93b).

עַל־זֹאת — *For this*. In the *Bris Amanah* (ch. 10) under Ezra's leadership, the people had sworn to bring the proper tithes (10:38). During Nehemiah's absence (v. 6) they failed to carry out their oath. Nehemiah returned and rectified the situation. He now requested that God credit him with leading the people when they swore. [See *Sotah* 13b: 'If someone completes a matter which another initiated, Scripture considers it as if the second had performed the entire matter.'] *For this*, i.e., for seeing to it *now* that the oath was fulfilled, Nehemiah requested credit for the original taking of the oath (*Malbim*).

וּבְמִשְׁמָרָיו — *For its watches*. Nehemiah had reestablished the watches of Levites to serve at the Temple [v. 11] (*Metzudos*).

on their place. [12] *And all Judah brought the tithe of the*
grain, wine, and oil to the storehouses. [13] *I appointed as*
treasurers over the storehouses: Shelemiah the Kohen, Zadok the scholar, and Pedaiah, of the Levites, assisted by Hanan the son of Zaccur, the son of Mattaniah; for they were considered trustworthy and it was for them to apportion [the shares] to their brethren.
[14] *Remember me, my God, for this; do not eradicate my kindnesses which I did at my God's Temple, for its watches.*
[15] *In those days I observed in Judah people treading on wine presses on the Sabbath, bringing sheaves and loading them on the donkeys; also wine, grapes, figs, and every [type of] load, bringing them to Jerusalem on the Sabbath day. I warned them on*
the day when they sold provisions. [16] *Also, the Tyrians*

◆§ Sabbath Desecration

15. בַּיָּמִים הָהֵמָּה — *In those days.* Like the neglect of the tithes [v. 10], the Sabbath desecration described here occurred while Nehemiah was away from Jerusalem [v. 6] (*Malbim*).

דֹרְכִים־גִּתּוֹת — *People treading on wine presses.* Pressing grapes for wine is a desecration of the Sabbath. It is a sub-category (*toladah*) of threshing (*Rambam, Hilchos Shabbos* 21:12), one of the 39 prohibited categories of labor (*Shabbos* 7:2).

וּמְבִיאִים הָעֲרֵמוֹת וְעֹמְסִים עַל־הַחֲמֹרִים — *Bringing sheaves and loading them on the donkeys.* They brought sheaves of grain from the fields and loaded them on the donkeys [on the Sabbath] (*Rashi; Metzudos*).

According to *Malbim* and *Ralbag,* they had already loaded the produce on the donkeys before the Sabbath. They now transgressed by having their animals carry the load on the Sabbath. [Causing an animal to work on the Sabbath is prohibited by the verse: *Do not do any work, you . . . and your animal* (*Exodus* 20:10).]

וְאַף־יַיִן עֲנָבִים וּתְאֵנִים וְכָל־מַשָּׂא — *Also wine, grapes, figs, and every [type of] load.* They also had their animals carry wine, grapes, figs, and other loads on the Sabbath (*Metzudos*).

וּמְבִיאִים יְרוּשָׁלַםִ — *Bringing them to Jerusalem.* [The loads of produce were brought to Jerusalem to be sold on the Sabbath.]

The Talmud (*Beitzah* 37a) asserts that the prohibition against doing business on the Sabbath is Rabbinic. *Ramban* qualifies this by remarking that conducting business as usual in every facet of weekday operation is Biblically prohibited (*Leviticus* 23:24; see also *Maggid Mishneh, Rambam, Hil. Shabbos* 21:1).

בְּיוֹם מִכְרָם צָיִד — *On the day when they sold provisions.* Nehemiah warned them on the market day, when they all gathered together (*Rashi; Metzudos*). The market day was on the Sabbath (*Ri Mitrani*).

יָשְׁבוּ בָהּ מְבִיאִים דָּאג וְכָל־מֶכֶר וּמוֹכְרִים
יז בַּשַּׁבָּת לִבְנֵי יְהוּדָה וּבִירוּשָׁלָםִ׃ וָאָרִיבָה
אֵת חֹרֵי יְהוּדָה וָאֹמְרָה לָהֶם מָה־הַדָּבָר הָרָע
הַזֶּה אֲשֶׁר אַתֶּם עֹשִׂים וּמְחַלְּלִים אֶת־יוֹם
יח הַשַּׁבָּת׃ הֲלוֹא כֹה עָשׂוּ אֲבֹתֵיכֶם
וַיָּבֵא אֱלֹהֵינוּ עָלֵינוּ אֵת כָּל־הָרָעָה הַזֹּאת
וְעַל הָעִיר הַזֹּאת וְאַתֶּם מוֹסִיפִים חָרוֹן
יט עַל־יִשְׂרָאֵל לְחַלֵּל אֶת־הַשַּׁבָּת׃ וַיְהִי
כַּאֲשֶׁר צָלֲלוּ שַׁעֲרֵי יְרוּשָׁלַםִ לִפְנֵי הַשַּׁבָּת
וָאֹמְרָה וַיִּסָּגְרוּ הַדְּלָתוֹת וָאֹמְרָה אֲשֶׁר
לֹא יִפְתָּחוּם עַד אַחַר הַשַּׁבָּת וּמִנְּעָרַי
הֶעֱמַדְתִּי עַל־הַשְּׁעָרִים לֹא־יָבוֹא מַשָּׂא
כ בְּיוֹם הַשַּׁבָּת׃ וַיָּלִינוּ הָרֹכְלִים וּמֹכְרֵי כָל־
כא מִמְכָּר מִחוּץ לִירוּשָׁלָםִ פַּעַם וּשְׁתָּיִם׃ וָאָעִידָה
בָהֶם וָאֹמְרָה אֲלֵיהֶם מַדּוּעַ אַתֶּם לֵנִים
נֶגֶד הַחוֹמָה אִם־תִּשְׁנוּ יָד אֶשְׁלַח בָּכֶם

16. וְהַצֹּרִים יָשְׁבוּ בָהּ — *Also, the Tyrians sat there.* Merchants from Tyre (*Ralbag*); or Tyrians who had settled in Jerusalem (*Metzudos*) — these gentiles sold their wares in Jerusalem on the Sabbath.

וּבִירוּשָׁלָםִ — *And in Jerusalem*! Even in Jerusalem, the city of the sacred Temple, they desecrated the Sabbath (*Metzudos*).

✤ Nehemiah Battles the Lords

17. וָאָרִיבָה אֵת חֹרֵי יְהוּדָה — *So I battled the aristocrats of Judah.* The common people, not the aristocrats, were guilty of desecrating the Sabbath. Nevertheless, the aristocrats were held responsible, since they could have admonished the people, but failed to do so (*Malbim*). [*Leviticus* 19:17 states, *Admonish your fellow and do not bear sin over him.* The verse means that one who fails to admonish his fellow bears the other's sin as if he had transgressed himself (see *Ramban;* see *Shevuos* 39a).]

וּמְחַלְּלִים אֶת־יוֹם הַשַּׁבָּת — *Desecrating the Sabbath day.* Nehemiah pointed out that they had desecrated the Sabbath in three ways: (1) by doing business on the Sabbath [v. 16]; (2) by having their animals carry loads of goods [v. 15]; and (3) by pressing grapes [v. 15] (*Ralbag*).

The Talmud (*Shabbos* 123b) remarks that the laws of *muktzeh* (מֻקְצֶה), literally *set apart* objects, were enacted as a result of Sabbath desecration at this time. Objects deemed *muktzeh* may not be moved on the Sabbath. Originally, the Rabbis of Nehemiah's time classified all utensils *muktzeh* except three: cake knife, table knife, and spoon. No other movable object could be handled. As people became

sat there and brought fish and every [type of] merchandise and sold [them] on the Sabbath to the sons of Judah — and in Jerusalem! 17 *So I battled the aristocrats of Judah, and said to them. 'What is this wicked thing that you are doing, desecrating the Sabbath day?* 18 *Did not your ancestors do this, and then our God visited all of this evil on us and on this city? And you bring additional wrath against Israel by desecration of the Sabbath!'*
19 *Then it came to pass that when the gates of Jerusalem cast shadows before the Sabbath, I gave word that the doors be closed; then I gave word not to open them until after the Sabbath, and I stationed some of my servants at the gates, [so that] no load would arrive on the Sabbath.* 20 *Then the merchants and sellers of all kinds of wares slept outside Jerusalem once, and then a second time.* 21 *So I warned them, and said: 'Why do you sleep next to the wall? If you repeat this, I will punish you!'*

more meticulous with Sabbath observance, the restrictions of *muktzeh* were eased, but not completely lifted. [See *Shabbos* ch. 17, and ArtScroll preface there.]

◆§ Nehemiah Closes the Gates

19. כַּאֲשֶׁר צָלְלוּ שַׁעֲרֵי יְרוּשָׁלַםִ לִפְנֵי הַשַּׁבָּת — *When the gates of Jerusalem cast shadows before the Sabbath.* This refers to late Friday afternoon (*Ri Mitrani; Metzudos*), or immediately after noon, when the sun begins to sink and shadows are cast to the east (*Malbim*).

לֹא־יָבוֹא מַשָּׂא בְּיוֹם הַשַּׁבָּת — *[So that] no load would arrive on the Sabbath.* I stationed my servants at the gates to prevent any load from coming through the smaller doors which opened in the wall (*Metzudos*).

20. הָרֹכְלִים — *The merchants.* A רוֹכֵל is one who peddles a number of different wares (*Ibn Ezra*). Another interpretation is that a רוֹכֵל is a seller of perfume (*Metzudos*).

Rashi to *Leviticus* 19:16 explains that רוֹכֵל is derived from the root רֶגֶל, *foot* (the letters 'כ' and 'ג' are interchangeable). A רוֹכֵל is a perfume peddler who travels on foot from city to city to sell his wares.

מִחוּץ לִירוּשָׁלָםִ — *Outside Jerusalem.* The vendors slept outside the walls waiting for the inhabitants of the city to open the gates and buy their wares on the Sabbath (*Rashi*). Alternatively: The vendors waited for the Jerusalemites to come out on the Sabbath and buy small objects which they could hide and bring into the city unnoticed (*Malbim*).

21. וָאֹמְרָה אֲלֵהֶם — *And said.* I said this to those merchants who slept outside the wall (*Rashi*).

מַדּוּעַ אַתֶּם לֵנִים נֶגֶד הַחוֹמָה — *Why do you sleep next to the wall?* Nehemiah was concerned that some of the people might go out to the merchants and make purchases on the Sabbath (*Metzudos*).

יָד אֶשְׁלַח בָּכֶם — *I will punish you* [lit. *I will send a hand against you*]. I will have

יג
כב־כה

כב מִן־הָעֵת הַהִיא לֹא־בָאוּ בַּשַּׁבָּת: וָאֹמְרָה
לַלְוִיִּם אֲשֶׁר יִהְיוּ מִטַּהֲרִים וּבָאִים שֹׁמְרִים
הַשְּׁעָרִים לְקַדֵּשׁ אֶת־יוֹם הַשַּׁבָּת גַּם־
זֹאת זָכְרָה־לִּי אֱלֹהַי וְחוּסָה עָלַי כְּרֹב
כג חַסְדֶּךָ: גַּם ׀ בַּיָּמִים הָהֵם רָאִיתִי
אֶת־הַיְּהוּדִים הֹשִׁיבוּ נָשִׁים °אשדודיות
כד °עמוניות מוֹאֲבִיּוֹת: וּבְנֵיהֶם חֲצִי מְדַבֵּר
אַשְׁדּוֹדִית וְאֵינָם מַכִּירִים לְדַבֵּר יְהוּדִית
כה וְכִלְשׁוֹן עַם וָעָם: וָאָרִיב עִמָּם וָאֲקַלְלֵם

°אַשְׁדֳּדִיּוֹת ק׳
°עַמֳּנִיּוֹת ק׳

you beaten or killed (*Ibn Ezra*). [Note Nehemiah's courage and faith in taking this step. He alienated the Tyrian merchants with all of the economic and political risk entailed, for the sake of strengthening religious observance.]

◆§ Nehemiah Commands the Levites

22. אֲשֶׁר יִהְיוּ מִטַּהֲרִים — *That they should purify themselves.* מִטַּהֲרִים is reflexive like מִתְטַהֲרִים, *purify themselves* (*Ibn Ezra*).

Nehemiah told the Levites to purify themselves ritually through immersion in the *mikveh* (*Metzudos*).

וּבָאִים שֹׁמְרִים הַשְּׁעָרִים לְקַדֵּשׁ אֶת־יוֹם הַשַּׁבָּת — *And come and guard the gates to sanctify the Sabbath day.* This refers to the Temple gates. Since the *Kohanim* were commanded to slaughter and burn the Temple sacrifices even on the Sabbath [see *Rambam, Temidin Umusafin* 4:9], Nehemiah felt it was necessary to introduce some special activity at the Temple to emphasize the sanctity of the Sabbath. For this purpose, he requested that *all* of the Temple guardians (instead of only some, as on weekdays) come on the Sabbath and guard the gates, in honor of the Sabbath (*Ralbag*).

According to *Metzudos*, Nehemiah requested that the Levites purify themselves and then honor the Sabbath by coming *before* the beginning of the Sabbath to guard the gates. [The group of Levites guarding the Temple was generally changed on the Sabbath. See *Rambam, Klei HaMikdash* 3:9.] The passage is rendered, *And guard the gates, then sanctify the Sabbath day*, i.e., *then, afterward*, initiate the sanctity of the day.

Ri Mitrani renders: *I told the Levites to purify themselves, and the guardians of the gates to come and sanctify the Sabbath.* The guardians of the Temple gates were told to sound the *shofar*, indicating to the people that the Sabbath was about to begin. In this way, they would *sanctify the Sabbath*, i.e., cause the people to sanctify it. [It was then the custom to blow the *shofar* late Friday afternoon to indicate the imminence of the Sabbath. See *Shabbos* 35b, *Orach Chaim* 256b.]

Malbim, however, interprets this verse as a reference to the guarding of the city gates, not of the Temple gates. Nehemiah instructed the Levites to purify themselves, and then guard the city gates in order to sanctify the Sabbath. The Levites, more zealous than others, were to guard against those who wished to enter the city to desecrate the Sabbath.

גַּם־זֹאת זָכְרָה לִּי — *This, too, remember for me.* As part of the *Bris Amanah*, the people had sworn to keep the Sabbath

From that time onward, they did not come on the Sabbath. [22] *Then I told the Levites that they should purify themselves and come and guard the gates to sanctify the Sabbath day. This, too, remember for me, my God, and be compassionate towards me according to Your abundant kindness.*

[23] *Also in those days I observed the Jews who had installed Ashdodite, Ammonite, and Moabite wives.* [24] *Half their children spoke Ashdodian, and did not know how to speak Hebrew; and likewise the language of each nation.* [25] *So I battled against them; then I cursed*

(10:32). Nehemiah had not arranged for them to take the oath. However, he asked for credit as if he had done so, because he now led the people in fulfilling it (*Malbim*; see comm. to v. 14).

וְחוּסָה עָלַי כְּרֹב חַסְדֶּךָ — *And be compassionate towards me according to Your abundant kindness.* Nehemiah asked for God's compassion and kindness in repaying him for his good deeds. God is not obligated to reward the righteous, since He provided them with life and the opportunity to perform their good works. It is only out of compassion and kindness that He rewards the righteous as if they were truly deserving (*Metzudos*; see *Job* 41:3).

☙ The Gentile Wives

23. גַּם — *Also.* In addition to withholding the tithes [v. 10] and desecrating the Sabbath [v. 17], the people also violated their oath that they would not marry gentile wives [10:31] (*Malbim*).

הֹשִׁיבוּ נָשִׁים אַשְׁדֳּדִיּוֹת עַמֳּנִיּוֹת מוֹאֲבִיּוֹת — *Who had installed Ashdodite, Ammonite, and Moabite wives.* They settled the gentile women into their homes, i.e., married them (*Metzudos*).

24. וּבְנֵיהֶם חֲצִי מְדַבֵּר אַשְׁדּוֹדִית — *Half their children spoke Ashdodian.* Many of their children spoke Ashdodian, like their Ashdodite mothers (*Rashi*; *Metzudos*).

Malbim, however, translates *Their children spoke half Ashdodian.* Their children spoke a jargon, half Ashdodian and half Hebrew, following each parent partially (cf. *Rambam, Tefillah* 1:4).

וְאֵינָם מַכִּירִים לְדַבֵּר יְהוּדִית — *And did not know how to speak Hebrew.* Either they did not speak Hebrew at all (*Rashi*; *Metzudos*), or they could not speak Hebrew *properly*, but rather spoke half Ashdodian and half Hebrew.

וְכִלְשׁוֹן עַם וָעָם — *And likewise the language of each nation.* Similarly many of the children of the other gentile women (Ammonites, Moabites) spoke the language of their mother's nation, but not Hebrew (*Metzudos*). According to *Malbim*, the last two phrases of the sentence, read ... [their children] *did not know how to speak Hebrew or the language of each nation.* The children could speak neither Hebrew nor the language of their mother's nation properly, since they spoke a confused jargon of both.

☙ Nehemiah Punishes and Admonishes the Sinners

25. וָאָרִיב עִמָּם — *So I battled against them.* I battled against those who took gentile wives (*Metzudos*).

וָאֲקַלְלֵם — *Then I cursed them.* First I battled them by arguing. Then I became more severe, and cursed them (*Malbim*).

יג וָאַכֶּה מֵהֶם אֲנָשִׁים וָאֶמְרְטֵם וָאַשְׁבִּיעֵם
כו בֵּאלֹהִים אִם־תִּתְּנוּ בְנֹתֵיכֶם לִבְנֵיהֶם וְאִם־
כו תִּשְׂאוּ מִבְּנֹתֵיהֶם לִבְנֵיכֶם וְלָכֶם׃ הֲלוֹא עַל־
אֵלֶּה חָטָא־שְׁלֹמֹה מֶלֶךְ־יִשְׂרָאֵל וּבַגּוֹיִם
הָרַבִּים לֹא־הָיָה מֶלֶךְ כָּמֹהוּ וְאָהוּב לֵאלֹהָיו
הָיָה וַיִּתְּנֵהוּ אֱלֹהִים מֶלֶךְ עַל־כָּל־
יִשְׂרָאֵל גַּם־אוֹתוֹ הֶחֱטִיאוּ הַנָּשִׁים הַנָּכְרִיּוֹת׃

The Talmud (*Moed Katan* 16a) understands that this was a curse uttered by Nehemiah to censure the sinners. According to *Ibn Ezra* and *Ralbag*, the curse refers to excommunication.

וָאַכֶּה מֵהֶם אֲנָשִׁים — *Then I beat some of their men.* When cursing did not deter them, I increased the severity of the punishment and beat some of them (*Malbim*).

Rashi, following the Talmud (*Moed Katan* 16a), explains that lashes were given as a warning and as a reminder of the severity of the sin. When egregious Torah desecration is rampant, the Rabbis may inflict as many lashes as they deem necessary for the situation at hand. [See *Shulchan Aruch Choshen Mishpat* 2:1. Also below, comm. to *If you give . . .*]

According to *Ralbag*, however, the men were given the thirty-nine lashes prescribed Biblically for the willful transgression of a Biblical commandment.

וָאֶמְרְטֵם — *And tore their hair out.* The hair was torn from their heads (*Metzudos*).

וָאַשְׁבִּיעֵם — *And I made them swear.* I made all of the Jerusalemites swear not to intermarry with gentiles (*Ibn Ezra*).

אִם־תִּתְּנוּ בְנֹתֵיכֶם לִבְנֵיהֶם — *If you give your daughters over to their sons.*

This was the oath Nehemiah forced upon them. The end of the statement is self-understood. 'If you give your daughters to their sons, or take their daughters — then you will be subject to the severe punishment meted out to those who violate their oath' (*Metzudos*; see *Rambam, Numbers* 14:21).

The Talmud (*Moed Katan* 16b) states that all of the measures taken by Nehemiah described in this verse — battling, invoking curses, beating, tearing out hair, and forcing an oath — are not Biblically prescribed. They were used for the needs of the moment, to punish the transgressors and prevent repetition of the sin. This teaches that a Rabbinical court may temporarily resort to any of these extreme measures when it deems them necessary to restrain egregious transgressors. [See *Rambam, Sanhedrin* 24:8.]

☙ Solomon's Sins

26. הֲלוֹא עַל־אֵלֶּה חָטָא־שְׁלֹמֹה מֶלֶךְ־יִשְׂרָאֵל — *Did not Solomon, king of Israel, sin over these?* Did not King Solomon's gentile wives cause him to sin? (*Metzudos*).

King Solomon married gentile princesses who had converted to Judaism. But because their intentions in converting were for personal benefit, and not purely for the sake of God, it is considered as if they had not converted, and as if Solomon had intermarried (*Rambam, Isurei Biah* 13:14-16).

I Kings 11:1-8 states that Solomon's gentile wives turned his heart away from God, and that he built altars for their idols. Solomon did not actually build the altars,

XIII
26

them; then I beat some of their men and tore their hair out, and I made them swear by God, 'If you give your daughters over to their sons, or if you marry their daughters to your sons, or to yourselves:
26 Did not Solomon, king of Israel, sin over these? There was no king like him among the many nations; he was beloved by his God, and God appointed him king over all of Israel — yet the alien wives caused even him to sin,

but because he failed to stop his wives from building them, he was punished as if he had built them (*Shabbos* 56b).

If Solomon could not keep from sinning after he married gentile women, how can *you* hope to refrain from sinning (*Rashi*)?

וּבַגּוֹיִם הָרַבִּים לֹא־הָיָה מֶלֶךְ כָּמֹהוּ — *There was no king like him among the many nations.* There was no monarch as wise as he. [*The wisdom of Solomon was greater than the wisdom of all of the men of the east, and the wisdom of all of Egypt: he was wiser than all men* (*I Kings* 5:9,10).] Yet his wives turned his heart (*Metzudos*).

There was no monarch as great and powerful as he. [*Solomon ruled over all the kingdoms, from the river of the land of the Philistines until the border of Egypt; they brought gifts and served Solomon all the days of his life* (*I Kings* 5:1). He was greater than all the kings of the earth in wealth and wisdom (*I Kings* 10:23).] Yet his wives turned his heart (*Malbim*).

וְאָהוּב לֵאלֹהָיו — *He was beloved by his God.* Solomon was a prophet [*God spoke to Solomon* (*I Kings* 3:5)] (*Ralbag*). Despite his great piety, his wives turned his heart (*Malbim*).

וַיִּתְּנֵהוּ אֱלֹהִים מֶלֶךְ עַל־כָּל־יִשְׂרָאֵל — *And God appointed him king over all of Israel.* He was so beloved by his God, that God appointed him king over Israel (*Metzudos*).

גַּם־אוֹתוֹ הֶחֱטִיאוּ הַנָּשִׁים הַנָּכְרִיּוֹת — *Yet the alien wives caused even him to sin.* Therefore you will certainly be caused to sin by your alien wives (*Rashi*).

The prohibition against intermarriage is Biblical, *For he* [the father of your gentile daughter-in-law] *will turn your son away from me . . .* (*Deut.* 7:4). Those who intermarried in Nehemiah's time did so with the intention of remaining loyal Jews. They thought that they would not be turned away from God, and that they were therefore exempt from the prohibition. To counter this erroneous thinking, Nehemiah cited the example of King Solomon. Despite his great power and piety his heart was turned (*Malbim*).

A different reason for Nehemiah's mention of King Solomon was to illustrate the far-reaching consequences of intermarriage. Because King Solomon's heart was turned from God by his gentile wives, he was punished with the loss of most of his kingdom to the usurper, Jeroboam son of Nebat [*because this was with you* (your gentile wives turned your heart) . . . *I shall tear your kingdom from you and give it to your servant* (*I Kings* 11:11)]. Jeroboam and the kings of Israel who followed him led the people into idolatry, and they were finally punished with exile. The kings of Judah followed the example of Jeroboam and his successors, and also led their constituents into idol worship, until the Temple was destroyed and the nation was exiled. Thus, Solomon's intermarriage eventually led to the downfall of the entire Jewish people (*Ralbag*).

יג
כז-לא

כז וְלָכֶם הֲנִשְׁמַע לַעֲשֹׂת אֵת כָּל־הָרָעָה הַגְּדוֹלָה
הַזֹּאת לִמְעֹל בֵּאלֹהֵינוּ לְהֹשִׁיב נָשִׁים נָכְרִיּוֹת:
כח וּמִבְּנֵי יוֹיָדָע בֶּן־אֶלְיָשִׁיב הַכֹּהֵן הַגָּדוֹל חָתָן
כט לְסַנְבַלַּט הַחֹרֹנִי וָאַבְרִיחֵהוּ מֵעָלָי: זָכְרָה לָהֶם
אֱלֹהָי עַל־גָּאֳלֵי הַכְּהֻנָּה וּבְרִית הַכְּהֻנָּה
ל וְהַלְוִיִּם: וְטִהַרְתִּים מִכָּל־נֵכָר וָאַעֲמִידָה
מִשְׁמָרוֹת לַכֹּהֲנִים וְלַלְוִיִּם אִישׁ בִּמְלַאכְתּוֹ:
לא וּלְקֻרְבַּן הָעֵצִים בְּעִתִּים מְזֻמָּנוֹת וְלַבִּכּוּרִים
זָכְרָה־לִּי אֱלֹהַי לְטוֹבָה:

27. וְלָכֶם הֲנִשְׁמַע — *So shall we listen to you?* This is understood as הֲנִשְׁמַע לָכֶם, *Shall we listen to you* (*Ri Mitrani*)?

King Solomon's heart was turned from God, despite his greatness, because of his gentile wives. So shall we listen to you, who are not as great as Solomon (*Metzudos*), when you claim that your hearts will not be turned (*Malbim*)?

A different translation is *Have you heard, to do all this great wickedness . . .?* Have you heard, among the admonitions of the Torah, anything that would permit you to do all this great wickedness? On the contrary, you should have learned from the disastrous results of Solomon's intermarriage to desist from this wickedness (*Ralbag*).

☙ Sanballat's Son-in-Law

28. וּמִבְּנֵי יוֹיָדָע — *One of* [lit. *and of*] *the sons of Joiada.* The translation follows *Rashi*.

לְסַנְבַלַּט — *Of Sanballat.* Sanballat was an oppressor of the Jews [see 2:10,19] (*Rashi*; *Metzudos*).

וָאַבְרִיחֵהוּ מֵעָלָי — *I drove him away from me.* Nehemiah drove away Joiada's son for a number of reasons:

(1) So that his father-in-law, Sanballat, would not have the opportunity to visit him in Jerusalem[1], where he could observe the affairs of the city and perhaps contrive to bring harm to the Jews (*Rashi*; *Metzudos*).

(2) Because his wife was a non-Jewess (*Ralbag*), and he refused to divorce her (*Metzudos*).

(3) Because he was too powerful for Nehemiah to punish as he had the others [v. 25]; Nehemiah could only drive him away (*Malbim*).

29. זָכְרָה לָהֶם אֱלֹהָי — *Remember them, my God.* Remember the wickedness of the sinners, and punish them for taking gentile wives (*Metzudos*). This request was for the punishment of Sanballat's son-in-law (*Malbim*).

Remember their good deeds [the deeds of those who drove out Sanballat's son-in-law] (*Rashi*).

עַל־גָּאֳלֵי הַכְּהֻנָּה — *For despising the priesthood.* According to *Rashi*, the interpretation is: Remember their good deeds in punishing Sanballat's son-in-law and those *Kohanim* who despised the priesthood.

The interpretation of *Metzudos* is *for*

1. According to Josephus [ch. 5], Sanballat later approached Alexander the Great and requested that he construct a Temple on Mount Gerizim [near the city of Shechem; see *Sotah* 32a], where his ousted son-in-law would officiate as *Kohen Gadol*. The request was granted.

27 *so shall we listen to you to do all this great wickedness,*
being faithless to our God by marrying alien wives?
28 *One of the sons of Joiada, the son of Eliashib the Kohen*
Gadol, was a son-in-law of Sanballat the Horonite; I
drove him away from me. 29 *Remember them, my God,*
for despising the priesthood and the covenant of the
priesthood and the Levites. 30 *I cleansed them from all*
that is alien and established the watches of Kohanim
and Levites, each at his work. 31 *Also for the wood*
offering, at prearranged times, and for the first fruits;
remember me, my God, for good.

despising the priesthood by marrying non-Jewish wives, and thus disqualifying themselves as *Kohanim* [see 7:64].

וּבְרִית הַכְּהֻנָּה — *And the covenant of the priesthood. Metzudos* interprets: for despising the covenant of the priesthood. In this covenant God promised that the *Kohanim* would perpetually serve at the Temple [*a covenant of eternal priesthood* (*Numbers* 25:13)]. They despised the covenant by marrying gentiles and disqualifying themselves from the priesthood (*Metzudos*).

Another interpretation is that the verse refers to God's promise that the descendants of the *Kohanim* would also be priests. [*It shall be for him* [Phinehas] *and his descendants after him, a covenant of an eternal priesthood* (*Numbers* 25:13).] The children of the *Kohanim* who married gentiles, however, could hardly be *Kohanim* since they were not even Jewish. Thus, the priests' intermarriage constituted a desecration of the covenant of the priesthood (*Malbim*).

וְהַלְוִיִּם — *And the Levites.* [The covenant of the Levites refers to God's promise that the Levites would always serve at the Temple. This is stated in *Numbers* 8:14 — *The Levites shall be mine.* The word *mine* signifies an eternal bond (*Sifri, Numbers* 92; *Chidushei R' Yitzchok Zev*).]

⇜§ Nehemiah Summarizes His Accomplishments

30. וְטִהַרְתִּים מִכָּל־נֵכָר — *I cleansed them from all that is alien.* Although some of the *Kohanim* and Levites had taken alien wives [v. 29], Nehemiah cleansed them from this by making them swear that they would no longer marry gentiles [v. 25] (*Metzudos*).

וָאַעֲמִידָה — *And established.* Only after I had purified them did I establish the watches (*Malbim*).

מִשְׁמָרוֹת לַכֹּהֲנִים וְלַלְוִיִּם — *The watches of Kohanim and Levites.* [This refers to the groups of *Kohanim* and Levites who served at the Temple. Each group was known as a watch. See comm. 12:7.]

אִישׁ בִּמְלַאכְתּוֹ — *Each at his work.* Each man was appointed to a specific job at a special time, and the system was followed precisely (*Metzudos*).

31. וּלְקֻרְבַּן הָעֵצִים — *Also for the wood offering.* Nehemiah enforced another part of the *Bris Amanah* (ch. 10) which the people were lax in upholding. The covenant included an oath to bring wood to be burnt on the altar [10:35] (*Malbim*; see comm. v. 14).

וְלַבִּכּוּרִים — *And for the first fruits.* Nehemiah established a specific time for bringing the first ripened of each fruit to the Temple (*Rashi*). This *mitzvah*, too, was one of the tenets of the *Bris Amanah* (10:36) which the people had neglected (*Malbim*).

זָכְרָה־לִּי אֱלֹהַי לְטוֹבָה — *Remember me, my God, for good.* Nehemiah listed his accomplishments so that the others might learn from him and emulate his example (*Ralbag*).

תם ונשלם שבח לאל בורא עולם

Appendices

Map of Jerusalem

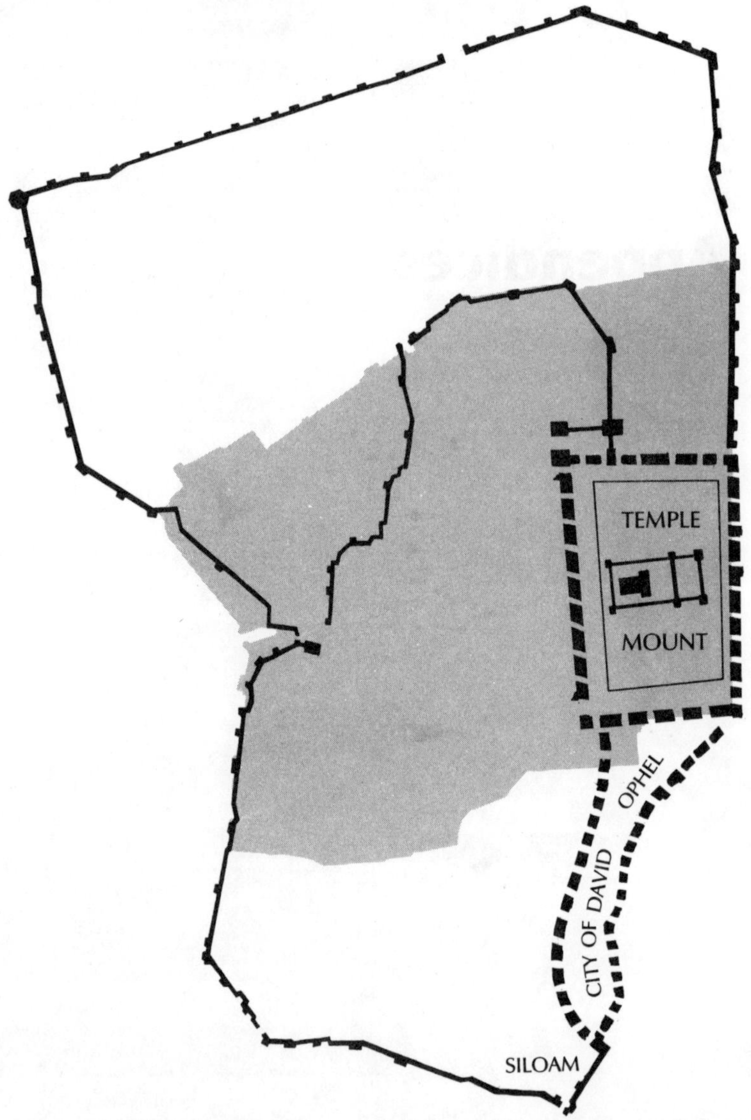

Walls rebuilt by Nehemiah (conjecture)

Walls at the time of the destruction of the Second Temple

Present-day walls of the Old City

Variations in Names in Nehemiah and Ezra			
Verse in Nehemiah	**Name**	**Verse in Ezra**	**Name**
7:7	Azariah	2:2	Seraiah
7:7	Raamiah	2:2	Reeliah
7:7	Mispereth	2:2	Mispar
7:7	Nehum	2:2	Rehum
7:15	Binui	2:10	Bani
7:24	Hariph		
		2:18	Jorah
7:25	Gibeon	2:20	Gibbar
7:26	people of Bethelehem	2:21	children of Bethlehem
7:28	people of Azmaveth	2:24	children of Azmaveth
7:29	people of Kiriath Ye'arim	2:25	children of Kiriath Arim
7:30	people of Haramah	2:26	children of Haramah
7:33	people of Nebo Aher	2:29	children of Nebo
7:43	Lehodiah	2:40	Hodaviah
7:45	the gatekeepers	2:42	children of the gatekeepers
7:47	Sia	2:44	Siaha
		2:50	Asnah
7:52	Nephishsim	2:50	Nephusim
7:54	Batzlith	2:52	Bazluth
7:57	Sofereth	2:55	Hassofereth
7:57	Ferida	2:55	Peruda
7:59	Amon	2:57	Ami
7:61	Addon	2:59	Addan

Variations in Populations in Nehemiah and Ezra

	Nehemiah		Ezra	
Family or City	Pop.	Verse	Pop.	Verse
Arah	**652**	7:10	**775**	2:5
Governor of Moab	**2818**	7:11	**2812**	2:6
Zattu	**845**	7:13	**945**	2:8
Binui	**648**	7:15	**642**	2:10
Bebai	**628**	7:16	**623**	2:11
Azgad	**2322**	7:17	**1222**	2:12
Adonikam	**667**	7:18	**666**	2:13
Bigvai	**2067**	7:19	**2056**	2:14
Adin	**655**	7:20	**454**	2:15
Hashum	**328**	7:22	**223**	2:19
Bezai	**324**	7:23	**323**	2:17
Bethlehem Netophah	**188**	7:26	**179**	*2:21;2:22
Beth El Ai	**123**	7:32	**223**	2:28
Lod Hadid Ono	**721**	7:37	**725**	2:33
Senaah	**3930**	7:38	**3630**	2:35
Asaph	**148**	7:44	**128**	2:41
Gatekeepers	**138**	7:45	**139**	2:42
Delaiah Tobiah Nekoda	**642**	7:62	**652**	2:60

* enumerated separately as 123 and 56 respectively.